Sourcebook o ation

"I am thrilled to have access to this great resource. It is with enthusiasm that I invite you to 'experience' this book if you want to get a better understanding of the historical and cultural contributions of key thinkers about the many fields of experiential education."

Paul Limoges, Chief Executive Officer, Association for Experiential Education

"A significant contribution to the field. Professors and educators of undergraduate and graduate experiential education and outdoor education programs will find this book practical and useful for their courses."

Scott Wurdinger, Minnesota State University

"This magnificent story of many people who define our collective and individual journeys brought back memories, and reminded me of why I am passionate about well-conceived experiential education."

Jude Hirsch, Georgia College & State University

"All the people discussed in this book have touched and transformed the lives of many. Tom Smith and Cliff Knapp have done an excellent job in showing the richness and diversity of the origins of experiential education."

Jean Berube, Gallaudet University

Experiential education is a philosophy and methodology for building knowledge, developing skills, and clarifying values by engaging learners in direct experience and focused reflection. To understand experiential education, what should one be reading? This volume introduces philosophers, educators, and other practitioners whose work is relevant to anyone seeking answers to this question. Following brief snapshots of John Dewey and Kurt Hahn, the book is organized in four sections:

- Philosophers and Educational Theorists
- Nature Educators and Outdoor Educators
- Psychologists and Sociologists
- School and Program Founders.

Each chapter focuses on an individual whose philosophy and practice exemplify a biographical and historical model for reaching a deeper understanding of experiential education. An appendix includes short biographical sketches of 45 additional people who deserve a closer look because of their contributions to the field of experiential education.

This sourcebook provides a much-needed overview and foundations for the field — for students in courses addressing experiential education, challenge education, outdoor experiential education, recreation education, and related fields; for learning theorists and curriculum specialists; for experiential educators; and for educational philosophers.

Thomas E. Smith, Founder/Director of the Raccoon Institute and Independent Psychologist/ Wilderness Guide, has taught psychology and education at colleges and universities and is a frequent presenter, consultant, and trainer at regional, national, and international conference workshops on experiential/adventure/challenge/outdoor education.

Clifford E. Knapp, Professor Emeritus, Northern Illinois University, has taught at all levels of education, elementary through graduate school, and is a frequent presenter at state, national, and international conferences offering workshops in experiential education and place-based education.

Sourcebook of Experiential Education

Key Thinkers and Their Contributions

Edited by

Thomas E. Smith, Ph.D.
and
Clifford E. Knapp, Ph.D.

Routledge
Taylor & Francis Group

NEW YORK AND LONDON

First published 2011
by Routledge
270 Madison Avenue, New York, NY 10016

Simultaneously published in the UK
by Routledge
2 Park Square, Milton Park, Abingdon, Oxon OX14 4RN

Routledge is an imprint of the Taylor & Francis Group, an informa business

© 2011 Taylor & Francis

Typeset in Minion by EvS Communication Networx, Inc.
Printed and bound in the United States of America on acid-free paper by Edwards Brothers, Inc.

Library of Congress Cataloging in Publication Data
Sourcebook of experiential education : key thinkers and their contributions
/ edited by Thomas E. Smith and Clifford E. Knapp.
p. cm.
Includes bibliographical references and index.
1. Experiential learning. 2. Educators—Biography. I. Smith, Thomas E. II. Knapp, Clifford.
LB1027.23.S596 2011
371.39—dc22
2010025156

ISBN13: 978-0-415-88441-9 (hbk)
ISBN13: 978-0-415-88442-6 (pbk)
ISBN13: 978-0-203-83898-3 (ebk)

Contents

Preface

It is not all that unusual in philosophy … to begin with the concrete, raise the issues of the concrete to a reflective and philosophical level, and then return to the concrete, interpreting and approaching the concrete and everyday in a new and fresh light.

David Strong (1995, p. 12)

This project began after one of our students asked the question, "If I want to understand the philosophy of experiential education, what should I be reading beyond Dewey [John Dewey, early 20th century educational philosopher] and Hahn [Kurt Hahn, mid-20th-century educational practitioner, and founder of the Outward Bound Schools] ?" Discussion of that question led us to thinking about the accusation often heard from critics of the developing field of experiential education (EE): "The field of EE is experience rich and theory poor." Those in the field of experiential education must answer those critics by establishing connections between program practices and the underlying theoretical postulates about education, growth, and learning. Richard Kraft (1981) wrote about the problem of defining EE's theoretical base:

> Attempts at definition have proven difficult, and many of us await a John Dewey or Jean Piaget to provide the legitimation we so desperately seek in the academic, corporate, and governmental worlds in which we work. Alas, after years of waiting, no messiah has come to lead us out of our wilderness. Perhaps that is because our theoretical roots, like our honorable history, is still there to be claimed. (p. 2)

Focus on the philosophical foundations of EE theory and practice is important if the field is to have greater impact on mainstream education. David Boud (1989) clarified this point: "Unless we are challenged to move beyond our existing practices then experiential education will remain forever peripheral to mainstream education" (p. 47). When questions arise about why experiential educators have had such a difficult time getting the field accepted in public educational systems, many agree with philosopher/educator Sean Blenkinsop's explanation: "Because we do not have a comprehensive and consistent enough philosophy of education to do the job that is currently being asked in the mainstream" (2006, p. vi).

This book is written for those who are interested in experiential learning and want to probe deeper into understanding why they value teaching and learning that way. The book is not an attempt to formulate a comprehensive philosophy for experiential education. However, we believe that this book, composed of selected biographies, will be helpful to people who are developing their own philosophies of experiential education. We agree with Gamaliel Bradford who wrote: "History is best understood through biography. People are the makers of history" (as cited in Gibson, 1936, p. 13). As Kraft suggested 30 years ago, our theoretical roots are still there to be claimed. In chapter 1 of this book we summarize some of the questions and issues that should be addressed by those who tackle the task of writing a comprehensive philosophy of experiential education.

Our purpose in compiling this sourcebook is simply to make a contribution to the field of EE by examining the lives and philosophies of people, other than John Dewey and Kurt Hahn. We are concerned with others who have made contributions to the field of experiential education. We begin with some concrete examples of historic and contemporary people who wrote about and/or practiced ideas about learning through experience. We think that reflection and discussion about these people and their ideas can help individual practitioners refine their personal philosophies of experiential education, and also contribute to that broader challenge of creating a comprehensive philosophy of the field.

We began this project by creating a list of people who contributed to the foundations of EE. This list soon grew to nearly 200, so we turned to experienced leaders in the field for help. We asked potential authors to write about:

1. someone they felt was important to the evolving field of EE,
2. someone they felt had influenced them in their professional development and shaped their personal philosophy of EE,
3. someone that they had a passion to write about.

The educators they chose to write about are the subjects of this book. In the end we collected papers on 37 people who were important in shaping the foundations of their practice. As the renowned outdoor educator, L. B. Sharp, used to say about his ongoing projects, we view this sourcebook as "never finished, just begun" (as cited in Carlson, 2002, p. 263). In the future, others may write additional biographies to cover more of the important thinkers and program builders.

We make no claim that this collection covers all of the important thinkers who have relevance for the field of experiential education, or that it even covers the "most important" thinkers. Compiling a list of "most important" thinkers that contributed to the philosophical foundations and program methodologies of EE would be a difficult task, and final decisions would certainly be based on personal value judgments. However, we believe that we have collected a valuable sourcebook of ideas about the foundations of experiential education.

We struggled with dividing the papers into subsections for the book, and ended up with four. There is a section about 11 philosophers and educational theorists; a section about 10 people who represent the field of nature study, outdoor and environmental education; a section of papers about six psychologists and sociologists who wrote about educational theory and practice; and a section about 10 program founders and practitioners—people who were "doers" as well as thinkers.

Most of the chapters begin with brief biographies, then focus on the educational ideas of the person(s) being considered, and conclude with their comments on the importance of that person to experiential education. As David Strong suggests in the opening quotation, we hope that the chapters may guide experiential educators to view their methodology "in a new and fresh light."

We would like to thank the many people who contributed to the finished product you now hold in your hands. We begin with the many students who asked us questions about experiential education and challenged us to think deeply about our philosophy of experiential learning. We also thank the contributing authors of the chapters that reveal the ideologies and practices of the many influential thinkers discussed in this book. We end our list of supporting people with thanks to the folks at Routledge/Taylor & Francis, including Naomi Silverman, Emilie Littlehales, Sioned Jones, Lynn Goeller, and Alanna Kolb. We express our gratitude to all those who made this book change from an idea to a reality.

Thomas E. Smith
Clifford E. Knapp

References

Blenkinsop, S. (2006) A letter from the chair of the JEE advisory committee. *The Journal of Experiential Education, 29,* vi–ix.

Boud, D. (1989). Some competing traditions in experiential learning. In S. W. Weil & I. McGill (Eds.), *Making sense of experiential learning: Diversity in theory and practice* (pp. 38–49). Bristol, PA: The Society for Research into Higher Education & Open University Press.

Carlson, J. A. (2002). *Lloyd Burgess Sharp: An oral history of a career that shaped outdoor education.* Unpublished doctoral dissertation, Stephen F. Austin State University, Nacogdoches, TX.

Gibson, H. W. (1936, January). The history of organized camping. *Camping Magazine,* 13–27.

Kraft, R. J. (1981, Spring). A call to action and reflection. *The Journal of Experiential Education, 4*(1), 1–6.

Strong, D. (1995). *Crazy mountains: Learning from wilderness to weigh technology.* Albany: State University of New York Press.

Acknowledgments

No volume of this size and scope can be compiled without the assistance of a great number of people. We would like to acknowledge some of those who helped us along this extended journey.

First, we want to pay tribute to the students we have encountered in our university classes and in the hundreds of workshops we have presented over the past 50 years. Their probing questions, eager participation, and positive comments have inspired us to continue to teach in experiential ways, and to think about the theoretical foundations of experiential education.

Second, we are indebted to the 32 experiential educators who accepted our invitation to write about one or more persons who influenced their philosophies of experiential education, and who they thought were important for the expansion and refinement of the theoretical foundations of the field. Without their contributions, this volume would not exist.

Third, we are grateful for the contributions of the 39 influential educators who are discussed in this book. They made an enormous difference in this world, and we must acknowledge them for their groundbreaking accomplishments.

Fourth, we would like to thank our families for their support during the years of creating this sourcebook. While we were away from home presenting workshops on this topic, or locked up with our computers, we were not always available to give them our love and support and share their lives.

Fifth, we appreciate the staff at Taylor & Francis/Routledge for their hard work in helping to change an idea into a physical reality. Without their efforts you would not be reading these acknowledgments now.

Sixth, and last, we are grateful to you, the reader, who acquired this sourcebook and parted the covers to read these pages. We hope that you leave this literary experience knowing more about the historical and theoretical foundations of experiential learning, and more about your personal philosophies of experiential education.

Thomas E. Smith
Clifford E. Knapp

1 Experiential Education and Learning by Experience

Thomas E. Smith, Clifford E. Knapp,
Jayson Seaman, and Steve Pace

In this chapter we provide a short history of the development of the field of experiential education and explain how it evolved in the United States into a broad and diverse profession. We then examine the meaning of the term and highlight some of the problems and issues facing experiential educators today. We hope that the contributing authors will help experiential educators spread the philosophy and methods of the field and take on a greater role in mainstream educational circles. We also hope that this book will help to propel the reader beyond the peripheral and beyond the philosophies of Dewey and Hahn.

Although there are many precedents in other geographical places, the contemporary approach to experiential education (EE) in America coincides with the beginnings of the adventure education movement in the 1970s when the Outward Bound schools, the National Outdoor Leadership schools, and Project Adventure were founded in the United States. These educational alternatives to traditional ways of teaching and learning reinforced the messages of earlier educators about the value of direct experience. These educators believed that students would learn certain concepts, skills, and values better if they occasionally moved away from their desks and books and were provided more opportunities for challenging small group experiences outside the classroom. This only made sense when learning through experience was the most effective and efficient way to meet particular objectives. A variety of challenging outdoor activities were collectively described as adventure education and later as experiential/challenge education. For example, ropes and team challenge courses, short- and long-term camping expeditions, rappelling, backpacking, rock climbing, canoeing, skiing, spelunking, initiative problems, environmental awareness activities, and community service learning gained in popularity as ways to develop individual self-concepts, group communication skills, and teamwork.

The last quarter of the 20th century saw rapid development of these adventure alternatives in schools and other educational institutions. As leaders of this movement recognized the positive impact of challenging group experiences on the psychological, social, and spiritual development of the participants, some educators and other helping professional noticed the parallels between adventure education and the emerging human potential movement. When counselors and therapists began to explore the potential of these outdoor strategies, programs of wilderness therapy, adventure-based counseling, and outdoor personal and group growth developed. The use of these adventure activities in teambuilding and leadership development attracted corporate human resource leaders and the movement expanded to the business world. By the turn of the 21st century, the scope and diversity of experiential education had broadened and professionals in the field continued to examine experiential theory and practice. Luckner and Nadler made this same point when describing experiential learning:

> These diverse perspectives cross a wide variety of disciplines and practices, which may include: traditional education, alternative education, outdoor-adventure education, career education, special education, therapy, social and cultural work, teambuilding and corporate training. (1992, p. 5)

Some critics of this developing field of experiential education have charged that the field is experience rich and theory poor. They accused EE leaders of adopting the Nike slogan "just do it," without thinking about the reasons for doing it. In the beginning some practitioners were guilty of leading adventure activities with a minimal understanding of the underlying objectives and purposes. In a new and emerging field, this leadership limitation can be easily understood, but not accepted. One explanation for this disconnect between theory and practice is that the *Journal of Experiential Education* was begun about 30 years ago and philosophical topics did not appear frequently enough in the early years of publication. This criticism can be countered by clarifying EE theory and bringing more consistency and congruency to EE practice. Understanding the link between educational theory and practice is important because sound theory provides the basis for valid practice.

The original theoretical base for the practice of EE was considered to be derived in part from John Dewey's educational philosophy. When Dewey established his Chicago laboratory school in 1896, he wanted his teachers "to provide children with experiences (cultivating a garden, for example, or a visit to a farm) that would lead to the gradual differentiation of the school subjects" (Tanner, 1997, p. 45). David Kolb's experiential learning cycle was also used extensively to explain how people learned: through experiencing, reflecting, generalizing, and applying the knowledge gained (Luckner & Nadler, 1992, p. 6).

> Clearly, the task of describing EE and its philosophical foundations continues to be challenging. The EE umbrella now spreads over a wide diversity of personal and professional philosophies and therefore reaching agreement on the meaning of the term is difficult. Still, it is important for EE leaders to think about clarifying definitions and theoretical underpinnings for their practice. Many Association for Experiential Education (AEE) committees have spent many hours attempting to clearly define EE. The most recent definition posted on the AEE Internet homepage is: "Experiential education is a philosophy and methodology in which educators purposely engage learners in direct experience and focused reflection in order to increase knowledge, develop skills and clarify values" (Association for Experiential Education, 2007, p. 1).

As EE leaders seek to define the field and clarify the theoretical foundations for the field, they need to consider several issues and questions. We offer the following questions and brief discussion of some of these issues to stimulate the thoughts of EE professionals.

Is it the process of individual and group reflection which makes an event in one's life become a memorable and useful experience? In their book, *12 Brain/Mind Learning Principles in Action* (2005), Caine, Caine, McClintic, and Klimek describe global experiences as "physiologically rich beginning events that evoke an impression of the 'whole' subject to be explored and engage the students in several simultaneous ways" (p. 127). These experiences are intended to stimulate interest, result in questions about the topic, and link it to the students' lives. They could include stories, simulations, ethical dilemmas, projects, artifacts, art, music, or poetry. When these types of events are reflected upon, they usually are more meaningful, understanding is expanded, and later applications are more clearly considered. In other words, when students undergo a careful process of reflection, an event in life is often transformed into a meaningful and memorable experience that can be applied more easily to similar situations in the future.

Should there be a distinction made among "experiential learning," "experiential education," and "schooling"? Learning is the personal, self-regulated acquisition of knowledge (concepts, skills, attitudes, values, and habits of mind) through a variety of ways and under different conditions. Learning occurs as a result of individual and group experiences provided by both formal institutions, such as schools, and through informal life situations occurring from birth until death. Bruner (1966) defined learning as the acquisition of the knowledge of results in a problem-solving situation when and where it can be "used for self correction." He believed that effective "instruction increases the appropriate timing and placing of corrective knowledge" (p. 50). For example, if a camper pitches a tent on a slope and rainwater washes underneath the shelter and wets the inside, the next time that tent is pitched he or she will search for a more level place if the lesson has been taught properly and learned well. Achieving an education can be viewed as the sum total of knowledge gained, usually resulting from formal instruction. Schooling is achieved through formal institutions established by most societies to pass on knowledge deemed important for living comfortably and productively in a particular culture. The term "experiential learning" may be redundant, for many believe that all learning is the result of lived experience in combination with personal reflection. Saying that someone quit school and received their education from life experience means that they had a different set of experiences than those provided by schools. Experience with books, lectures, and other mediated instruction will always be important parts of learning, but many other strategies for stimulating learning can result in lasting knowledge. Christian Itin (1999) suggests that distinguishing between learning and education is important because using the terms interchangeably makes meaningful discussion more difficult.

Is there a significant difference between learning through experience inside the classroom or outside the classroom? The similarities and differences of learning inside or outside the classroom and the school building must be acknowledged. Historically, EE was most often associated with outdoor learning, and many still consider the outdoor classroom as an important educational setting. When practitioners in the humanistic education movement who had their roots in the human potential movement of the 1960s, '70s, and '80s became involved with the EE movement, they pointed out that meaningful experiential activities could also be facilitated in the classroom. Perhaps distinguishing between the outside classroom and the inside classroom is less relevant now because experiential learning occurs in both places

Does experiential learning always have to involve active, whole-body participation? Human experience can be received either actively or passively. In some life events the individual is more passive-receptive (as in reading a book or listening to a lecture), and at other times a person is more active-interactive (as in planting a tree or climbing over a wall). Some educational activities demand whole body movement and the need for mind/body coordination (as in hiking a forest trail or rappelling down a rock cliff). Some educators now use the term "active learning" to describe this kinesthetic, hands-on/minds-on way of attaining knowledge. Gibbons and Hopkins (1980) suggested that discussions of experience-based learning would profit from defining activities along a passive-active continuum. "They recommend that "by creating a scale with clearly defined categories we can not only make the nature of the field and the distinctions between different kinds of programs clearer, but we can solve other problems as well ... a term that does not distinguish between a bus tour and a mountain climbing expedition is too vague" (p. 32).

Should the evolving field be described as "adventure programming" instead of "adventure education"? When John Miles and Simon Priest edited a second edition of their book, *Adventure Education* (1990), they re-named it *Adventure Programming* (1999), noting that the new title "more accurately reflects the terminology of the profession as it has evolved over the past decade" (p. xiii). We find this distinction thought provoking, for it raises the question about whether or not the field should be called experiential programming. This change would take experiential education outside the realm of formal education as it is usually thought of in our society.

Should educators view EE as a philosophy and/or a methodology? Throughout the years, there have been many attempts to define EE, usually by describing the educational processes that are involved. For example, in one of the early articles in the *Journal of Experiential Education*, Joplin (1981) attempted to clarify the concept of EE by postulating a five-step model—focus, action, support, feedback, and debrief. Such descriptive models may clarify the methodology, but do not explain the nature and depth of the underlying EE philosophy. The currently accepted AEE definition states that EE is both a philosophy and a methodology.

Christian Itin (1999) suggests that it is better to think of EE as a philosophy, not just a collection of active-learning strategies because this may help in moving the field into the mainstream of educational reform. He suggests the following definition of the philosophy of experiential education:

> Experiential education is a holistic philosophy, where carefully chosen experiences supported by reflection, critical analysis, and synthesis, are structured to require the learner to take initiative, make decisions, and be accountable for the results, through actively posing questions, investigating, experimenting, being curious, solving problems, assuming responsibility, being creative, constructing meaning, and integrating previously developed knowledge. (p. 93)

In spite of Itin's insistence that EE should be considered a philosophy, this definition does not outline that philosophy in sufficient detail. His opening words seem to imply that EE is a methodology based on a holistic philosophy, and then he describes the nature of EE as a methodology.

Is it helpful to think of EE as a theory of instruction? A theory of instruction "sets forth rules concerning the most effective way of achieving knowledge" and "provides a yardstick for criticizing or evaluating any particular way of teaching or learning" (Bruner, 1966, p. 40). A theory of instruction must be concerned with both learning and development and must be congruent with the theories of learning and development to which it subscribes.

According to Bruner (1966), a theory of instruction has four features. It should:

Specify the experiences which most effectively implant in the individual predisposition toward learning.

Specify the ways in which a body of knowledge should be structured so it can be most readily grasped by the learner.

Specify the most effective sequences in which to present the materials to be learned.

Specify the nature and pacing of rewards and punishments in the process of learning and teaching. (pp. 40–41)

The AEE has listed 12 principles of practice. (Luckmann, 1996, p. 7) as a way of defining experiential education. These principles specifically relate to all of the above features of a theory of instruction as described by Bruner (1996), especially the first three. The last feature about rewards and punishments is dealt with more generally. Some of the principles acknowledge that learners are accountable for the results of their experience and should assume responsibility for constructing meaning. One principle recognizes that educators are responsible for setting boundaries and supporting the learners as they facilitate the learning process. Rewards and punishments in experiential education usually take the form of immediate feedback to learners after they participate in an event. For example, if hikers forget to take raingear and it rains, they will get feedback in the form of wet clothing and hopefully their reflection on that experience will lead them to take corrective action the next time.

What is the relationship between EE philosophy and EE goals? In the "official" AEE definition it states that the purpose of EE is to "increase knowledge, develop skills, and clarify values" (Association for Experiential Education 2007, p. 1). This statement opens the door to discussions about the purposes of education. Should the aims of education be mainly for achieving intellectual or psychological/social development? Perhaps both aims should be achieved in order to create a well-rounded individual. To the extent that EE states goals for only personal growth and value clarification, it is subject to all the criticisms that have been leveled at progressive education by the traditionalists over many years. Certainly, when the EE methodology is applied to programs of counseling and therapy, psychological goals such as improving the self-concept and social adjustment are the main foci. When EE methodology is applied to classroom teaching and a curriculum composed of writing, reading, or mathematics skills, the academic aims of experiential education are paramount.

Holistic educator, Ron Miller asked, *What Are Schools For?* (1990), and reviewed the cultural influences and answers to that question throughout history. The development of EE theory involves answering the broad question, "Why do we do what we do?" Individual practitioners need to narrow their inquiry by asking: "Why do I do what I do?", "Why do I do it the way I do it?", and "What do I hope to accomplish by doing it this way?"

Has experiential education become trivialized and misunderstood by some leaders as Dewey feared it might be? Roberts (2005) elaborates on this issue in his article and labels this shallow execution of unrelated activities as "experience-as-technique" (p. 14). By this he explains: "meaningful activity is tightly bound (in both time and space), rationally constructed, and efficiently controlled. Experience becomes not organic, interactive, and continuous but rather something scripted, timed, and located" (p. 15). Roberts is critical of short initiatives or challenges, such as riding a zip line or climbing a wall, that are separated from the main flow of educative experiences. Dewey would call this deviation from the main educational content as mis-educative. Do some experiential educators simply select an activity for students because they think it is fun, but not think deeply about how it fits with the ongoing curriculum or planned objectives for individual and group development? Is simply having fun a valid objective apart from other more "serious" or academic objectives?

What are the similarities and differences between EE and other educational reform movements? Although the AEE membership is a professionally diverse group, there is a danger of becoming isolated from other professional organizations and other educational reform movements. Some critics describe AEE conferences as gatherings of like-minded folks who already share common theories and practices. They believe that EE leaders should interact more with other professionals who think and act differently. The search for a more definitive philosophy of EE may require awareness of a variety of other ideological and methodological approaches to teaching and learning. Some important alternatives are: holistic education, humanistic education, character education, affective education, confluent education, transpersonal education, global education, peace education, cooperative learning, project-based education, and place-based education.

Although this book does not outline a comprehensive philosophy of EE, we hope it offers food for thought for those who want to think more deeply about what they do and why they do it. We agree with Richard Kraft (1999) who stated: "Experiential education would appear to be uniquely poised to help overcome the current deficiencies of both traditional schooling and much of vocational-technical training as it occurs today" (p. 186).

References

Association for Experiential Education (AEE). (2007). Retrieved June 28, 2007, from http://www.aee.org
Bruner, J. S. (1966). *Toward a theory of instruction*. New York: W. W. Norton.
Caine, R. N., Caine, G., McClintic, C., & Klimek, K. (2005). *12 brain/mind learning principles in actions: The fieldbook for making connections, teaching, and the human brain*. Thousand Oaks, CA: Corwin.
Ewert, A. (2005). Reflections on experiential education and the journal: Possible pathways to the future. *The Journal of Experiential Education, 28*, vii–xi.
Flavin, M. (1996). *Kurt Hahn's schools & legacy: To discover you can be more and do more than you believed*. Wilmington, DE: Middle Atlantic Press.

Gibbons, M., & Hopkins, D. (1980). How experiential is your experience-based program? *The Journal of Experiential Education 3,* 135–140.

Itin, C. (1999). Reasserting the philosophy of experiential education as a vehicle for change in the 21st century.*The Journal of Experiential Education, 22*(2), 91–98.

Joplin, L. (1981). On defining experiential education. *Journal of Experiential Education, 4,* 17–20.

Kraft, R. J. (1999). Experiential learning. In J. C. Miles & S. Priest (Eds.), *Adventure programming* (pp. 181–186). State College, PA: Venture.

Luckmann, C. (1996). Defining experiential education. *The Journal of Experiential Education 19,* 6–7.

Luckner, J. L. & Nadler, R. S. (1992). *Processing the experience: Strategies to enhance and generalize learning.* Montecito, CA: True North Leadership.

Miles, J. C., & Priest, S. (Eds.). (1990). *Adventure education.* State College, PA: Venture.

Miles, J. C., & Priest, S. (Eds.). (1997). *Adventure programming.* State College, PA: Venture.

Miller, R. (1990). *What are schools for?* Boston: Holistic Education.

Roberts, J. W. (2005). Disney, Dewey, and the death of experience in education. *Education and Culture, 21,* 12–30.

Tanner, L. N. (1997). *Dewey's laboratory school: Lessons for today.* New York: Teachers College.

Who were John Dewey and Kurt Hahn, and why were they considered to be influential as guides to forming a philosophy of experiential learning? This collection of papers is about educational theorists and practitioners whose ideas may contribute to the expansion and refinement of the theory and practice of experiential education. The collection is seen as going beyond the fundamental ideas of the two people who are most often considered as laying the foundation for contemporary experiential education, John Dewey and Kurt Hahn. Therefore, we solicited two experienced leaders in the field to write brief overviews of the ideas of Dewey and Hahn.

JOHN DEWEY'S INFLUENCE AND LEGACY

Jayson Seaman

Given the way Dewey's ideas are often presented in the literature, one might know him primarily as a learning theorist concerned with making education as hands-on and as relevant to children and to the real world as possible. Clearly, Dewey's influence on education, especially experiential education, has been immeasurable. However, he was first and foremost a philosopher, and to overlook his broader philosophy is to miss the points he made about education. In this brief introduction, I will discuss Dewey's interrelated philosophical and educational ideas before turning to the prospect of moving *beyond* him and his thinking.

Dewey's Life

Dewey was born in Vermont in 1859. He graduated from the University of Vermont at age 20, taught at public schools in Pennsylvania and Vermont, and then completed a PhD from Johns Hopkins University at 25. He worked as a professor of philosophy for 10 years at the University of Michigan before moving to the University of Chicago. After leaving Chicago because of a dispute over his laboratory school, Dewey spent the rest of his career at Columbia University. He was a prolific writer up until his death in 1952 (Field, 2007).

Dewey's Philosophy

Dewey's contributions covered nearly all aspects of human existence, including aesthetics (1934/1980), epistemology (1949), psychology (1896/1975), and political and social theory (1954). His underlying pragmatism influenced his views on education in several key ways. He rejected the "spectator" theory of knowledge, arguing that the only way we can know the world is by interacting socially in it. His early training in psychology, coupled with an interest in Darwinian theory, led him to see how society and individuals co-evolved. Synthesizing these viewpoints, Dewey concluded that knowledge was a tool for acting in the world and, through acting, for changing the conditions for our future. The quality of our knowledge is therefore supremely important in order to achieve "intelligent planning, deliberation, and calculation" (Dewey, 1910/1997, p. 15). This sensibility informs Dewey's emphasis on practical human activity and on science as a way of inquiring into—and experimenting with—social conditions to achieve favorable results.

Dewey's philosophy also contained important moral and political dimensions. For instance, in his educational texts and elsewhere, he strongly criticized capitalism for arranging social conditions mainly to serve "private advantage and power" (1938, p. 81), describing his own politics as a kind of "radical liberalism" and "fighting liberalism" (1935/1991). He believed individual freedoms were realized *through* our association with one another, a view that influenced his deep commitment to democracy as a form of government, a mode of interaction among individuals, and even as a basis for knowledge acquisition (Garrison, 1995).

Dewey's Educational Views

"I believe that all education proceeds by the participation of the individual in the social consciousness of the race." It is with these words that Dewey began his *Pedagogic Creed* (1897). Such was the charge of schooling: To structure the conditions for students to *participate* in social activity, and in so doing, master the knowledge and dispositions required to shape civilized society in thoughtful ways. Failure to do so would "result in adoption of superficial measures which in the end will only render existing problems more acute and more difficult to solve" (1938, p. 77).

Dewey challenged the dominant educational theories of his day (Kliebard, 1995). He rejected arbitrary subject-matter boundaries (i.e., social studies, math, science) and believed instruction should start from the practical human problems that were encountered by previous generations. He also rejected some of the views of his child-centered colleagues. He too wanted to capture students' interests, but he charged that "nothing can be more absurd educationally than to make a plea for a variety of active occupations in school while decrying the need for progressive organization of information and ideas" (1938, p. 84). The teacher's job was twofold: (a) "to clarify, build up, and *put in order the content of experience,* so that in time it will grow to include the systematic body of facts which the adult's consciousness already possesses" (quoted in Tanner, 1997, p. 45, italics added), and (b) to interpret the child's "powers, interests, and habits we must know what they mean. They must be *translated into terms of their social equivalents*—into terms of what they are capable of in the way of social service" (1897, p. 77, italics added). Dewey's theory of education was developmental in two senses, then he believed that curriculum should be ordered sequentially so it would follow the evolution of Western civilization as a way of life, and pursued actively in order to ignite the emerging capacities and interests of the child. For a short time, his laboratory school at the University of Chicago served as a crucible where these ideas were tested, refined, and disseminated (Tanner, 1997).

It is in the context of his curriculum theory that Dewey used the term "experience". He wrote: "Unless experience is so conceived that the result is a plan for deciding upon subject matter, upon methods of instruction and discipline, and upon material equipment and social organization of the school, it is wholly in the air" (1938, p. 28). The curricular principles of *continuity* and *interaction* were central to this concept, as the "longitudinal and lateral aspects of experience" (1938, p. 44). Thus, it was by engaging in carefully structured social "occupations" that matched the problems faced by previous generations as well as the dawning capacities of the child, and by reflecting carefully on the *meaning* of the solutions to individuals and to society, that children would become educated through *experience* (Seaman, 2010).

Beyond Dewey and Back Again

For Dewey, education was a reciprocal process of social and individual change. Experiential educators have long shared this sentiment, but the richness of Dewey's concept of *experience* is lost if it is reduced to simply "learning by doing" followed by reflection. Interestingly, Dewey later thought he might substitute the term "culture" for "experience" in his writing (Glassman, 2001). This indicates the breadth of the term for Dewey; what would it mean for theory and practice if we called our field *cultural education* instead of *experiential education*?

Should we move *beyond* Dewey in our thinking? Yes, in my view, for several reasons. Dewey's full vision for experience in education may simply be too cumbersome—he struggled with it himself at the lab school (Jackson, in Dewey, 1956/1990). Also, his theories have been criticized persuasively from several different perspectives (e.g., Bowers, 2005; Egan, 2002; Margonis, 2003; Popkewitz, 1998). Finally, times have changed since Dewey's era. A piecemeal implementation of his vision may be all we can hope for, given how entrenched and efficiency-minded the educational system has become (see Tyack & Cuban, 1995). Other theorists may now offer better guidance under these conditions (Miettinen, 2006).

But scholars might also proceed tentatively. It is highly doubtful that Dewey's ideas have been exhausted. Given the broad scope of the term "experience" for Dewey, it is not clear that a modern usage of *experiential* refers to the same thing. He might applaud the success we've achieved at making hands-on learning a central part of education for many students. However, his awareness of the economic basis of social life (and even of private thinking) and his focus on rigorous, scientific inquiry have not been emphasized in experiential education. Hopefully, by introducing the theorists in this book to our understanding of Dewey, we might reflect on our use of his ideas and come to understand them in fresh, new ways.

References

Bowers, C. A. (2005). *The false promises of constructivist learning theories: A global and ecological critique.* New York: Peter Lang.

Dewey, J. (1897). My pedagogic creed. *The School Journal, LIV*(3), 77–80.

Dewey, J. (1980). *Art as experience.* New York: Perigee. (Original work published 1934)

Dewey, J. (1991). *Liberalism and social action.* Amherst, NY: Prometheus. (Original work published 1935)

Dewey, J. (1938). *Experience and education.* New York: Macmillan.

Dewey, J. (1954). *The pubic & its problems.* Athens, OH: Swallow.

Dewey, J. (1975). The reflect arc concept in psychology. In J. A. Boydston (Ed.), *John Dewey: The early works* (Vol. 5). Carbondale: University of Southern Illinois. (Original work published 1896)

Dewey, J. (1990). *The school and society/The child and the curriculum.* Chicago: University of Chicago. (Original work published 1956)

Dewey, J. (1997). *How we think.* Mineola, NY: Dover. (Original work published 1910)

Dewey, J., & Bentley, A. F. (1949). *Knowing and the known.* Boston: Beacon.

Egan, K. (2002). *Getting it wrong from the beginning: Our progressive inheritance from Herbert Spencer, John Dewey, and Jean Piaget.* New Haven, CT: Yale University Press.

Fallace, T. D. (2008). John Dewey and the savage mind: United anthropological, psychological, and pedagogical thought, 1894–1902. *Journal of the History of the Behavioral Sciences, 44*(4), 355–359.

Field, R. (2007). John Dewey [Electronic Version]. *The Internet Encyclopedia of Philosophy*. Retrieved December 19, 2007, from http://www.iep.utm.edu/d/dewey.htm

Garrison, J. (1995). Deweyan pragmatism and the epistemology of contemporary social constructivism. *American Educational Research Journal, 32*(4), 716–740.

Glassman, M. (2001). Dewey and Vygotsky: Society, experience, and inquiry in educational practice. *Educational Researcher, 30*(4), 3–14.

Kliebard, H. M. (1995). *The struggle for the American curriculum, 1893–1958* (2nd ed.). New York: Routledge.

Margonis, F. (2003). The path of social amnesia and Dewey's democratic commitments [Electronic Version]. *Philosophy of Education*. Retrieved December 19, 2007, from http://www.ed.uius.edu/eps/PES-Yearbook/2003/2003toc.htm

Miettinen, R. (2006). Epistemology of transformative material activity: John Dewey's pragmatism and cultural-historical activity theory. *Journal for the Theory of Social Behavior, 36*(4), 389–407.

Popkewitz, T. S. (1998). Dewey, Vygotsky, and the social administration of the individual: Constructivist pedagogy as systems of ideas in historical spaces. *American Educational Research Journal, 35*(4), 535–570.

Tanner, L. N. (1997). *Dewey's laboratory school: Lessons for today*. New York: Teachers College.

Tyack, D. B., & Cuban, L. (1995). *Tinkering toward utopia: A century of public school reform*. Cambridge, MA: Harvard University.

KURT MATTHIAS ROBERT MARTIN HAHN

Steve Pace

Although he never completed an academic degree beyond his secondary schooling, Kurt Hahn (1886–1974) was one of the most influential educators of the 20th century. His passion for developing the character and morality of youth led him to start a number of innovative educational programs, including Outward Bound. Hahn was the second son of German Jews. His father was a successful industrialist, and his mother a compassionate woman who believed in the goodness of all people. His education was in the traditions of the German gymnasiums, and after graduation in 1904 he spent nearly a decade as a roving student. With financial support from his father, he traveled to England to study the classics at Christchurch and Oxford; and he also attended the universities of Berlin, Heidelberg, Freiberg, and Gottigen in Germany.

Through the years, Hahn became obsessed by the social declines or social diseases that he observed in society. Hahn believed that every child is born with innate spiritual powers and an ability to make correct judgments about moral issues, but in the progression through adolescence, the child loses these powers because of the diseased society and the impulses of adolescence. In his introduction to the book, *Outward Bound: The Inward Odyssey, Vol. II* (Zelinski, 1991), Anthony Richards described Hahn's ideas about the "declines" of youth through the adolescent years.

The decline in fitness due to the modern methods of locomotion.
The decline of initiative and enterprise due to the widespread disease of spectatoritis,
The decline of memory and imagination due to the confused restlessness of modern life.
The decline of skill and care due to the weakened tradition of craftsmanship.
The decline of self-discipline due to the ever-present availability of stimulants and tranquilizers.
The decline of compassion due to the unseemly haste with which modern life is conducted.
 (p. 3)

When in England, Hahn visited Cecil Reddie's Abbotsholme, one of the "new schools" that advocated character development in the school agenda (James, 2000). His developing educational philosophy was also influenced by Lord Baden Powell's Boy Scout programs, and by the new private schools in Germany that had been started by Herman Leitz. Hahn became interested in developing educational programs that focused on moral development as well as physical and intellectual development.

Hahn worked in the German Foreign Office during World War I, and "by the end of the war he became a private secretary to Prince Max of Baden, a German federal prince and heir to the grand Duchy of Baden" (Stetson, n.d., p. 2). The two men shared an understanding of the importance of Plato's ideas on education. Plato had suggested that a new element—character building—be added to educational curricula. Kurt Hahn agreed, and many think of his educational approach as basic "character education." However, Hahn also believed in the importance of physical conditioning and learning academic subjects. As part of his concern for physical well being, he believed that every child has both a natural physical aptitude and a natural physical inaptitude. Both provide opportunities: one to develop strength and the other to overcome weakness. This was the source of another of Hahn's aphorisms, "There is more in you than you think" (Neil, n.d.). Hahn's goal was to provide an "ideal pasture" for these innate powers and abilities to manifest themselves (Richards, n.d.).

In 1920, with Prince Max as his benefactor, Hahn began a small private school in the castle in Salem, Germany, and he became an activist for educational and social reform. As the Nazi party rose to power in the late 1920s, Hahn's libertarian political stance led to trouble with the authorities; and after being arrested and imprisoned for protesting Germany's youth movement, he fled to England in 1933. Within a year, he started the Gordonstoun school in Scotland, from which he built his reputation as an innovative educator (Stetson & Blair, n.d.).

"Kurt Hahn's educational philosophy was a collage of what he considered the best ideas drawn from as many sources as possible. Hahn used material that was already proven to work rather than experiment with something new. However, his success lay in the selection and unique combination of the principles that he decided to 'borrow'" (Richards, n.d., p. 2). A historic document summarizes what Hahn called, "The Seven Laws of Salem" (Flavin, 1996, p. 15):

First Law: Give the children opportunities for self-discovery.
Second Law: Make the children meet with triumph and defeat.
Third Law: Give the children the opportunity of self-effacement in the common cause.
Fourth Law: Provide periods of silence.
Fifth Law: Train the imagination.
Sixth Law: Make games important but not predominant.
Seventh Law: Free the sons of the wealthy and powerful from the enervating sense of privilege.

It is important to note that the building of character, the development of morality, is but a first step in the educational process for Hahn. In his Harrogate Address on Outward Bound in 1965, Hahn suggested that the impact of an Outward Bound experience on the individual "is apt to evaporate, leaving no trace on future conduct, unless the Outward Bounders, in their normal surroundings, will translate it into action—in other words, unless they seek and find opportunities for a demanding active service of use to their fellow men" (Hahn, 1965, p. 6).

Although Kurt Hahn died in 1974 his ideas are as current today as they were in his prime. "He taught that education must enable young people to effect what they have recognized to be right, despite hardships, despite dangers, despite inner skepticism, despite boredom, and despite mockery from the world" (Neil, n.d.).

This book is based on the notion that it is important for experiential education to look at the ideas of educational theorists and practitioners that go "Beyond Dewey and Hahn" for theoretical foundations. While I agree that will be valuable for the field, I would suggest that what we find beyond Kurt Hahn can never diminish the importance of what we can find within Kurt Hahn.

Perhaps the core of Hahn's beliefs can be summed up in a quote by one of his students: "We are better than we know. If we can be made to see it, perhaps for the rest of our lives, we will be unwilling to settle for less" (Stetson & Blair, 1996, p. x).

References

Hahn, K. (1965). Harrogate address on outward bound. Retrieved December 20, 2007, from http://www.kurthahn.org/writings/gate.pdf

Flavin, M. (1996). *Kurt Hahn's schools and legacy: To discover you can be more and do more than you believed*. Wilmington, DE: Middle Atlantic Press.

James, T. (2000). Kurt Hahn and the aims of education. Retrieved June, 2005, from http://www.kurthahn.org/writings/james.pdf

Neil, J. (n.d.). Kurt Hahn quotes. Retrieved December 17, 2007, from http://wilderdom.com/Hahn.htm

Richards, A. (1991). Introduction. In M. Zelinski (Ed.), *Outward bound: The inward odyssey*. New York: Beyond Words. Retrieved December 18, 2007, from http://www.outward-bound.org/lic_sub3_history.htm

Richards, A. (n.d.). Outward bound: The founder's story. Retrieved December 17, 2007, from http: //www.outwardbound.net/about/history/kurt-hahn.html

Stetson, C. (n.d.). An essay on Kurt Hahn founder of outward bound. Retrieved, October, 2006, from http://www.kurthahn.org/writings/stet.pdf

Stetson, C. P., & Blair, P. S. (1996). Journey with Kurt Hahn. Fourways, Gauteng, South Africa: Outward Bound Trust of South Africa.

Zelinski, M. (Ed.). (1991). *Outward bound: The inward odyssey*. New York: Beyond Words.

Part I

Philosophers and Educational Theorists

The value of any theory is, in the long run, determined by practical application.

John Dewey, 1895

A comprehensive philosophy of experiential education (EE) is dependent on individual prac- titioners developing their personal philosophies and then dialoguing with others in the field. Looking to the ideas of philosophers in general, and educational philosophers in particular, seems to be an appropriate starting point for building a philosophy of experiential education. One problem is that there are many disagreements about the various definitions of philosophy advanced by scholars (Harrison-Birket, 2001). Two references may be helpful:

1. The *Penguin Dictionary of Philosophy* suggests that philosophy should be distinguished from science because the questions involved cannot be answered empirically, and from reli- gion because there is no place for faith or revelation in philosophy (Mautner, 2005).
2. The *Oxford Companion to Philosophy* concludes that philosophy is basically just critical thinking (Honderich, 2005).

One might also think of philosophy as a particular set of beliefs and values, and then do some critical thinking about questions of importance in developing an educational theory.

1. "What is learning" and "how do people learn?"
2. "What is teaching" and "how should teachers teach?"
3. "What is the purpose of education" and "what is worth knowing and studying?"
4. "What is the relationship of the schools to society at large and to the world?

Answering these questions in terms of beliefs and values gives rise to one's personal theory of education, and reaching a consensus in the field of EE results in a philosophy of EE. Arriv- ing at a consensus about a single definition may be difficult, or perhaps impossible, because of the diversity of personal and professional philosophies of those who consider themselves to be experiential educators. Still, clarification of one's personal philosophy is valuable because it can make one a more effective practitioner.

As experiential educators contemplate these questions, it is impossible to leave the com- plexity of philosophy behind. There is value in understanding the focal points of philosophy as defined throughout history. Most scholars would agree that there are four main areas of phi- losophy. *Metaphysics* involves the study of the nature of the world, the nature of reality, and the organization of the universe (cosmology). *Epistemology* involves thinking about how we know what we know, and seeks distinctions between true knowledge and belief. Important parts of epistemology include the study of logic, reasoning, semantics, and the rules of rational thought.

Axiology is the study of values and valuation, and includes ethics and aesthetics. Ethics involves critical thinking about what is good, what is right, and the value judgments of people. Aesthetics asks questions about the nature of beauty. *Ontology* involves the study of being in general. In recent times, it has been suggested that questions about the processes of human growth and development, formerly discussed as part of ontology, should be considered as a fifth category of philosophy.

Educational philosophy is primarily related to epistemology, but the development of an educational philosophy also involves attention to the other branches of philosophy. For example, John Dewey's metaphysical assumptions gave rise to his pragmatism, which was the core of his functional psychology and educational philosophy. His assumptions about ethics and human growth and development influenced his suggestions on school processes and curriculum content. This complexity creates problems for anyone developing a personal philosophy of education, because while they may agree with the tenants of a particular educational theory, they may find disagreement with some of the underlying philosophical foundations. Critical thinking about theories of education has to involve the analysis of core questions of philosophy if one is to overcome incongruencies and diversity of opinions.

Historically, a number of educational theories have been offered by philosophers and educators, and then adopted by those field practitioners who agreed with them. College courses in educational philosophy typically examine the prominent theories and then compare and contrast them. Through the years there have been many scholarly debates about the similarities and differences between theories. Summarizing the various educational philosophies in a few lines does not do them justice, but any search for broader theoretical foundations of EE should certainly include attention to them and their proponents.

John Dewey's progressive view can be considered as the centerpoint of educational philosophy in the 20th century, for most other theories supported, expanded, criticized, or suggested alternatives to his approach. *Progressivism* begins with a psychological theory of human growth and learning that is usually based on *constructivism*, which emphasizes the role of individuals in constructing their own knowledge and values—their own realities. Most constructivists do emphasize methods of teaching or content of school curriculum; they seek to understand the learning process from the study of the developmental process. Jean Piaget's work on the development of cognitive and perceptual processes in children is recognized as important to constructionist theory (Piaget, 1955), as is Lev Vygotsky's (1978) work on the development of language and the important link between language and learning. Jerome Bruner's (2006) ideas on education are based on a constructivist philosophy, as is Albert Bandura's (1976) social learning theory.

Progressivism has been described as John Dewey's brand of constructivism, concerned with how the learner constructs knowledge from experience, reflection, and experimentation. Progressives recommend that classrooms be more student-centered than teacher-centered. This suggests that educational programs should focus on process as well as content, and feature teaching students how to learn as well as what to learn.

In describing and defending John Dewey's philosophy of education for EE, April Crosby suggested that the epistemological assumptions underlying EE "are much more reliable than those underlying more traditional theories of education" and that implies that "students educated according to these assumptions are better prepared to deal with the world than are students educated according to traditional epistemology" (1984, p. 4).

In protest against Dewey's pragmatic education, William Bagley (1874–1946) wrote on essentialism in the early years of the 20th century (Bagley, 1934). Essentialism rests on the assumption that information is the key to a good education, and assumes that there is a core body of knowledge that needs to be mastered if one is to be considered educated. These classrooms are most often teacher centered, with the teacher/authority passing on information and essential skills. Arguments of "back to basics" are usually associated with essentialism, and many contemporary educational theorists still suggest that the "non-essentials" should be taken out of the school curriculum (Sizer, 1997).

Another alternative to progressive education is called *perennialism*, which is based on the belief that there is wisdom in the great philosophical, literary, and scientific thinkers of history, and that a good education involves understanding that wisdom. These educators teach students about the great books (Hutchins, 1959) and the great ideas of history. These classrooms are also teacher centered, with instruction delivered by lecture, coaching, or Socratic questioning, and the curriculum emphasizes reading, writing, recitation, and debate. Big ideas, not isolated facts, are important, and there is value in learning for its own sake. Mortimer Adler's Paideia Proposal for educational curriculum is an example of a perennialist's approach to education (Adler, 1988).

Before the dust had even settled on Dewey's progressive philosophy of education, some of his followers suggested that his argument that education should prepare people for productive lives in society did not go far enough. They argued that, like the perennialists, there was value in transmitting knowledge about the existing culture and the democratic system. Their disagreement with the notion that education should involve teaching the child how to conform to societal norms, and accept particular social and political orientations, led to development of *reconstructionism* as an educational philosophy.

George Counts (1899–1974) advocated the child-centered classroom, but thought that teachers should empower students to lead society instead of follow it. He suggested that education should instill a critical social consciousness, not the rugged individualism that was advocated by traditionalists. He dared teachers to be truly progressive (Counts, 1932). Like Counts, Theodore Brameld (1904–1987) was a social activist who suggested that the goal of education should be to create citizens of the world. He was a forerunner of the philosophy of global education that has developed over the past 25 years (Brameld, 1956). Ivan Illich (1926–2002) was an anarchist who argued that institutions of education are forerunners to the institutionalization of all society, and led to total dis-empowerment of the individual. He advocated for less government regulation of the schools (more power to the people), and learning networks that existed outside organized education.

A widely read reconstructionist was Paulo Freire (1921–1997) whose seminal book, *The Pedagogy of the Oppressed* (1970), has had major influence on educational theory and practice, especially in third world countries. His theory of *critical pedagogy* challenges the schools to abandon the "banking" concept of education, where students are viewed as empty vessels waiting to be filled with the wisdom of authoritarian teachers. He believed the aim of education should be to empower students to move into the world and challenge oppressive societal and political forces. He argued that educational reform must precede societal reform. The influence of Freire on educational theory has increased during the past two decades, and many EE theorists have already examined his philosophy (Breunig, 2005). Henry Giroux is recognized as one of the founding theorists of critical pedagogy in the United States (Giroux, 1988).

A humanistic paradigm for education developed in the 1960s, championed by psychologists, sociologists, educators, and spiritual leaders who considered themselves as part of the human potential movement. *Humanism* as an educational philosophy, rooted in the work of Carl Rogers, Abraham Maslow, Kurt Lewin, Fritz Perls, and others who were bonded together as a "third force" in American psychology. The humanists have had a significant impact on the developing practices of EE. The cornerstone of humanism as an educational philosophy lies in believing in a basic growth hypothesis—a tendency of all living organisms to become what they are programmed by genetic predisposition to become. Carl Rogers called it a "formative tendency" (Rogers, 1978). Humanists believed the role of educators should be as facilitators of the growth and learning drive that is inherent in all humans.

Although philosophical existentialism includes diverse opinions about metaphysics, epistemology, axiology, and ontology, there is a shared respect for individualism. This leads to a strong rejection of the essentialist's approach to education, for individuals are responsible for determining their own notions of truth, beauty, and the meaning of life. *Existentialism* as an educational philosophy developed in the 1960s, putting more emphasis on experiences that help students discover their individuality, their true or "authentic" being. Perhaps, more than any other educational theory, the existential approach gives students latitude in their choice of what to study, and even whether to study at all (Smith, 2008). This emphasis on personal choice is balanced by guiding students to understand the parallel personal responsibilities involved in their decisions.

Later in his life, Abraham Maslow (1971) advocated for a "fourth force" in American psychology which would study experiences that go beyond ordinary ego functioning. This became known as transpersonal psychology, and it gave rise to an educational philosophy that can be called *transpersonalism*. In this approach, there is room for the spiritual and mystical experiences of the mind, for classroom activities involving body relaxation, stretching and breathing, and for facilitating body-mind experiences using centering, meditation, tai chi, and other esoteric practices. EE programs that offer solo experiences parallelling the Native American vision quest would find support in transpersonalism. Because most American educators cling to conservative perennialist and essentialist philosophies, ideas about transpersonal education have had limited impact in the public schools. Still, this theory should be of interest to EE professionals (Hendricks, 1976; Moore, 1997).

This collection could have included chapters on most of those educators/philosophers mentioned above, because their ideas would be helpful as EE practitioners build personal and professional philosophies of education. There are chapters on some of these important educational philosophers in this collection, and Appendix I offers brief biographical sketches of many others. There are eight chapters in the section to follow:

Chapter 2—Aristotle, Plato, and Socrates: Ancient Greek Perspectives on Experiential Education
Chapter 3—Rousseau and Pestalozzi: Emile, Gertrude, and Experiential Education
Chapter 4—Sir Patrick Geddes: "*Vievndo Discimus*"—By Learning We Live
Chapter 5—Alfred North Whitehead: Educational Emergence
Chapter 6—Martin Buber: Dialogue, Relationship, the Other, and the More-Than-Human World
Chapter 7—Paulo Freire: Critical Praxis and Experiential Education
Chapter 8—Maxine Greene: The Power of the Possible
Chapter 9—Eleanor Duckworth: The Teacher's Teacher

References

Adler, M. (1988). *Reforming education: The opening of the American mind*. New York: Macmillan. Bagley, W. C. (1934). *Education and emergent man*. New York: T. Nelson & Sons.
Bandura, A. (1976). *Social learning theory*. New York: Prentice-Hall.
Brameld, T. (1956). *Toward a reconstructed philosophy of education*. New York: Dryden.
Breunig, M. (2005). Turning experiential education and critical pedagogy theory into praxis. *Journal of Experiential Education, 28*(2), 106–122.
Bruner, J. (2006). *The process of education*. Cambridge, MA: Harvard University Press.
Counts, G. (1932). Dare progressive education be progressive? *Progressive Education, 9*(4), 257–263. Retrieved October 2006, from http://courses.wccnet.edu/~palay/cls2002/counts

Crosby, A. (1984). A critical look: The philosophical foundations of experiential education. *Journal of Experiential Education, 4*(1), 1–7.

Freire, P. (1970). *Pedagogy of the oppressed.* New York: Continuum International.

Giroux, H. (1988). *Teachers as intellectuals: Toward a critical pedagogy of learning.* New York: Bergin & Garvey.

Harrison-Birket, A. (2001). *Mastering philosophy,* 2nd ed. New York: Palgrave Macmillan.

Hendricks, G. (1976). *Transpersonal education: A curriculum for feeling and being.* New York: Prentice-Hall.

Honderich, T. (2005). *Oxford companion to philosophy,* 2nd ed. New York: Oxford University Press. Hutchins, R. (1959). *An introduction to the great books* (Vols.1–2). New York: Encyclopedia Britannica.

Illich, I. (1999). *Deschooling society.* New York: Marion Boyars.

Maslow, A. (1971). *The further reaches of human nature.* New York: Viking.

Mautner, T. (2005). *The penguin dictionary of philosophy,* 2nd ed. New York: Penguin.

Moore, T. (1997). *The education of the heart.* New York: Harper.

Piaget, J. (1955). *The child's construction of reality.* London: Routledge and Kegan Paul.

Rogers, C. (1978). The formative tendency. *Journal of Humanistic Psychology, 18*(1), 23–26.

Sizer, T. (1997). *Horace's hope: What works for the American high school.* New York: Mariner Books.

Smith, T. (2008). A thin line of Socratic wisdom: Individual choice and responsibility in learning. In *Raccoon's Droppings* (pp. 211–260). Lake Geneva, WI: Raccoon Institute.

Vygotsky, L. (1978). *Mind in society: Development of higher psychological processes,* 14th ed. Cambridge, MA: Harvard University Press.

2   Aristotle, Plato, and Socrates

Ancient Greek Perspectives on Experiential Learning[1]

Paul Stonehouse, Pete Allison, and David Carr

The intention of this chapter is to briefly sketch several of Socrates and Plato's contributions to experiential education, and then, in more detail, examine Aristotle as a progenitor of the experiential learning cycle and a potential catalyst for a moral renaissance within outdoor education. Special attention will be given to Artistotle's notion of practical wisdom, and his arguments about transforming experience into informed judgment. We understand learning through experience to be a theory of education that broadly encompasses many contexts. One context is outdoor education, which uses the outdoor environment as the locus for learning experientially. Our expertise lies with the area of outdoor education, but our references to the philosophy of experiential learning in this chapter are intended to be relevant for a more general readership.

Socrates and Plato

The contributions of Socrates, Plato, and Aristotle to the philosophies of experiential learning are well documented (Kraft, 1985, pp. 9–10; Crosby, Warren, Sakofs, & Hunt, 1995, pp. 6–8; Wurdinger, 1997, pp. 1–6; Hunt, 1999, pp. 115–117). We want to explore some aspects of their philosophies that we believe to be interesting and informative to current thinking and practices, although in a short chapter it is only possible to sketch some general ideas.

Socrates (469–399 BC) was a veteran of the Peloponnesian war, a father, husband, and master debater. He was also Plato's teacher, and we know of Socrates chiefly through Plato's dialogues. Much scholastic debate surrounds the possibility of separating their views (Blackburn, 1996, pp. 355–356). Socrates was a paragon to philosophers, who were literally lovers of wisdom (see *Phaedo*, *Crito*, and *Apology* in Plato, trans. 2002). In valuing truth above all else, even in death (he died by imbibing hemlock while under arrest), Socrates established a high standard for all educators in their pursuit of understanding.

Perhaps Socrates' greatest contribution to experiential learning was his *elenctic* method. Plato calls the Socratic method *elenchus* (*Apology* 21c-e, 23a), meaning a way of asking questions that helps the interlocutor know what they know and do not know (Long, 2002, p. 55). Here, the skillful teacher only facilitates learning, thoughtfully assessing where the student is, and prompting the student's own discovery. The point of all these questions is captured in his often quoted line, "An unexamined life is not worth living" (*Apology* 38a), where Socrates proffers reflection, the linchpin of the experiential pattern of inquiry, as indispensable to living well (Wurdinger, 2005, p. 8).

৵৵৵

Plato's influence on experiential learning comes particularly through the adventure vein, illustrated by Kurt Hahn's implementation of many ideas from The Republic (Plato, trans. 1987; James, 1995, p. 35). Describing what experiential educators would call holistic education, Plato says the two branches of education, one philosophical, broadly meaning intellectual pursuits, and the other physical, are not intended the one to train body, the other mind, except incidentally, but to ensure a proper harmony between energy and initiative on the one hand and reason on the other, so we may venture to assert that anyone who can produce the perfect blend of the physical and intellectual sides of education and apply them to the training of character, is producing harmony of far more importance (411e–412a). In Greek, "Plato" (427–347 BC), means "broad," and was allegedly a nickname for the breadth of his shoulders (Laertius, 1979). He was born an Athenian aristocrat and was greatly influenced by Socrates' life and death. He founded a school which he called The Academy. Life at The Academy highlights an indirect but important association to experiential learning, particularly relevant to the outdoor education sector. Academy is the Greek word for leisure, which in Latin is scola, in English is school (Pieper, trans. 1998, pp. 3–4). For the Greeks, the re-creative activities of reflection, exercise, and study were the epitome of leisure. Pertinent to outdoor educators and often related or associated with fields such as recreation and leisure studies, the Greek ideal of leisure is more than a mere vacation (literally to be unoccupied); it is "a disposition of receptive understanding, of contemplative beholding, and immersion—in the real" (Pieper, trans. 1998, p. 31). That the Greeks associated school with leisure, Plato's Academy being an exemplar, may be the source of the conviction often held by those involved in experiential learning, that learning can, and should, be enjoyable.

When one speaks of philosophical influences on experiential learning, it is generally implied that certain attributes of experiential learning have their roots in particular schools of philosophical thought or in specific philosophers' beliefs. However, there is another positive form of influence. Much like Socrates' metaphorical self-appellation, the gadfly (*Apology* 30e–31a), Plato, in several places, intellectually buzzes, bites, and irritates his modern readers into defining their positions. For example, Plato's pejorative views of democracy are both stimulating and potentially challenging for those involved in experiential learning who usually hold democratic values to be central to their practice:

> I dare say that a democracy is the most attractive of all societies. The diversity of its characters make it look very attractive... [But], we said that no one who had no exceptional gifts could grow into a good man unless he were brought up from childhood in a good environment and trained in good habits. Democracy with a grandiose gesture sweeps all this away and doesn't mind what the habits and background of its politicians are; provided they profess themselves the people's friends. (*The Republic*, 1987, 557c, 558b)

Instead of a democratic society, governed by the elected, Plato envisioned a state ruled by philosopher kings (guardians). Philosopher kings were chosen over a five-decade selective process. The candidate pool initially consisted of *all* citizens and was gradually reduced throughout a rigorous education, primary, physical training, mathematics, philosophy, and a 15-year internship. One could only become a philosopher king through successfully enduring the whole course. Far more than intellectual ability, philosopher kings had to prove themselves morally, having an appropriate motivation for power, as well as a flawless public *and* private moral character. At the very least, Plato causes the modern experiential practitioner to pause and reflect how citizenship education can be better refined and more intentional.

Another area where Plato acts as a gadfly to experiential learning is in his epistemological convictions. Plato, through Socrates says:

> Now, how about the acquirement of pure knowledge? Is the body a hindrance or not, if it is made to share in the search for wisdom? What I mean is this: Have the sight and hearing of men any truth in them, or is it true, as the poets are always telling us, that we neither hear nor see any thing accurately? And yet if these two physical senses are not accurate or exact,

the rest are not likely to be, for they are inferior to these. In thought, then, if at all, something of the realities becomes clear to it? (*Phaedo*, trans. 1966, 65a–c)

Plato developed a concept of Ideal Forms to cope with several conundrums he found in experience. For example, although the potter's pot is never truly round, we conceptualize roundness as an ideal; or just as no human institution is completely just, we hold an ideal, an abstract and theoretical form of justice (Blackburn, 1996, pp. 143–144). Although we cannot seem to provide a general definition for "justice," it must exist, for we often agree when we see it. Thus, Plato posited that "justice," and other ideals, existed in an alternate reality to our own, a reality of the Ideal Forms. Plato, mistrusting the physical, for it is only a poor reflection of the realm of the Forms (see the cave analogy in the *Republic*, 1987, 514a–521b), uses unassisted reason to gain "pure knowledge," and thus is considered a rationalist (Blackburn, 1996, p. 381). We offer this example as helpful for experiential educators, because we need to consider the limits of what can be known experientially and appropriate learning strategies for educating complexities inaccessible to experience (Higgins, 2009, p. 47).

Plato thought knowledge could be discovered through dialectical discussion. By dint of intellectual debate and examination, one could increasingly approach "the truth," as represented by the Ideal Forms. This pursuit of knowledge of the ideal, resulted in a tendency towards general definitions as found in many of the dialogues.

One definition of particular interest to the outdoor experiential practitioner is that of virtue (*Meno*, trans. 2002, p. 77a). We highlight virtue because ethics and values were a significant motivation in the inception of outdoor education in the 20th century. For example, Outward Bound, drawing its inspiration from William James' "Moral Equivalent of War" (1949, pp. 311–328) was interested less in skills development and more in moral formation (Hunt, 1996, p. 15). This is captured grammatically in Lawrence Holt's comment about sailing training at Aberdovey, the first Outward Bound School in Wales, which he said must be less about training for the sea than through the sea (Miner & Boldt, 1981, p. 33). Critiquing the increasing tendency towards algorithmic, assembly line, product-oriented outdoor experiential learning programs, Loynes, contemplating alternative models, briefly considers bringing back an ethical emphasis, a moral paradigm, for outdoor education (2002, pp. 119–120). Bowles, in personal communication with Loynes, remembers the early Hahn's ethical agenda, before his ideas were marketed, saying: "I firmly believe that the work of Kurt Hahn is waiting for an informed re-appraisal" (Loynes, 2002, p. 119). The ethical vision Bowles references, is Hahn's hope that education through service could instill a love for humanity (Richards, 1981, pp. 22–23). Facilitating the development of compassion was at the core of Hahn's mission, and he considered it the most urgent of the societal declines (Hahn, 1960, p. 7). He believed that Samaritan service—the compassionate passerby whose selfless care to a person of different ethnicity extended the domain of neighbour to all humankind—provided a vehicle to stir compassion once again (Hahn, 1958, p. 6):

Our conscience is always struggling against what seem irresistible temptations—of greed, of prestige, of malice of comfort. Over these temptations conscience could triumph every time if it could call to its help a counterforce, an ally. Compassion is that ally, the most powerful that conscience can have; compassion that is forever in vigilant readiness to dominate the inner life. (Hahn, 1940, p. 6)

Plato's influence on Hahn (Richards, 1981, pp. 49–56) lies behind this moral renaissance that Bowles (in Loynes, 2002, p. 119) suggests. For the early Greeks, the ethical life was a life of virtue. For Socrates, and to a significant degree Plato, virtue is obtained through knowledge: "It is from defect of knowledge that men err, when they do err, in their choice of pleasures and pains - that is, in the choice of good and evil" (*Protagoras*, trans. 1967, 357d). Aristotle enters here because he fundamentally disagrees with Plato's approach to virtue and the good in general, introducing his critique with this statement, "though we love both truth and our friends [Plato], reverence is due to the truth first" (*Aristotle*, trans. 1999, I 6§1).

Aristotle

Aristotle (384–322 BC) was born in the Greek colony of Stagira. His father, Nicomachus, was physician to the King of Macedonia (Denise, White, & Peterfreund, 2005, p. 22). Early exposure to his father's habits of scientific observation is thought to be a significant reason for his drifting from Plato's idealism.

In 367 BC, Aristotle was sent to Plato's Academy in Athens where he spent the next 20 years, until Plato's death (Crisp, 2000, p. vii). Plato and Aristotle appear to have had great admiration for one another (I 6§1). Plato nicknamed Aristotle "the mind," but did think of him as something of a dandy, for paying more attention to clothes "than was becoming for a sincere lover of wisdom" (Milch & Patterson, 1966, p. 6; Thomas, Thomas, & Lewis, 2001, disc one, track 13).

At Plato's death in 347 BC, Aristotle left for Asia Minor under invitation from the philosopher King Hermeias, whose niece, Pythias, he married and with whom he had a daughter, also named Pythias (Blackburn, 1996, p. 24). Persian military pressure in 345 BC interrupted this fruitful time of biological study, and he moved to the Isle of Lesbos, later hearing that his friend and patron Hermeias had been executed. Aristotle so valued friendship, which accounts for a fifth of *The Nicomachean Ethics*, that he wrote a eulogistic hymn to Hermeias which he sung after dinner every evening (Pakaluk, 2005, p. 20).

In 343 BC biological studies in Lesbos where again interrupted when King Philip of Macedonia wished that Aristotle tutor his son, Alexander (Denise et al., 2005, p. 22). Although only teaching Alexander for four years, Aristotle stayed in Macedonia for eight. His wife died tragically during this time (Hughes, 2001, p. 3), and Aristotle later lived with Herpyllis, with whom he had a son, Nicomachus (Blackburn, 1996, p. 24).

Aristotle, now 49 (335 BC), moved back to Athens and founded the Lyceum, which would last for eight centuries (Milch & Patterson, 1966, p. 7), where he taught and researched for 11 years (Hughes, 2001, p. 3). While this decade was thought to be Aristotle's most prolific, the height of his mental powers (Denise et al., 2005, p. 22), his prowess apparently did not extend to his physical conditions. In his early 50s he is described as balding, pot-bellied, thin-legged, still with a boyhood lisp, restless, preferring to deliver lectures while walking under the colonnade, earning his school the name "peripatetics" (Thomas et al., 2001, disc 1, track 16; Blackburn, 1996, p. 24).

Aristotle's student, Alexander, by then known as Alexander the Great, died in 323 BC; anti-Macedonia sentiment swept over Athens. Aristotle's Macedonian association soon landed him on trial for impiety (Crisp, 2000, p. xxxvi). Unwilling to let Athens sin against philosophy a second time, and unlike Socrates, he chose exile to the island of Euboea (Hughes, 2001, p. 3; Denise et al., 2005, p. 23). A year later, now 63 (322 BC), after making arrangements for Herpyllis and Nicomachus (Irwin, 1999, p. xiii) and freeing his slaves, the gentle and unperturbed philosopher died of a digestive illness (Crisp, 2000, p. xxxvii; Thomas, et al., 2001, disc 1, track 20–21).

Aristotle is credited with having one of the largest libraries in the Greek world (Denise et al., 2005, p. 22) and to having written over 400 works ranging from the "nature of reality, physics, knowledge, the mind, language, biology, physiology, astronomy, time, theology, literature, rhetoric, the nature of human happiness, and much else" (Crisp, 2000, p. vii). Only a third of his work has survived, but it alone requires 1.5 million words to translate. "An account of Aristotle's intellectual afterlife would be little less than a history of European thought" (Barnes, 1982, p. 86).

To support our discussion regarding the renewal of a moral paradigm for outdoor education, the primary Aristotelian text of interest is the eponymous *Nicomachean Ethics*. It is such renown that it is simply referred to as *The Ethics* (Aristotle, trans. 1999). Aristotle's ethical enterprise is not to provide a moral argument, but to make us good (II 1§1). His is a search for "the good" for humankind (I 1–2). Although Plato has suggested that the search should endeavor to identify a universal Ideal Form of the Good, Aristotle finds this impractical:

> It is a puzzle to know what the weaver or carpenter will gain for his own craft from knowing this Good Itself, or how anyone will be better at medicine or generalship from having gazed on the Idea Itself. For what the doctor appears to consider is not even health [universally], but human health, and presumably the health of this [particular] human being even more, since he treats one particular patient at a time. (I 6§16)

This passage captures the fundamental difference between Plato and Aristotle, beautifully portrayed in Raphael's *The School of Athens*, where Plato's finger reaches for the sky, and Aristotle's hand motions towards the ground. Plato searched for general truths, Aristotle looked to apply truth in context. Like Plato, reason plays an immense role in determining the good for Aristotle, but unlike Plato, understanding is in large part gleaned from and applied to experience.

In order to distill Aristotle's contribution to a moral paradigm within outdoor education, it will be helpful to sketch his argument, thereby providing exposure to its main tenants and vocabulary. Aristotle believed all animate objects to have a *telos*, a purpose they were created to fulfill. *Eudaimonia,* often translated as happiness, a flourishing life, fulfillment, or well-being is the *telos* that Aristotle generally identifies for humans. How this *eudaimonia* is reached, is connected to the function, the *ergon*, of the being. The *ergon* is related to how something is supposed to function, what is natural to it. Like Socrates and Plato before him, Aristotle stressed the rational function of the human species (Denise et al., 2005, p. 23). For humans to live eudaimonistically, they must live in accordance with right reason (VI 13§4–5). To live "excellently" in harmony with our reason, is to live "virtuously," which means excellence in Greek. Thinking virtuously requires the intellectual virtues (found in Book VI), while acting virtuously requires what are called the moral virtues (found in Books II–IV). These two sets of virtues are interdependent for they cannot operate without one another (X 8§3), and they make up an agent's virtue. The sum of this virtue, or lack thereof (vice), over a life-time, forms a person's character (I 10§11).

Aristotle's ethic is a character-ethic, based on his concept of virtue. It is important at the outset to note the criticisms that character has received within outdoor experiential learning contexts as early as the 1970s (Drasdo, 1973/1998, p. 28; Roberts, White & Parker, 1974, pp. 148–150) and more poignantly in recent years (Brookes, 2003a, 2003b). These criticisms raise valid questions about the amorphous nature of the concept of character, and the lack of evidence that it is enhanced through outdoor experiential techniques.

For Aristotle, virtue is: "a state that decides, consisting in a mean, the mean relative to us, which is defined by reference to reason, that is to say, to the reason by reference to which the prudent person [the person with *phronesis*] would define it" (II 6§15). It is Aristotle's intellectual virtue *phronesis* that provides the judgment that discovers the mean. Aristotle describes *phronesis* as the "eye of the soul" (VI 12§10). Irwin translates *phronesis* as "prudence" (1999, p. 345), Crisp as "practical wisdom" (2000, p. xxiv), Pakaluk as "intelligence and foresight in action" or "sagacity" (2005, pp. 214–215), and Hughes as "moral discernment" (2001, p. 224). It is important to note that although the mean is reached through intellectual activity under the auspice of *phronesis*, this in no way precludes the affective, but to the contrary assumes its necessity for proper moral function. "[V]irtues are concerned with actions and feelings says Aristotle in II 3§3 (see also II 6§10, 12; II 9§1; III 1§1; X 8§2).

For Aristotle, developing *phronesis* is a cyclic matter of reflection and experience. Here we see the beginnings of what Dewey detailed as the pattern of inquiry (Dewey, 1973, pp. 223–239;

Wurdinger, 2005, p. 8). Experience provides the raw material for reflection. As knowledge is gleaned from each particular experience, more general understanding is developed. When a particular morally salient instance presents itself, the *phronimos,* the person with *phronesis* draws on previous knowledge amassed through former experience, and makes an informed contextual judgment.

Aristotle identifies two significant spheres within experience, which foster this growth in *phronesis,* and virtue in general, the shared life and practice. In the shared life, he recognizes that virtue is learned through community—family, education, and friendship. *The Ethics* does not advocate a self-help approach, but instead recognizes growth in *phronesis* to be a community affair (Pakaluk, 2005, p. 98; X 9§14). Aristotle's suggestion that "partners in deliberation" (III 3§10) are needed to fully understand, supports the experiential education practice of small group interactive processing. These references to real-life ethical instruction are only part of Aristotle's understanding of moral education—a part that has been further developed by Taylor (1991) in some useful ways.

Arts and literature can also enrich and inform moral dialogue (Carr, 2005, p. 149). Aristotle blended fiction and non-fiction into his teaching, drawing on dramatists and tragedians such as Euripides (III 1§8) and Homer (III 3§18; III 8§10; III 11§1). This emphasis on the potent role of narrative and story raises a question that may be useful to experiential educators such as- Could interaction with literature be a vicarious "primary experience?" (Dewey, 1973, p. 254). As a moral agent experiences the shared life, both fictionally and non-fictionally, the reflective process orchestrated by *phronesis* garners new understanding, informing future practice.

The other significant sphere for growth in *phronesis* is practice. For Aristotle, an act is virtuous only when it is done from an established state of character. Gradually, as right reason, according to the *phronimos,* is achieved, and as the moral virtues, having to do with appetitive control, are refined and heed this reason, a moral agent becomes predisposed to strike the virtuous mean. This predisposition, is just that, a disposition, a state. Practicing virtue is key to this habituation: "We become just by doing just actions and become temperate by doing temperate actions" (II 4§1). For Aristotle, habituation is not mindless, but a "cognitive shaping" through time, allowing the agents to act from their accrued states (Sherman, 1991, p. 7). Habits then, are established patterns of judgment, towards or away from virtue, not robotic conditioning. As practice occurs the reflective process, via *phronesis,* refines understanding, informing practice the next time round.

It is worth noting here that judgment, phronesis, is often placed at the core of experiential models of outdoor education. For example, it is experience processed in the mill of reflection and feedback that yields refined insight—the kind of insight that satisfies our hunger for understanding, develops our body of knowledge, and strengthens our capacity for sound judgment (Drury, Bonney, Berman, and Wagstaff, 2005, p. ix). Aristotle's comprehensive and sophisticated discussions of character, virtue, and *phronesis,* are pertinent to current scholarship within the field of experiential learning. For example, the "situationist" critique, which draws largely on social psychological research, is claiming behavior to be situationally bound—that there are no traits of character that a person carries between situations (Brookes, 2003a, 2003b; Fenwick, 2000, pp. 11–14). Brookes' critique particularly targets outdoor adventure education, "the idea that personal traits (character) can be acquired 'in one setting'—which will then persist in other settings, remains foundational to much outdoor adventure education theory, research and promotion" (2003a, p. 49). Brookes' observations, and research citations, seem to match the belief that significant character formation does not appear to happen in on-off adventure courses.

Aristotle's understanding of character, based on dispositions of judgment, developed through *a lifetime* (I 10§11) of experience, seems to explain this paucity of transformation, moral and otherwise, better than the situationist critique. For the situationists tends to reduce the palette of moral response to one empirical dilemma-fraught assessment, and greatly simplify the complexity of human morality (Milgram, 1963; Swanton, 2005, pp. 30–33). Following in Aristotle's philosophy, a one-, two-, or three-week expedition is insufficient to permanently inculcate virtue.

Implications for EE Philosophy

What outdoor experiential learning *can* do well is to provide a new way of seeing by creating space for participants to better know themselves and others, and to become more aware of their own moral journey. In Aristotelian terms, experiential learning can create opportunities for students and educators to develop their *phronesis*. In conclusion, this chapter has highlighted the influence of early Greek thought on experiential learning. Whether it is Socrates' contemplative questions, Plato's leisure-oriented holistic curriculum, or Aristotle's reference to the role of experience in character development, as educators we benefit from exposure to these philosophical roots. The value of this encounter comes not merely in confirming our beliefs and positions, but also in challenging them as seen in Plato's epistemological rationalism. Finally, the ancient emphasis on virtue has increasing contemporary relevance for the renewed ethical interests within the associated fields of experiential learning.

Note

1. Two different types of notation are used in this chapter to cite works of antiquity. Plato's works use Stephanus pagination (e.g., *Apology* 38a). Here, the work cited is Plato's *Apology*. The number "38" is page 38 of the Stephanus edition. The letter "a" represents section a on page 38. When citing Aristotle's *Nicomachean Ethics* (e.g., VI 5§2), the following notation is used. The Roman numeral is the book within the *Nicomachean Ethics* (VI), the number after the Roman numeral (5) is the chapter within the book. The number after the "§" symbol is the section within the chapter.

References

Aristotle. (1999). *Nicomachean ethics* (T. Irwin, Trans. 2nd ed.). Indianapolis, IN: Hackett.

Barnes, J. (1982). *Aristotle*. New York: Oxford University Press.

Blackburn, S. (1996). *The Oxford dictionary of philosophy*. New York: Oxford University Press.

Brookes, A. (2003a). A critique of neo-Hahnian outdoor education theory. Part one: Challenges to the concept of "character building". *Journal of Adventure Education and Outdoor Learning, 3*(1), 49–62.

Brookes, A. (2003b). A critique of neo-Hahnian outdoor education theory. Part two: The "fundamental attribution error" in contemporary outdoor education discourse. *Journal of Adventure Education and Outdoor Leadership, 3*(2), 119–132.

Carr, D. (2005). On the contribution of literature and the arts to the educational cultivation of moral virtue, feeling and emotion. *Journal of Moral Education, 34*(2), 137–151.

Crisp, R. (2000). *Nicomachean ethics*. Cambridge, UK: Cambridge University Press.

Crosby, A., Warren, K., Sakofs, M. S., & Hunt, J. (1995). A Critical Look: The Philosophical Foundations of Experiential Education. In K. Warren, M. S. Sakofs, & J. Hunt (Eds.), *Theory of Experiential Education* (3rd ed., pp. 3–13). Dubuque, IA: Kendall/Hunt.

Denise, T. C., White, N. P., & Peterfreund, S. P. (2005). *Great traditions in ethics* (7th ed.). Belmont, CA: Thomson/Wadsworth.

Dewey, J. (1973). *The philosophy of John Dewey. Two volumes in One: 1) The structure of experience; 2) The loved experience* (J. J. McDermott, Ed.). Chicago: University of Chicago Press.

Drasdo, H. (1998). *Education and the mountain centres* (2nd extended ed.). Penrith, Cumbria, UK: Adventure Education. (Original work published 1973)

Drury, J. K., Bonney, B. F., Berman, D., & Wagstaff, M. (2005). *The backcountry classroom: Lessons, tools, and activities for teaching outdoor leaders* (2nd ed.). Guilford, CT: Falcon/Globe Pequot Press.

Fenwick, T. (2000). Expanding conceptions of experiential learning: a review of the five contemporary perspectives on cognition. *Adult Education Quarterly, 50*(4), 243–272.

Hahn, K. (1940). The love of enterprise, the love of aloneness, the love of skill. Retrieved June 27, 2007, from http://kurthahn.org/writings/liverpool.pdf

Hahn, K. (1958). Forty-eighth annual dinner of old centralians. Retrieved June 27, 2007, from http://kurthahn.org/writings/oldcentral.pdf

Hahn, K. (1960). Outward Bound. Retrieved June 27, 2007, from http://kurthahn.org/writings/obt1960.pdf

Higgins, P. (2009). Into the big wide world: Sustainable experiential education for the 21st century. *Journal of Experiential Education, 32*(1), 44–60.

Hughes, G. J. (2001). *Routledge philosophy guidebook to Aristotle on ethics.* London: Routledge.

Hunt, J. (1996). Character-based ethics. *Zip Lines: The Voice for Adventure Education, 29,* 12–15.

Hunt, J. (1999). Philosophy of adventure education. In J. C. Miles & S. Priest (Eds.), *Adventure programming* (pp. 115–122). State College, PA: Venture.

Irwin, T. (1999). *Nicomachean ethics* (2nd ed.). Indianapolis, IN: Hackett.

Kraft, R. J. (1985). Towards a theory of experiential education. In R. J. Kraft & M. Sakofs (Eds.), *Theory of Experiential Learning* (2nd ed., pp. 7–38). Boulder, CO: Association for Experiential Education.

James, T. (1995). Kurt Hahn and the aims of education. In K. Warren, M. S. Sakofs, & J. Hunt (Eds.), *Theory of experiential education* (3rd ed., pp. 33–43). Dubuque, IA: Kendall/Hunt.

James, W. (1949). *Essays on faith and morals* (R.B. Perry, Ed.). New York: Longmans.

Laertius, D. (1979). *Lives of the eminent philosophers* (D. Hicks, Trans., Vol. 1 & 2). Cambridge, MA: Harvard University Press.

Long, A. A. (2002). *Epictetus : A stoic and Socratic guide to Life.* New York: Oxford University Press.

Loynes, C. (2002). The generative paradigm. *Journal of Adventure Education and Outdoor Learning, 2*(2), 113–125.

Milch, R., & Patterson, C. H. (1966). *Aristotle's Nicomachean ethics: Notes, including Aristotle's life, Aristotle's works.* Lincoln, NB: Cliffs Notes.

Milgram, S. (1963). Behavioral study of obedience. *Journal of Abnormal and Social Psychology, 67,* 371–378.

Miner, J. L., & Boldt, J. R. (1981). *Outward Bound USA: Learning through experience in adventure-based education* (1st ed.). New York: Morrow.

Pakaluk, M. (2005). *Aristotle's Nicomachean ethics: An introduction.* Cambridge, UK: Cambridge University Press.

Pieper, J. (1998). *Leisure, the basis of culture* (G. Malsbary, Trans.). South Bend, IN: St. Augustine's Press.

Plato. (1966). *Plato in twelve volumes* (H. N. Fowler, Trans. Vol. 1). Cambridge, MA: Harvard University Press.

Plato. (1967). *Plato in twelve volumes* (W. R. M. Lamb, Trans. Vol. 3). Cambridge, MA: Harvard University Press.

Plato. (1987). *The Republic* (H. D. P. Lee, Trans. 2nd ed.). New York: Penguin.

Plato. (2002). *Five dialogues* (G. Grube, Trans. 2nd ed.). Indianapolis, IN: Hackett.

Richards, A. (1981). *Kurt Hahn, the midwife of educational ideas.* Unpublished doctoral thesis, Department of Education, University of Colorado, Boulder.

Roberts, K., White, G. E., & Parker, H. J. (1974). *The character-training industry: Adventure-training schemes in Britain.* Newton Abbot, Devon, UK: David & Charles.

Sherman, N. (1991). *The fabric of character: Aristotle's theory of virtue.* New York: Oxford University Press.

Swanton, C. (2005). *Virtue ethics: A pluralistic view.* New York: Oxford University Press.

Taylor, C. (1991). *The ethics of authenticity.* London: Harvard University Press.

Thomas, H., Thomas, D. L., & Lewis, E. (2001). *Living biographies of great philosophers* [sound recording]. Ashland, OR: Blackstone Audiobooks.

Wurdinger, S. D. (1997). *Philosophical issues in adventure education.* Dubuque, IA: Kendall/Hunt.

Wurdinger, S. D. (2005). *Using experiential learning in the classroom: Practical ideas for all educators.* Lanham, MD: Scarecrow Education.

3 Rousseau and Pestalozzi
Emile, Gertrude, and Experiential Education

Thomas E. Smith

Jean-Jacques Rousseau was a Swiss/French philosopher, writer, and political theorist living in the 18th century. He is recognized as a brilliant, unconventional, controversial, and sometimes-paranoid thinker. His predominant thesis was that human beings are basically good, whereas society is basically evil. His classic novel about the education of a young man named Emile presents, what is considered by many, one of the great educational treatises of history. He argued that because society endorses educational programs that create good citizens—compliant and uncritical sheep for the flock—the public schools undermine free-thinking, creativity, and individuality. His argument was restated in the 20th century by a number of educational reformists (Goodman, 1960; Illich, 1971; Gatto, 1991).

Rousseau suggests that education should occur outside the school and grow out of the experiences that children encounter on a day to day basis. *Emile, or On Education*, was first published in 1762 (Rousseau, 1991a), but is still widely read and discussed by educational theorists (Brubacher, 1962; Smith & Smith, 1994; Soetard, 1995; Palmer, Bressler, & Cooper, 2001). The story is about the growth and education of a young man, guided by Rousseau, according to the principles of "natural education." The teacher (Rousseau) took the boy to the country, to be protected from the corruptive vices of the city, and gave him the freedom to discover what it means to be "good" and to follow his own heart. Emile learned to live naturally, to open his senses to the realities of the world, and to learn according to the laws of nature and human nature.

John Heinrich Pestalozzi was a schoolmaster and educational reformer 34 years younger than Rousseau. He sought to put Rousseau's ideas about education in nature into practice. He was only in his late 20s when he opened an orphanage where he tried to teach neglected children, and throughout the next 25 years, he experimented with various educational approaches.

The purpose of this chapter is to describe the life and work of these two important historical figures, and suggest that they established significant philosophical foundations for the contemporary field of experiential education.

Brief Biography of Rousseau

Jean-Jacques Rousseau (1712–1778) was born in Switzerland, but eventually became a philosopher, composer, writer, and political theorist in France. His ideas influenced leaders of both the French and American revolutions, and also provided some theoretical postulates for socialism and communism. He first attracted wide-spread attention with his essay, *Discourses on the Sciences and the Arts* (1749) in which he described the harmful effects of the existent social system (Soetard, 1995). A few years later he published a book, *On the Origin of Inequality* (1755), which offered further criticism of society (Rousseau, 1984). When he was 50 years old, he published two controversial books, one on politics, *The Social Contract* (Rousseau, 1964), and the other on education, *Emile, or On Education* (Rousseau, 1991a). Both of these books were seen as subversive by the church and the governments of France and Switzerland. They were banned in both countries, and as a result an arrest warrant was issued for Rousseau. He became a fugitive for the rest of his life (Damrosch, 2005).

Rousseau's childhood was complicated by the death of his mother shortly after his birth. The relationship with his father centered mostly around shared readings. According to one biographer (Damrosch, 2005), many of the books they read were from his mother's collection of romantic novels. Years later, in his autobiography, Rousseau confessed that those readings "gave me bizarre and romantic notions of human life, which experience and reflection have never been able to cure me of" (Damrosch, 2005, p. 15). He appropriately used the word "cure," because his life was filled with psychological problems, especially in his social relationships. By the age of 60, his letters and other writings had overtones of emotional distress that bordered on paranoia. He escaped to England for a while in the late 1770s and was helped by the famous English philosopher David Hume (Edmonds & Eidinow, 2006). However, when he began to suspect the honesty of that friendship, he returned to Europe. As the years passed, Rousseau came to mistrust most of his human contacts, and often spoke of his dependence on the loyalty of his dog, Sultan (Edmonds & Eidinow, 2006).

In spite of his lifetime of psychological and social difficulties, Rousseau's thoughts on political and educational reform were brilliant. Based on his assumption about the inherent goodness of humankind, he refers to the species as *the noble beast*. "There is no original perversity in the human being" (Rousseau, 1956, p. 40). Humans were born in goodness but doomed to be corrupted by society and civilization. According to Rousseau, politicians and societal leaders put their private interests and ambitions ahead of the good of society, and they then create social institutions that corrupt future generations. Humans are socialized and culturally indoctrinated to such an extent that they lose touch with their basic goodness, their basic senses, and an inner awareness of self-freedom and self-responsibility. They come to accept conformity over individuality.

Rousseau on Education

Rousseau believed the solution to this sorry state of societal affairs lies in appropriate individualized education. Just as plants are shaped by cultivation, humans are shaped by education. He believed that everyone could discover or recover their basic goodness with a proper education. Like Plato, Rousseau saw the purpose of education as developing good citizens who could live in balance with others in society. His definition of good citizens was creative, free-thinking, highly moral people. His hope for the future was that appropriate education could create enough free-thinking and moral people to move into political leadership, and then create a moral society.

This line of thought leads to a problematic paradox for Rousseau; one cannot educate a person toward higher morality and good citizenship within a corrupt and immoral society. He argued that because society's schools were part of the problem, they could not be part of the solution. Teaching should not involve indoctrination about the desirable characteristics and virtues as defined by an immoral society. It was this argument that led to his conflict with the church, which supported institutionalized education to teach children how to overcome their basic evil nature. Rousseau believed that people have to break free of societal institutions and their influences.

Rousseau's notions about "natural education" suggested children have a natural inclination to demonstrate activity, curiosity, creativity, and discovery of their own essential goodness. The teacher's role is to guide the student to experiences, during which this natural tendency toward growth and moral development will unfold. Emile, Rousseau's educational charge, was encouraged to learn by experience, by trial and error, and to draw his own conclusions about life. He believed children need to grasp ethical principles through concrete experiences, which is something very different from memorizing verbal formulas. Today, Rousseau would be a strong supporter of education away from the desk and away from the school building.

Although children may need a little guidance as they learn, Rousseau warns:

> But let it be very little, and avoid the appearance of it. If he goes wrong, do not correct his errors. Say nothing til he sees them and corrects them himself; or at most, arrange some practical situation which will make him realize things personally. If he never made mistakes he would never learn properly. (Rousseau, 1956, p. 76)

Rousseau's "natural education" for Emile led him to recognize that there are developmental stages for different types of learning. He writes, "We must view the man as a man and the child as a child" (1991a, p. 34). For the young Emile, "Geography, history, languages and literature are all beyond his undeveloped understanding" (p. 31). "Emile at the age of twelve will scarcely know what a book is. But at least, I will be told, he must be able to read. I agree. He must be able to read when he needs to read. Before that it will only be a bother to him" (p. 51).

According to Rousseau, the appropriate method of instruction for the young child is to provide him with natural experiences and natural objects to explore, and he should be allowed to follow his personal interests. The emotions that develop throughout childhood are also important, and must never be left behind. "The man who gets the most out of life is not the one who has lived it longest, but the one who has felt life most deeply" (1991b, p. 15).

In the middle years, physical and sensory education becomes important. "Our first masters of philosophy are our feet, our hands, and our eyes. The senses are the first faculties to take form and mature in us. They should therefore be the first to be cultivated" (1991a, p. 54). By mid-adolescence Emile is ready to learn about ideas and judgment:

> To begin with, our pupil had only sensations, now he has ideas; he only had feelings, now he judges; for from the comparison of several sensations, whether successive or simultaneous, and the judgment passed on them, there comes a sort of mixed or complex sensation which I call an idea. It is the particular way of forming ideas that gives its character to the human mind. (1991a, p. 91)

For Rousseau, humans are not completely mature until they understand their role in society and become socially involved. This creates another paradox—that of the person needing to be individualistic as well as social. He postulates that experiences of personal growth and self-discovery will lead to higher morality, including awareness of the potential of a moral society and acceptance of one's responsibility to create that society. It is through awareness and understanding of self that one comes to awareness and understanding of others.

Brief Biography of Pestalozzi

Johann Henrich Pestalozzi (1746–1827) was born in Zurich, Switzerland. He did not start school until he was nine years old, but eventually completed his studies at the University of Zurich. He started out as a student of theology, but later transferred into law. His interest in education began when he tutored his own son. His early beliefs were that the best model for education was maternal love. The love, support, encouragement, and moral guidance that a mother gives her children prepares them to become good citizens. There is a direct connection between maternal love and an individual's moral development, and Pestalozzi reportedly suggested that maternal love was the first agent in education of the child (Spring, 1994).

Pestalozzi on Education

Pestalozzi's interest in education led him to open an orphanage farm for neglected children at Neuhof. He was fascinated by Rousseau's *Emile*, and, in developing the educational program, he sought to put Rousseau's ideas about natural education into practice. Like Rousseau, he believed that children should learn through activity and through manipulating things, not just words. He even argued that books have little value in the primary years of education. He recognized that some children learn better by direct handling of objects and others by direct observation and reflecting to reach conclusions. He wrote of the importance of "sense perception" and "object lessons," and suggested that teachers should get students involved in real life and sensory awareness experiences.

Like Rousseau, Pestalozzi's method was quite "learner-centered," as opposed to "content-centered" (Silber, 1965; Soetard, 1994). Pestalozzi might be considered as one of the grandfathers of student-centered education. Although his efforts at Neuhof were unsuccessful and the program went bankrupt after five years of operation, the experience led to his re-direction of his life toward educational experimentation.

Like Rousseau, one of Pestalozzi's early writings was a novel about Leonard and Gertrude, written in the 1780s and revised in the 1790s, which included ideas on schooling (Silber, 1965). He published academic papers throughout the last quarter of the 18th century, but his work was not widely circulated. Then, in 1801 he published his seminal work, *How Gertrude Teaches Her Children*, and that book is still being reprinted (Pestalozzi, 1973). In that book, he outlined his "psychological method of instruction," which has since been called "the Pestalozzi method" (Barlow, 1977).

Shortly after the publication of *How Gertrude Teaches Her Children*, Pestalozzi moved to a castle at Yverdon and started another private school. The educational program involved field trips, group work, and ability grouping that allowed for the accommodation of individual differences of development. Pestalozzi believed that children should not be fed facts and data as if filling empty vessels; they should be guided to find answers by using their own powers of observation, analysis, and reason. The aim of education should be to educate the whole child, and thus schooling should involve activity—"the hands," affective processes—"the heart," and cognitive processes—"the head" (Silber, 1965). Pestalozzi's suggestion that teachers should be concerned with the harmonious development of the whole child makes him one of the grandfathers of holistic education. His arguments represented a fundamental shift from the thinking of traditional educators who saw the schools solely as an institution for the development of intellect (Gutek, 1999).

William H. Kilpatrick, a progressive educator who was a contemporary of John Dewey, offered a summary of Pestalozzi's thoughts about education: Within each child there is "a little seed which contains the design of the tree, so educators need only take care that nothing stops nature's march of developments" (1951, p. 5). Personality is sacred, and there is an inner dignity in each child just as for each adult. The foundation for those who work as educators should be love. Without love neither the physical of the intellectual powers of the child will develop naturally. Education is a matter of the heart, not just the brain. Learning should be based on direct, concrete observation and experience. New learning must be followed by action. "Life shapes us and the life that shapes us is not a matter of words, but actions" (p. 3).

The extensive reflection and observational research that Pestalozzi used to develop his methods impressed people, and he is often considered as the first to make a scientific study of education (Gutek, 1999). He believed there was a unified science of education that could be learned by teachers, although there was certainly not a rigid list of rules to follow. The traditional university did not have a school of education until after Pestalozzi's research and writing. It is ironic that when teacher training institutions developed, most of them tended to advocate rigid and authoritarian techniques for teaching. As Pestalozzi continued to experiment with his ideas, the school at Yverdon attracted students and teachers from many nations, including Fredrich Froebel, from Germany, who was to become the founder of kindergarten education.

Pestalozzi's educational philosophy is important to contemporary pedagogies of progressive education, humanistic education, holistic education, person-centered education, and experiential education. He recognized the importance of balancing individual growth with social development, and wrote about the schools as a way of improving the conditions of every person and every society.

Implications for EE Philosophy

There are more similarities than differences in the educational philosophies and methodologies of these two significant figures in educational history:

1. Both believed that education should have individual and social goals. There should be attention to the cultivation of each child's individuality and morality, at the same time as there was attention to developing good citizens for society. Pestalozzi had great hope for the schools. He felt that these goals could be achieved by teachers who were properly trained, and he was to have considerable influence on the development of teacher training programs. On the other hand, Rousseau believed that goals for individual growth would be ignored by schools that were organized and funded by the state, and could only be accomplished apart from the schools—apart from the political-social corruption of society. His ideology had influence on the free school and alternative school movements.
2. Both Rousseau and Pestalozzi advocated that education should be accessible to all children, and that it was appropriate to move away from the traditional academic curriculum to educational and training programs that were more practical and appropriate for the poor.
3. Both men recognized that children are different from adults, and different from each other, that children pass through different stages that require different teaching strategies, and that they pass through those stages at different rates. Educators should recognize these complex developmental differences and develop programs accordingly. Pestalozzi suggested that books may not be appropriate until the child is 10 years old.
4. Both emphasized the value of experiential learning, and they advocated getting students actively involved in the learning process. Children have a natural tendency to explore and manipulate objects and natural phenomena—a natural tendency to learn. Teachers should recognize the natural curiosity of the child and let it be a guide to their instruction. Both Rousseau and Pestalozzi believed in multi-sensory learning and recognized the value of the outdoor classroom. Classroom textbooks were less important than direct interaction with others and the natural world during the early years of schooling.
5. Both believed that the educational process should be child-centered, not content-centered. They believed that the teacher should be a guide or facilitator, not an instructor. Teachers should create climates of openness and trust wherein students can feel safe and secure in their personal growth and learning. They believed that to teach a child, one must love and understand that child.
6. A final similarity should be noted. Both Rousseau and Pestalozzi were great examples of the reflective practitioner. While both were involved with action, teaching, and experience, they were also keen observers and were continually reflecting on their experiences and observations.

Although the history of philosophy begins with the ancient Greeks—Socrates, Plato, and Aristotle—the 17th century was of great importance to this field. Locke, Berkeley, Hume, Hegel, and Kant all wrote during that period, and contemporary philosophers still discuss and debate their ideas. Twentieth-century developments in philosophy can be seen as extensions of, or reactions against, those giants of the past. The history of the theory and practice of experiential education runs parallel to that. Plato and Aristotle laid important foundations, but it was Jean-Jacques Rousseau and Johann Pestalozzi who championed the experiential cause in the 17th century. Their ideas on the growth and development of children, the importance of learning by experience from interaction with natural objects and the natural environment, and the role of schools and teachers in society, set the stage for John Dewey and the progressive education movement of the 20th century. Experiential educators should still discuss and debate their ideas because the issues they discuss are still relevant.

References

Barlow, T. (1977). *Pestalozzi and American education.* San Francisco: Este Es Press.

Brubacher, J. (1962). *Modern philosophies of education.* New York: McGraw-Hill.

Damrosch, L. (2005). *Jean-Jacques Rousseau: Restless genius.* New York: Houghton Mifflin.

Edmonds, D., & Eidinow, J. (2006). *Rousseau's dog.* New York: Harper-Collins.

Gatto, J. (1991). *Dumbing us down: The hidden curriculum of compulsory schooling.* New York: New Society.

Goodman, P. (1960). *Growing up absurd.* New York: Random House.

Gutek, G. (1999). *Pestalozzi and education.* New York: Waveland.

Illich, I. (1971). *Deschooling society.* New York: Harper & Row.

Kilpatrick, W. (1951). Preface. In J. Pestalozzi, *The education of man—Aphorisms* (pp. ix–xii). New York: Philosophical Library.

Palmer, J., Bressler, L., & Cooper, D. (2001). *Fifty key thinkers in education: From Confucius to Dewey.* New York: Routledge.

Pestalozzi, J. (1973). *How Gertrude teaches her children.* New York: Gordon.

Rousseau, J. (1956). *The Emile of Jean Jacques Rousseau: Selected, translated and interpreted by William Boyd.* London: Heinenann. (Reprinted by Teachers College Press in 1991).

Rousseau, J. (1964). *The social contract*, translated by M. Cranston. London: Penguin.

Rousseau, J. (1984). *On the origins of inequality* (M. Cranston Trans.). London: Penguin.

Rousseau, J. (1991a). *Emile or on education* (A. Bloom. Trans.). New York: Basic Books.

Rousseau, J. (1991b). *Emile for today: The Emile of Jean Jacques Rousseau: Selections* by (W. Boyd. Trans. & Ed.). New York: Teachers College, Columbia University Press.

Silber, K. (1965). *Pestalozzi: The man and his work* (2nd ed.). London: Routledge & Kegan-Paul.

Smith, L., & Smith, J. K. (1994). *Lives in education: A narrative of people and ideas* (2nd ed.). New York: St. Martins Press.

Soetard, M. (1994). Johan Henrich Pestalozzi. *Prospects: The Quarterly Review of Comparative Education, 24*(1) 297–310.

Soetard, M. (1995). Jean-Jacques Rousseau. In Z. Morsy (Ed.) *Thinkers on Education, Volume 4* (pp. 188–202). Paris: UNESCO.

Spring, J. (1994). *Wheels in the head.* New York: McGraw-Hill.

4 Sir Patrick Geddes

"*Vivendo Discimus*"—By Living We Learn

Peter Higgins and Robbie Nicol

To write about Patrick Geddes' (1854–1932) contribution to educational philosophy and practice (epitomised in his motto "*Vivendo discimus*") is a daunting task, not simply because of his achievements in the field of education, but because one is continually distracted by accomplishments of a similar scale in an astonishing diversity of other areas. Indeed one need look no further than the titles of books about him to realise this. Examples include: *The interpreter: Geddes, The Man And His Gospel* (Defries, 1927); *The Worlds of Patrick Geddes: Biologist, Town Planner, Re-educator, Peace-warrior* (Boardman, 1978); *Patrick Geddes: Social Evolutionist and City Planner* (Meller, 1990), *Think Global, Act Local: The Life And Legacy of Patrick Geddes* (Stephen, 2004). If one reads these and other texts on Geddes (e.g., Kitchen, 1975; Stephen, 2004), it is easy to conclude that his zeal for learning and action remained undiminished throughout a career of international significance. His accomplishments and legacy are perhaps best understood in the context of the period during which he lived and worked, spanning the latter part of the Victorian era and the early 20th century. His range of interests is exemplified through archival records which show that he knew personally or was in correspondence with a number of influential United Kingdom and international intellectuals, artists, poets, educationalists, scientists, and policy makers of the time including, Thomas Huxley, Charles Darwin, Mahatma Ghandi, John Dewey, Cecil Reddie, Lewis Mumford, Hugh MacDairmid, Charles Rennie Mackintosh, Kurt Hahn, and Fridtjof Nansen.

Geddes' work in education should be seen as integral with his belief in people living and working in harmony with their communities. He adapted the work of the French philosopher Frederic Le Play to construct the epithet, "place, work, folk", as a means of encouraging awareness of the significance of this relationship and in acknowledgement of the potentially negative influence of the urban and rural environment (see Meller, 1990, p. 34). In this sense he is rather different from many educational philosophers; for him education had to be located in such a context. Despite the radical nature of this approach, not to mention the fact that he never completed a university degree, the British establishment sought to recognise his "civic and educational services to society," and he was offered a knighthood in 1912, but he refused for "democratic reasons" (Boardman, 1978, p. 219). He was again offered a knighthood in 1931 (the year before he died) "for services to education" and, after some emotional struggle, finally accepted it "on business grounds" as he felt it would aid the projects he was working on (Boardman, 1978, p. 423).

His philosophical arguments also led to development of the concept of "environmental sustainability" (even though he did not use this or any other specific term), and also to the idea much beloved by environmentalists, to "think global, act local". These concepts pervade his most significant book, *Cities in Evolution*, first published in 1915. In this sense his legacy in environmentalism may be more significant than that in education or other fields.

Biography

Good accounts of Geddes' life and the influences on his upbringing can be found in most of the published biographies and associated materials. Whilst Kitchen (1975) and Boardman (1978) provide well-researched early accounts of his life and works, Geddes has continued to attract attention in published books (e.g., Meller, 1990; Stephen, 2004, 2007) and dedicated Web sites (Ballater Geddes Project, n.d., a, b) and through the Sir Patrick Geddes Memorial Trust (2007) which probably offer the most easily accessible sources of information on his early years and work. There is a useful chronology in an appendix in Stephen (2004). The following account is drawn from these sources.

Patrick (baptised Peter) Geddes was born on October 2, 1854, in Ballater, a small town on the banks of the River Dee in Scotland. He was the fifth of five children, two of whom died in infancy. His parents (Alexander Geddes and Janet Stevenson) were not wealthy. His father was a regular soldier (a Gaelic speaker from the Highlands of Scotland) who eventually rose to the rank of Sergeant Major and Quartermaster. Patrick was three years old when the family moved to Kinnoul Hill on the outskirts of Perth in Central Scotland, where from the age of nine he went to school at Perth Academy.

This period in Geddes' development is noted as significant by biographers and by Geddes himself. According to Stephen (2004), he described his childhood as "growing up in a garden" (p. 21), and noted that his father gave him his first lessons in mathematics through the planting of potatoes. His relationship with his father seems to have been pivotal in providing the local forays and subsequent walking tours in the Scottish Highlands that fostered Patrick's appreciation of the landscape, ecology (though the term and concept had not yet been developed), and his approach to education and society. The indulgence in Patrick's creative education by his parents also would have been unusual in its day. For example, his father built a shed in the garden to allow him to conduct chemistry experiments. One year before his university studies he spent mornings at cabinet-making and afternoons attending the School of Art.

He spent a further year in and around Perth studying the sciences, sometimes walking up to 25 miles a day to do so. He studied chemistry under a local analyst and geology with a tutor (James Geikie, who became very well known in the field) before subsequently enrolling to study biology at Edinburgh University where he lasted a week before leaving dissatisfied with the teaching methods (Stephen, 2004, p. 23). He encountered a book by the eminent scientist and Darwin supporter Thomas Huxley. On reading the first few pages of *Lay Sermons* he instantly "knew that its author was the teacher for him" (Boardman, 1978, p. 26). At the age of 20 he set off for London to the Royal School of Mines (later to become Imperial College) where he was taught by and clearly impressed Huxley who, amongst other things, encouraged him to write an article contradicting Huxley's research, and also sent him on to various scientific establishments including the Sorbonne and the University of Paris. While based at the marine station in Brittany, he again showed creative scientific talent, writing a significant article on protozoa. In Paris Geddes came into contact with Frederic Le Play, whose influence stimulated his interest in social development and in particular the role of geography and occupation.

In his mid-20s Geddes was sponsored by the British Association to join a scientific expedition to Mexico, where he suffered an illness which resulted in a loss of sight for several weeks. The consequence of this is well documented by biographers, and it seems that he spent the time in deep reflection on his ideas, putting them into order to assist future learning and communication. He referred to the diagrammatic structures he developed as "thinking machines" (Meller, 1990, p. 45). The blindness also seems to have convinced him that a career spent looking down a microscope was not practical.

His return to Scotland led to several years of various brief or part-time academic posts in and around Edinburgh (including as a lecturer in zoology) during which time he married (Anna Morton) and started a family. Eventually, in 1889, a patron endowed a personal Chair in Botany for him at the University of Dundee, where one of his first acts was to establish a botanical garden for teaching purposes. Although his appointment was only for three months a year, it provided Geddes with the opportunity to further develop his interests and work across a growing range of disciplines, but at the cost of financial instability. For example this was the same year he published an influential monograph, *The Evolution of Sex* (Geddes & Thompson, 1889), which amongst other themes addressed the controversial socio-cultural issue of women's role in society (Meller, 1990, p. 7). The book directly influenced the views of a minister of the Australian government who subsequently pioneered women's suffrage (Boardman, 1978, p. 436).

During part of this period Geddes lived in the "Old Town" of Edinburgh, and it seems that the manifest urban decay of this area spurred him and Anna to set about renovating the area and enlisting neighbours in support. Together they found neglected or derelict areas in the city, then surveyed, planned and planted gardens and play areas in them (with education as well as recreation in mind). Amongst his other projects, he set up mixed-community student hostels in the city. His determination that these should be educational as well as functional is clear in that the students were expected to govern themselves. The hostels were also were used for summer schools where Geddes offered courses in "seaside zoology" and "garden botany" to both young men and women (Stephen, 2004, p. 31).

At the same time he accomplished major projects such as the radically innovative design of the Edinburgh zoological gardens and the building of the "Outlook Tower" on the High Street. This structure was designed to give an overview of the city from its high vantage point and at the same time educate the visitor by drawing attention to the form and function of the city, life and work within it, and further to give a broad perspective on Britain and the world. (For further information see Meller, 1990; Maclean, 2004; Ballater Geddes Project, n.d., a, b; Gillon, n.d.). These experiences were again formative in that Geddes developed ideas of place, community and communal action which were later to emerge in his writing and other work.

As in other periods of his life in the early 20th century, Geddes experienced some financial discomfort. He increased his local and UK teaching to support his family and ventures, and also took on work in Cyprus. However, perhaps through his approach to education, their children developed into fine young people and eventually his son Alasdair (aged 23) accompanied Patrick (aged 60) on his first visit to India in 1914.

After 1914 Geddes spent much of his life abroad (Leonard, 2004) including three extended visits to India where he was appointed to a specially created Chair of Sociology and Civics at Bombay University. There his work was primarily in planning towns, but with a focus on developments that were compatible with the landscape and culture. In Calcutta he collaborated with the philosopher Rabindranath Tagore towards the "creation of a university that would blend Eastern and Western philosophical and educational systems and would bring about an enlightened education for the future" (Leonard, 2004, p. 50). In India, in Palestine (where he planned the city of Tel Aviv), in several European countries, and in America, Geddes remains better known than in the United Kingdom.

In the year of departure for his second visit to India (1915–17), this time with his wife Anna, Patrick published *Cities in Evolution*. This is a remarkable discourse on the development of cities and their potential as social and educational places which, if planned and built correctly, can satisfy these objectives whilst enhancing their role in housing and industry. The book resonates with Geddes' global vision, locally applied. Although it cannot be said that he had the modern concept of "environmental sustainability" in mind, his work gave credence to the concept.

In 1917 whilst serving in the war in Europe, Alasdair was killed by shrapnel and soon after Anna died from an illness in Calcutta. These personal tragedies devastated Patrick who was already in despair at the insanity of war. Despite this setback in his mid-60s, Geddes retained his drive to sustain existing projects and develop new ones.

In 1919 he retired from his Chair at Dundee University giving an inspiring farewell lecture before returning to India (see Defries, 1927, and Geddes, 1949, for the text). He left India for health reasons in 1924 and moved to Montpellier in France. Moving in his 70s is a striking decision, but understandable as his early visits to Europe were formative in his development and, Leonard argues (2004, pp. 44–48), here he had found his intellectual home. He encountered followers of the influential sociologists Frederic Le Play and Auguste Compte (a philosopher sociologist best known for the development of Positivism). He also had contacts with Ernst Heinrich Haeckel (naturalist, zoologist, fellow follower of Darwin, and writer of a very early book on ecology), and peaceful anarchists (who were also social geographers) such as Elisée Reclus. These men were instrumental in the development of Geddes' ideas of bioregionalism, community evolution and regeneration through education and mutual co-operation that are part of his intellectual legacy. Geddes died in Montpellier in 1932.

Geddes, the Re-educator

> Intellectual education involves general and sensory, imaginative and artistic education: Re-education, Re-creation and thus Re-construction and the concept of Culture in its literal sense, of 'to cultivate.' (Geddes, 1919, as cited in Geddes, 1949, p. 216)

This brief biography serves not only to introduce Geddes' contributions and legacy to society, but also demonstrates his personal philosophy of education in and through action. His life and works resonate with a belief in an ability to embrace new knowledge and experiences, to learn from these, and then to inform and lead others through example and teaching. It is this culmination of applying learning to action and learning from action that gives substance to, and provides a model for experiential education.

Furthermore, it is clear that he saw learning not simply as an end in itself, but that through learning/education social transformation can and perhaps should occur. This is in clear contrast to, for example, abstract models of experiential learning (e.g., the "Kolb cycle") where learning is independent of a values context. Geddes' vision encompasses the idea that education can be used to engage with society, and perhaps change it. This social transformative approach, which has much in common with the subsequent work of Paulo Freire is never more evident than when Geddes demonstrates his belief in the capacities of children.

> Hence, at every level is needed the euthanasia of external and centralised authority, with the corresponding calling forth of the resources, aptitude, and insight of teachers and parents, and, most of all, each school and group of children—as students and workers, as playmates and artists, learning and loving—in short, as more fully living. *Vivendo discimus*. (Geddes, 1905, p. 193)

Educational Philosophy and Principles

In common with earlier educational philosophers such as Comenius (1592–1670) and Pestalozzi (1746–1827), Geddes' holistic approach to education was based on learning *via* the "three Hs"—"Heart, Hand and Head" (Geddes, 1919, as cited in Geddes, 1949, p. 228; Boardman, 1978, p. 224) rather than the "three Rs"—Reading, wRiting and aRithmetic. Geddes' "three Hs" related to affective, physical, and intellectual development which, he insisted should be emphasised in learning in *that order of priority* "for in that order they develop" (Geddes, 1949, p. 228). He made a point of employing this approach with his own children and students. This concept of the integration of affective and intellectual learning with a physical dimension resonates with experiential education, the progressive education movement, and both environmental and outdoor education.

According to Meller (1990, p. 22) Geddes' approach to learning owes much to his father who nurtured his love of nature through long walks in the Scottish Perthshire countryside. These early experiences eventually resulted in the focus of his academic positions at Edinburgh and Dundee University where his enthusiasm for the natural world and student learning were obvious. One of his students commented:

> I liked him best when we were in the country on excursions, for he was then like a schoolboy. He was untiring, regardless of the weather, and content with little in the way of food even on the longest jaunts. And although he did not give us much in the way of preparation for degree examination—that was left to his assistant—he did far more by taking us into the open out-of-door, exposing us to undreamt-of beauties and making us ask the how and why of nature. (Miss B. D. Craig, as cited in Boardman, 1978, p. 111)

The themes of science, evolutionary biology, and ecology are central to Geddes' approach to knowledge, learning, and teaching. It is not so much that he taught these as subjects, in an interdisciplinary fashion, but more that they were the basis for understanding human development, society, community, and culture.

> Star wonder, stone and spark-wonder, life-wonder and folk-wonder: these are the stuff of astronomy and physics, of biology and the social sciences. Hence the fundamental place of Nature study, and of our Surveys. To appreciate sunset and sunrise, moon and stars, and the wonders of the winds, clouds and rain, the beauty of the woods and moon and fields—here are the beginning of the natural sciences. Set the child observing nature, not with labelled and codified lessons but with its own treasures and beauty feasts—as of stones, minerals, crystals, of living fishes and butterflies, of wild flowers and seeds! Above all, the cultivated plants and the kindly domesticated animals. We adults have all been more or less starved and stunted: in schools we were even made artificial defectives, for want of such observations; and with our intelligence unawakened through nature's work and play. Each child needs its own plot in the school garden, and its own bench in the workshop; it should also go on wider and wider excursions, and these increasingly of its own choice. We need to give everyone the outlook of the artist, who begins with the art of seeing, and then in time we shall follow him into the seeing of art, even the creating of it. (Geddes, 1919, cited in Geddes, 1949, p. 216)

His thoughts about subject areas were often illustrated through his "thinking machines"—diagrams which showed the relationships between concepts/subjects and disciplines. The best known of these relates to "place, work, folk" and the discipline-based corollaries of "geography, economics, anthropology" (Meller, 1990, pp. 46–47). In this example he used grids to make the relationships between them explicit, though he also used other diagrammatic representations. Through the development of such devices Geddes "hoped to initiate and educate others to accept the need for educational reform and to pursue a synthesis of all knowledge" (Meller, 1990, p. 45). Although these were designed to prompt creative thinking and creative acts he was, according to Meller (1990), "unable to persuade others to follow what he hoped was the path towards solving the problems that arose" and they were "to prove his Achilles' heel" (p. 45). (see Boardman, 1978; Meller, 1990; and Stephen, 2004, for further details of Geddes' "thinking machines").

As a polymath and interdisciplinarian, Geddes "raged against increasing specialisation in modern studies, suggesting instead that students should be encouraged to have an encyclopaedic comprehensiveness in their approach to knowledge" (Meller, 1990, p. 44). His frustration was aimed at schools and universities alike for their failure to embrace the principles of what became an *experiential* approach to education. He ridiculed "the current Nature-starvation of school and college, with their verbalism and empaperment" and "moral starvation", insisting that "we must cease to think merely in terms of separated departments and faculties, and must co-relate these in the living mind (Geddes, 1919, as cited in Geddes, 1949, p. 228).

Geddes' Contributions to Knowledge and to Experiential Education

Patrick Geddes' contributions to knowledge and the field of education were consistently inter-disciplinary. The following examples give some insights.

The Regional Survey: Geddes' biographers consistently highlight the significance of his upbringing in rural Perthshire (Scotland) and his love of biology, geography, and their interdisciplinary nature. According to Maclean (2004), this "stemmed from his evolutionary biological outlook; it was organic, saw no major clash between the human and natural sciences" (p. 85). Through his desire for integrated understanding of the sciences and civics, Geddes' love of geography evolved and he came to see it as "the only complete science—the synthesis as the mother of them all" (Geddes in Maclean, 2004, p. 85). This coupled with his educational and social convictions led quite naturally to the belief that, through active participation in geographical research and understanding an informed citizenry would develop the skills and knowledge necessary for social improvement. "Geddes' role was to teach them to see for themselves, to learn for themselves and to act on their own initiative" (Maclean, 2004, p. 86) and his favoured approach to doing so was through "regional survey" of an area—essentially an evaluation, based on observation and research—which was a necessary precursor to any social or planning decisions.

The Outlook Tower: In 1892 Geddes took over a high, centrally located building in the centre of Edinburgh and developed it into an educational resource. The Outlook Tower was, essentially "a multifunctional building: to assist the 'understanding' of the geographer, the historian, the sociologist and the social worker, in other words a centre for civic and regional survey" (Maclean, 2004, p. 87). The five floors of the building, which were visited from the top down, displayed in turn the city, Scotland, Britain and its empire, United States, Europe, and, finally, the world. Each of these contained educational displays which were often interpreted for visitors by Geddes when he visited the tower. The key point of the project, essentially a "regional survey" that could be adapted to anywhere on Earth, was that it provided visitors with a structured means of learning about their environment and demonstrated a "concentric approach to geography, leading from the local to the regional to national to the global" (Maclean, 2004, p. 89). Geddes' social ambitions were a driving motivation and he intended that it would lead to local involvement in social and planning decisions, and associated improvements in the quality of their environment.

The Valley Section: This is one of the most significant and adaptable of Geddes' educational concepts. As noted earlier, the French social geographer Elisée Reclus was an inspiration for Geddes and was "the source for Geddes' attempt to create a general unit for the study of a region" (Meller, 1990, p. 40). Geddes devised a generalised diagram of a river valley from source to sea and placed on it the "trades" which evolved appropriate to the location in the section, from miner and woodman in the hills to the shepherd, peasant, farmer, and fisher as one moves further down the valley (for diagrams see Meller, 1990, p. 41; Maclean, 2004, p. 90.). The diagram was not intended to be a static representation but evolutionary, showing how over time the "trades changed; the farmer became the baker, the hunters furriers, the shepherd the wool mill worker, etc. stressing "the interdependence of the city or organism, and its region and habitat" (Maclean, 2004, p. 90). For Geddes, the Valley Section held a myriad of possibilities in the teaching of other subjects (e.g., mathematics—see Maclean, 2004, p. 91) as well as geography.

Influence on Scottish educational policy: Geddes' promotion of education through geography led to a number of disciples promoting his approaches in both formal and informal education which were essentially practical and outdoors. Their activities are well documented by biographers. Maclean (2004) highlights Geddes' influence on UK geographers and local (Scottish) educational policy makers, teachers, and teacher-educators, pointing to a number of Scottish individuals who clearly adhered to Geddes' exhortation to commit to practical outdoor learning through nature study, the Valley Section and Regional Survey. [For example, the influential text-book *Environmental Studies: A Concentric Approach* (Masterton, 1969) which was written a generation later, and policy documents such as the 1965 memorandum on *Primary Education in Scotland* (Scottish Education Department, 1965) which accorded with the Geddes' rationale for "child-centred and activity-based" and outlined a Scottish progressive education system (Maclean, 2004, p. 111)].

Nature study and the origins of outdoor education: One of Geddes' followers, Dr. Cecil Reddie, who studied with him in Edinburgh between 1878 and 1882, was responsible for the first attempt in the United Kingdom to formalise "the outdoors" into an educative medium when he founded Abbotsholme School in 1889 (Parker & Meldrum, 1973). Reddie was particularly concerned to exercise both mind and body through community and other work with a view to engendering social responsibility. Central to this philosophy was that educational objectives were more readily achieved in pleasant surroundings. It was a philosophy inspired by the Romantic movement, of which one of the chief characteristics was a passionate concern regarding the relationship between human beings and the natural environment, and Geddes' views on education wherein "the child's desire of seeing, touching, handling, smelling, tasting and hearing are all true and healthy hungers, and these should be cultivated" (Geddes in Maclean, 2004, p. 85.). In accord with Geddes, Reddie felt it was crucial that these senses were applied to, stimulated by, and educated in the outdoors, and his admiration for him led to a request for Geddes to write an educational report on Abbotsholme which he did in 1904 (Meller, 1990, p. 55). As the earliest "progressive school" in the United Kingdom, its role has been significant in this movement and in the development of education outdoors.

Sustainability: A century ago Geddes made the point that "by leaves we live": For example how many people think twice about a leaf? Yet the leaf is the chief product and phenomenon of life: this is a green world, with animals comparatively few and small, and all dependent on the leaves. By leaves we live. Some people have strange ideas that they live by money. They think energy is generated by the circulation of coins. Whereas the world is mainly a vast leaf colony, growing on and forming a leafy soil, not a mere mineral mass; and we live not by the jingling of our coins, but by the fullness of our harvests. Moreover, the leaves made the coal: coal is but plant-life fossilised; and hence the coalminers are the modern masters of energy (Geddes, 1919, as cited in Geddes, 1949, pp. 216–217).

Many of us were indeed taught by our "chemistry masters that oxygen in the air is a matter of 'inorganic chemistry' whereas the whole of it is but the ever-increasing waste-product of plant-life" (Geddes, 1919, as cited in Geddes, 1949, p. 216). However, global climate change has brought home the fundamental importance of understanding the role of plants in producing oxygen from our major industrial and human waste product—carbon dioxide.

Even though he did not use the term "sustainability," Geddes' understanding of the concept and its significance is obvious. His characteristic interdisciplinary approach, and his originality in thinking and teaching clearly parallels the recommendations of contemporary advocates of sustainable development and sustainability education. This is all the more remarkable in light of the contemporary thinking which generally adopted a reductionist approach.

Implications for EE Philosophy

"Obstacles and stumbling blocks to understanding had been swept away, and we felt as on a mountain top. I remembered what an American (Earl Barnes, I think) had remarked to me of Geddes: That he was 'a very wise man, with his feet on the ground, and his head in the air'" (Defries describing Geddes' final lecture in Dundee, cited in Geddes, 1949, p. 230). Although Geddes achieved many things in his lifetime, many projects were left incomplete. Though this may be a reason for his lack of visibility amongst the great polymaths of the 20th century, it may also be due to the very qualities that made him a great educational philosopher and educator. He had an energetic and mercurial interest in almost everything, a commitment to learning through the senses and personal experiences, and was able to make intellectual leaps within and across disciplines. He may also have been somewhat neglected by experiential educators in part because of his achievements in other fields, but also because he offered no simple recipes, preferring instead to focus on reality and complexity. However, thanks to the efforts of biographers from the 1970s onwards he has, some 150 years after his birth, enjoyed something of a recent revival in his homeland and elsewhere.

Although his legacy in the form of city plans and buildings is extensive and found in many parts of the globe, it is the intellectual ideas behind these and his commitment to education that constitute his lasting contribution. Geddes is a rarity, a towering philosopher who could conceptualise complex ideas in simple phrases, and who developed many of his ideas into educational, civic and architectural projects. These qualities, and his epithets (e.g., "Heart, Hand, Head"; "Place Work, Folk"; and "By Living, We Learn") resonate with the ideas and purposes of contemporary experiential educators. Furthermore, his palpable commitment to the concepts of "sustainability" and "thinking global and acting local" draw the student into a deeper engagement with the man and his ideas.

During his lifetime the world became increasingly industrialised, but the rapid acceleration caused by globalization, population growth, wealth in the "developed" world were at an early stage, and there was no reason for scientists to turn their attention to the issue of global climate change. Nonetheless, his observation that "by leaves we live" (Geddes, 1919, as cited in Geddes, 1949, p. 216) is a scientific fact which he developed into an educational exhortation. This idea urges respect for earth systems and a re-assessment of our values, priorities, and actions. In this, as in other areas, he seems to have been prescient. Through promoting the understanding of the natural world upon which we depend and the social context in which we live, and advocating an experiential means of doing so, he has established the goal and offered a means of achieving it. Whilst Geddes would be proud of such a legacy, were he alive today, he would surely be urging government and individual action on education, social justice, communities, and, perhaps most of all, sustainability.

In reporting Geddes' final lecture at Dundee University in 1919, Defries (1927, as cited in Geddes, 1949, p. 230) describes the concluding exchanges:

> Then the young soldier-chairman rose and said: 'The Professor has given us a method by which to live and teach and work, and a fuller comprehension of life as a whole.' Cheers followed this declaration. An old lady next to me said: 'He has been talking to the next generation—it is too much for us.'

Almost 100 years and several generations have passed since Geddes' final lecture. Geddes would surely hope that we will listen carefully to his message, and act (on living, teaching, working, and sustainable development) with some urgency.

References

Ballater Geddes Project. (n.d., a). Retrieved December 4, 2007, from http://www.ballaterscotland.com/geddes/

Ballater Geddes Project. (n.d., b). Retrieved December 4, 2007, from http://www.ballaterscotland.com/geddes/geddesexhib04web.pdf

Boardman, P. (1978). *The worlds of Patrick Geddes.* London: Routledge and Keegan Paul.

Defries, A. (1927). *The interpreter: Geddes, the man and his gospel.* London: Routledge.

Geddes, P. (1905). An educational approach — a technical approach. In J. E. Hand (Ed.), *Ideals of science and faith* (pp. 170–216). London: George Allen.

Geddes, P. (1915). *Cities in evolution.* London: Williams & Norgate.

Geddes, P. (1919). Final lecture at the University of Dundee [published in 1949 reprint of *Cities in evolution*]. London: Williams and Norgate.

Geddes, P. (1949). *Cities in evolution* (rev. ed.). London: Williams & Norgate.

Geddes, P., & Thompson, J. (1889). *The evolution of sex.* Edinburgh: Walter Scott.

Gillon, J. (n.d.). *Patrick Geddes and the Outlook Tower.* Retrieved December 4, 2007, from http://members.fortunecity.com/gillonj/patrickgeddesandtheoutlooktower/

Kitchen, P. (1975). *A most unsettling person.* London: Gollancz.

Leonard, S. (2004). Finding Geddes abroad. In W. Stephen (Ed.), *Think global, act local: The life and legacy of Patrick Geddes* (pp. 41-60). Edinburgh: Luath Press.

Maclean, K. (2004). Patrick Geddes: Regional survey and education. In W. Stephen (Ed.), *Think global, act local: The life and legacy of Patrick Geddes* (pp. 85–116).Edinburgh: Luath.

Masterton, T. (1969). *Environmental studies: A concentric approach.* Edinburgh: Oliver & Boyd.

Meller, H. (1990). *Patrick Geddes: Social evolutionist and city planner.* London: Routledge.

Parker, T., & Meldrum, K. (1973). *Outdoor education.* London: Dent.

Scottish Education Department. (1965). *Primary education in Scotland.* Edinburgh: Her Majesty's Stationery Office.

Sir Patrick Geddes Memorial Trust. (2007). Retrieved December 4, 2007, from http://www.patrickgeddes.trust.co.uk/

Stephen, W. (Ed.). (2004). *Think global, act local: The life and legacy of Patrick Geddes.* Edinburgh: Luath.

Stephen, W. (Ed.). (2007). *A vigorous institution: The living legacy of Patrick Geddes.* Edinburgh: Luath.

5 Alfred North Whitehead

Educational Emergence

Jasper S. Hunt

I first heard the name Alfred North Whitehead in 1975. I was ending my junior year at The Evergreen State College in Olympia, Washington, and was looking ahead to my final year there. I had decided I wanted to do a senior capstone project that would focus my academic interests on a topic of significance. I had developed a close relationship with one of my teachers, Dr. William F. (Willi) Unsoeld, so I approached him about doing a special project. He liked the idea a lot because the college did not require a formal senior capstone project. Willi was a professor of philosophy and religion as well as experiential education. I asked him whom he considered the most important philosopher of the 20th century. He sat back in his chair and thought carefully for several minutes, then looked at me and said, "Alfred North Whitehead." So began my long relationship with Whitehead, which would culminate in my doing my PhD dissertation at the University of Colorado, Boulder, in 1983, comparing Whitehead and John Dewey. My fascination with Whitehead continues after 32 plus years, and I find his thinking as captivating and interesting now as I did in 1975.

Biography

Whitehead was born in 1861 in England and died in 1947 in the United States in Cambridge, Massachusetts. Whitehead was originally a mathematician and taught mathematics and philosophy of science at Cambridge University and the University of London. In 1924, when he was 63 years old, Whitehead was invited to join the philosophy faculty at Harvard University. He taught at Harvard until 1939. It was during his tenure at Harvard that he devoted himself to philosophy. Whitehead was a "mathematician's mathematician" and a "philosopher's philosopher." I say that because his work in mathematics and philosophy was highly technical and much of it is accessible only to people with strong intellectual backgrounds in either mathematics or western philosophy. Indeed, when I first began my study of Whitehead under the tutelage of Willi Unsoeld, I was stopped dead in my tracks for a time. Willi insisted that the only way to understand Whitehead was to understand the central problems of Western philosophy involving metaphysics, epistemology, axiology, ontology, and philosophy of religion. So, I had to drop Whitehead and instead immerse myself, under Unsoeld's direction, in the pre-Socratics, Plato, Aristotle, Descartes, Locke, Hume, and Kant in order to appreciate the problems that Whitehead was confronting in his philosophical work.

In addition to his mathematical and philosophical focus, Whitehead wrote and thought deeply about general problems in education and philosophy of education. Whitehead's own education was in the elite English universities of the time. All of his teaching was in traditional settings, although his time at the University of London can be viewed as progressive for its time. The University of London attempted to bring formal education to a much wider audience than the traditional English universities served. Whitehead wrote several essays on educational matters and some of the key ones were brought together in a work titled *The Aims of Education*

(Whitehead, 1929). Although his views on education are not made explicit in his formal philosophical writings, one can see the implications for teaching in many places in his philosophical work.

Inert Ideas

An excellent way to engage Whitehead's thinking on education is to consider his notion of *inert ideas*.

> In training a child to activity of thought, above all things we must beware of what I will call "inert ideas"—that is to say, ideas that are merely received into the mind without being utilized, or tested, or thrown into fresh combinations. In the history of education, the most striking phenomenon is that schools of learning, which at one epoch are alive with ferment of genius, in a succeeding generation exhibit merely pedantry and routine. The reason is, that they are overladen with inert ideas. Education with inert ideas is not only useless: it is, above all things, harmful—Corruptio optimi, pessima. Except at rare intervals of intellectual ferment, education in the past has been radically infected with inert ideas. (Whitehead, 1929, pp. 1–2)

To take an idea and then to present it to a student in isolation from any sort of experiential context is to make that idea inert. As defined in the *American Heritage Dictionary of the English Language*, to be inert is to be "unable to move or act" (Morris, 1973, p. 672). As an educational matter, an inert idea is one that is imposed upon a student without taking account of that student's situation. The idea then risks being irrelevant to that student in that situation. An inert idea does not result in making a difference in a student's life. It is merely "received into the mind" in isolation. Note here that it is not the idea itself that is inert; there are no inherently inert ideas in Whitehead's philosophy. Ideas become inert because of the lack of connectivity within a person's educational perspective. There must be a dynamic relationship between an idea and a person for that idea to become important and useful. If there is no dynamic relationship, then the idea becomes inert *to that person*. An inert idea for one person may not be inert at all to another person. There is, therefore, a relativity of inert ideas depending upon people and perspectives.

> Dead knowledge is the danger. It is the peculiar danger of scholarship, of universities; and it is considered quite respectable. You "know" a great deal, that is supposed to suffice. Now what is wanted is "activity in the presence of knowledge." Novel viewpoints; knowledge applied to experience. (Whitehead, 1954, p. 368)

Experiential educators know that useful knowledge must involve a dynamic process of action with reflection. Failure to take account of the action-reflection dynamic is to inculcate inert ideas, or as Whitehead put it "dead knowledge."

In order to avoid the danger of teaching inert ideas, Whitehead developed an emergent view of education which has at its core the rhythmic nature of learning. Whitehead believed that education must proceed according to certain basic patterns of emergence, which constitute a rhythm in the becoming of the student. The idea of rhythm grounds Whitehead's philosophy of education.

> It is that the development of mentality exhibits itself as a rhythm involving an interweaving of cycles, the whole process being dominated by a greater cycle of the same general char-

acter as its minor eddies. Furthermore, this rhythm exhibits certain ascertainable general laws which are valid for most pupils, and the quality of our teaching should be so adapted as to suit the stage in the rhythm to which our pupils have advanced. (Whitehead, 1929, p. 27)

The rhythm of educational emergence is actually constituted by three very broad stages of the development of mentality. Mentality is a characteristic of human beings and how they become. The progression of education is itself rooted in the emergence of mentality.

> Lack of attention to the rhythm and character of mental growth is a main source of wooden futility in education. I think that Hegel was right when he analyzed progress into three stages, which he called Thesis, Antithesis, and Synthesis; though for the purpose of the application of his idea to educational theory I do not think that the names that he gave are very happily suggestive. In relation to intellectual progress I would term them, the stage of romance, the stage of precision, and the stage of generalization. (Whitehead, 1929, p. 17)

It is interesting and important to note that from the beginning, Whitehead's philosophy of education was rooted in a theory of the emergence of the students, as opposed to basing the educational theory on ideas external to the students. Hence, it is fundamental to this educational philosophy that its foundation be based upon a conception of *experience*.

Romance

Romance is the starting point of education for Whitehead. The stage of romance constitutes the confrontation of the student with something new, which is given to experience. Romance confronts the student with a very broad totality, undifferentiated by much rigor. Romance is appealing and vague. Romance presents the student with broad possibilities for discovery and wonder.

> The stage of romance is the stage of first apprehension. The subject-matter has the vividness of novelty; it holds within itself unexplored connections with possibilities half-disclosed by glimpses and half-concealed by the wealth of material. In this stage knowledge is not dominated by systematic procedure. Such system as there must be must be created piecemeal ad hoc. We are in the presence of immediate cognizance of fact, only intermittently subjecting fact to systematic dissection. (Whitehead, 1929, pp. 17–18)

Precision

The stage of *precision* in Whitehead's educational theory makes the transition from general, vague fascination with something as a whole, to the discernment disclosed through analysis. Precision takes the source of interest generated by romance and submits it to the methods of detailed inquiry applicable to a given set of circumstances. The goal of precision is to make that which is vague and inchoate, clear and distinct.

> The stage of precision also represents an addition to knowledge. In this stage, width of relationship is subordinated to exactness of formulation. It is the stage of grammar, the grammar of language and the grammar of science. It proceeds by forcing on the students' acceptance a given way of analyzing the facts, bit by bit. New facts are added but they are the facts which fit into the analysis. (Whitehead, 1929, p. 18)

Generality

Generality in many ways is the ultimate goal of education in Whitehead's view. Generality is the ability of the student to take the interest generated by romance and the tools of analysis generated by precision, and transfer them to a wider scope than had been previously possible.

> We have now come to the third stage of the rhythmic cycle, the stage of generalization. There is here a reaction towards romance. Something definite is now known; aptitudes have been acquired; and general rules and laws are clearly apprehended both in their formulation and their detailed exemplification. The pupil now wants to use his new weapons. He is an effective individual, and it is effects that he wants to produce. He relapses into the discursive adventures of the romantic stage, with the advantage that his mind is now a disciplined regiment instead of a rabble. (Whitehead, 1929, pp. 36–37)

Whitehead's stages of educational development should not be interpreted as a set sequence of steps which must be taken on the path to knowledge. The three stages constitute a cycle and there is a constant overlapping and interplay of the three stages in the development of a student. Whitehead anticipates the perception that his three stages are a rigid prescription for educational progress.

> My second caution is to ask you not to exaggerate into sharpness the distinction between the three stages of the cycle. I strongly suspect that many of you, when you heard me detail the three stages in each cycle, said to yourselves—How like a mathematician to make such formal divisions! I assure you that it is not mathematics but literary incompetence that may have led me into the error against which I am warning you. Of course, I mean throughout a distinction of emphasis, of pervasive quality, romance, precision, generalization are all present throughout. But there is an alternation of dominance, and it is this alternation which constitutes the cycle. (Whitehead, 1929, pp. 27–28)

The key words here are "alternation of dominance." Whitehead's point is that at a given time in the life of a student, that student needs to confront educational materials from the perspective which will encourage that student to continue on with education. This does not mean that the student at the romantic stage shouldn't be encouraged towards precision, or that a student at the precise stage should not be romantic. It is just a matter of emphasis as to which stage should be dominant at a given time. The rhythm of education implies that all three stages should be constantly overlapping and supplementing each other in the students' educational experiences.

There is a key term from Whitehead's metaphysics that is very useful for understanding his educational views. That term, "the *fallacy of misplaced concreteness*" is used in Whitehead's philosophical writings to refer to the tendency to take a particular component or aspect of experience, and then elevate that element to a degree of metaphysical finality that is unwarranted.

> One form is what I have termed, elsewhere, the 'fallacy of misplaced concreteness.' This fallacy consists in neglecting the degree of abstraction involved when an actual entity is considered merely so far as it exemplifies certain categories of thought. There are aspects of actualities which are simply ignored so long as we restrict thought to these categories. Thus the success of a philosophy is to be measured by its comparative avoidance of this fallacy, when thought is restricted within its categories. (Whitehead, 1978, p. 3)

Although in the context from which this quote comes, the fallacy of misplaced concreteness is used in the highly technical discussion of Whitehead's metaphysics, nevertheless I think it is extremely useful in the field of education.

So far in this chapter four key educational ideas have been presented: the avoidance of inculcating inert ideas, and the importance of romance, precision, and generality in the educational cycle. One can take the fallacy of misplaced concreteness and apply it to all four areas. The fallacy would be committed if an educator were to focus on any of the four concepts at the exclusion of the other three and without regard to the situation of the learner.

Experiential educators are often confronted with the problem of emphasizing content or process. On one side is the argument that experiential teaching methodologies need only be focused on the academic content of the subject matter. On the other side is the argument that process is everything and that content is really not very important to experiential educators. Whitehead would suggest that both sides, if presented as representing the totality of education, have committed the fallacy of misplaced concreteness within the educational context. The same can be said of the rhythmic cycle of romance, precision, and generality. Failure to account for the proper place of all three can result in committing the fallacy of misplaced concreteness.

Being and Becoming

Whitehead is often classified as a "process philosopher." Indeed the title of his magnum opus, *Process and Reality* (Whitehead, 1978), lends support to this classification. The roots of this classification lie in the problem posed by the Pre-Socratic philosophers and carried on throughout Western philosophy. The ancient Greek philosopher, Parmenides, argued that the ultimate nature of reality is "being" and that the world given to perception as in flux is not what the world really is. Typically, in the Greek tradition, "being" would lie in areas like mathematics and other intellectual abstractions. On the other hand, the ancient Greek philosopher Heraclitus argued the opposite of Parmenides. Heraclitus suggested that the world of appearances, the world of flux, is what the world ultimately is, and that the quest for permanence of "being" is doomed to failure. This old philosophical problem has been addressed in Western philosophy by Plato and Aristotle and on down through the ages to modern philosophers with many, varied attempts to reconcile "being" with "becoming." The reason Whitehead is classified as a process philosopher is that his solution to the being/becoming problem lies in his detailed analysis of the two concepts as inextricably tied together with the becoming of any occasion of experience from the tiniest sub-atomic particle to the most massive physical structures in the universe. It is beyond the scope of the intent of this chapter to go into detail about Whitehead's metaphysics and cosmology. However, there is a key point from the technical work that is very applicable to the field of education.

Whitehead tells us that *how* an actual entity *becomes* constitutes *what* that actual entity is; so the two descriptions of an actual entity are not independent. Its "being" is constituted by its "becoming." This is the "principle of process" (Whitehead, 1978, p. 23).

One can focus on the metaphysical problem of being/becoming as a matter of interest only to technical philosophers or one can focus on the problem as it relates to educational practice. The process of education is what gives rise to the product of education. In Whitehead's language *how* we educate students will have a direct result on *what* they become. I'll never forget Willi Unsoeld's admonition to developing experiential educators that they never, ever separate the process of education from the content of education. Unsoeld argued that the "perfect" educator is one who is able to achieve the proper balance between academic content and the process by which that content is taught. The notion of academic content is flexible. The content may be mathematics or it may be a top-roped rock climbing site. However, regardless of the specific nature of the content, experiential educators must be aware of the balance between process and content in their instructional plans. Failure to achieve that balance will most often result in inert ideas being generated in students.

In order to prevent education from simply becoming the inculcation of inert ideas into students, Whitehead's theory stresses the importance of basing education on the experiences of the students, or as the existentialists would term it, the lived situations of the students. Education viewed as experience-based means that the ideas that are deemed important to know, should be presented in such a way as to enlighten the lives of the students involved. The point is that experience should not be a chopped-up affair, with total disconnections from moment to moment, with no principle of unity. Experience is essentially a coherent unity as should the educational plan be. Whitehead's often repeated proposition is relevant here: "The many become one and are increased by one" (Whitehead, 1978, p. 21). The "many," comprising the subjects, the content of education, should only be presented as they fructify in the "one" of the student's own experience. Otherwise, education risks committing the fallacy of misplaced concreteness by concentrating on inert ideas, rather than the lived experience of students.

> The solution which I am urging is to eradicate the fatal disconnection of subjects which kills the vitality of our modern curriculum. There is only one subject-matter for education, and that is 'Life'—in all its manifestations. Instead of this single unity, we offer children—Algebra, from which nothing follows; Geometry, from which nothing follows; Science, from which nothing follows; a couple of Languages, never mastered; and lastly, most dreary of all, Literature, represented by plays of Shakespeare, with philological notes and short analyses of plot and character to be in substance committed to memory. Can such a list be said to represent Life, as it is known in the midst of living it? The best that be said of it is, that it is a rapid table of contents which a deity might run over in his mind while he was thinking of creating a world, and has not yet determined how to put it together. (Whitehead, 1929, pp. 6–7)

Whitehead is particularly critical of the misuse of standardized tests in education. I find it very interesting that his writing in the first quarter of the 20th century raised warnings about standardized tests, given that the United States in the first quarter of the 21st century has, under the power of the centralized federal government, committed itself almost 100% to basing educational evaluation on standardized tests (e.g., "No Child Left Behind" legislation).

> It is for this reason that the uniform external examination is so deadly. We do not denounce it because we are cranks, and like denouncing established things. We are not so childish. Also, of course, such examinations have their use in testing slackness. Our reason of dislike is very definite and very practical. It kills the best part of culture. When you analyze in the light of experience the central task of education, you find that its successful accomplishment depends on a delicate adjustment of many variable factors. The reason is that we are dealing with human minds, not with dead matter. The evocation of curiosity, of judgment, of the power of mastering a complicated tangle of circumstances, the use of theory in giving foresight in special cases—all these powers are not to be imparted by a set rule embodied in one schedule of examination subjects. (Whitehead, 1929, p. 5)

Whitehead's concern with such tests is that they are inherently composed of inert ideas, given that they are written with no knowledge of the particular students who are taking the tests. It is not testing per se that Whitehead objects to; rather it is imposing tests ex cathedra, without consideration of a student's life situation. Whitehead goes so far as to argue that no student should ever be examined except by the particular teacher who knows and has worked with that student.

And I may say in passing that no educational system is possible unless every question directly asked of a pupil at any examination is either framed or modified by the actual teacher of that pupil in that subject. The external assessor may report on the curriculum or on the performance of the pupils, but never should be allowed to ask the pupil a question which has not been strictly supervised by the actual teacher, or at least been inspired by a long conference with him. (Whitehead, 1929, p. 5)

Implications for EE Philosophy

There is much more that could be written about Alfred North Whitehead as a source of educational theory for contemporary experiential educators. For example: Whitehead developed a complex and fascinating philosophy of religion and theology that has educational implications. He stresses the importance of solitude as foundational in religious experience. Many experiential education programs incorporate periods of solitude into their program offerings. His theory of God is a fairly radical departure from orthodox theology, which traditionally conceives of God as remote and metaphysically different from the rest of reality. Rather, Whitehead's theory of God has the deity having real relations with the world and, indeed, the realities of the emerging world influence the ontology of the deity. His speculative philosophical system has within it ideas that are germane to educators. Although he affirms the importance of philosophical speculation, Whitehead is an empiricist and insists upon grounding speculation within the context of the lived experience.

Alfred North Whitehead offers a comprehensive, systematic philosophy. Experiential educators who want to explore theoretical avenues will find Whitehead a most exciting and rewarding source of inspiration. I will conclude that Willi Unsoeld's recommendation to study Whitehead was excellent and after several decades I still find Whitehead's philosophy of value in my teaching. I am profoundly grateful to Professor Unsoeld for pointing me in this direction.

References

Morris, W. (1973). *The American heritage dictionary of the English language.* New York: Houghton Mifflin.

Whitehead, A. N. (1929). *The aims of education.* New York: Macmillan.

Whitehead, A. N. (1954). *Dialogues of Alfred North Whitehead.* Westport, CT: Greenwood.

Whitehead, A. N. (1978). *Process and reality* (corrected ed.) D. W. Griffin & D. W. Sherburne (Eds.). New York: The Free Press.

6   Martin Buber
Dialogue, Relationship, the Other, and the More-Than-Human World

Sean Blenkinsop

In this chapter I will focus on a narrow range of Buber's philosophy, which, I think, is most relevant to experiential education both historically and for the field today (for more extended discussions see Blenkinsop 2004, 2005). I will focus on Buber's notion of relationship, particularly his philosophy of dialogue. I will follow Buber's understanding of relationship as it occurs with one other person, and as it occurs with the "more-than-human world," to borrow a phrase from Abram (1996). These two kinds of relationship will form a thread through a discussion of Buber's life and then his philosophy. I will also offer two experiential activities that I use in my teaching to help students make these philosophical ideas clear.

Part 1: The Life Lived

Born in Vienna in 1878, Martin Buber grew up under the influence of three adults: his grand-parents Adele and Solomon, and his father, Karl, all three of whom were committed to the betterment of individual persons and the community as a whole. Karl was a lover of the earth and "genuine human contact with nature" (Friedman, 1981, p. 12). Devoted to his estates and to agriculture, Karl influenced Martin in his relationships with other people, but also with the world around him.

> The relationship of my father to nature was connected with his relationship to the realm that one customarily designates as the social. It was solicitude … in the personal sense,… of active responsible contact that could rise here to full reciprocity. (Buber, 1967, p. 23)

Martin began school at the age of 10 and a year later had an encounter that was fundamental to his understanding of the Other and of *Thou*. He tells of sneaking into his grandparents' barn in order to stroke a horse, and continues:

> … [I] … felt the life beneath my hand, it was as though the element of vitality itself bordered on my skin, something that was not I, was certainly not akin to me, palpably the other, not just another, really the Other itself; and yet it let me approach, confided itself to me, placed itself elementally in the relation of Thou and Thou with me. (Buber, 1967, p. 38)

The significance of this experience of profound connection and the sensation of being in relation is Buber's first documented interaction with the Other. It is this and similar personal experiences, occurring as moments of discernable clarity, that Buber will later remember as he builds his philosophy of dialogue. In Buber's conception of dialogue, two individuals may come together, without the loss of the *I* (italics simply indicates Buber's I in relation), yet truly confirm the Other as *Thou*. Thus the relation of *I/Thou* becomes an existence encompassing both *I* and *Thou* but existing between the two.

Buber entered the university in Vienna to study philosophy. There he gained further insights into the human encounter with the more-than-human world. The first discovery was the experience of "the true actuality of the spirit" of books "as a 'between'" (Buber, 1967, p. 50). Here, an immature Buber experiences a connection with a non-living entity, the words of an author, which parallels his "in between" experience with the horse. Buber claims that something is created in between himself and the "spirit" of the book. This insight is useful for the educational relationship in two ways; first for the way we engage with the more-than-human world and second for the way we engage each other. Students can engage so that the more-than-human becomes a unique interaction that may add experiences, act as a mirror for, or offer insights to the student. This process expands the realm of possibility and can provide a challenge. Buber also witnessed how his own engagement was encouraged through interaction with a specific teacher in this process of learning and discovery.

Buber's second discovery was the Burgtheatre. An entranced Buber discovered the "spokenes [sic] of speech, sound becoming 'Each-Other'" (Buber, 1967, p. 51). The theatre involved people creating, choosing, and becoming through the spoken word and through the projection of themselves into the characters. Buber believed this was occurring through the communion of dialogue witnessed and sanctioned by others in a public forum.

Buber distinguished two types of actors, a distinction which foreshadows his later separation of *I/It* and *I/Thou*. The first type, corresponding to the *I/It* relationship, acquires the fullness of the character in absolute imitation, knowing all that has and will come to pass. This actor is external to the character and examining it as though in the past tense. This Buber describes as "exclusion" and is the "orientation" way of being. The second type of actor uses "the wings of the moment," life experiences, and existence from within to "step into the character's skins" and become that character. This kind of acting he calls "empathy."

However, both of these relationships are in the realm of *I/It* and it is the truly great actor, who is able to be both simultaneously, who offers us insight into the *I/Thou*. Buber calls this "inclusion" which, unlike empathy, "does not mean giving up one's own side of the relationship." The ability to see the other, understand and embrace the other without giving up the self is the true penetration of being, true dialogue, the *I/Thou* (Buber, 1969, p. 12). So, the actor both "becomes" his character and stays himself.

Buber often referred to marriage as the "exemplary bond," and his marriage to Paula, whom he met at the university, was the truest example of relationship that he had with another person. It was the model for much of his discussion on dialogue and probably the one upon which he fashions his understanding of the *I/Thou*. Martin and Paula came together as two individuals and a relationship and chose to commit thoughtfully to their relationship, worked through issues, and supported each other to grow and learn in their independent projects. Buber describes this love as being truly dialogical and distinguishes it from the monological, "Luciferic" love where the individual is simply pre-occupied with the self.

As a well-educated young man in a community that honored scholarship, Buber began to feel himself trapped between two realms, the political and the scholastic. With respect to the political, he found himself being sought out by people in search of advice, support, or insight. Buber felt that he was unprepared and inadequate to be the kind of community leader and teacher these people were seeking. This sense of unpreparedness rose in part because his image of the teacher, which shaped his educational philosophy, was directly connected to childhood experiences of encountering the *zaddik*. The *zaddik* is "the true helper" (Buber, 1967, p. 72), a simple individual, a "living double kernel of humanity: genuine *community* and genuine *leadership*" (Buber, 1967, p. 73). It was this image of the *zaddik* that shaped Buber's understanding of what a teacher should be and made the role all the more daunting.

In response to a sense of unpreparedness, Buber withdrew himself into the rarified air of solitary contemplation. Looking back on his life, Buber surmised that this process of self-examination and self-reflection was a phase he had to go through in order to become himself. In many ways we see this life paralleling how experiential educators use reflection to support individual becoming and might explain the kind of responsibility we see as educators for this combination of "genuine *community* and genuine *leadership.*"

It was during this period of sequestration that Buber received, though not fully, an unknown young man in search of personal guidance. Shortly after this meeting, Buber learned that the man committed suicide and Buber, overwhelmed by this invasion of the "everyday" into his isolation, realized that he had failed in a very real way to deal with the world. He had lacked "presence" for the young man, failing to understand, engage with, and encounter that unique individual who was reaching desperately to Buber for help. From then on Buber gave up his detached, other-worldly, mystical way of life. He thenceforth believed that we exist in this world, subject to finite time and space, and it is here where the mystical and the religious take place. Referring to the world he writes: This moment is not extracted from it, it rests on what has been and beckons to the remainder which has still to be lived. You are not swallowed up in a fulness[sic] without obligation, you are willed for the life of communion (Buber, 1967, p. 94). Buber acknowledges that by 1905, after his movement through and out of mysticism, "the Hasidic tradition had grown for me into the supporting ground of my own thinking" (Buber, 1967, p. 118). Between 1907 and 1919 Buber worked on the philosophy of dialogue and the dialogical relationship, and in 1922, after two years of isolated study dedicated solely to Hasidic material, he published, his famous second draft of *I and Thou* (Buber, 1970).

Buber's biography is essential to understanding his thought. The steps that led Buber to understanding the *I/Thou* came through his experiences with his caregivers, with nature, and with the world around. The challenge of the intellect, the importance of the word, the experience of mysticism and of its limits, and the recognition that he belonged to the real world but with the potential to reach towards the Other were significant encounters on his educational journey to his mature work.

As experiential educators we recognize the importance of encounters, of relational experiences, with other people and with animals, text, stage productions, and the more-than-human. The ideas of the *I/Thou* relationship and the role of teacher in both community and leadership resonate in deep ways with experiential educators. By extending Buber we may see the outline of an epistemology beginning to take shape. It is this outline that has potentially significant implications for ongoing relevance to experiential education. Buber learned in and through relationship and this has implications for how we come to know. If knowledge is a shared creation, a substance of relation in the "in between," then what does it mean to know? What does the knower become and how do we create knowledge with our students? However, these questions need more of Buber's philosophy and are beyond the purview of this paper. Our time is better spent continuing our journey with two activities that I use to help students understand and experience the nature of relationship with the individual other and with the more-than-human world.

Part 2: Two Activities

The Knife-Edged Ridge: A Way into Understanding the I/Thou

Picture this: you are high in the mountains and have been mountaineering through some magnificent terrain for the last few weeks. You are gingerly making your way along a knife-edged ridge. The ridge runs for as far as you can see, and you are trying to forget the fact that on one side of the ridge there is a 3,000-foot drop into nothingness while on the other the slope is even more precipitous, but thankfully there is only a drop of 2,000 feet before a hard stop on the valley floor. You are gently edging your way along this narrow ridge, being thoughtful about your foot placement, and wondering why you ever found mountaineering a good idea in the first place. Then, wonder of wonders, you discover another expeditioner coming along the ridge towards you from the other direction. And now you have to pass each other because neither of you wants to go back from where you have come.

In some ways this is a classic experiential activity—traffic jam on a log, the wobbly-woozie, or you could even use a High-V—but it comes directly out of Buber's writings as an image to consider when conceptualizing the *I/Thou*. There is a way that each person on the "ridge" has to encounter, embrace both themselves and the Other, in order to be successful that captures, if briefly, the relationship that Buber is aiming at. We all know, having done activities like these many times, that we need to respond exactly to what the other person is doing, we need to be "present" and, in fact, if it works well, neither *I* nor *Thou* is lost but there is also a third relation that occurs between us—*I/Thou*.

Buber believes that life is relationship and he begins *I and Thou* with his primary distinction, the "twofold attitude," *I/It* vs. *I/Thou*.

> Man can treat the world … as an "It"—an orderly, comprehensible collection of things of objects to be experienced and used. He then becomes aware of himself as a subject differentiated from these objects, as an 'I' dealing with 'Its' … our conceptual knowledge is of this sort. When we behold what confronts us in the world, we deal with it by treating it as an object which can be compared and assigned a place in an order of objects, described and analyzed objectively, filed away in our memory to be recalled when needed. (Buber, 1970, p. 90)

The *I/It* relationship as "an attitude toward the world" lacks mutuality, because "the 'I' remains separate" and "we lose in being unable to relate to anything" (Hendley, 1978, p. 141). The *I/It* is passive and takes place within the individual, thereby separating subject from object, and not "between" the individual and the other. The *I/It* relationship objectifies, made so from within the individual, and alienates the world that Buber believes must be revered and related to because only in saying "*Thou*" does the *I* truly come into being.

Buber sees *I/Thou* as paradoxically existing outside time and space since it occurs in "the actual and fulfilled present" (Buber, 1970, p. 63), but lacks the detached *I* placing the encounter into either time or space. Remembering Buber's encounter with the horse as a child helps to understand this concept of a fulfilled present being "non-temporal." However, this does not mean that Buber is advocating for a complete removal of the *I/It*. *I/It* and *I/Thou* operate in concert and both have necessary functions since we are living in a temporal world and it is impossible to sustain oneself in the non-temporal. Buber simply wants to disavow prioritizing *I/It* to the exclusion of *I/Thou* because *I* is different between *I/It* and *I/Thou* and *I/It* is the wrong path to take to the self.

For Buber, the human is responsible for the temporal, however the *I/Thou* offers insight into the eternal through the encounter with the other, entering relationship, and engaging in dialogue. The self is illuminated through history, personal work, and the process of dialogue. A reality in which relationship and dialogue exist between the individual and other people and between the individual and the world beyond is neither completely within nor completely outside the individual; that is what Buber means by *I/Thou*.

In his essay *Distance and Relation* (1951), Buber explains his perception of how human relations develop. He maintains that all children are born with the ability to relate. Very early they then learn the "primal setting at a distance," that is, they learn to separate themselves from objects, thereby creating an *It*. Thereafter follows the "entering into relation." This means *I/Thou* must be present before *I/It*, since "setting at a distance" implies distance from something, which Buber calls the *Primitive Thou*. Buber believes that children arrive as the "innate Thou" (1970,

p. 78), and only later does the need to distance oneself appear. All children are born in relation and need to "regain/return" to *I/Thou* consciously after "setting at a distance" the world. "The process of becoming … is the movement between the attitude of *I/Thou* to *I/It* and back to *I/Thou*" (Koo, 1964, p. 114).

Buber claims that through such things as technology, science, and institutionalization today's world is in a situation of ever-increasing "*I/Itness*" moving farther from relation. Though we live constantly within potential reach of the *Thou*, and it is, as Buber says, always "coming towards us and touching us," yet we "have become inept and uneager for such living intercourse" (Buber, 1970, p. 92). However, there is hope, since "all of these *Thou*'s which have been changed into *Its* have it in their nature to change back again into presentness" (Friedman, 1960, p. 63), a change which can be accomplished by learning again to revere the world and its objects.

I/Thou implies a dialogue that, spoken or silent, must be genuine and inclusive whereas *I/It* is a monologue. Inclusion, as Buber realized when watching the great Burgtheatre actors, means that two types of skills come together. The first skill entails coming to know one another, as we stand on that knife-edged ridge, in strengths and weaknesses, necessities and possibilities, and not losing the self. The second skill, empathy, involves the individual "becoming" the other and losing oneself. It is in dialogue that *I* is discovered and deepened, because the other, knowing our actuality and our project can act as a mirror, a questioner, a supporter, and a challenger; the other is able to ask "where art *Thou*?" However, relationship requires effort and confirmation. To confirm someone, which Buber failed to do in the case of the young visitor who committed suicide, is to encounter him in his own concreteness and it occurs through "making present," which "means to imagine quite concretely what another … is wishing, feeling, perceiving, and thinking … it is through this … that we grasp another as a self" (Friedman, 1956, p. 97).

Relationship plays a major role in experiential education. There are discussions happening continuously around the nature of relationships between parents, teachers, students, administrators, and the community at large. However, Buber is asking a question which is seldom considered: What do we mean by relationship? Buber is offering a lens through which educators must examine themselves, but we have still just explored relationship with another human. We are going to have to get a little closer to Buber's God, the God of Hasidism, if we are going to explore what might be the life-blood of experiential education: relationship to the more-than-human world.

Shekina: The Divine Indwelling: Relationship with the More-Than-Human World

"The sparks which fell down from the primal creation into the covering shells and were transformed into stones, plants, and animals" (Buber, 1958, p. 37).

One of my favorite environmental activities of all time is Rainbow Chips. It comes from the work of the Institute for Earth Education and Steve Van Matre (1990, pp. 84–85). The activity itself is quite simple involving you giving out small "chips" of construction paper in a variety of rainbowesque colours and having students find natural things that match those colours. Now I acknowledge that that activity fits into the larger work of environmental education, but in this case I use it to help students make sense of the Hasidic concept of the *shekina*.

Of course, no activity is worth its salt without, as Van Matre rightly points out, a little magic. So, we add a story. These days I use a story that I was given about 15 years ago by two Anishinaabe boys I was working with who didn't like the Institute's version. Since then I have heard a similar story appear in other places, but I am pretty sure I first heard it from these two boys and that it came out of their culture.

The story: Once upon a time, the world was black, without any color. The only exception occurred during those rare rainstorms when the sun shone and two perfect, parallel rainbows would appear. The animals and plants were intrigued by this brilliant color and so one day when the rainbows appeared Raven decided to investigate and flew off towards them. Unfortunately, Raven ended up flying too close and managed to shatter the upper rainbow into an infinite number of pieces which cascaded all over the earth, transforming everything they landed upon. This is why there is color on the earth, why ravens remain black, and why on some perfect, rainbow days you can see the remains of a second rainbow just above the first.

There are two aspects to Buber's God. The first, like the intact rainbow, is his own completeness that exists "above" while the second is the "shattered" unity, the *shekina*, the "exiled glory of God" (Buber, 1958, p. 81), that is spread out, in little pieces, within each and every animal, vegetable, and mineral on the earth a piece of the *shekina* "burns." In Hasidism people are responsible for finding, drawing forth, and "re-connecting" these scattered pieces, and they must approach each and every object with the intent of uncovering that spark, uniting it with their own and, ultimately, uniting all the sparks and returning them, like a bride, to God "so that she is again together with her bridegroom" (Buber, 1988, p. 216). Unfortunately, sparks can be hidden through both ignorance and choice and this creates a prison, a shell, around them.

> The sparks are to be found everywhere. They are suspended in things as in sealed-off springs; they stoop in the creatures as in walled-up caves, they inhale darkness and they exhale dread; they wait. (Buber, 1958, p. 103)

"The good is held captive in the shells" (Buber, 1958, p. 221), but, the spark is released, through the genuine encountering of the other. It is at that moment of insight and connection that dialogue is occurring.

> After a descent during which I had to utilize without a halt the late light of a dying day, I stood on the edge of a meadow. I pressed my stick against a trunk of an oak tree. Then I felt in twofold fashion my contact with being: here, where I held the stick, and there, where it touched the bark. Appearing to be only where I was, I nonetheless found myself there, too, where I found the tree. At that time dialogue appeared to me. (Buber, 1964, p. 47)

These encounters are not a call to pantheism, but an understanding that the world and humans are made sacred through relationship. Buber has also emphasized these natural encounters for children in his essay *Education* (Buber, 1968), and, for confirmation, draws upon the importance Hasidism places on reverence for all things, including tools, in order to draw forth these sparks or put the rainbow back together.

As an older man, Buber looked out his window at the great tree and experienced a real sense of relationship. "What I encounter is neither the soul of the tree nor a dryad, but the tree itself" (Buber, 1970, p. 59). There is a challenge here that he struggles with; if "relation is reciprocity" then "does the tree then have consciousness, similar to our own" (Buber, 1970, p. 58)? Buber has experienced a relationship with the tree, but the tree has not, and cannot reciprocate in the human way. However, that also means the tree cannot obfuscate relationship in a human way either, so the significance of the encounter to the tree is immaterial.

The relationship was important to Buber's own personal project, so important as to change his existence, and lead him to recommend relationship, moments of encounter, with nature to all children. Educators must not interpret this as meaning that any awareness of an object amounts to relationship. As we have seen in Buber's own experience, the relationship he is describing with the more-than-human is a rare and fleeting experience, but was of profound importance and must not be ignored.

Buber eventually defines three spheres of relation. The first is "life with nature," which lacks language, and it is here that we encounter the more-than-human, such as that which Buber encountered when he pressed his stick against the tree. At such moments of intense awareness, the pure other reaches towards us and allows us to glimpse both true relationship and ourselves as human.

> It is the I of pure intercourse with nature. Nature yields to it and speaks ceaselessly with it; she reveals her mysteries to it and yet does not betray her mystery. It believes in her and says to the rose: "So it is Thou"—and at once shares the same actuality with the rose. Hence when it returns to itself, the spirit of actuality stays with it; the vision of the sun clings to the blessed eye that recalls its own likeness to the sun, and the friendship of the elements accompanies man into the calm of dying and rebirth. (Buber, 1970, p. 116)

The second sphere of relation is "life with man." It involves language and can be made manifest through the *I/Thou*. The third is "life with spiritual beings," whom we cannot "hear" but by whom we are "addressed," as Buber was by the tree and his cat ("The domesticated animal has not … received the gift of the truly 'eloquent' glance from *us* … what it has from us is only the ability … to turn this glance upon us brutes" (Buber, 1970, p. 145), and whose immanence enable us to create, to think, and to act.

Buber has two reasons for concern about the way in which humankind perceives nature. First, because "whoever knows the world as something to be utilized knows God in the same way" (Buber, 1970, p. 156) and second, because to delude ourselves that the normal adult relationship is ideal is to totally misunderstand the very real challenge of relationship—that is the struggle to achieve unity within yourself, with others, and out into the broader community. Buber does not want us to solely objectify Nature, to solely approach nature in the one-directional monological way of *I/It*. Rather he wants us to understand that any approach made to a specific object holds with it the possibility of engaging with the spark situated within, that can provide insight at the moment and assist the recipient towards a better understanding of self.

For Buber, the self is discovered and nurtured by means of continually more reflective and conscious relationships, so that the individual becomes a person "in between" others, human and more-than-human. This then offers relevance and challenge to experiential educators who can explore levels of rapport between learners, other humans, the natural world, and encountered objects such as text and art. However, a teacher cannot force a student either into relationship or to learn, the impetus for relationship with the more-than-human world remains with each individual. That does mean that at least in experiential education the student has the option to enter relationship with the more-than-human.

At the very least, nature is ever present and provides the possibility of glimpses into relationship that the flawed humans around us, even those doing the best they can, may not be able to give. It is up to us to turn into relationship with nature. Buber believes that the human must find the spark within everything and join those sparks together, and it is only through entering relationship that one can achieve that. So, rather like a silent teacher, nature waits with the offer of relationship until we, the students, finally decide to recognize its presence and reach out in return. The role of nature cannot be overlooked or underestimated.

Implications for EE Philosophy

For experiential educators, the purpose of drawing Buber out in this way is to acknowledge our focus on relationship, to add increased philosophical depth to the work we love, and to challenge us to think deeply about these relations in which we are immersed and although often unseen and unacknowledged are fundamental to our becoming human. Buber believes the discovery and development of one's relationship to this larger unity, or connective web, in which we exist, affects our ability to develop better relationships with the objective world around us. If he is correct, this means that experiential educators are positioned to offer insight into something that needs to become widely understood by humankind, and soon. We must consider the question of that which surrounds our students. We must face the question of green space, the more-than-human, and whether or not a person's ability to make connections to the larger world is impeded by a sticky layer of tarmac over the landscape. Beyond this Buber argues that this process of being thoughtful, reverential, of the more-than-human helps us to re-connect the shattered rainbow. One wonders if that can be augmented through allowing students to more fully understand themselves, each other, and the world they encounter every day.

Ultimately, Buber's mandate to educators in this object-filled world is to be more thoughtful, more aware, of the more-than-human other, and of how the world *is* in relation to educator and students. Experiential educators know this process of dialogue and relationship and have a sense that it changes the student's very self if allowed to happen. Buber's thought provides a clearer sense of why.

References

Abram, D. (1996). *The spell of the sensuous: Perception and language in the more-than-human world*. New York: Pantheon.

Blenkinsop, S. (2004). Martin Buber's education: Imitating God, the developmental relationalist. In C. Higgins (Ed.), *Philosophy of education yearbook, 2004* (pp. 79–87). New York: Columbia University Press.

Blenkinsop, S. (2005). Martin Buber: Educating for relationship. *Ethics, Place, and Environment, 8*(3), 285–307.

Buber, M. (1951). Distance and relation. *Hibbert Journal, XLIX*(2), 105–113.

Buber, M. (1958). *Hasidism and modern man* (M. Friedman, Trans.). New York: Harper.

Buber, M. (1964). *Daniel: Dialogues on realization* (M. Friedman, Trans.). New York: Holt, Rinehart and Winston.

Buber, M. (1967). *Encounter: Autobiographical fragments*. La Salle, IL: Open Court.

Buber, M. (1968). *Between man and man* (R. G. Smith, Trans.). New York: Macmillan.

Buber, M. (1969). *Buber and the theatre* (M. Friedman, Trans.). New York: Funk & Wagnalls.

Buber, M. (1970). *I and thou*. W. Kaufmann (trans.). New York: Charles Scribner's.

Buber, M. (1988). *The origin and meaning of Hasidism* (M. Friedman, Trans.). Atlantic Highlands, NJ: Humanities Press International.

Friedman, M. (1956). Martin Buber's philosophy of education. *Educational Theory, 6*(2), 95–104.

Friedman, M. (1960). *Martin Buber: The life of dialogue*. New York: Harper & Row.

Friedman, M. (1981). *Martin Buber's life and work* (3 vols.). New York: E.P. Dutton.

Hendley, B. (1978). Martin Buber on the teacher/student relationship: a critical appraisal. *Journal of Philosophy of Education, 12*, 141–148.

Koo, G. (1964). The structure and process of self. *Educational Theory, 14*(2), 111–132.

Van Matre, S. (1990). *Earth education ... a new beginning*. Warrenville, IL: The Institute for Earth Education.

7   Paulo Freire
Critical Praxis and Experiential Education

Mary Breunig

In the preface of *Pedagogy of the Oppressed*, Paulo Freire (1921–1997) writes about a factory worker responding to a specific situation of injustice that was being discussed during one of the training courses that Freire conducted. Freire (1970, p. iv) writes that the factory worker said, "I can't say that I've understood everything you've said just now, but I can say one thing—when I began this course I was naive, and when I found out how naive I was, I started to get critical."

I had a somewhat similar awakening when I first read Freire. I was introduced to Paulo Freire's work by Jasper Hunt while I was working toward a master's degree in experiential education at Minnesota State University in Mankato. What has developed into revelations and insights about Freire's work and its intersection with the field of experiential education began with reflective skepticism about why it was that we were reading *Pedagogy of the Oppressed* (1970) in the first place. I naively believed that the coursework for my master's degree would involve rock-climbing adventures and canoe expeditions. I was naive about the field of experiential education, believing that all experiential education happened outdoors and involved some form of hands-on learning. I have since become critically awakened about the ways in which Freire's educational ideals intersect with and influence the field of experiential education.

Alongside John Dewey and Kurt Hahn, Paulo Freire is frequently cited as the third person whose educational ideals had a strong influence on the field of experiential education. All three were concerned with the active involvement of students in real experience and liberation. All three saw education as needing the experience of the students to be a central part of the educational process (Experiential Education, n.d.; Itin, 1999). For all three the ultimate aim of education was about developing and enhancing people's capacities to participate in active citizenship. While Dewey and Freire largely overlap in their theories of experiential learning, they depart on the larger ideological purposes of education, with Freire focusing more on critical reflection on race, class, and power (Deans, 1999). "For Freire, education is about the content to be taught, the process by which it is taught, and the resulting consequences for the person within their social context" (Itin, 1999, p. 93).

This chapter provides an overview of the life and work of Paulo Freire. His educational ideals will be discussed, experiential education will be briefly defined, and that will be followed by a section on the ways in which Freire's liberatory pedagogy intersects with the field of experiential education in theory and in practice.

Biography

The Brazilian educator, Paulo Freire, is among the most influential educational thinkers of the late 20th century. He was born in Recife, a port city of northeastern Brazil on September 19, 1921. Freire attests that his parents taught him at an early age to prize dialogue and to respect the choices of others—both key elements in his understanding of adult education (Collins, 1977). His parents were middle class but suffered financial reverses so severe during the Great Depression that Freire learned what it was to go hungry. It was during his childhood and as a result of that hardship that Freire determined to dedicate his life to the struggle against hunger (Collins, 1977).

After the family finances improved a bit, Freire was able to enter the University of Recife where he enrolled in the Faculty of Law and also studied philosophy and the psychology of language while working part-time as an instructor of Portuguese in a secondary school. During this same period, he was reading the works of Marx and also Catholic intellectuals (Collins, 1977). In 1944, Freire married Elza Maia Costa Oliveira. They had three daughters and two sons. As a parent, Paulo's interest in theories of education began to grow, leading him to do more extensive reading in education, philosophy, and the sociology of education than in law.

His early work experiences in public service as a welfare official and later as director of the Department of Education and Culture of the Social Service in the State of Pernambuco brought him into direct contact with the urban poor (Collins, 1977). The educational and organizational assignments he undertook there led him to begin to formulate a means of communicating with the dispossessed that would later develop into his dialogical method for education. His involvement in education also included directing seminars and teaching courses in the history and philosophy of education at the University of Recife, where he was awarded a doctoral degree in 1959 (Collins, 1977).

In the early 1960s, numerous reform movements flourished simultaneously in Brazil as socialists, communists, students, labor leaders, populists, and Christian militants all sought their own socio-political goals. It was during this time that Freire became the first director of the University of Recife's Cultural Extension Service which brought literacy programs to thousands of peasants in the northeast. Later, from June 1963 up to March 1964, Freire's literacy teams worked throughout the entire nation. They claimed success in interesting adult illiterates to read and write in as short a time as 30 hours (Collins, 1977).

The secret of this success is found in the resistance of Freire and his co-workers to merely teaching the decontextualized skills of reading and writing. Instead, they presented the idea of participation in the political process through knowledge of reading and writing as a desirable and attainable goal for all Brazilians. Freire's liberatory methods were incontestably political and when the Brazilian military suppressed all progressive movements, Freire was thrown into jail for his so-called "subversive" activities (Collins, 1977). In prison he began his first major educational work, *Education as the Practice of Freedom*. This book, an analysis of Paulo's failure to effect change in Brazil, had to be completed in Chile, because Freire was sent into exile in 1964 (Collins, 1977).

Later, Freire worked under the auspices of the World Council of Churches in Geneva. In 1969, he taught at Harvard University and 10 years later returned to his own country under a political amnesty. In 1988 he was also appointed Minister of Education for the City of Sao Paulo—a position which made him responsible for guiding school reform within two-thirds of the nation's schools. Freire died of heart failure in Sao Paulo, Brazil, on May 2, 1997 (Collins, 1977).

Freire and Education

Freire's most well known work is *Pedagogy of the Oppressed* (1970). Throughout this and subsequent books (*Pedagogy of the City*, 1993; *Pedagogy of Hope*, 1994; *Pedagogy of Freedom*, 2001), he argues for a system of education that emphasizes learning as a political act—as a means for all people to be liberated.

Freire was not only one of the key figures in the Latin American liberation movement that attempted to alleviate the oppression of those in poverty, and he was also regarded as the inaugural philosopher of critical pedagogy (McLaren, 2000). His work with the poor in Brazil introduced him to the lives of impoverished peasants. His experiences compelled him to develop educational ideals and practices that would serve to improve the lives of these marginalized people and to lessen their oppression. Freire began to explore an approach to teaching and learning that would in essence dismantle the "banking model" of education, which supported the dominant ideological perspective that students were open repositories to whatever knowledge the teacher deemed important and noteworthy to deposit on any particular day (Freire, 1970). Freire's (1970) definition of the banking model of education closely parallels other forms of "traditional pedagogy" whereby the teacher teaches and the students are taught.

> the teacher is the "knower" and the student is the "open repository" into which the teacher pours knowledge.
> the teacher disciplines and the students are disciplined.
> the teacher (or institution) chooses the curricular content, and the students adapt to it.
> the teacher is the subject of the learning process, while the students are mere objects.
> knowledge is assessed through standardized exams.
> the act of knowing is assessed through a student's ability to recite and memorize the information that is transmitted.

In contrast, Freire's problem-posing model of education valued the importance of student experience and a dialogical method of teaching and learning whereby the student and the teacher were mutually engaged in the production of knowledge and the process of teaching and learning. In this sense, Freire was advocating for a social justice-oriented, experiential education. His own life experiences helped him understand the ways that schooling was often used by dominant interests to validate their own privilege and to maintain the marginalization of others' interests. As Joe Kincheloe (2004) suggests, Freire understood schools to be impediments for the education of the poor, and thus sought to find strategies for students to intervene in what he considered to be a dehumanizing process. Freire (1970) referred to this educative process as liberatory action or praxis. Praxis starts with an abstract idea (theory) or an experience and incorporates reflection upon that idea or experience that then translates into purposeful action. "Praxis in education aims to bridge the gap between theory and transformational action that effectively transforms human existence" (Gur-Ze'ev, 1998, p. 467).

Freire argued that people need to engage in a praxis that incorporates theory, action, and reflection as a means to work toward social change and justice. For Freire, liberatory or problem-posing education was intentionally oriented to issues of social justice as described above. One of the key applications of this form of pedagogy was in adult literacy programs.

He devised a literacy program that was based on the ideal of problem-posing pedagogy as well as the practical needs of his students. Reading materials were directly related to the world of work his students knew firsthand. He encouraged his students to use their newly acquired literacy skills as a means to understanding the conditions of their labor and the interests being served by their work. Freire developed the notion of reading the word and the world as a means to the possibility of "rewriting" a less oppressive world (Freire & Macedo, 1987).

One of the key elements of this educative process was that people develop conscientization (Freire, 1970). Conscientization is an ongoing process by which a learner moves toward critical consciousness. This process is the heart of liberatory education. It differs from "consciousness raising" in that the latter frequently involves "banking" education—the transmission of pre-selected knowledge. Conscientization means breaking through prevailing mythologies to reach new levels of awareness—in particular, awareness of oppression, being an "object" in a world where only "subjects" have power. The process of conscientization involves identifying contradictions in experience through dialogue and becoming a "subject" with other oppressed subjects—that is, becoming part of the process of changing the world (Freire, 1970).

Freire's problem-posing or liberatory pedagogy was thus intentionally directed toward developing a critical consciousness in an individual as a mean to bring about a more socially just world.

Defining Experiential Education

There are numerous published definitions of experiential education (Joplin, 1981; Luckmann, 1996; Itin, 1999). The Association for Experiential Education (AEE; 2004) defines experiential education as both a philosophy and methodology in which educators purposefully engage with learners in direct experience and focused reflection to increase knowledge, develop skills, and clarify values.

Central to the definition of experiential education is the distinction between experiential education as methodology and experiential education as philosophy. This distinction suggests that there is a difference between experiential learning and experiential education.

Knapp (1992) explains that experiential learning consists of four distinct segments: "(a) active student involvement in a meaningful and challenging experience, (b) reflection upon the experience individually and in a group, (c) the development of new knowledge about the world, and (d) application of this knowledge to a new situation" (pp. 36–37).

Kolb (1984) described the experiential learning cycle as a four step process: (a) Concrete Experience, (b) Observation and Reflection, (c) Forming New Knowledge, and (d) Application and Testing Concepts in New Situations. This cycle helps illustrate how experience, reflection, new knowledge, and application can be employed as a way of teaching experientially. Many experiential educational initiatives are based on this learning cycle, but do not prescribe an intended learning outcome or aim. In essence, employing the experiential learning cycle without an intended educational aim represents experiential learning as methodology, implying that there is a certain way of teaching that makes the learning experiential (Breunig, 2005a). Experiential learning thus informs a number of educational methodologies (e.g., adventure education, service learning, cooperative learning, active learning, and place-based learning).

Experiential education as philosophy employs both methodology (experiential way of teaching) and philosophy as part of the educative process. Experiential education as philosophy implies that there is an intended aim toward which the experiential learning process is directed. In essence, recent research on experiential education (Breunig, 2005a; Itin, 1999), the recent focus of many experiential education conferences, and experiential education curriculum suggests that one intended aim of experiential education for the 21st century should be focused on its potential as a vehicle for social change.

Liberatory Pedagogical Praxis and Experiential Education

In light of some of the above information, there is something to be learned from the intersection of the justice-oriented intention of Freire's liberatory pedagogical praxis and its potential implications on the field of experiential education.

Praxis and the Experiential Learning Cycle

There is resonance between Freire's notion of praxis and the experiential learning cycle. As previously mentioned, praxis starts with an abstract idea (theory) or an experience and incorporates reflection upon that idea or experience that then translates into purposeful action (Freire, 1970). Both Freire and Kolb additionally emphasize the importance of starting with the student's experience and previous preparation.

For experiential education practitioners, understanding praxis and the experiential learning cycle can aid in lesson-planning. Designing lessons for an outdoor or an indoor environment can begin with either an experience or with theoretical knowledge. If a student starts with an experience, the experience can be enhanced by reflection and by encouraging the student to form concepts and generalizations (theory). The student can then be encouraged to refine her initial experience, hopefully making that particular experience more educative as a result. If a student were to start with an abstract concept or with theory, then that student is encouraged to apply that theory experientially and to reflect upon both the theoretical knowledge and the experiential knowledge that she has gained in order to learn from that experience.

An experiential educator could choose to apply Freire's notion of praxis and/or the experiential learning cycle when teaching a lesson on paddling a canoe. The educator could hand the student a paddle and put her in a boat on calm water and encourage her to experience what happens when she attempts to steer the boat. The educator would then ask the student to come back onto land and introduce the student to some of the "paddling theory," including the physics of paddling a boat. The student can then apply both the experiential and theoretical knowledge to her paddling praxis. In contrast, the educator could choose to start with the paddling theory before encouraging the student to experience it. In either case, the experiential educator can apply both praxis (experience, action, and reflection) and the experiential learning cycle in her teaching.

Problem-posing Education (Liberatory Pedagogy)

Freire (1970) argues that the central purpose of a reflective and action-oriented praxis must be directed toward transformation and liberation. He believes that one of the greatest obstacles to the achievement of liberation is that oppressive reality acts to submerge human beings' consciousness, arguing for conscientization which will be discussed in more detail later in this section. Freire believes that a problem-posing method of education that values the importance of student experience and a dialogical method of teaching and learning whereby the student and the teacher are mutually engaged in the production of knowledge and the process of teaching and learning can aid in a person's liberation.

Similar to Dewey, Freire's problem-posing or liberatory method of education begins with the experiences of the students. Freire asserts that through dialogue the teacher-of-the-students and the student-of-the-teacher cease to exist. A new term thus emerges: teacher-student with students-teachers. There is resonance with this in Steven Simpson's (2003) book entitled, *The Leader Who is Hardly Known: Self-less Teaching from the Chinese Tradition*. Simpson advocates for experiential educators to reflect upon the dilemma of what it means to be a "leader" or a "facilitator." He argues that, an educator is not just a leader or just a facilitator, but is a leader-facilitator, reminding us that providing some vision while allowing students some freedom should be done with such subtlety that the students feel as though the educator was hardly involved.

Freire (1970) asserts that "By imposing their [the leaders] word on others, they falsify that word and establish a contradiction between their methods and their objectives. If they are truly committed to liberation, their action and reflection cannot proceed without the action and reflection of others" (p. 107). Freire argues that it is insufficient for students to master content without applying it toward the purpose of liberation and transformation.

Both Freire and Simpson are advocating for many of the same ideals that Dewey and the progressivists argued for, including experience, teacher as guide, genuine reflection, and the importance of purpose, to name a few. Freire goes on to assert that manipulation (e.g., bribing students with marks or grades) and prescription (e.g., essentially "spoon feeding" students a narrow view of knowledge and truth) cannot be components of a liberatory praxis.

In light of the above, it is imperative that experiential practitioners identify and act upon their praxis in purposeful ways. For example, if an outdoor leader is facilitating a group of students and that group of students has a theoretical understanding and accepting of Leave No Trace camping principles and practices—dispose of waste properly and leave what you find (Leave No Trace, n.d.), but is not applying that knowledge in praxis, then it is the obligation of that leader to point out the incongruence between the group's espoused values and beliefs and their actions.

Both Freire and Simpson would also caution the budding outdoor leader to try to avoid patronizing and/or manipulative behavior. In reference to the above example, the outdoor leader of the trip may consider posing a series of critical queries to point out the lack of congruence between values and beliefs or may consider facilitating an activity that could serve as a metaphor to instruct students about how to act upon their ideals.

Freire also asserts that if leaders are truly committed to liberation, their praxis cannot proceed without the praxis of others (Freire, 1970). The experiential practitioner may have a greater knowledge base and more experience than the students, but that should not be the only experience that is valued. Liberation begins with dialogue and authentic dialogue happens when the experiential practitioners ask themselves what they will dialogue with the participants about, avoiding prescription of that dialogue and ensuring that dialogue begins with the experience of the participants. On an outdoor trip, this may be as simple as avoiding assumptions about participants' previous preparation and asking them what they already know and to demonstrate that, and then facilitating an experience that builds upon that.

Conscientization

According to Freire (1970), the earlier that dialogue begins, the more truly revolutionary an experience will be: "Revolutionary leaders cannot think without the people, nor for the people, but only with the people" (p. 112). The purpose of a dialogical-liberation is to transform an unjust reality. Developing a critical consciousness, or what Freire refers to as conscientization, is an essential component of authentic dialogue. Consider, for example, the story in the opening paragraph of this chapter. The worker in the story reported that his critical consciousness about worker injustices was being awakened as a result of the course that he took with Freire. This is what Freire refers to as conscientization.

Likewise, experiential education theory often focuses on the ways in which outdoor and experiential education can serve to develop people's critical thinking skills (Breunig, 2005b; Brookfield, 1995; Itin, 1999). Taken together, both Freire and experiential education theorists assert that developing a critical consciousness will provide individuals with the opportunity to take action against the oppressive elements of reality and to, in essence, engage in justice-oriented work.

In practice, an experiential educator may wish to probe participants to question the ways in which outdoor pursuits can attend to issues of environmental and social justice. For example, if a young male participant is displaying a great deal of confidence, and perhaps even entitlement, with some of the decision-making processes, a facilitator may wish to subtlety attempt to find ways to encourage his voice to be less dominant and to encourage other voices to be heard. Assigning each individual to serve as the "leader of the day" is one means to deliberately attempt to share some of the authority. Having an individual "leader of the day" will also encourage each individual voice, each individual epistemology, and various leadership styles to come to the fore. Those individuals who may feel oppressed or may come from a background where they have been marginalized in the past will then be provided with an opportunity to have their voices heard. Setting ground rules that directly introduce students to a democratic process at the outset of a wilderness trip is another means to frontload the group with information about how to negotiate power and authority while on the trip.

This liberatory effort of providing for equity can be discussed with the group. A facilitator could use an evening debriefing session to encourage people to critically reflect upon their experiences with being the "leader of the day." The facilitator could use a series of critical queries to discuss the ways in which oppression and marginalization silence certain voices and even prevent people from being asked to serve in a leadership role. The experiential educator could then encourage participants to discuss the ways in which leadership can be used to either oppress or to liberate, encouraging each participant to identify a way in which he or she will directly apply some newfound learning about this to his or her work or home life.

In this way, a facilitator can model liberatory praxis and can encourage participants' conscientization about their own praxis. Ideally, the result would be that participants would continue to develop their critical consciousness and to engage in liberatory actions and praxis.

Implications for EE Philosophy

There is a great deal of resonance between the work of Paulo Freire and some of the forefathers of experiential education, including John Dewey and Kurt Hahn as well as between some of the present day goals of experiential education theory and the theory of Paulo Freire.

Some of the key concepts that can be directly applied in practice include praxis and the experiential learning cycle, the problem-posing method of education, and conscientization. If, indeed, both liberatory pedagogy and experiential education assert that the aim of their educative practices is to bring about a more socially just world, then there is value in developing an understanding of both of these theories and in engaging in a reflective praxis that acts upon the theoretical underpinnings of these pedagogies.

References

Association for Experiential Education (AEE). (2004). *What is experiential education?* Retrieved February 23, 2004, from http://www.aee.org

Breunig, M. (2005a). Turning experiential education and critical pedagogy theory into praxis. *Journal of Experiential Education, 28*(2), 106–122.

Breunig, M. (2005b, November). *Developing peoples' critical thinking skills through experiential education theory and practice.* Paper presented at the Association for Experiential Education 32nd Annual Conference Proceedings, Tucson, Arizona.

Brookfield, S. (1995). Through the lens of learning: How the visceral experience of learning reframes teaching. In D. Boud, R. Cohen, & D. Walker (Eds.), *Using experience for learning* (pp. 21–32). Berkshire, UK: Open University.

Collins, D. (1977). *Paulo Freire: His life, works & thought.* Mahwah, NJ: Paulist.

Deans, T. (1999). Service-learning in two keys: Paulo Freire's critical pedagogy in relation to John Dewey's pragmatism. *Michigan Journal of Community Service Learning, 6,* 15–29.

Experiential Education. (n.d.). Retrieved May 1, 2007, from http://en.Wikipedia.org/wiki/Experiential Learning

Freire, P. (1970). *Pedagogy of the oppressed.* New York: Continuum.

Freire, P. (1993). *Pedagogy of the city.* New York: Continuum.

Freire, P. (1994). *Pedagogy of hope.* New York: Continuum.

Freire, P. (2001). *Pedagogy of freedom: Ethics, democracy, and civic courage.* New York: Rowman & Littlefield.

Freire, P., & Macedo, D. (1987). *Literacy: Reading the word and the world.* London: Routledge.

Gur-Ze'ev, I. (1998). Toward a nonrepressive critical pedagogy. *Educational Theory, 48*(4), 463–486.

Itin, C. M. (1999). Reasserting the philosophy of experiential education as a vehicle for change in the 21st century. *The Journal of Experiential Education, 22*(2), 91–98.

Joplin, L. (1981). On defining experiential education. *The Journal of Experiential Education, 4*(1), 17–21.

Kincheloe, J. L. (2004). *Critical pedagogy.* New York: Peter Lang.

Kolb, D. A. (1984). *Experiential learning: Experience as the source of learning and development.* Saddle River, NJ: Prentice Hall.

Knapp, C. (1992). *Lasting lessons: A teacher's guide to reflecting on experience.* Charleston, WV: ERIC Clearinghouse on Rural Education and Small Schools.

Leave No Trace (n.d.). Retrieved May 1, 2007, from http.//www.nols.edu/leavenotrace

Luckmann, C. (1996). Defining experiential education. *The Journal of Experiential Education, 19*(1), 6–8.

McLaren, P. (2000). Paulo Freire's pedagogy of possibility. In S. Steiner, M. Krank, R. Bahruth, & P. McLaren (Eds.), *Freirean pedagogy, praxis and possibilities: Projects for the new millennium* (pp. 1–21). New York: Falmer.

Simpson, S. (2003). *The leader who is hardly known: Self-less teaching from the Chinese tradition.* Oklahoma City, OK: Wood 'N' Barnes.

8 Maxine Green
The Power of the Possible

Laurie S. Frank

Maxine Greene has been cited in the *New York Times* as "one of the leading educational philosophers of the past fifty years" (Kohl, 2007, p. xi). This chapter focuses on three of Maxine Greene's major themes:

1. Freedom and the individual's responsibility to become situated in the quest for freedom. This involves a focus on mystification as a barrier to freedom, Greene's belief that freedom can only be attained in the social context of community, and her emphasis on social justice as it pertains to freedom.
2. Imagination and the arts, and how they can provide experiential opportunities to see the world from multiple perspectives and help individuals "wake up" to alternative choices for action.
3. Education, experience and consciousness and the responsibility of the teacher and the role of education in helping students question what is going on around them and to start their own journey toward freedom.

The chapter then touches on Greene's thinking as it relates to experiential education.

Biography

Born in the early part of the 20th century, Maxine Greene has always been a thinker and a writer. Although she describes her original family as one that "discouraged intellectual adventure and risk" (1998, p. 9), from the age of 7 she wrote stories on anything that would accept pencil lead or ink. In her late teens, she became politically involved after meeting people in Europe who were heading to Spain to fight against fascism, and this had a profound impact on her thinking. She returned to the United States to finish her undergraduate degree in 1938.

After receiving her doctorate in education from New York University in 1955, she spent most of her career on the faculty at Teachers College, Columbia University, "establishing herself as a lone female voice among her male philosophy of education colleagues who found her 'too literary'" (The Maxine Greene Foundation for Social Imagination, the Arts & Education, n.d.). She remembers that the "biggest compliment I received in the old days was that I was 'a woman who thought like a man'" (Greene, 1998, p. 257). These experiences with sexism helped to clarify her thinking about social justice, freedom, and the viewing of multiple perspectives through the arts.

Greene, in her distinguished career, has authored seven books, dozens of articles, and she has received numerous academic awards and honorary degrees. She is past president of the American Educational Research Association, Philosophy of Education Society, and the American Educational Studies Association.

Currently, Greene is the William F. Russell Professor (emerita) in the Foundations of Education Department at Teachers College. In 2004 the College created the Maxine Greene Chair for

Distinguished Contributions to Education. She continues to speak throughout the United States and Europe, and has hosted periodic salons at her home, which are open to anyone who is interested, to discuss contemporary literature. Greene also continues to conduct workshops as the Philosopher-in-Residence of the Lincoln Center Institute for the Arts in Education.

Maxine Greene continues to inspire people interested in awakening the minds and spirits of their students, as well as those who are interested in teaching and acting in the realm of social justice. When she founded the Maxine Greene Foundation for Social Imagination, the Arts, and Education in 2003, Greene explained her vision for the foundation:

> To generate inquiry, imagination, and the creation of art works by diverse people. It has to do so with a sense of the deficiencies in our world and a desire to repair, wherever possible. Justice, equality, freedom—these are as important to us as the arts, and we believe they can infuse each other, perhaps making some difference at a troubled time. (The Maxine Greene Foundation for Social Imagination, the Arts & Education, 2007, p. 2)

Freedom and Responsibility

> This is one way of conceiving of what freedom signifies—the freedom to alter situations by reinterpreting them and, by so doing, seeing oneself as a person in a new perspective. Once that happens, there are new beginnings, new actions to undertake in the world. (Greene, 1988, p. 90)

Maxine Greene's life work encompasses what might be, and what is not yet. It is about the power of the possible, which is rooted in the idea of freedom. Human beings are capable of reflection and can view the world critically if they are able to become "wide-awake" and view the world from a variety of perspectives. A person's perspective is based on her or his life history and experiences, and, because it is seen from one angle (the self), it is always incomplete. People become situated by differentiating between the self, the world, and other people. Greene was influenced by existential philosophers, including Jean-Paul Sartre, Hannah Arendt, and Maurice Merleau-Ponty. In essence, existentialism espouses that each individual human being has the responsibility for creating meaning in her or his life. In Greene's existential view, the world does not swirl around us, but the "knower as person" exists in a concrete situation, seeing the world from that vantage point (1973, p. 137). Once a person can do this, he or she is empowered, is autonomous, and can make real choices. Greene explains:

> From the perspective of the system or the cosmos, things seem to happen automatically, irresistibly. From a human perspective nothing is fully predictable or determined. All kinds of things are possible, although none can be guaranteed. When risks are taken, when people do indeed act in their freedom, a kind of miracle has taken place. Arendt reminds us that we ourselves are the authors of such miracles, because it is we who perform them—and we who have the capacity to establish a reality of our own. (1988, pp. 55–56)

On Becoming "Wide Awake"

To illustrate how Greene applies her philosophy in the area of experiential educational learning, an example of urban youth activities will be examined. There are people in the United States who are thrown away—who live in places where poverty is high, where violence is a daily occurrence, and where young people deal drugs, steal cars, and drop out of school. The Earth Conservation Corps (ECC) went into such a place in the shadow of the nation's capital—a neighborhood called Anacostia.

As he stood in front of a dump, Bob Nixon, founder of ECC, describes Anacostia in this way: "They didn't just dump trash here, they dumped people here. There are, you know, 90 percent of the public housing communities in Washington are, you know, within a mile and a half of this dump right here" (O'Neill, 2007). The neighborhood is littered with garbage and the Anacostia River is one of the most polluted rivers in the United States, full of raw sewage and other debris. The ECC hires young people to clean up the community. In the process, many of them have a transcendent experience. Most start out taking the pollution and debris for granted, not caring. Then something happens. Their perspectives change. As they learn about nature and how to detect pollution, and work together to clean up their neighborhood, they start to see their surroundings in a different light. On one trip down the river, Darius Phillps, an ECC member, sees the natural habitat that used to be hidden from him:

> Basically like five, ten minutes away, I live from here. This is my heritage. And to be a part of something so beautiful, it's overwhelming when you look at it around here, and you can say that I'm a part of something so beautiful. (O'Neill, 2007)

According to Nixon, some of these young people turn into activists, "untangling all sorts of environmental injustices" such as reporting the dumping of illegal sewage into the river. (O'Neill, 2007). Some become guides, helping children learn about nature and their neighborhood. Daniel Zwerdling, National Public Radio (NPR) reporter who interviewed ECC members, states that when "Corps members talk about their work and how it'll affect their future, they sound as if there's no limit to what they can do" (O'Neill, 2007). Some go on to college, and some see ECC as a stepping-stone for jobs with the Environmental Protection Agency or the Park Service (O'Neill, 2007).

These young citizens also grieve for their colleagues and friends in ECC who are lost to gun violence and illness. On average, one ECC member dies every year. When Corps members are shot or die of undiagnosed diseases, instead of resorting to revenge or despair, these young people find a way to make something good come of it. They recommit themselves to doing good work for their community (Phillips, in O'Neill, 2007), and, in one instance, they procured a piece of land in their neighborhood to turn into a park. It will be called the "Diamond Teague Memorial Park," named after a leader in the Corps who was shot to death on his front porch.

How are these young people able to transcend the oppression and ugliness of their realities? How are they able to move beyond what could be taken-for-granted as an objective reality, and act, together, in a created reality? Maxine Greene would say that they have become "wide-awake" to their subjective realities, and are making intentional choices to act. Greene says that it "seems eminently clear that the freedom of wide-awakeness has to be expressed in intentional action of some kind. The one who drifts, who believes that nothing matters outside of his or her own self-preservation, can hardly be considered to be free" (1978, p. 153). Maxine Greene would say the young people in the Earth Conservation Corps were realizing their freedom.

Confronting Mystification

> The new cultists of efficiency, the would-be scientific managers, create their own mystifications by attempting to describe education as a technocratic operation, dependable because linked to what is most controllable and "real." This is one way of the many indications of the importance of working against what Dewey called a "social pathology" and to do so with as much passion as can be mustered. (Greene, 1978, p. 63)

In the United States today, we are bombarded with messages about "what is" and what "ought to be." Much of what is portrayed in the media and by our politicians is a "mystification" or "surface reality" (Greene, 1978, p. 54) that many people take for granted as objectively true. Greene states that "it is not simply that the public is lied to and deliberately deluded, it is that the explanations provided mystify and falsify by imparting an objective and a 'natural character' to the issues of the day" (1978, p. 63).

When people accept these messages at face value, it can cause indifference, apathy, disempowerment. The result is an affront to freedom. Arendt described "dark times" punctuated by "highly efficient talk and double-talk" and marked "by a camouflage spread by the establishment or system" (Arendt, in Greene, 1988, p. 113). Greene cautions, "Whether it is mystification by the media, a cynicism due to the wars and corruptions of the recent past, a wishful thinking, an unquenchable desire for comfort and for certainty, Americans generally do not perceive the 'darkness' Arendt described" (Greene, 1988, p. 114).

To transcend the effects of mystification, it is necessary to wake up to the world and start seeing it from a variety of vantage points. This can be accomplished if we pay attention to "our nagging sense that things ought not to be this way" (Greene, 1973, p. 49) … or we can be jolted into awareness through works of art that help us see a situation from a new perspective. It can also occur when we come together with others to authentically ask questions and choose to act. Humans have the unique "capacity to surpass the given and look at things as if they could be otherwise." (Greene, 1988, p. 3)

The Social Dimension of Freedom

This is what we shall look for as we move: freedom developed by human beings who have acted to make a space for themselves in the presence of others, human beings become "challengers" ready for alternatives, alternatives that include caring and community. And we shall seek as we go, implications for emancipatory education conducted by and for those willing to take responsibility for themselves and for each other. We want to discover how to open spaces for persons in their plurality, spaces where they can become different, where they can grow. (Greene, 1988, p. 56)

When speaking of freedom, the existential philosopher, Jean-Paul Sartre focused on the individual. When he speaks of an individual using his or her freedom of action, Sartre "means that one wills a world that bends to his or her desires" (Rasheed, 2002, p. 394). Maxine Greene develops Sartre's idea by bringing the concept of freedom into the domain of the community, where each person's subjective reality is brought to bear in the inter-subjective realm. The influence of John Dewey and others from the Progressive era is apparent when Greene says: "Freedom of mind and freedom of action were functions of membership and participation in some valued community. It is important to hold in mind that the *person*—that center of choice— develops in his/her fullness to a degree he/she is a member of a live community" (1988, p. 43).

This social dimension of freedom sheds light on the concept of "negative freedom," which is "the right not to be interfered with or coerced or compelled to do what they did not choose to do" (Greene, 1988, p.16). To Greene, this is not true freedom. Freedom involves *praxis*—acting together to influence reality, "a transformation of that situation to the end of overcoming oppressiveness and domination. There must be collective self-reflection; there must be an interpretation of present and emergent needs; there must be a type of realization" (Greene, 1978, p. 100). According to Greene, this can only be accomplished in concert, in community, with others.

To Maxine Greene, then, the pursuit of freedom is a social undertaking as well as a dialectic, or "the coming together, not the merging, of the self and the other" (Taliaferro, 1998, p. 91). Greene talks about the "subject/object relationship and the realization that freedom can be achieved only in an ongoing transaction, one that is visible and legible to those involved" (1988,

p. 83). As people begin to "wake up" and identify the objective obstacles to freedom, they can come together in inter-subjective space, and proceed "out in search of meaning and transcendence, moving out to change their world" (Greene, 1978, p. 209).

Freedom and Social Justice

Freedom, according to Greene, is a quest, an existential project which means it is a lifetime of confronting walls (Taliaferro, 1998). The young people in the ECC came together to name their obstacles, their walls, and rose in action together. There are a plethora of examples like this throughout U.S. history where people came together to address issues of social justice. The actions of these small groups even ballooned into wholesale movements, such as the Abolitionist movement, Civil Rights movement, the Suffrage movement, the many fronts in the movement for rights for those who are gay, lesbian, bisexual, and transgendered. Even today, people in the United States are witnessing the emergence of movements to address such issues as global warming, health care, immigration, and, of course, unveiling the mysticism that is brought on when officials talk about the "war on terror."

Imagination and the Arts

Denise Taliaferro (1998), in a chapter on the work of Maxine Greene involving "double consciousness," describes the dialectic process.

> The Self is the combination of identities we choose to claim, and the Other is the combination we choose not to claim. Because the Self and Other are in dialectical relation, we are all, at one and the same time, both. Yet, we are all not both in the same way. People who are oppressed from positionalities of race, gender, class, sexual orientation, age, disability, or some other nexus see their Self through the eyes of the Other. In contrast, those who are in a position of privilege where certain identities are concerned, see their Other through the eyes of the Self. (p. 91)

Taliaferro goes on to note that "from an oppressed positionality the double-consciousness emerges," where people can see the self from the perspective of the other (p. 92). When in a position of privilege one does not naturally have "double-consciousness." Maxine Greene, however, demonstrates how freedom can be "perceived through reconciliation between the Self and the Other" by "repositioning the self in relationship to others" (p. 93). This is done through the imagination.

Imagination is a means to help us construct a coherent world. Greene states that "imagination is what, above all, makes empathy possible" (1995, p. 3). When we are able to cross those spaces and experience empathy with others, "we can look in some manner through strangers' eyes and hear through their ears" (1995, p. 3). Without this ability we would be fixed in our own realities. Using imagination allows us to make a connection not only with others, but to see how the other realities impact our own, and "how the very act of imagining shapes our own realities" (Taliaferro, 1998, p. 94). Greene stresses the importance of imagination: "Of all our cognitive capacities, imagination is the one that permits us to give credence to alternative realities. It allows us to break with the taken for granted, to set aside familiar distinctions and definitions" (1995, p. 3).

In this way, Maxine Greene shows how she can be situated as White and a woman and use her imagination to become attuned to alternative realities, realities she could not experience directly. She is able to model how people can come together in a pluralistic community to open spaces, break with what is taken-for-granted, and create something new.

As we attempt to make sense ... we might well look through some of the perspectives provided by literature and other arts. This is partly because an engagement with an imaginative form can lead, as no other engagement can, to a recapturing of our authentic perspectives on the world. (Greene, 1978, p. 119)

For Greene, the imagination interacting with works of art is another way to access multiple perspectives, and even give us a reason to "wake up." Interacting with a work of art by "bracketing out" (1978, p. 2) the everyday world and tapping into the "realm of possibility" can ... offer alternative ways of structuring experience, as dreams and other kinds of imaging do. Engaging with them, the individual gains no factual information ... he (sic) may well see facets of his own experience afresh; he may even re-evaluate some of his knowledge to self consciousness 1973, p. 16).

In other words, the interaction with the work of art in this way is an experience, an experience from which learning can take place, and an avenue from which people can expand the scope of their lived realities.

Greene's focus on the arts, especially literature, offers a way for people to achieve "wide-awakeness." If people can seek out these perspectives "consciously and critically, and for meanings to be perceived from the vantage points of persons awake to their freedom," then "perceptive encounters with works of art can bring human beings in touch with themselves" (Greene, 1977, pp. 123–124). In this way, the work of art can act as a mirror to the self and as a window to the other. When people are equipped with their imaginations and are open to new ways of seeing, he or she can travel to new places, enter new aesthetic spaces, and "locate himself or herself in an intersubjective reality reaching backwards and forward in time" (p. 123). Greene encourages every educator to pack her or his bags for the trip toward freedom because it is the wide-awake teacher who can spark students on their own freedom-trail.

Role of Education

It is through and by means of education, many of us believe, that individuals can be provoked to reach beyond themselves in their intersubjective space. It is through and by means of education that they may become empowered to think about what they are doing, to become mindful, to share meanings, to conceptualize, to make varied sense of their lived worlds (Greene, 1988, p. 12).

In 1988, in *The Dialectic of Freedom*, Greene painted a picture of schools in trouble. Since then schools are showing signs of losing even more ground. George Wood, principal of Federal Hocking High School and director of The Forum for Education and Democracy sums it up this way:

For nearly twenty years we have ventured down this radical path of school reform that has led to more students being pushed out of school, more retentions of students, more dropouts, a narrowing of the curricula, and dissatisfaction on the part of teachers, students, and parents. NCLB [No Child Left Behind], which institutionalizes these narrow and inaccurate measures of school performance in unprecedented ways, only makes it worse. (n.d., p. 34)

Teachers, like anyone else, are subject to mystification and objectification. If left unquestioned, the era of No Child Left Behind, testing, and standardized instruction can turn teachers into technicians, leading to the dehumanization of education. If educators are not careful, they will buy into a "paradigm having to do with a monolithic system and individuals who are totally controlled" (Greene, 1973, p. 45), and in which the person is subordinated to the system.

"People who feel anonymous and unimportant are unable to assume responsibility for effecting change," and young people who feel this way are what we call "unmotivated." They "appear to their teachers to be apathetic, disinterested, dull" (pp. 46–47). According to Greene, teachers have profound influence on students, which can be either empowering or dis-empowering.

The teacher who can help young people attune to their own consciousness is one who can take on the persona of "stranger"—someone who, like the person returning from a long trip, sees their world with new eyes, the eyes of a stranger. This person notices hitherto unseen details, and views the world with wonder and curiosity. This teacher reflects on her or his philosophy of education, which "begins in wonder, philosophy always begins in wonder. The individual must be moved to ask questions about the universe, to engage in dialogue with himself (sic) about the world as it impinges on him and about the explanations others provide" (1973, p. 21). This teacher, who is thus "wide-awake," is the only person prepared to reach students to begin the process of questioning and gaining their freedom. As Greene points out, this is not an easy task:

> To create the kinds of social conditions that provoke and sustain autonomy demands the most critical consciousness of the forces that seduce people into acquiescence and mind-lessness. It requires a profound self-understanding on the part of the teacher, who has to live in a kind of tension simply to function as a free agent, to make choices appropriate to the often unpredictable situations that arise. (1978, p. 248)

Greene uses Camus' novel, *The Plague*, as a metaphor for working in the schools, where the "plague" represents "evasion and indifference" (1973, p. 281). In that book people had a choice to succumb to the plague or fight it—one was either a victim of it or a volunteer in fighting it. In our schools, indifference and evasion are endemic. The wide-awake teacher has a choice to make—do you throw up your hands in surrender or do you take a stand? Even if the "plague" subsides, it will never fully go away, so vigilance is required to address it when it returns. The wide-awake teacher is free to make a choice to make a difference.

Greene's Thinking and Experiential Education

> To find ourselves 'in the delight of experiencing' requires a transaction with the world, an ongoing transaction with 'qualities and forms.' This kind of transaction may be thought of in terms of acts of consciousness, meaning a series of moments in which we grasp what is given, in which we thrust into the world. (Greene, 1978, p. 200)

Many people mistake activity—the doing of things—with experiential education. Maxine Greene reminds us that experiential education is really an internal process by which people can "wake up" and construct a coherent world for one's quest for freedom and transformation by integrating a variety of perspectives and vantage points. This process can be accomplished through the coming together in community, through dialogue and the asking of questions, through interfacing with art and literature. It is when people can truly get outside their own reality, using a uniquely human capacity for imagination that transformation can take place. In this way, a person starts with her or his own experience, and then, in the process of "waking-up," chooses to venture outside her or his own place and vantage point while constructing a more holistic image of one's reality. The doing of things may provide a needed spark, but it is not an end in itself. At its base, experiential education is a constructivist process that takes place from the inside out, helping each individual make sense of their world.

One of Maxine Greene's principal themes has to do with consciousness, and the viewing of the world through multiple realities. It is about reflection and the process of discovering the "meaning of our experience ... which constitutes reality" (1978, p. 173). Consciousness, in this sense, is not a passive act, but one that requires "imagining, intuiting, remembering, believing, judging, conceiving, and (focally) perceiving" (1978, p. 14). It is through these acts of consciousness that human beings can connect with the world. It is an experiential process.

As a proponent of Dewey, Greene summarizes one of his ideas:

> The individual exists within a continuum of experience, a vital matrix in which all things are interrelated—the individual and society; mind and matter; thought and the phenomena of the world. 'Experience' is of as well as in nature. It is not experience which is experienced, but nature. Things interacting in certain ways are experience. (1973, p. 127)

Experiential education, in all its manifested forms, uses reflection to make meaning from the lived world. This, in turn, allows people to take conscious action. Whether one is engaged in inquiry, encountering a new reality in the out-of-doors, exploring the meaning of a literary masterpiece, or exercising one's right to free expression, the experiential process invites people to find their place, or situation, in the world. Maxine Greene asserts, "the point is that learning must be a process of discovery and recovery in response to worthwhile questions rising out of conscious life in concrete situations. And the learning must in some way be emancipatory" (1978, p. 19).

Like the young people in the Earth Conservation Corps who came together and chose to act in concert to change their world, everyone has the capacity to wake up, reach out, and be free. It is about the power of the possible.

Implications for EE Philosophy

As a person who considers herself an experiential educator, I am challenged by Maxine Greene's call to action. Being "wide awake" in a system that may fail to recognize the value and process of experiential education is, at best, difficult. Once the experiential process of "waking up" has begun, though, there is no going back. Through my own experiences, my willingness to see the world from a variety of perspectives, and my ability to develop empathy through the use of my imagination, my world changed forever. Along with the excitement of seeing the world anew, heartache and sadness became part of my being because it became impossible to ignore injustice.

I have had the privilege of visiting over 100 schools about North America. It is clear to me that the educational system is struggling, and yet there is amazing education occurring in every school. Some individual educators have embraced experiential education and the *process* of learning, but many have become (by choice or circumstance) isolated in their schools. Once "awake" the next truly courageous act is to find allies in the pursuit of freedom, enabling action to take place. Maxine Greene tells us that we are not alone—cannot be alone. It is only in the presence of others that we can create genuine change.

Maxine Greene's ideas give us all an impetus to get started. Once you begin reading about the power of the possible, there is no going back.

References

Camus, A. (2002). *The Plague*. New York: Penguin Modern Classics.

Greene, M. (1973). *Teacher as stranger: Educational philosophy for the modern age*. Belmont, CA: Wadsworth.

Greene, M. (1977). Toward wide-awakeness: An argument for the arts and humanities in education. *The Humanities and the Curriculum*, 79, 119–125.

Greene, M. (1978). *Landscapes of learning.* New York, NY: Teachers College.

Greene, M. (1988). *The dialectic of freedom.* New York, NY: Teachers College.

Greene, M. (1998). An autobiographical remembrance. In W. F. Pinar (Ed.), *The passionate mind of Maxine Greene: I am not yet* (pp. 256–257). Bristol, PA: Falmer Press, Taylor & Francis.

Kohl, H. (2007). Foreword. In M. Greene *The public school and the private vision: A search for America in education and literature* (pp. xi–xiv). New York, NY: The New Press.

O'Neill, J. D. (Executive Producer). (2007, July 6). *Bill Moyers Journal* [Television broadcast]. New York: Public Affairs Television, Inc.

Rasheed, S. (2002) The existential concept of freedom for Maxine Greene: The influence of Sartre and Merleau-Ponty on Greene's educational pedagogy [Electronic version]. *Philosophy of Education,* 394–401.

Taliaferro, D. M. (1998). Signifying Self: Re-presentations of the double consciousness in the world of Maxine Greene. In W. F. Pinar (Ed.), *The passionate mind of Maxine Greene: I am not yet* (pp. 89–98). Bristol, PA: Falmer Press, Taylor & Francis.

The Maxine Greene Foundation for Social Imagination, the Arts & Education. (n.d.). Retrieved July 9, 2007, from: http://www.maxinegreene.org/aboutmaxinegreene.html

Wood, G. (n.d.). The Forum for Education and Democracy, http://www.forumforeducation.http

9   Eleanor Duckworth
The Teacher's Teacher

Andrew J. Bobilya and Brad Daniel

> In my entire life as a student, I remember only twice being given the opportunity to come up with my own ideas, a fact I consider typical and terrible. (Duckworth, 2006, p. 125)

Eleanor Duckworth is an educational theorist and professor of education at the Harvard Graduate School of Education. Her interests center on teaching, learning, and the educational experiences of students and teachers. She has worked in the United States and abroad in the areas of teacher training, curriculum development, and program assessment. She has authored numerous articles and books on teaching and learning including, *The Having of Wonderful Ideas and Other Essays on Teaching and Learning* (2006), *Tell Me More: Listening to Learners Explain* (2001), and *Teacher to Teacher: Learning from Each Other* (1997). This chapter is based on a review of Duckworth's written works, an interview she graciously granted to the authors on September 5, 2007, and subsequent correspondence with Dr. Duckworth.

Biography

Born in Montreal in 1935 and raised in Nova Scotia, Duckworth's journey into the field of education began after she left graduate school, where she was studying psychology. She had already spent three years studying in Geneva with Jean Piaget and Barbel Inhelder. Piaget was a philosopher and developmental psychologist known for his studies of cognitive development and learning in young children (Piaget, 1953, 1955). Inhelder was a psychologist and Piaget's student. She was research director of his lab, and co-author of many of his books. Duckworth had originally decided to do graduate work in psychology because, "I thought the world needed social scientists to keep scientific and technical developments under human guidance." However, having already studied with Piaget and Inhelder, she found the doctoral program she was later engaged in of little interest, and left it (Duckworth, personal communication, October, 14, 2007). Duckworth was offered a position in elementary school science curriculum development, largely because of having studied with Piaget whose work and reputation were becoming well known. She continues to use Piaget's ideas to develop teaching and research methods that relate directly to how children learn. She bases her work on Piaget's theory of the nature of intelligence and on Piaget and Inhelder's clinical interviewing methods. Inhelder called this research approach "critical exploration," a term which Duckworth continues to use to refer to her own work. Her work in curriculum development, teacher training methodology, and projects of educational research and program development was marked by Piaget's theory of learning, which provided a framework that allows children to create their own ideas and knowledge. As her experience and expertise developed through the years, she has advised educational programs throughout the world.

In her Geneva training, Duckworth had learned how to give children interesting things to think about, and to listen to what they had to say. This approach to research revealed much about their thoughts and ideas. In the course of her work with the Elementary Science Study, *ed* that, as she paid attention to children's ideas, the children also became interested in *their* ideas, and in whatever subject matter gave rise to them. She saw that teachers could *make* use of that same questioning and listening approach to engage and further the learn*ing of their* students and to some degree develop curriculum for them. Through her efforts in various educational pursuits, Duckworth discovered that by listening carefully to students she could determine what they do and do not understand. She urged teachers to follow the learning process of students. She resumed her doctoral work at the University of Geneva in 1977, and received her doctorate in educational sciences. For a number of years, she served as an interpreter for Piaget's lectures in North America. Professor Duckworth continues to teach courses at Harvard including "Teaching and Learning: The Having of Wonderful Ideas," "Curriculum Based on Understanding," and "The Work of Jean Piaget" (Duckworth, personal communication, October 14, 2007). She also remains active in the field of teacher education and conducts workshops around the world. For example, she led an interactive workshop at Peking University in the summer of 2007 titled, "Holding Magical Thoughts" (EN News, 2007). She continues to challenge the ways in which teachers think about learning—both their own and that of their students. Duckworth expresses her love for teaching teachers:

> I love to teach teachers. I love to stir up their thoughts about how they learn; about how on earth anyone can help anyone else learn; about what it means to know something. There are two main reasons that I love to teach teachers in particular. One is that teachers are as interested as I am in how people learn, so the dialogue is deeply felt. The second is that I always learn from them in return, when I see the endless variations on how they use what they learn in their own teaching. (Duckworth, 2006, p. 173)

Teaching teachers has been, and continues to be her motivation for a lifelong career in education. She is currently a board member for The Center for Collaborative Education and is involved with the Cambridge United for Justice with Peace organization. She also serves as a contributing editor for the *Journal of Mathematical Behavior* and is on the editorial board for the *McGill Journal of Education*.

The Educational Process

For Duckworth, the process of learning—in which a student struggles to understand something—is a part of the knowing itself. In working with students, she "focuses not on telling information or facts, but on helping people learn in a way that what they have learned belongs to them and will be accessible to them in a situation where it would be appropriate (Duckworth, personal communication, October 14, 2007).

> The essential element of having the students do the explaining is not the withholding of all the teacher's own thoughts. It is, rather, that the teacher not consider herself or himself the final arbiter of what the learner should think, not the creator of what the learner does think. The important job for the teacher is to keep trying to find out what sense the students are making. (Duckworth, 1997, p. 133)

Eleanor Duckworth's philosophy about how students learn best translates to learning at all ages. Her work has been instrumental in challenging the role of the teacher as one who imparts knowledge. The having of wonderful ideas is what Duckworth considers to be the essence of intellectual development (Duckworth, 2006). These wonderful ideas can only be constructed in an educational environment that does not propose what children ought to learn on a given day. Rather, the student and teacher are co-learners working alongside each other in the educational process. This pedagogy calls on the teacher to find activities and lessons that engage children and will take their thoughts further. Congruent with constructivism, Duckworth believes

> Much education is learning other people's ideas which doesn't help you develop much confidence in your own ideas ... Students get their own ideas as they truly make sense of whatever you are offering them. [This] helps them expand their connections to the world. It expands their minds and expands their sense of what is possible for them. It expands respect for other learners. It expands their coming to ideas that are useful to them." (Duckworth, personal communication, September 5, 2007)

It is not possible for a teacher to determine what a student will learn. What teachers can do is create situations most likely to help a student learn. "Teaching is helping people learn, and you have not taught if people have not learned. Teaching is not telling" (Duckworth, personal communication, September 5, 2007). She urges teachers to provide "a setting that suggests wonderful ideas to children—different ideas for different children—as they are caught up in the intellectual problems ..." (Duckworth, 2006, p. 7). She states that there are two aspects of providing occasions for wonderful ideas:

> First, the right question at the right time can move children to peaks in their thinking that result in significant steps forward and real intellectual excitement; and, second, although it is almost impossible for an adult to know exactly the right time to ask a specific question of a specific child—especially for a teacher who is concerned with 30 or more children— children can raise the right question for themselves if the setting is right. (Duckworth, 2006, p. 5)

The fostering of an environment where students and teachers believe that it is alright to question other's thoughts contributes greatly to increased learning regardless of the subject matter or the age of the student. David Hawkins, a mentor of Duckworth's, said of curriculum development, "You do not want to cover a subject; you want to uncover it" (Hawkins, 2000, as cited in Duckworth, 2006, p. 7). To cover a subject implies a simplification that obscures more than reveals, but to uncover a subject suggests a realization that unexpected knowledge may emerge.

The Role of the Teacher in the Learning Process

Duckworth believes that teachers are facilitators of learning rather than just imparters of knowledge. "The teacher's responsibility is to set things up so that learners have a chance to learn" (Duckworth, personal communication, September, 5, 2007). She recognizes that all *teachers* are not *school teachers*, and writes, "By *teacher* I mean someone who engages learners, who seeks to involve each person wholly—mind, sense of self, sense of humor, range of interests, interactions with other people—in learning" (Duckworth, 2006, p. 186). The teacher's goal should be to construct an educational environment that gives rise to wonderful ideas in the students, and such a setting does not propose what children ought to know a priori. She acknowledges that the process of helping children to have wonderful ideas on their own can be very difficult for teachers, because they are usually expected to have a plan as to how things should proceed—expectancies that can actually inhibit the creating of wonderful ideas. For this educational process to unfold, teachers must trust their own judgment. If teachers are made to feel bound by the requirements of a textbook, and believe that their success as a teacher will be marked by the completion of lesson plans, and the scores that their students attain on tests, then deviations on the part of the students will be deemed inappropriate and inconvenient. Duckworth believes that if teachers have confidence in the potential of each child, and children are encouraged to pursue the having of wonderful ideas, regardless of whether those ideas are deemed "wonderful" by the outside world, they will be more likely to someday discover an idea that no one else has had before (Duckworth, 2006, p. 14). She admits that her educational philosophy and pedagogy require a shift in thinking, and she offers this advice:

> First, teachers themselves must learn in the way that the children in their classes will be learning. Second, the teachers work with one or two children at a time so they can observe them closely enough to realize what is involved for the children. Last, it seems valuable for teachers to see films or live demonstrations of a class of children learning in this way, so that they can begin to think that it really is possible to run their class in such a way. A fourth aspect is of slightly different nature. Except for the rare teacher who will take this leap all on his or her own on the basis of a single course and some written teachers' guides, most teachers need the support of at least some nearby co-workers who are trying to do the same thing, and with whom they can share notes. An even better help is the presence of an experienced teacher to whom they can go with questions and problems. (Duckworth, 2006, p. 9)

She proposes that teachers think of their work as research, as calls for them to do "critical exploration in the classroom" (Duckworth, 2006, p. 159). The "teaching/researcher" role comes naturally according to Duckworth, as the teacher and researcher are asking the same questions:

> What do you think and why? How do other people really think about these matters? Which ideas build on which others and how? This kind of research need not take place in a classroom. But it does require, as a researcher, someone who knows a subject matter well enough to engage a great variety of learners, that is, it requires someone who is a good teacher. (Duckworth, 2006, p. 186)

Duckworth's emphasis on observational research is no doubt the result of her study with Piaget and Inhelder. She believes that the job of school teachers could be reconstrued so that, observational research and writing would be a part of the job (Duckworth, 2006). Teaching and research form a continual dance for this truly passionate teacher.

She recognizes, in addition, that looking honestly at what the child is actually learning as a result of the teacher-student interaction requires the teacher to be open to self-evaluation—and she knows how difficult this is. She calls on teachers to consider their role as researchers, not in order to become published researchers, but because they care enough about the students' learning process and their role in it to continually observe and evaluate. She does think it is important that teachers make their observations and knowledge accessible to others through writing and contributing to theoretical and pedagogical discussions on the facilitation of human learning.

The Role of the Student in the Learning Process

Because the students' learning must, by definition, be the focus of the teaching, a teacher's job is to put students in contact with subject matter, and to work hard to keep the contact alive. In her work with teachers, she continually designs situations where they will think about learning from the student's perspective. Through her years of teaching teachers, Duckworth has observed the impact that examination of the learning process from the perspective of the student can have on their teaching. Duckworth also believes that it is important for teachers, as students, to exchange ideas with others. There is always risk in sharing one's ideas and values with others in an attempt to clarify them. "The courage to submit an idea of one's own to someone else's scrutiny is a virtue in itself—unrelated to the rightness of the idea" (Duckworth, 2006 p. 67). It is worth a teacher's while to help students learn to risk sharing what they think and be open to the questioning of their peers. This process lies at the foundation of their ability to form their own ideas and to see how their ideas relate to the ideas of others.

Duckworth often has her students at Harvard place themselves in the role of the student in the learning process. She wants them to continually learn about the process of learning as well as the process of teaching. One class project involves the students, who may be experienced teachers themselves, observing the moon over the course of the semester, and keeping a written record of the moon's shape, orientation, location, and apparent movements. From these observations the teachers try to reconstruct what must be moving around what, in what ways—a very difficult task of spatial reasoning, visualization, and checking ideas against data. This challenges her students to identify their own learning process as they observe one small piece of the natural world and then track how their understandings change over the course of the semester. Just as it is valuable for students to know how it feels to come to their own understanding, not through being told answers, but through the power of their own minds, so it is valuable for teachers to do the same thing. When teachers recreate their own learning process, and discover the possibilities within their own "not knowing," they begin to understand the potential power of their students' minds as well. "The virtues involved in not knowing are the ones that really count in the long run. What you do about what you do not know is, in the final analysis, what determines what you *will* know" (Duckworth, 2006, p. 67). In addition, the eventual sharing among students who have all been engaged in the same moon observation project enhances understanding of the ways other people give meaning to the same experience. One student in her class said, "I needed time for my confusion"—a phrase that has become a touchstone for Duckworth. She explains that she asks the teachers in her classes to observe the moon as an example of learning any complex knowledge. Her intent is to help the teacher as student understand that all of us need time for thinking through our confusion if we are to arrive at clear and adequate ideas. She urges teachers to continue to raise questions with students, even about what appears to be a right answer in order to determine how to see where an answer holds up well, and where it does not. Among other things, this questioning assists students in learning the connectedness of one idea to another, and their understanding of the world is then broadened.

On Experiential Education

When asked if she considers herself to be an experiential educator, Professor Duckworth replied, "If something is to be educational, it has to be experiential, so, yes, I do. People learn through what they experience" (Duckworth, personal communication, September, 5, 2007). She emphasizes that there is value in the process of experiential education as learners are forced to wrestle with their own ideas about a subject matter.

> Experiential education as I do it in a classroom, also has great potential impact on my students; a very sweeping impact is that people realize that they can learn in areas that they thought were not possible, they never could, or that was not the way their mind worked. I think that it is very important that people get to have a great sense of confidence in their own minds. A lot of education, when you're just learning what passes for education, when you are learning other people's ideas, doesn't help you develop much confidence in your own ideas. I think experiential [education] does that. When you give students the subject matter itself instead of words about the subject matter and stick with it while they pass through confusion and ideas that later they will reject and feelings that they can't do anything with yet and finally get their own minds around these. They come up with their own ideas as they try to make sense of whatever you're offering them; they come to see that those ideas can work out and can be of interest to other people and stay with them and help them

expand their connections to the world. (Duckworth, personal communication, September, 5, 2007)

Duckworth believes that in order for students to learn, they must be offered opportunities to be in contact with phenomena related to the area to be studied—not to read or see what someone else thinks about the phenomena, but to really have the students make sense of it for themselves. Consistent with experiential education philosophy and constructivist theory, the student is the creator of meaning and the teacher's role is to understand the student's meaning and take it further, instead of imposing their own. Duckworth believes that this is the only way to have a real effect on what the students learn (Duckworth, personal communication, October 14, 2007). With respect to experiential education, Duckworth recalls two individuals who had the greatest influence on her—Mike Savage and Dr. David Hawkins, both with whom she worked at the Elementary Science Study (Duckworth, personal communication, September, 5, 2007).

Implications for EE Philosophy

Professor Duckworth is concerned about the state of public education today, believing that there is "not much of a role for experiential learning… [Education] is in the grip of standardized multiple choice tests" (Duckworth, personal communication, September, 5, 2007). She believes that instead of subjecting students to a standardized test that assesses whether they know the "right" answer, students should be given opportunities to learn through presenting their own work and asking questions of each other's work that develop the ability to think. Given the current emphasis on standardized tests as the primary means of assessment, the role of the teacher becomes even more difficult as he or she seeks to create settings that encourage the formation of wonderful ideas while being pressured to teach the right answers.

> Knowing the right answer requires no decisions, carries no risks, and makes no demands. It is automatic. It is thoughtless. Knowledge of the right answer ahead of time is, on the whole, more valued than ways of figuring it out. True, intelligence tests require that certain things be figured out, but the figuring out doesn't count. If the figuring out leads to the right answer, then of course the right answer counts. But no tester will ever know and no score will ever reveal whether the right answer was a triumph of imagination and intellectual daring, or whether the child knew the right answer all along. (Duckworth, 2006, p. 63)

Duckworth believes that in order to foster an environment where students engage in learning, the teacher must provide occasions where surprise, puzzlement, excitement, patience, caution, and honest attempts and wrong outcomes are seen as legitimate and important elements of learning (Duckworth, 2006). This is how students begin to develop a broad, deep, solid basis for what they know instead of constructing the quickest route to the right answer. Duckworth believes that education in the 21st century needs to value the meaning that students give to the events that are shared. The role of a teacher becomes even more messy as she/he attempts to understand the students' perspectives while also trying to understand their own. This process assumes that questioning another person's ideas is a good thing—even questioning the teacher in order to better understand one's thoughts and feelings about a particular experience. The role of a teacher is a high calling to which Duckworth shares these final words of encouragement:

> What I have learned from the teachers with whom I have worked is that, just as there is no simple solution to the arms race, there is also no simple answer to how to work with children in the classroom. It is a matter of being present as a whole person, with your own thoughts and feelings, and of accepting children as whole people, with their thoughts and

feelings. It is a matter of working very hard to find out what those thoughts and feelings are, as a starting point for developing a view of a world in which people are as much concerned about other people's security as they are about their own. (Duckworth, 2006, p. 123)

Eleanor Duckworth's educational philosophy may well be seen as having roots in the ideas of John Dewey, but she clearly stretches his ideas in many ways. We hear loud and clear in her words the call for

recognizing the student as the center of learning,
a holistic focus on the entire person,
a challenge for teachers to guide students to wrestle with what they believe and why,
an appreciation of observation and interaction with the natural world, and
an emphasis on experiential learning.

Author's Note

We are grateful to Dr. Duckworth for taking the time to speak with us on the telephone and her continued editorial support throughout the writing of this manuscript. The opportunity to speak with her made the writing of this piece come alive as we were able to check our interpretation of the ideas she was sharing. Thank you for sharing your *wonderful ideas*!

References

Duckworth, E., (Ed). (2001). *Tell me more: Listening to learners explain*. New York: Teachers College.

Duckworth, E. (1997). *Teacher to teacher: Learning from each other*. New York: Teachers College.

Duckworth, E. (2006). *The having of wonderful ideas and other essays on teaching and learning* (3rd ed.). New York: Teachers College.

EN News. (2007). Retrieved October 19, 2007, from http://ennews.pku.edu.cn/news.php?s=181832895

Piaget, J. (1953). *The origins of intelligence in children*. London: Routledge & Kegan Paul.

Piaget, J. (1955). *The child's construction of reality*. London: Routledge & Kegan Paul.

Part II

Nature Study, Outdoor and Environmental Education

Our society is teaching young people to avoid direct experience in nature. That lesson is delivered in schools, families, even organizations devoted to the outdoors.

Richard Louv, 2008

The next part of this book includes chapters that have roots in three major educational movements of the 20th century in the United States. These are the nature study, outdoor education, and environmental education movements. Although educational terminology often changes with time, these three movements can be characterized by specific philosophies, goals, objectives, and pedagogy. The people discussed in this section are only a few of the many who could represent these movements and exemplify how they are important to the philosophical foundations of experiential education.

Nature Study

The philosophical roots of nature study were first planted by European educators such as Comenius (1592–1670), Rousseau (1712–1778), Pestalozzi (1746–1827), Froebel (1782–1852), and Agassiz (1807–1873) (Ward & Leonard, 1956). The nature study movement in the American public schools flourished between 1890 and 1920 (Minton, 1980). The movement was a reaction by some against what was perceived to be wrong with the school curriculum and teaching methodology at the time. These criticisms were mainly directed at the way science was taught, but because the advocates believed in integrated, cross-discipline teaching, nature study infused other subjects as well. Nature study was an example of early school reform in the public schools and some of its influence remains today in various experiential education programs.

Influential nature study authors of the early 20th century were Wilbur S. Jackman (1855–1907), Clifton F. Hodge (1858–?), Anna B. Comstock (1854–1930), and Liberty Hyde Bailey (1858–1954). We can view the movement by looking at the writings of Liberty Hyde Bailey, who taught at Cornell University and was a prominent author and educator. In 1897, Bailey was charged with encouraging nature study in the rural schools in the state of New York, partly because of political and economic concerns about the steady population movement from the country to the city. Bailey described the purpose of the project as follows: The animus of the endeavor is to cause the child to love nature and thereby to be content with country life. There is no other corrective of agricultural ills than this (Bailey as cited in Ward & Leonard, 1956, p. 5).

Bailey defined nature study as a process involving "seeing the things that one looks at, and the drawing of proper conclusions from what one sees. Its purpose is to educate the child in terms of his environment, to the end that his life may be fuller and richer" (1904b, p. 11). He wrote in broad descriptive terms about the movement being an "outgrowth of an effort to put the child into contact and sympathy with its own life" (p. 21).

Bailey believed that nature study should involve the objects that pupils meet outdoors such as stones, flowers, twigs, birds, and insects. Pupil interest in these objects should be an important consideration in planning lessons. He was not in favor of a rigid curriculum.

> The best way to teach nature-study is, with no hard and fast course laid out, to bring in some object that may be at hand and to set the pupils to looking at it. The pupils do the work, they see the thing and explain its structure and its meaning. (Bailey, 1904b, p. 12)

Bailey suggested that teachers should avoid giving students definitions and using model flowers or leaves because lessons should always begin with real things and phenomena, not with abstract ideas. He suggested that the true method was to say, "Go and find me a flower … and let us see what it is" (1904b, p. 12). He wanted teachers to follow three steps:

The first was to have students accurately observe something.
The second was to help them understand why the thing was so, or what it meant.
The third essential step was to cultivate the student's desire to know more.

According to Bailey's theory of instruction, the results of these steps should be the development of the students' personal interest in the world of nature.

Bailey was a sharp critic of public schools, as he understood them at the turn of the century. He stated:

> It is a fact, however, that our teaching has been largely exotic to the child; that it has begun by taking the child away from its natural environment; that has concerned itself with the subject matter rather than with the child. (Bailey, 1904a, p. 21)

He was also critical of the over-use of books as ways to expose pupils to knowledge:

> First of all, we put our children into books, sometimes even into books that tell about the very things at the child's door, as if a book about a thing were better than the thing itself. Books are only secondary means of education. We have made the mistake of considering them primary. (1904a, p. 23)

This focus on first-hand, practical experience is also evidenced in this quotation of Bailey's: "A young man who has spent all his time in the schoolroom is usually hopelessly helpless when he encounters a real circumstance" (1904a p. 24). Bailey believed "that much of our teaching is unrelated to the circumstances in which the child lives" (1904a, p. 26). To summarize his criticisms, he mentions five dangers of the predominant teaching methods he observed: (a) giving too much attention to teaching facts; (b) making instruction too long and laborious; (c) merely telling or explaining instead of letting the child do work within his own realm; (c) clinging too closely to the book habit; and (c) using secondary sources such as museums and collections instead of having contact with actual things.

Bailey believed that public elementary schooling was largely unrelated to the lives of children in the local community. He thought books and other forms of mediated teaching technologies were over used at the expense of direct experiences with nature, both in and out of the classroom. He felt that schools were not preparing young people for life, especially when the study of science at higher grade levels focused on unrelated factual information and the lessons were too long and uninteresting. He believed that children were losing their enthusiasm for learning other school subjects because of how they were taught.

The nature study movement was designed to overcome perceived weaknesses in public education. The goal of achieving a more meaningful curriculum through contextual learning in the community is still being championed by some educators today. Nature study's aims and recommended methodologies still survive, although the field is seldom called by that name. The term faded from common use in most schools in the 1920s, and other terminology was introduced to describe the teaching of direct experiences inside and outside the classroom. For example, terms such as "conservation education" introduced in the 1930s, "outdoor education" introduced in the 1940s, "environmental education" introduced in the 1960s, "experiential education" introduced in the 1970s, and "place-based education" introduced in the 1990s supported many of the values and methods of the nature study movement.

At the turn of the 20th century, Bailey felt strongly about the importance of his approach to nature study and predicted that the term might fall into disuse if educators didn't fully understand it. Prophetically he wrote, "But the name matters little so long as we hold to the essence" (1904b, p. 13).

Outdoor and Environmental Education

Outdoor education and environmental education are separate, but closely related movements within education. They share some common content and processes, while being distinctive in some other important ways. Various interpretations have appeared in the literature, but their original purposes have changed very little since their inceptions.

During the late 1800s, some educators realized that education could be improved by taking students out of the classroom to learn appropriate and required concepts, skills, attitudes, and values. Some of the early outdoor educators used camp settings during the regular school year to meet academic objectives, as well as to improve students' social development and recreational skills.

The term "outdoor education" emerged in the United States in the early 1940s and describes the instructional use of natural and cultural areas to meet student learning objectives in a variety of subject-matter disciplines through direct experiences. This type of school-based, contextual learning involving the local surroundings has also been referred to as taking field trips, excursions, journeys, or doing field studies.

The classic definition, developed by William B. Stapp and his graduate students, appeared originally in a 1969 issue of *The Journal of Environmental Education*: "Environmental education is aimed at producing a citizenry that is knowledgeable concerning the biophysical environment and its associated problems, aware of how to help solve these problems, and motivated to work toward their solution" (Stapp, 1998, p. 34).

Some historians point to Rachel Carson's book, *Silent Spring* (1962), as helping to create the first Earth Day in April 1970. Spurred by federal legislation during the 1960s and 1970s, outdoor and environmental education expanded in public and private schools across the nation. In fact, some critics accused educators of simply changing the names of their outdoor science, nature study, or outdoor education programs and adopting the then current term, "environmental education." This practice of changing the names of these closely related fields in order to modernize the program content, methodology, or focus continues today.

Some of the practices in outdoor and environmental education programs do overlap. Although both fields are interdisciplinary, one difference is that outdoor education can be applied to any subject matter discipline that can be more effectively taught and learned outside. According to Lloyd B. Sharp (1895–1963), a pioneer in outdoor education, the key principle is: "that which ought and can best be taught inside the schoolrooms should there be taught there, and that which can best be learned through experience dealing directly with native materials and life situations outside the school should there be learned" (Sharp as cited in Knapp, 1996, p. 77).

For example, outdoor education could mean teaching the concept of an acre by measuring a playing field (mathematics); or visiting a park to write poetry or draw pictures inspired by the setting (language arts and art); or recording the information found in a cemetery to learn about past events (history); or testing the pH to determine if a nearby stream is acid or alkaline (science); or climbing a hill to calculate student heart rates (physical education).

Environmental education, on the other hand, can take place inside or outside the classroom, and can include local as well as global perspectives, but the focus is usually on studying ecology and resource issues such as water, air, and soil pollution, solid waste and toxic disposal, urban sprawl and population, deforestation, endangered plants and animals, or drought and flooding, especially at upper grade levels. The line separating outdoor and environmental education becomes blurred when teachers take students outside to increase nature awareness or study culture's impact on ecosystems. It makes little sense to argue over what label applies to these kinds of outdoor lessons when their purposes and methods blend.

Both outdoor education and environmental education are offered mainly through schools, nature centers, and outdoor residential facilities, and the instructional methodologies are selected from the general field of education. Environmental and outdoor educators primarily advocate experiential learning strategies, although both fields draw from conventional instructional technologies such as textbooks, periodicals, computers, videos, and overhead transparencies as well. These educators stress the importance of contextual, direct, and unmediated experiences used often in problem-based learning situations. Students are encouraged to use a variety of senses in exploring the content to maximize active engagement and learning. For more details about instructional methods in these fields, refer to the fifth edition of *Teaching in the Outdoors* (Hammerman, Hammerman, & Hammerman, 2001). This classic book has been in continuous print since 1964.

Summary

Nature study, outdoor education, and environmental education have operated as significant educational reforms since the early 1900s, and all recommend use of outdoor settings and experiential education strategies. All three of these educational movements have faced the same problems and controversies that experiential education does now. Debates have centered on questions of definition and purpose, relationship to the regular school curriculum, and the best practices for facilitating learning. As the evolving field of experiential education seeks to improve both theory and practice, the writings of past and present nature study, outdoor education, and environmental education professionals can be of value. There are many historic and contemporary figures whose ideas and writings could be reviewed to examine their philosophies (see Appendix I). There are eight chapters in this section:

Chapter 10: Jean Louis Rodolphe Agassiz: Nature and Experiential Education
Chapter 11: Alexander von Humboldt: Expeditionary Scientist
Chapter 12: Anna Botsford Comstock: Beyond Science—Learning About Self and Nature Through Field Experience
Chapter 13: Charles A. Eastman and Luther Standing Bear: Two Early Indian Writers and Educators
Chapter 14: Aldo Leopold: Teaching in the Spirit of the Land Ethic
Chapter 15: Lloyd B. Sharp: Trailblazer in Outdoor Education
Chapter 16: Rachel Carson: Inspiring A Sense of Wonder
Chapter 17: Sigurd Olson and Paul Shepard: Experiential Education and Ancient Rhythms

References

Bailey, L. H. (1904a). The nature-study movement. In State of New York Department of Agriculture (Ed.), *Cornell nature-study leaflets: Being a selection, with revision, from the teachers' leaflets, home nature-study lessons, junior naturalist monthlies and other publications from the College of Agriculture, Cornell University, Ithaca, N.Y., 1896–1904* (pp. 21–29). Albany, NY: J. B. Lyon Company.

Bailey, L. H. (1904b). What is nature-study? In State of New York Department of Agriculture (Ed.), *Cornell nature-study leaflets: Being a selection, with revision, from the teachers' leaflets, home nature-study lessons, junior naturalist monthlies and other publications from the College of Agriculture, Cornell University, Ithaca, N.Y., 1896–1904* (pp. 11–20). Albany, NY: J. B. Lyon Company.

Carson, R. (1962). *Silent spring.* Boston: Houghton Mifflin.

Hammerman, D. R., Hammerman, W. M., & Hammerman, E. L. (2001). *Teaching in the outdoors* (5th ed.). Danville, IL: Interstate.

Knapp, C. E. (1996). *Just beyond the classroom: Community adventures for interdisciplinary learning.* Charleston, WV: ERIC Clearinghouse on Rural Education and Small Schools.

Minton, T. G. (1980). *The history of the nature-study movement and its role in the development of environmental education.* Unpublished doctoral dissertation, University of Massachusetts, Amherst.

Stapp, W. B. (1998). The concept of environmental education. In H. R. Hungerford, W. J. Bluhm, T. L. Volk, & J. M. Ramsey (Eds.), *Essential readings in environmental education* (pp. 33–35). Champaign, IL: Stipes.

Ward, W. B., & Leonard, N. B. (Eds.). (1956, Fall). [Special issue] *Cornell Nature Study Leaflets: 1896 to 1956, 50*(1).

10   Jean Louis Rodolphe Agassiz
Nature and Experiential Education

Clifford E. Knapp

Biographical Background

Imagine being born in the early 1800s in rural Switzerland and being home schooled by your parents until the age of 10. Continue to imagine that your parents encouraged you to explore the area around your home and collect birds, fishes, and small mammals and keep them for study. You learned how to hunt, trap, fish, boat, and hike in the area and you loved being outdoors discovering nature's secrets. That's how the life of Jean Louis Rodolphe Agassiz (pronounced AG-a-see) began after his birth in Motier, Switzerland, in 1807. Louis (as he was usually called by family and friends) grew up with his brother, Auguste, and sisters, Olympe and Cecile, exploring the surrounding waters, mountains, and glaciers and satisfying his thirst for knowledge about natural history. His enthusiasm for learning about nature was extraordinary. He was later considered to be "an illustrious savant" and "the originator and source of so many new ideas" by Alexander von Humboldt, one of the leading scientists of the day. As a youth he said, "My highest ambition was to be able to designate the plants and animals of my native country correctly by Latin name, and to extend gradually a similar knowledge in its application to the productions of other countries" (Agassiz in Lurie, 1988, p. 9). As a youth he was especially interested in fish, rocks, minerals, fossils, and plants.

Louis was the son of Rodolphe, a Protestant pastor, and Rose Mayor, the daughter of a physician. His native language was French; later he learned some Latin, German, Italian, Greek, and English. At the age of 10 he entered a nearby school for boys at Bienne. There he developed his interest in languages that later became an asset as he traveled the world. At 11 he began to record his observations of nature in a journal, a practice he continued for much of his life (Faber & Faber, 1991). At 15 he entered the Academy at Lausanne where he received his first formal lessons in zoology and visited his first museum. Collecting specimens for museums was to become one of his life-long goals. Lurie, one of Agassiz's biographers, stated: "At fifteen, Agassiz had three essential attributes that would help him in his ambition: an insatiable curiosity about nature, a good knowledge of languages, and an intense desire to succeed" (1988, p. 12). He had other habits of mind that guided him in his quest to "serve the cause … and enlarge the boundaries of science" (1988, p. 40, 43) and become "the first naturalist of his time" (1988, p. 71). He was optimistic about the future, self-confident, had a boundless imagination, intense intellectual curiosity, a dedication to learning, and demonstrated immense drive and physical energy. At the age of 17 he entered a medical school in Zurich with his brother and stayed for two years. In those days, medical knowledge was synonymous with science knowledge and learning science was his first love. While rooming with his brother, he kept up to 40 birds in their room. The birds perched on a large pine tree he had erected inside. His desire to collect zoo and museum specimens hadn't cooled since childhood.

In 1826, at 19, he went to the University of Heidelberg to study physiology, anatomy, and botany. There he assumed a broader view of natural history. He commented that he had "never thought of the larger and more philosophical view of nature as one great world" (Agassiz in

Lurie, 1988, p. 21). When he met Alexander Braun and Karl Schimper, he teamed with these like-minded Heidelberg students and explored the countryside almost daily. Braun described Agassiz as a person who "is familiar with almost all the known mammalia, recognizes birds from far off by their song, and can give a name to every fish in the water" (1988, p. 22).

In 1827 he attended the University of Munich for three years to continue his study of science with his friends, Braun and Schimper. As roommates, they gave each other nicknames based on their natural history interests: "Braun was 'Molluscus,' after a current fascination with shells, Schimper was 'Rhubarb' for a botanical flair, and Agassiz was 'Cyprinus,' the carp, a fish notable for its fecundity, rapid growth, large size, and great appetite" (Lurie, 1988, pp. 34–35). Dollinger, one of his German biology professors, taught him to observe accurately, a skill that he would pass along to his students for the rest of his life. Observation skills were useful to Agassiz in his roles as paleontologist, ichthyologist, geologist and embryologist. Agassiz earned a doctorate of philosophy of natural history in 1829 at the University of Erlangen (Lurie, 1988). He also earned a doctor of medicine degree a year later at the University of Munich. One of the theses he defended was that the physiological organization of women was more complicated than and superior to that of men. He continued to respect women as students and taught many female schoolteachers throughout his life. As a teacher, he wanted women as well as men to study a natural history curriculum in schools.

During this time, he traveled over much of Switzerland and Germany collecting fishes and later wrote a monograph on the natural history of freshwater fishes of Central Europe. During many of these trips, he preferred going to the fish markets to find new specimens, rather than visiting with people. He once discovered a new species of carp at a fish market. In 1829 Agassiz's first book, Brazilian Fishes, was published. He dedicated it to a French scientist, Georges Cuvier, who Agassiz admired very much. At Munich he deepened his "personal and intellectual self-assurance derived from experience" (Lurie, 1988, p. 31).

After returning briefly to Switzerland, Agassiz looked for other challenges. He set his sights on Paris where his science hero, Cuvier, worked and where he could study at a great natural history museum. He studied fossil fish so intensely that they even entered his dreams. He pondered for weeks over the details of a preserved fish partially imbedded in stone. For two nights he saw the complete fossil in his dreams, but could not remember what it looked like when he awoke. On the third night he took a pencil and paper to bed and when a dream image of the fish appeared, he woke up and sketched it. The next day when he managed to separate the fish from the stone, he found that his sketch matched the real fish's skeletal structure. Cuvier was not only a great influence on Agassiz's scientific skill development, he helped shape his philosophy of nature and theology. Based on observations, Cuvier saw "no evidence of animals having developed from other animals, or having produced animals higher than themselves" (Lurie, 1988, p. 60). Agassiz held this belief for most of his life and it was the primary basis for his challenge to many of Darwin's ideas about evolution. Unfortunately, in 1832, Agassiz's mentor, Cuvier, died suddenly and Louis eventually decided to return to Switzerland.

In 1832 Agassiz became a professor of natural history at the Lyceum of Neuchatel in Switzerland. At age 25 his formal education had ended; he had two doctorates, a published book, and many ideas for more scientific investigations. He lectured on botany, zoology, geology, and on the philosophy of nature. When he taught certain subjects, he preferred to lecture outdoors where he could get a panoramic view of the land and illustrate the course content with direct experiences. He was probably the first naturalist to make plaster casts of specimens to preserve collections and share them with his students (Cooper, 1945). Because of his extensive study of glaciers, he was known for a while as "the Father of Glaciology" (Academy of Natural Sciences in Philadelphia, n.d.). He stayed at Neuchatel for 14 years before going to America.

Agassiz arrived in Boston in 1846 and began to lecture at various places around the country. This famous naturalist from Europe was much in demand and spoke to packed auditoriums.

"Americans cried for instruction, and Agassiz could not resist their pleas. He was living in the fullest enjoyment of his talent for imparting a love of nature to all who would listen, and their numbers seemed to grow every day" (Lurie, 1988, p. 128). A short time later, he was employed at Harvard University in Cambridge, Massachusetts, and his first wife, Cecile, had died in Germany. By that time he had a son, Alexander, and two daughters, Pauline and Ida. When Agassiz later married Elizabeth Cary in 1850, he was able to bring his daughters to the United States to join his son who had already arrived.

Agassiz's fascination with collecting for and exploring museums led naturally to his desire to establish a museum at Harvard in 1853. He had already established a network of wealthy Bostonians and other leading scientists and he used these connections to raise money for the project. He pursued this goal along with others such as writing a comprehensive history of American fishes; influencing the direction of science at learning institutions; stimulating the scientific minds of Harvard students; reporting on a trip to the Florida reefs; and lecturing on natural history to a public hungry for his ideas. Lurie summed up the professor's obsession with taking on new projects before finishing old ones: "Agassiz's spirit needed the constant refreshment of new ideas representing grander projects than those that had preceded them" (1988, p. 195). By 1857 he had laid the political and financial groundwork for establishing a great museum that would captivate his attention for most of his life. By 1859 construction was begun and on November 13, 1860, the Museum of Comparative Zoology (also known as the Agassiz Museum) was opened to the public. Agassiz was appointed the director and one of his dreams to educate people by having direct access to specimens was finally realized. "Agassiz had for his use the greatest number of and variety of natural history materials ever assembled in the United States" (Lurie, 1988, p. 251).

During Agassiz's time at Harvard University, he continued to lecture and publish scientific books and articles. Even during the last year of his life, he launched a new project for educators that would bring together his life goals for combining research, teaching, and public service. From May to July of 1873 Agassiz supervised the completion of building the Anderson School of Natural History on Penikese Island off the coast of Massachusetts. On July 6, two days before a group of 50 schoolteachers were scheduled to arrive, he discovered that the dormitory was not separated into male and female rooms. Co-educational sleeping quarters was not the kind of natural history study that he planned for these men and women teachers, so a partition was quickly constructed. The success of the summer school left Agassiz in high spirits for further work at the museum that fall. On December 2nd he lectured in Fitchburg, Massachusetts, and on December 5th he attended his wife's birthday party. The next morning he complained of not feeling well and he fell asleep, never to regain his faculties. He died on December 14, 1873, at the age of 66. He was buried in Mount Auburn Cemetery and a 2,500-pound boulder from the mountains in Switzerland, where he explored glaciers, marked his grave. Much of the country mourned the passing of one of the greatest naturalists of his day.

Agassiz accomplished many of his life ambitions, including achieving the reputation as a principal spokesperson for natural history in the United States. He developed a theory about early glaciers that changed the way scientists viewed geologic evidence of ancient ice sheets. He assembled a large collection of specimens in one of the leading museums in the nation. He published 23 important scientific books and numerous periodical articles (Cooper, 1945). He was one of the founders of the National Academy of Sciences. He served on the Board of Regents of the Smithsonian Institutions in Washington, D.C. He was influential in founding Cornell University, a prominent institution promoting teaching and research in natural history. He supported women in their role as students at a time when many educational institutions did not. Many of his students went on to become important leaders in science and natural history (Lurie, 1988). Finally, he gained fame as a professor who preferred teaching indoors and outdoors with real specimens whenever possible instead of using the contemporary methods of rote memorization and recitation. Agassiz's career was truly remarkable because of all these accomplishments.

Thoughts on Agassiz's Educational Philosophy

Agassiz's life as a teacher illustrated his philosophy of education that was based primarily upon experiential learning. His teaching was guided by how he had learned best – through having direct experiences in nature and by using real scientific objects. Louis had many talents, but teaching was recognized as one of his greatest strengths. He wanted to dedicate his life to instructing his "young countrymen" in the mysteries of nature and awakening in them "the taste for science and observation so neglected among us" (Agassiz, in Lurie, 1988, p. 45). When asked the question about what he regarded as his greatest work, he replied, "I have taught men to observe" and in the preamble to his will he described himself as "Louis Agassiz, Teacher" (Agassiz in Cooper, 1945, p. 1).

His many students recognized his desire to share what he knew, but his least favorite ways of teaching were by asking them to listen to indoor lectures, memorize and recite content, or read about what others wrote about specimens before examining them directly. He believed that "lectures and constant supervision were old-fashioned techniques" (Lurie, 1988, p. 177). When he did lecture, he admitted, "without [museum] collections, lectures will remain deficient" (Agassiz in Lurie, 1988, p. 214). "He continually preached his doctrine, "Read nature, not books" (Cooper, 1945, p. 27). For example, when Agassiz taught Shaler, his graduate student, about the structure of a fish, he gave only brief directions: "Find out what you can without damaging the specimen; when I think that you have done the work I will question you" (Agassiz in Cooper, 1945, p. 41). Shaler was not allowed to use any scientific equipment, books, or talk to anyone else. Then Agassiz left Shaler alone for seven days. After over 100 hours of study, Shaler told Agassiz what he had learned. At the end of the hour, Agassiz said, "That is not right" and he left. Shaler discarded his first notes and studied the fish for another week, working 10 hours each day. Agassiz was finally satisfied. Then Shaler said that his teacher placed a half a peck of fish bones before him to "see what I could make of them, with no further directions to guide me" (Cooper, 1945, p. 42). After two months of study, Shaler had reconstructed the bones of six fish species with only occasional supervision. Only after being convinced that Shaler had learned a lot, did Agassiz allow him to learn from indirect, secondary sources. Once Agassiz was convinced that his students could accurately observe, compare, classify, and analyze, then he assisted them generously by providing other necessary, available resources.

Joseph Le Conte recalled his first experiences as a student under Agassiz. His professor gave him one thousand shells and told him to separate them into different species. Le Conte worked for one week and rarely saw his teacher. When Agassiz reviewed the results of Le Conte's efforts, he told him that he had improved the current level of scientific knowledge by creating a better classification system (Lurie, 1988).

Agassiz's natural history students were taught to appreciate the proper place of books in their education, but he warned them that books were sometimes incorrect and the most authoritative source of learning was accurate observation of the book of nature. He told teachers: "Train your pupils to be observers, and have them provided with the specimens about which you speak. If you can find nothing better, take a house-fly or a cricket, and let each hold a specimen and examine it as you talk" (Agassiz in Cooper, 1945, p. 82).

Agassiz did not encourage the learning of isolated facts. He said, "It is a fallacy to suppose that an encyclopaedic knowledge is desirable. The mind is made strong, not through much learning, but by the thorough possession of something" (Agassiz in Cooper, 1988, p. 81). He admitted that it was "much more important … to the naturalist to understand the structure of a few animals, than to command the whole field of scientific nomenclature" (Agassiz, 1885, p. 58).

He always cautioned teachers to "have the courage to say, 'I do not know'" (Agassiz in Cooper, 1945, p. 83).

Another student, Burt G. Wilder, who eventually joined Agassiz on the staff of the school at Penikese Island and later taught zoology at Cornell University, said: "Agassiz was pre-eminently a teacher. He taught his assistants; he taught the teachers in the public schools; he taught college students; he taught the public, and the common people heard him gladly" (Wilder in Cooper, 1945, pp. 48–49). Wilder recalls, "At one of the later lectures, after speaking about fifteen minutes, he invited his hearers to examine living salmon embryos under his direction at one table, and living shark embryos under mine at another" (Wilder in Cooper, 1945, p. 51).

At that time in history when the predominant teaching strategies were reading, rote memory, and recitation, Agassiz had the courage to be different. He had faith in his students' ability to learn how to observe and compare through firsthand contact with specimens, either in museums or in natural contexts. He also knew that students could learn in groups by sharing their knowledge with others when they were ready. His maxim, "read nature, not books" showed his belief in the values of sensory and active learning. He especially wanted to include women public school teachers among his students and he gave many staff development workshops for them. When his wife, Elizabeth, started a school for young women near Harvard to raise funds for her husband's museum, Agassiz enthusiastically helped make natural history a primary requirement in their education (Lurie, 1988, p. 200).

Implications for EE Philosophy

From the many examples in Agassiz's life as a scientist and teacher, it is obvious that he has influenced modern experiential education philosophy. His students taught others and they continued the chain by teaching others over the generations. To show how Agassiz's life provided a foundation for today's educators, some of his accomplishments will be placed on a continuum of experience developed by Gibbons and Hopkins. Maurice Gibbons and David Hopkins outlined a scale of "experientiality" in an article explaining their belief that "some experiences ... are more experiential than others" (1980, pp. 135–140). Their contention is that the construct, "experiential education," is vague and of little value if it includes a wide range of different activities under the same name. They begin with activities that are highly mediated by the teacher and with students as mostly passive learners and end with more direct learning in community contexts involving students in active, engaged ways. Gibbons and Hopkins wanted to demonstrate that experiences could be categorized on a five-point scale according to how accurately they reflected life outside a traditional classroom setting. To help solve this problem of multiple types of experiences subsumed by a single, abstract term, they created a five-point continuum representing the degrees of "fullness of experience involved." They believe that the "fullest" types of experiences are those that reflect an ideal way of learning using the whole community and surrounding area as classrooms.

The continuum begins with the "Receptive Mode" whereby direct experiences or representations of them presented to mostly inactive students. Two examples, of this would be when Agassiz lectured about glaciers as the students observed the terrain outdoors during a geography lesson or when he sketched representative samples of organisms on the blackboard to teach about classification. The students watched either a real or mediated visual example in order to understand the lesson content.

Next on this continuum is the "Analytic Mode." In this mode "students conduct field studies in which they apply theoretical knowledge and skill in order to study some event, analyze some aspect of the environment or solve some practical problem" (Gibbons & Hopkins, 1980, p. 136). One example of this mode is when Agassiz went on a cruise off the coast of Nicaragua late in his career. He tried to find out if organisms gathered at great depths in the ocean were related to those gathered nearer the surface. He wanted to test Darwin's theory of evolution by gathering specimens from the ocean. At this point in his life, he was more open minded about Darwin's theory of evolution and wanted to find evidence to either support or refute it. "That Agassiz was never able to gather evidence of the sort he required on this journey, or to study the materials he collected in an intensive fashion, was tragic" (Lurie, 1988, p. 374). Another example of the Analytic Mode is when Agassiz and his students searched for grooves carved in bedrock and for deposits of glacial erratics or moraines to support his ice age theory. The students were more engaged in discussions and physical movement during these lessons.

The third point on the continuum, the "Productive Mode," occurs when "students generate products, activities and services which have been assigned or are of their own devising" (1980, p. 136). A good example of this is Shaler's discovery of six different species of fish after Agassiz gave him a quantity of fish bones or Le Conte's improvement in the system of shell classification when Agassiz gave him the shell collection and the directions to separate them into groups of different species.

The fourth point on the continuum is labeled, the "Developmental Mode" wherein "students pursue excellence in a particular field by designing and implementing long-term programs of study, activity and practice" (1980, p. 136). There were many of Agassiz's graduate students who went on to leadership positions in the sciences after graduation. One example was Frederick Ward Putnam who eventually headed the Cambridge Peabody Museum and the American Museum of Natural History, as well as joined the faculty of the Penikese Island School for teachers. Another example of Agassiz's impact on the study of nature was his consultation with officials when Cornell University was founded. Many fine naturalists graduated from Cornell and they eventually influenced the field of nature study.

The last and closest point to engaged and active experiential learning on the scale of experientiality is the "Personal Growth Mode." At this level "students learn to understand themselves and their relationships with others. They accomplish the tasks presented by their stage of development toward maturity and make contributions to the lives of others" (1980, p. 136). This often occurs more easily after formal schooling ends. The entire life of Louis Agassiz best represents this point on the continuum. As a youth he set broad and ambitious goals and when he died at age 66 he had accomplished almost all of them. His life was not without pain, loss, disappointment, conflicts with some colleagues and students, and unmet objectives, but he did accomplish a great deal. His most notable achievement was his success as a teacher who recognized that the best kind of education was one based upon direct experiences with reality, whether in museums or outdoors where he believed the Creator had designed all of nature. His life inspired many teachers during his lifetime and after his passing.

At the turn of the 20th century, Agassiz was one of the most well-known naturalist teachers in the United States. When Northern Illinois State Normal School opened its doors to 173 aspiring, young teachers in 1899, Agassiz's plaster bust looked out on them from an auditorium wall. There were 11 other images on the walls where the students met an hour each day for general exercises. These included role models such as U.S. presidents, Washington, Lincoln, and Grant; Herbart, the father of pedagogy; Mann, who established the first Normal School; Froebel, the founder of Kindergartens; Comenius, creator of the first illustrated textbook; and Pestalozzi, Swiss educational reformer. The purpose for placing these people in the auditorium was to inspire the students as they prepared for the teaching profession (Northern Illinois University, 2004). This acknowledgement reflects the impact that Agassiz made on educational thought at that time and the importance placed on his ability to inspire great teaching and positive values in others.

Another example of Agassiz's influence on others was the formation of The Agassiz Association and creation of a regular nature column in *St. Nicholas: A Magazine for Young Folks* in 1880. "Local chapters of the association were set up all over the country and beyond, and by May 1883, the organization reported that it had five thousand members in places ranging from Brunswick, Maine, to Dallas, Texas, to Greeley, Colorado, to Valpariso, Chile" (Adkins, 2004, p. 37).

Agassiz saw both the unity of and the interrelationships among the academic divisions of knowledge. He recognized that the discipline of science was connected to others. He believed: "It cannot be too soon understood that science is one, and that whether we investigate language, philosophy, theology, history, or physics, we are dealing with the same problem, culminating in the knowledge of ourselves" (Agassiz in Cooper, 1945, pp. 83–84). Experiential educators also understand the significance of the unity of knowledge and are represented in all academic disciplines. Agassiz was an important pioneer in establishing a part of the philosophical and psychological foundations for present-day experiential educators. His teachings still live on.

After his death poet James Russell Lowell wrote:

The beauty of his better self lives on
    In minds he touched with fire, in many an eye
    He trained to Truth's exact severity;
    He was a Teacher: why be grieved for him
    Whose living word still stimulates the air?

(Lowell in Cooper, 1945, n. p.)

References

Academy of Natural Sciences in Philadelphia. (n.d.). *Louis Agassiz (1807–1873)*. Retrieved January 16, 2007, from http://www.ucmp.berkeley.edu/history/agassiz

Adkins, K. (2004). Foundation stones: Natural history for children. In S. I. Dobrin & K. B. Kidd (Eds.), *Wild things: Children's culture and ecocritism* (pp. 31–47). Detroit, MI: Wayne State University.

Agassiz, E. C. (Ed.). (1885). *Louis Agassiz: His life and correspondence by Agassiz and Agassiz*. Retrieved May 4, 2006, from http://www/gitemberg.org/catalog/world/readfile?fk_files=8929&pageno=58

Cooper, L. (1945). *Louis Agassiz as a teacher*. Ithaca, NY: Comstock.

Faber, D., & Faber, H. (1991). *Nature and the environment: Great lives*. New York: Charles Scribner's Sons.

Gibbons, M., & Hopkins, D. (1980). How experiential is your experience-based program? *The Journal of Experiential Education, 3*(1), 135–140.

Lurie, E. (1988). *Louis Agassiz: A life in science*. Baltimore: The Johns Hopkins University.

Northern Illinois University. (2004). *Altgeld hall: The dawn of a new century*. DeKalb, IL: Northern Illinois University Offices of Public Affairs, Publications, Media Imaging and Document Services.

11 Alexander von Humboldt
Expeditionary Scientist

Brad Daniel

Devoted from my earliest youth to the study of nature, feeling with enthusiasm the wild beauties of a country guarded by mountains and shaded by ancient forests, I experienced in my travels, enjoyments which have amply compensated for the privations inseparable from a laborious and often agitated life.

Alexander von Humboldt (1907, Vol. 2, p. ix)

Biography

Friedrich Wilhelm Heinrich Alexander von Humboldt, more commonly known simply as Alexander von Humboldt, is a seminal figure in the history of scientific exploration, although many in the modern era know relatively little about the man and his numerous achievements. He was born on September 14, 1769, into an aristocratic family in Berlin, Germany. Humboldt was a skilled observer of nature and scientific explorer, an expeditionary scientist who was particularly adept at recognizing patterns in the natural world through observation and experimentation. Rather than simply making observations, Humboldt was an accomplished scientist who was meticulous in demanding precise measurements. He usually could be found studying in a field or a desert or on a mountain slope. His expeditions explored many places, including Mexico, Europe, Siberia, Venezuela, Ecuador, Colombia, Peru, and Cuba.

Humboldt's life was spent traveling, experiencing, and researching various places around the globe while accumulating a diverse array of scientific knowledge. In his 76th year, he began the remarkable and daunting task of contemplating and summarizing his vast knowledge of the natural world and the universe. In his words, he sought "to develop the physical phenomena of the globe, and the simultaneous action of the forces that pervade the regions of space" (Humboldt, 1997, p. 23). This crowning achievement, titled Cosmos, was published in five volumes, the last of which was incomplete and was published posthumously in 1862. A lifelong bachelor, he died on May 6, 1859 at the age of 89.

The Scientist

Humboldt made significant contributions to a wide array of scientific fields, including volcanology, botany, geology, meteorology, geophysics, astronomy, anthropology, zoology, oceanography, climatology, geography, physiology, and mineralogy. He could also be described as an ecologist because of his emphasis on finding the interconnections among all aspects of the biotic (living) and abiotic (nonliving) worlds—despite the fact that Ernest Haeckel did not coin the term "ecology" until the mid-1860s. An integrative thinker, Humboldt's breadth of knowledge and experience allowed him to identify the interconnections among various scientific fields and bodies of knowledge. His work was foundational to the disciplines of physical geography, field meteorology, and biogeography. In fact, his work helped to lay the groundwork for relatively new fields, such as earth systems science.

During his life, Humboldt was known as a naturalist, world traveler, inventor, natural historian, and cosmic theorist. His cosmic theories connected nature's abiotic and biotic features and emphasized their interdependence. Humboldt desired to "recognize the general connections that link organic beings" and to "study the great harmonies of nature" (Sachs, 2006, p. 2).

Humboldt's contributions to natural science were as broad as his personal and professional interests. He was a scientific generalist, interested not only in understanding the nuances of each scientific field, but also the interconnections among them as observed in the natural world. Regardless of the topic, his approach was consistent. Whether exploring drainage basins of the Orinoco and Amazon River systems or climbing high Andean peaks, he was a keen observer of the natural world, noting not only individual plants and animals, but also natural patterns and processes. Over the course of his life, this ability allowed Humboldt to make many astute observations. He theorized on a wide variety of natural phenomena, including the periodicity of meteor showers, existence of alpine life/altitudinal zones, genesis and path of tropical storms, magnetic properties of rocks, problems of altitude sickness, impact of clear-cutting on soil erosion, origin of the earth's crust, and existence of isotherms (lines drawn on a weather map or chart linking all points of equal or constant temperature). He also reported on the relationship between volcanic formation/location and subterranean fault lines and fissures. He was not satisfied with simply making observations but, rather, subjected those ideas and observations to rigorous scientific measurement. His thorough and precise nature helped provide a basis for developing new ideas and revising old ones by encouraging shifts in current scientific thinking.

One rather well-known example of Humboldt's ability to observe, synthesize information, and theorize concerns the relationships among altitude, latitude, and temperature. He contributed influential research linking these three geographic factors to plant and animal distribution, and this research helped to lay the foundation for the field of biogeography. From his travels to the high Andes, Humboldt formulated a theory of the relationship between latitude and elevation with respect to temperature. He postulated that the average temperature drops one degree Fahrenheit for every degree of latitude traveled toward the pole and one degree Fahrenheit for every 300 feet rise in elevation. Thus, with respect to temperature, ascending a mountain 300 feet is nearly equivalent ecologically to traveling one degree North in latitude. This relationship between temperature and elevation and temperature and latitude, known as Humboldt's Rule, affects the distribution of plants and animals. For example, spruce-fir forests, which are more characteristic of Canada, grow above 5000–5500 feet in elevation in the North Carolina Mountains, but they grow at increasingly lower elevations as one travels higher in latitude. Humboldt's Rule has influenced research into life zones, field meteorology, and the location of biomes.

Doubtless, the work of Humboldt has deeply affected the careers of many; yet, most of the scientists, philosophers, artists, and writers that were influenced by Humboldt are much better known than he was. Those who have written about Humboldt have described him in a variety of ways. Charles Darwin once called him "the greatest scientific traveler who ever lived" and stated that Humboldt had inspired his own career in science (Helferich, 2004, p. xvii). Ralph Waldo Emerson wrote, "Humboldt was one of those wonders of the world who appear from time to time as if to show us the possibilities of the human mind, a universal man" (Sachs, 2006, p. 4). John Muir, no stranger to nature-oriented exploration, wrote, "How intensely I desire to be a Humboldt!" (Sachs, p. 27). Historian Aaron Sachs wrote of Humboldt, "It is quite possible that no other European had so great an impact on the intellectual culture of nineteenth-century America" (2006, p. 4). Humboldt supported, encouraged, and mentored young and rising scientists, such as Louis Agassiz, Asa Gray, and Joseph-Louis Gay-Lussac. He also encouraged the collaboration of scientists from all disciplines.

The fact that Alexander von Humboldt was one of the foremost natural scientists of the early 19th century is evidenced by the number and variety of things named after him. These include plants (e.g., a lily, an orchid, an oak, a willow, and several neotropical trees and shrubs), animals (e.g., a skunk, squid, dolphin, and penguin), natural features (e.g., an ocean current, a bay, a river, an asteroid, glaciers, and mountain ranges), towns and counties (in South Dakota, Tennessee, Kansas, Nebraska, Minnesota, Iowa, Nevada, California, and Saskatchewan, Canada), parks and forests (in Chicago, Cuba, and Peru), and institutions (e.g., the Humboldt Tropical Medicine Institute at Cayetano Heredia University in Lima, Peru, and Humboldt State University in Arcata, California).

Humboldt on Learning, Education, and Personal Growth

Alexander von Humboldt personified the axiom "travel broadens a person in a variety of ways." Traveling and exploring the natural world contributed to his personal development. Expeditionary science, as practiced by Humboldt, combined many elements useful for personal growth. These included the challenges afforded by subjecting oneself to new and unique experiences, the adventures of climbing high peaks in the Andes or boating Amazonian tributaries, the perspectives afforded by being exposed to different people and cultures from around the world, and the knowledge gained from exposure to diverse habitats, environments, flora, and fauna. As he traveled the outer landscape, new ideas were stimulated on his inner landscape. Humboldt wrote:

> The traveler experiences new sensations; he enjoys the happiness of seeing well around him. But this enjoyment, as we ourselves experienced, is not of long duration. There is doubtless something solemn and imposing in the aspect of a boundless horizon, whether viewed from the summits of the Andes or the highest Alps, amid the expanse of the ocean or in the vast plains of Venezuela and Tucuman. Infinity of space, as poets in every language say, is reflected within ourselves; it is associated with ideas of a superior order; it elevates the mind which delights in the calm of solitary meditation. (Humboldt & Bonpland, 1907, Vol. 3, pp. 78–79)

While travel creates anxiety for some, Humboldt thrived on new experiences and places. In *Cosmos*, he noted, "It is an inherent attribute of the human mind to experience fear, and not hope or joy, at the aspect of that which is unexpected and extraordinary" (Humboldt, 1997, Vol. 3, pp. 78–79).

Humboldt believed that scientific knowledge was to be used for the good of all people and that the benefits of such knowledge should be shared equally among all social groups, including indigenous people (Sachs, p. 6). His thinking was influenced greatly by the "deep feeling of awe and appreciation for the great variety of landscapes and cultures that his obsessive traveling enabled him to experience" (Sachs, p. 13). For Humboldt, a scientific expedition was not simply an endeavor to collect data, but to observe and define the problems of the total culture he visited. He was not shy about expressing his opinions and suggesting avenues for change. Such was the case with his opposition to slavery, which he shared publicly and often through many correspondences to then-President Thomas Jefferson. He wrote:

> Reason can everywhere enlighten reason; and its progress will be retarded in proportion as the men who are called upon to bring up youth, or govern nations, substitute constraint and force for that moral influence which can alone unfold the rising faculties, calm the irritated passions, and give stability to social order. (Humboldt & Bonpland, 1907, Vol. 2)

This passage illuminates many of the ideas held by Humboldt regarding human potential, intelligence, and education. He noted the similarities between people encountered on his travels and encouraged open, active inquiry as a means for mutual understanding, personal growth, and the fulfillment of human potential.

Humboldt had a desire to "see new things deeply, in context, and in connection to everything else he's seen and learned" (Sachs, 2006, p. 49). This led him to express concern over a variety of humanitarian, social, and political issues including:

> ... the deepening gulf between classes; the division of labor; the overspecialization of professions and, in the intellectual arena, the increasing separation between science and art; the constant tension surrounding race and ethnicity; the hardening of separate gender roles; explosive regional differences; and, especially, the apparent divide between civilization and nature. (Sachs, 2006, p. 30)

While Humboldt appreciated both the beauty and complexity of nature, the primary lens through which he sought to understand it was that of science. He encouraged scientists to see in the natural world those unifying patterns, properties, and processes that "cut through the apparent dissimilarities among phenomena in order to lay bare the underlying unity of all nature (Helferich, 2004, p. xvi). As Sachs has noted, "[T]heories of universal chaos teach us that certain global patterns, beautiful in their connectedness, do exist." Humboldt was one of the first scientists to begin to see and describe those patterns (Sachs, 2006, p. 51).

Many current scientific explorations and discussions attempt to identify unifying processes, including the pursuit of a "Grand Unified Theory of Science" and the naturalist E. O.Wilson's concept of consilience. Humboldt encouraged scientists not to look only at the individual threads in nature's tapestry, but to constantly examine how those threads are intertwined to produce the whole tapestry. He wrote, "The discovery of an unknown genus seemed to me far less interesting than an observation on the eternal ties which link the phenomena of life, and those of inanimate nature" (Sachs, 2006, p. 12).

Humboldt and Experiential Education

Experience clearly played a key role in Humboldt's education and in formulating his own philosophy of life. He continually searched for experiences with different cultures, new places, and emerging ideas. His personal narratives indicated that he valued new experiences as well as the feelings, ideas, and thoughts that were stimulated by such encounters. They helped to shape his thinking on a variety of topics from scientific discoveries to social issues, such as justice and equality.

Humboldt's approach to scientific expeditions mirrored his own philosophy of learning in which one must experience broadly and, then, integrate those experiences with other life experiences. He believed that "open minded travel was the key to science" (Sachs, 2006, p. 53). Humboldt lived out L. B. Sharp's famous exhortation, "That which can best be learned through experience dealing directly with native materials and life situations outside the school should there be learned" (1943, p. 363). Thus, the first step to understanding anything about the natural world is intense observation. As Helferich wrote, "[O]nly through travel, despite its accompanying risks, could a naturalist make the diverse observations necessary to advance science beyond dogma and conjecture" (2004, p. 27).

Humboldt's field observations led him to question and to discern interconnections among various components. Field-based observation, experimentation, and experiential learning formed the foundation of his pedagogy. To understand nature systemically requires one to go beyond mere reductionist experiments conducted in the classroom. Instead, it requires one to experience the rhythms and pulses of nature by immersing oneself within it, to observe it first-hand, and to see what new questions and observations arise as a result. Humboldt knew this and considered field experience extremely valuable to the student of science.

Expeditions, as employed in experiential education, offer significant learning experiences. The expedition structure incorporates many of the polarities involved in personal growth, including "the tensions of solitary reflection versus social interaction, of venturing out versus coming home, of the security of familiar terrain versus the thrill of unknown lands" (Daniel, 2003, p. 254). Although Humboldt undoubtedly confronted difficult circumstances during his expeditions, he was both consistent and courageous in meeting the related challenges. In addition to contributing to scientific knowledge, his expeditions played a crucial role in his own personal growth as he indicated when he wrote the following:

> The contemplation of the individual characteristics of the landscape, and of the confrontation of the land in any definite region of the earth, gives rise to a different source of enjoyment, awakening impressions that are more vivid, better defined, and more congenial to certain phases of the mind. At one time the heart is stirred by a sense of the grandeur of the face of nature, by the strife of the elements, or, as in Northern Asia, by the aspect of the dreary barrenness of the far-stretching steppes; at another time, softer emotions are excited by the contemplation of rich harvests wrested by the hand of man from the wild fertility of nature, or by the sight of human habitations raised beside some wild and foaming torrent. (Humboldt, 1907, Vol. 2, p. 25)

Humboldt's work and his personal life modeled many of the core ideas of experiential education. These include the value of stepping out of one's comfort zone by subjecting oneself to new and unique experiences with other cultures and places; the adventure and challenge afforded by exploring the natural world through various modes of travel; and the importance of reflecting on experience in order to draw out deeper meaning and to integrate that meaning with one's life. This cycle forms the foundation of experiential learning theory. Humboldt exemplified the understanding that, in order to fully realize the benefits of an experience, it must be processed in meaningful ways. He was thoughtful in his attempts to bring disparate events and knowledge together to create a cohesive whole. In fact, his expeditions followed a familiar three-step pattern (separation, initiation, and return) similar to that described in Joseph Campbell's mythic journey. A three-phase process is also discussed in transformation theory. These steps are described in various bodies of literature, including transpersonal psychology (Brown, 1989), vision questing (Foster & Little, 1992), and adventure therapy (Gass, 1993).

Campbell (1968) popularized the notion that personal transformation takes place in three steps, separation, initiation, and return. The steps involve creating a fundamental, repeating pattern that is common to many cultures and academic disciplines. The content of each step is extraordinarily similar. In stage one, the participant is separated from the familiar, such as family, home, and friends. In stage two, the participant is involved in some direct, existential experience, which, often, is new or unique. In stage three, the participant returns home to family, community, and friends. Each stage is experiential, engaging the heart, challenging the mind, and testing the spirit. Humboldt's expeditions followed this pattern. He wrote:

> ... perhaps they would return from that vicarious journey a bit changed—a little more adventurous, a little more trusting of their internal compass spurred on by an uncertain longing for what is distant and unknown, for whatever excited my fantasy: danger at sea, the desire for adventures, to be transported from a boring daily life to a marvelous world. (in Helferich, p. xxi)

Throughout the 19th and early 20th centuries, science became specialized into smaller and smaller subdivisions. As science expanded, fieldwork and the direct experience of the natural world lost its appeal to some; instead, greater emphasis was placed on learning science in the laboratories. In response to this trend, Theodore Roosevelt noted that "the average unfortunate student who has taken up scientific work in the colleges [has] been carefully trained not to do the field work which in the past has aided in producing men like Humboldt" (Sachs, p. 237). Additionally, this specialization makes it difficult for many students to understand the connections among the fields. Today, many schools, colleges, and universities have cut back or eliminated their field-based science programs due to concerns over risk, liability, fees, cost-effectiveness, and transportation issues.

Humboldt's life was one of discovery through direct experience. A large subset of experiential education deals with outdoor experiences, and Humboldt reminds us that outdoor experiences are holistic learning experiences because they provide opportunities for growth in a variety of ways. Not only was Humboldt a field scientist, he set a world altitude record while attempting to climb the Chimborazo volcano, Ecuador's highest summit, at over 19,200 feet. He did this while studying plant and animal distribution on high alpine slopes. His focus on personal experience, open-mindedness, and integrative thinking is a good example for today's experiential educators.

Implications for EE Philosophy

Sachs (2006) offers this overview of his motivations: "We may never completely understand our relationship to the world, but that relationship compels us to keep exploring" (p. 36).

Alexander von Humboldt was many things—scientist, educator, explorer, keen intellect, truth seeker, and careful observer. His life and accomplishments remind us to wonder as we wander, to ponder as we explore, to experience new things and integrate them with what we already know, and to consider the connections of the individual thing to the greater whole.

We can learn from Humboldt, who was a leader in experiential education before the field formally existed. His time spent in the natural world inspired him and others, whose appetites for scientific knowledge were stimulated and never fully sated. He continually questioned his assumptions and challenged his conclusions with precise measurements and a search for more physical data. Coupled with his precision, however, was a global mentality that sought to understand the interconnected patterns and processes inherent in nature and human nature. He had an uncanny ability to shift back and forth with seeming effortlessness between micro and macro scales. His exemplary life inspired others to live life fully and learn, looking not solely within the confines of individual disciplines, but also to consider it all—the inner-workings and inspirational "majesty and greatness of the creation" (Humboldt, p. 23). In essence, Alexander von Humboldt exemplified experiential education as he sought to understand the inhabitants and functions of the entire cosmos.

References

Brown, M. H. (1989). Transpersonal psychology: Facilitating transformation in outdoor experiential education. *Journal of Experiential Education, 12*(3), 47–56.

Campbell, J. (1968). *The hero with a thousand faces.* Princeton, NJ: Princeton University.

Daniel, B. (2003). *The life significance of a spiritually oriented, Outward Bound-type wilderness expedition.* Unpublished doctoral dissertation, Antioch New England Graduate School, Keene, NH.

Foster, S., & Little, M. (1992). *Vision quest: Personal transformation in the wilderness.* New York: Simon and Schuster.

Gass, M. A. (1993). *Adventure therapy: Therapeutic applications of adventure programming.* Dubuque, IA: Kendall/Hunt.

Helferich, G. (2004). *Humboldt's cosmos*. New York: Penguin.

Humboldt, A.V., & Bonpland, A. (1907*). Equinoctial regions of America: Personal narrative of travels to the equinoctial regions of America during the years 1799–1804* (T. Ross, Trans.; Vol. 2). London: George Bell & Sons. Retrieved July 1, 2007, from http://www.globusz.com/ebooks/Equinoctial2/00000015.htm

Humboldt, A. V., & Bonpland, A. (1907). *Equinoctial regions of America: Personal narrative of travels to the equinoctial regions of America during the years 1799–1804* (T. Ross, Trans.; Vol. 3). London: George Bell & Sons.

Humboldt, A. V. (1997). *Cosmos: A sketch of the physical description of the universe* (E. C. Otte, Trans.; Vols. 1–5). Baltimore, MD: Johns Hopkins University.

Sachs, A. (2006). *The Humboldt current: Nineteenth-century exploration and the roots of American environmentalism*. New York: Penguin.

Sharp, L. B. (1943). Outside the classroom. *The Educational Forum, 7*(4), 361–368.

12 Anna Botsford Comstock

Beyond Science—Learning About Self and Nature Through Field Experience

Janice L. Woodhouse and Christopher D. Wells

Anna Botsford Comstock (1854–1930) developed nature-study materials for elementary teachers to use in their classrooms and put considerable effort into convincing teachers and school administrators about the importance of teaching nature study. She is best known for writing the book, *Handbook of Nature-Study*[1] (Comstock, 1911/2010), which is a compilation of the nature-study lessons she and others developed. This chapter provides a brief historical overview of Comstock's career, a description of her philosophy and methods of teaching nature study, and a discussion of the experiential foundations of that practice.

Biography

Anna Botsford was born in a log cabin in Cattaraugus County, New York, during the post-pioneer stages of the development of the region. She was the only child of a father "skilled in the various industries of the farm" (Herrick & Smith, 1953, p. 56) and a Quaker mother who had a "passionate love of beauty in nature" (p. 57). Accounts of her childhood reveal a broad, experiential education, both formal and nonformal.

She described the places of her childhood with a detail for the sights, smells, sounds, and textures that reflects an astute ability to observe her surroundings. She lived connected to the landscape in all aspects of her life. During the Civil War, she helped make wound dressings, stockings, and wristlets for the troops (Herrick & Smith, 1953). She helped her mother with the keeping of the household: knitting, sewing, piecing a quilt, cleaning milk pails, and digging potatoes for the next day's meal. "My hours of great happiness were when [mother] could go into the fields and woods with me. She taught me the popular names of sixty or more flowers and of a dozen constellations.... Her delight over the beauty of a fern, a sunset, or a flower made me appreciate them too" (Herrick & Smith, 1953, p. 57).

Anna also recalled a period of her life at about age 10 when she was "naughty"—running away from a teacher she believed was "unfitted for teaching ... [and whose] discipline was capricious" (Herrick & Smith, 1953, p. 66). Other stories, from this time and later in life, reveal an intelligent woman who was clear about her beliefs and who stood firmly for her convictions.

As there was no public high school in Cattaraugus County, her parents boarded her at Chamberlain Institute and Female College,18 miles away in Randolph, New York. Anna recorded this experience as very positive, feeding her ambition for a university education.

Finding a Career and a Husband in the Woods at Cornell

By Needham's (1946a) account, Anna Botsford arrived at Cornell University in 1875 to study English and history, and opted to round out her studies by taking a course in invertebrate zoology. Cornell was only six years old then, and there were few women students and no women faculty. Because she enjoyed both the content of the zoology course and the way her instructor,

John Comstock, taught it, she then enrolled in his field and laboratory entomology course. During the entomology course, Botsford and Comstock began to take a number of field trips—many of which were not requirements of the course—to study insects living on the campus. She wrote to her mother, "Did I tell you that Mr. Comstock sits next to me at table at his own request? He is very pleasant and the very essence of kindness. This afternoon he invited me to go and gather moss and autumn leaves in the gorge. We had a charming time" (Herrick & Smith, 1953, p. 86).

Botsford and Comstock were married in October 1878. Throughout their 52-year marriage, they would meld their "love for nature with professional devotion to the study of living things" (Champagne & Klopfer, 1979, p. 300). While she continued her studies at Cornell University, Anna Comstock assisted her husband with his entomological research and publications; in her spare time, she completed her baccalaureate coursework and graduated in 1885 (Needham, 1946b). Like many women both then and now, Comstock had to balance personal and professional obligations and goals. Describing her weekly routine during the first years of their marriage, Comstock wrote, "My week is systematized as follows: Monday forenoon do the washing, afternoon, laboratory; Tuesday, laboratory; Wednesday forenoon, iron, afternoon, odds and ends of housework; Thursday, cook and bake, afterwards laboratory; Friday, laboratory; Saturday sweep and dust the house from top to bottom and mop the kitchen" (Herrick & Smith, 1953, p. 104). She did not complain about the distractions of housekeeping, she simply declared, "I had a conviction that in order to know how to manage a house, I ought to do all the work myself" (p. 101).

In an effort to produce high-quality illustrations for a textbook that her husband was writing, she took a course in wood engraving at Cooper Union in New York City, where she trained as a student of master-artist, wood engraver John P. Davis. Her work as a wood engraver was highly respected, and, as a result, she was later elected to the American Society of Wood Engravers (Needham, 1946b). This skill and her work at Cornell with John led to involvement in a project that would be a cornerstone of the Nature-Study Movement.

How Ya Gonna Keep 'em Down on the Farm?

During the 1890s, farming for many in New York State became unprofitable, resulting in a large migration of young people from the farms to the cities. Needham (1946b) describes a nature-study project, developed by the faculty of Cornell's College of Agriculture and carried out in part by Anna Comstock, to interest future farmers in the value of living and working in a rural environment and to make farming more economically feasible. The project included the introduction of nature study as a subject to be taught in rural schools and the formation of Junior Naturalist Clubs. Anna Comstock, College of Agriculture faculty, and others wrote a series of publications called *Nature-Study Leaflets*[2] to be used by the teachers in rural schools. Comstock used her skills as a wood engraver to illustrate the leaflets and also organized classes at Cornell to train rural teachers to lead nature-study classes. She spoke about the value of nature study at teachers' meetings throughout the state of New York and at universities in New York, Virginia, and California. Comstock concurrently developed a very successful and highly respected correspondence course for teachers who were widely scattered geographically. The course trained them to teach their students about nature through the direct observation of natural phenomena (Kohlstedt, 2005).

In 1898, Comstock received an appointment as Assistant Professor of Nature Study in the Cornell University Extension Division and was the first woman given the title of professor at Cornell (Comstock, 1911/2010). However, a year later, in response to the objections of certain trustees to having a woman professor, she was demoted to lecturer. Finally, in 1913, her professional title was restored. She was one of the first four women admitted to the Sigma Xi national honor society for the sciences in 1888 (Kappa Alpha Theta Notables, n.d.) and was named one of

America's 12 greatest living women in a 1923 survey by the League of Women Voters (National Wildlife Federation, n.d.). In 1930, Hobart College honored her with the degree of Doctor of Humane Letters (Herrick & Smith, 1953). She continued to teach at Cornell through the summer session of 1930, conducting classes in her home two weeks before her death on August 24. Comstock was inducted into the Conservation Hall of Fame in 1988 (National Wildlife Federation, n.d.).

An Experience-Based Pedagogy of Place

Anna Botsford Comstock's contribution to the Nature-Study Movement, and thus to the foundations of experiential education, is most visible in the now classic, 930-page *Handbook of Nature-Study*, first published in 1911. It has gone through 24 editions, has been translated into eight languages, was most recently reprinted in 2010, is used as a college text, and is available at popular bookstores. The *Handbook of Nature-Study* contains hundreds of lessons about animals, plants, the earth, and sky. The first part of the book provides an explanation of the goals and benefits of nature study for the teacher and the student, suggests the incorporation of instructional technology such as microscopes and field glasses, and describes ways to relate nature study to other subjects such as geography, language arts, history, and arithmetic.

Anna Botsford Comstock was a student of Liberty Hyde Bailey,[3] and therefore the foundations of her beliefs about nature study mirrored many of his. However, through spending years working directly with teachers in the public schools, she developed her own philosophy about what nature study should include, how it should be taught, and how it should be experienced by the student.

Comstock was a pioneer in putting into writing and disseminating the content and practice of working with students in the outdoors—exploring their "place" and using direct experience to make meaning of the world around them. Although the terms "experiential" and "place-based" were not used to discuss teaching methods during Comstock's time, they are inherently a part of the approach she used and advocated. In the following section, we examine Comstock's writings as they reflect several principles of experiential education practice (Association of Experiential Education, 1995). We do this cautiously, without making assumptions about her intentions, realizing that we risk amplifying (and possibly distorting) the significance of her work.

Principle: The educator recognizes and encourages spontaneous opportunities for learning (Association of Experiential Education, 1995).

Comstock (1911/2010) believed that nature study should be taught in a way that makes it interesting to students and provides them with a hands-on opportunity for learning. She felt that occasionally there is a need to use posters and blackboard drawings to explain the details of things found in nature, but that the most valuable learning comes from direct observation of nature in the field.

She was committed to the principle that "the time to study any living thing is when you chance to find it" (Comstock, 1904, p. 57). It should not be made a drill. The lesson should be "short and sharp" (Comstock, 1911/2010, p. 6), 10-minutes to a half-hour in length, and be focused on simple observation of some life form found in its context.

Anna Comstock explained in the preface to the *Handbook* that each lesson in the book was written independently over a number of years, and that as a result, they make no reference to one another. No plan was ever undertaken to relate the lessons to one another since, in Comstock's opinion, each lesson should be taught independently as the opportunity arises to make observations in nature, rather than as part of a planned series of lessons.

Principle: The learner is actively engaged in posing questions, investigating, experimenting, being curious, solving problems, assuming responsibility, being creative, and constructing meaning (Association of Experiential Education, 1995).

The primary method for teaching each lesson in the *Handbook* begins with background material to educate teachers about the topic. Then, once they are familiar with the subject matter of the lesson, teachers are to share the "leading thought"[4] given in the lesson with their students. Students should then be given an opportunity to observe the phenomena suggested in the lesson and to use those observations to develop an understanding of the leading thought. The lessons encourage direct observation and experimentation with local phenomena. "Make the lesson an investigation and make the pupils feel that they are investigators" (Comstock, 1911/2010, p. 23).

To help the student feel like an investigator and make meaning from their investigations, questions are posed in each lesson to help the student connect what is observed within a broader context of the greater ecology. Although Comstock did not use such language to express her thoughts, or use the terms "habitat" or "ecology," these concepts are implied. For example, she explains, "The child through nature-study … learns about the life of the bird, whether it be a chicken, an owl, or a bobolink; he knows how each bird gets its food and what its food is, where it lives, where it nests, and its relation to other living things" (Comstock, 1911/2010, p. 21), including the human aspects of the environment.

Most of the questions posited in the lessons are to help students sharpen their observations and reflect upon their experience. A typical example comes from a lesson about the red-winged blackbird: "What is the song of the redwing? Describe the way he holds his wings and tail when singing, balanced on a reed or some other swamp grass. Does he show off his epaulets when singing? What note does he give when he is surprised or suspicious? When frightened?" (Comstock, 1911/2010, p. 119). These questions stimulate the child to pose other questions. They also stimulate curiosity and creative thought: "Nature study cultivates the child's imagination since there are so many wonderful and true stories that he may read with his own eyes, which affect his imagination as much as does fairy lore" (p. 1). Comstock knew this was possible from her own experience as a child and from working with children and teachers. The Comstocks never had children of their own, and she never had a course in curriculum development or instruction, yet she learned about both through her many visits to elementary schools throughout western New York State when she guided nature-study lessons with children and teachers (Champagne & Klopfer, 1979). This direct experience in the classroom helped her to develop her approach: "Many methods were tried and finally there was evolved the method followed in [*the Handbook of Nature-Study*]" (Comstock, 1911/2010, p. viii). The longevity of the *Handbook* demonstrates the reliability of her perceptions and predictions about how children learn when given thoughtful guidance.

Problem-solving skills are encouraged through questions such as these posed for the study of birds' nests in winter: "Of what materials is the lining made, and how are they arranged?… How are the materials of the nest held together, that is are they woven, plastered, or held in place by the environment?" (Comstock, 1911/2010, p. 47). These questions require observation *and* conjecture: Connecting what is seen with what is imagined would result if certain elements interact. In other words, what could make this happen?

Creativity is stimulated by the consistent inclusion of poetry in the lessons. In addition, Comstock wrote about the integration of nature study with language arts and drawing. She disagreed with those who claimed that children disliked English writing exercises. She declared this was not the case when children wrote about something they had experienced and "when they are interested in the subject and write about it to a person who is interested" (Comstock, 1911/2010, p. 16).

Comstock's education taught her a conventionally scientific approach to understanding nature. Her thesis at Cornell was "The Fine Anatomy of the Interior of the Larva of *Corydalus cornutus*" [a hellgrammite—the larval form of the Dobson Fly] (Herrick & Smith, 1953, p. 149). She spent much of her life with her husband in the field examining, identifying, and discovering insect species. However, she did not believe that learning scientific names, limiting students to a scientific articulation of experience, or drawing exact re-creations of natural phenomena were the best ways to keep children engaged and learning: "We might as well declare that a child should not speak unless he put his words into poetry as to declare that he should not draw because his drawings are not artistic" (Comstock, 1911/2010, p. 17). She also was critical of the belief that nature study and science were synonymous inquiries. Indeed, she believed that "error in this respect has caused many a teacher to abandon nature-study and many a child to hate it" (p. 5). The nature-study lessons encourage a learning style that today is called "free expression" of experience, without grading that expression against imposed criteria. At the same time, her expectations of what could or should be learned were bold—even rigorous. She apologized for the length (930 pages) of the *Handbook*, but noted, "it does not contain more than any intelligent country child of twelve should know of his environment" (p. xi).

Principle: Experiential learning occurs when carefully chosen experiences are supported by reflection, critical analysis, and synthesis (Association for Experiential Education, 1995).

Besides the questions included in each lesson that guided investigation and reflection, Comstock encouraged the use of field notebooks. This field notebook could be any blank book that would fit in a pocket. Comstock believed a field notebook should not be compulsory, but an option for students to use in recording their observations. The student should be encouraged to write, or draw, or collect, and record freely their experience and their thoughts about that experience. The field notebook "should be considered the personal property of the child and should never be criticized by the teacher except as a matter of encouragement; for the spirit in which the notes are made is more important than the information they cover" (Comstock, 1911/2010, p. 13).

Principle: The results of the learning are personal and form the basis for future experience and learning (Association for Experiential Education, 1995).

Comstock believed that knowledge of the natural world would enable the learner to be more self-reliant and thus, a better problem-solver. She believed that nature study has multiple purposes: that it should provide practical and helpful knowledge "so that [the child] is not so helpless in the presence of natural misfortune and disasters" (Comstock, 1911/2010, p. 1). "The object of the nature teacher should be to cultivate in the children powers of accurate observation and to build up within them understanding" (p. 1). She also believed that this study would cultivate the imagination, develop a regard for what is true and the power to express it, and develop a love of the beautiful and a "sense of companionship with life out-of-doors and an abiding love of nature" (p. 2).

Other personal benefits of Comstock's approach to teaching nature study included mental and physical health. Comstock was aware of the relationship between physical activity and health: "This is an age of nerve tension, and the relaxation which comes from the comforting companionship found in woods and fields is without doubt, the best remedy for this condition" (Comstock, 1911/2010, p. 2). Similarly, she advocated such time in nature for the teachers whose "nerves were at such a tension that with one more thing to do they must fall apart" (p. 3). Comstock was quite sympathetic with this stress condition and spent time teaching and writing about how nature study would address this problem, concluding that "without planning or going on a far voyage, she [the teacher] has found health and strength" (p. 3).

Her claims about the broader benefits of experiential and place-based education may have been more intuitive and based on observation and experience than on careful scientific analysis. Recent research validates these claims (e.g., DeLay, 1996; Finkel & Monk, 1995; Louv, 2005; Taylor & Kuo, 2006; see also the Children & Nature Network Web site).

Implications for EE Philosophy

We have discussed the relevance of Comstock's practice to some of the principles of experiential education. It is also important to emphasize her recognition of the impediments that teachers faced with regard to teaching nature study and using experiential education methods. Comstock noted, that at the time her book was written, nature study had not become a core part of the curriculum in elementary schools because teachers were, as a whole, not trained to teach it, and they did not have adequate time for it in their teaching schedules. It is interesting to note that 100 years later, teachers still face the same challenges regarding teaching children about their environment (King, 2002; Parlo & Butler, 2007).

Comstock's focus on the teacher as nature educator—a unique contribution at the time—is exemplified by the care she took to use common, rather than scientific, terminology when writing the *Handbook*, thus making each of the lessons usable to the untrained teacher who did not know what there was to see in nature or how to find out. She used her talent to create a bridge between the expert naturalist/scientist and the teacher who may not have had much training in any of the sciences. Comstock criticized an educational system that locked teachers and students into teaching and learning about phenomena for which they had no passion. She believed that "naughtiness in school is a result of the child's lack of interest in his work, augmented by the physical inaction that results from an attempt to sit quietly" (Comstock, 1911/2010, p. 4).

It is impossible to measure the full impact of Anna Botsford Comstock's work or to exact the philosophical basis of that work. She did not discuss her beliefs and methods in terms of a philosophy. That was not her orientation. She was educated at a time when the pragmatism of Locke, Rousseau, Darwin, Pierce, and James may have guided the curriculum (Ozman & Craver, 1995); her approach to educating teachers and students certainly reflects attributes of pragmatism: centrality of experience, an emphasis on process, and doing what works best to achieve desired ends. Comstock made a path for others to follow; she focused on what was wanted and needed in the contexts of the time. It is the challenge and opportunity for those who followed her path to assess the philosophical underpinnings of her work and the foundations it laid for education beyond the classroom.

We do know that Comstock trained hundreds of rural teachers in nature study each year from 1898 until 1930 (Champagne & Klopfer, 1979; Gordon, 1956). We know that her focus on rural schools soon broadened to include urban areas (Hitt, 1961). We know that, in some years between 1898 and 1908, there were over 800 Junior Naturalist Clubs, an outgrowth of Comstock's work developed under the direction of John W. Spencer. These clubs enrolled between 20,000 and 35,000 students annually (Gordon, 1956) and were formed in Egypt, England, France, India, Japan, and the United States (Hitt, 1961). We know that nature study and many of its aims and recommended methodologies still survive, although the field is seldom called by that name. We know that current programs in outdoor and environmental education have roots in the Nature-Study Movement (Knapp, 2002; Minton, 1980; Palmer, 1957). We know that experiential education is imbedded in both of those fields.

Comstock was a leader in structuring learning experiences for particular and well-articulated outcomes, although she lived during an era when education was not examined as empirically as it is today. Thus, to claim that her work helped lay the foundation of experiential education is an exercise in connecting the dots between her philosophy and practice and today's theory—dots that are blurry and inexact. However, certain truths are clear and frame the main point of this chapter: that, although Comstock did not use the term "experiential education" in her writing, it was what she advocated and practiced. The story we tell in this chapter invites consideration of that observation.

It is also notable that the American Nature Study Society (ANSS), founded in 1908, became the leading organization serving and strengthening the Nature-Study Movement. Bailey and Comstock both served as presidents of the organization. This society still exists today and maintains national and international partnerships with other nature-study and environmental education groups. Congruent with the school reform visions of the pioneers of this movement, ANSS still stresses "student-centered learning using hands-on teaching materials and field experiences"

(American Nature Study Society, n.d.). The organization continues to advocate that nature study is a bridge "between the natural sciences, social sciences, and humanities, and grounds them in real-world experiences" (American Nature Study Society, n.d.).

Notes

1. There is great discrepancy about whether or not the term "nature study" should be hyphenated. In this chapter, the words "nature study" are hyphenated when used as an adjective (e.g., nature-study lessons), but not when used as a noun (e.g., methods of teaching nature study). Exceptions to these rules appear in the text when the terms are used in quotations or references in prior publications; in those cases, the authors defer to the way the term was written in those publications.
2. The *Nature-Study Leaflets* were first called *Teachers' Leaflets: For Use in the Rural Schools*, and were issued quarterly by Liberty Hyde Bailey under the auspices of the Experiment Station Extension. The leaflets became a state-supported responsibility of the College of Agriculture at Cornell in 1896. The first leaflet (No. 1), "How a Squash Plant Gets Out of the Seed," was written by Bailey. The leaflets were printed for over 50 years (Gordon, 1956).
3. Bailey, a botanist, was invited to Cornell to give a series of lectures in 1887. The U.S. Congress had recently passed the Hatch Act authorizing an annual appropriation of $15,000 to each state for agricultural experimentation. Cornell decided to use the funds to establish a chair of practical and experimental horticulture, and offered the position to Bailey. Bailey, raised on a farm, always saw agriculture as an academic discipline. He also was committed to making the science of living things comprehendible to nonacademic people. To him, the fundamental purpose of education was to serve the people, and he believed that the resolution of agricultural problems was as important as cultural, ethical, and legal issues. Through the extension movement and its bulletins, lectures, demonstrations, and farm visits, Bailey built support for his programs among New York State farmers and in the state legislature (Cornell University Library, n.d.). Bailey was one of the early leaders of the Nature-Study Movement. For more information about the involvement of Bailey and Comstock in the Nature-Study Movement, see Bailey (1904a, b) and Knapp and Woodhouse (2006).
4. Comstock used the term "leading thought." Today, we would call this a main concept. For example, "The earthworm is a creature of the soil and is of great economic importance" (Comstock, 1911/2010, p. 424).

References

American Nature Study Society (ANSS). (n.d.). Leading the way to the future through environmental education. Retrieved April 17, 2006, from http://hometown.aol.com/anssonline

Association of Experiential Education (AEE). (1995, February). AEE adopts definition. *The AEE Horizon*, *15*, 1.

Bailey, L. H. (1904a). The nature-study movement. In State of New York — Department of Agriculture (Ed.), *Cornell nature-study leaflets: Being a selection, with revision, from the teachers' leaflets, home nature-study lessons, junior naturalist monthlies and other publications from the College of Agriculture, Cornell University, Ithaca, N. Y., 1896–1904* (pp. 21–29). Albany, NY: J. B. Lyon.

Bailey, L. H. (1904b). What is nature-study? In State of New York – Department of Agriculture (Ed.), *Cornell nature-study leaflets: Being a selection, with revision, from the teachers' leaflets, home nature-study lessons, junior naturalist monthlies and other publications from the College of Agriculture, Cornell University, Ithaca, N.Y., 1896–1904* (pp. 11–20). Albany, NY: J. B. Lyon.

Champagne, A. B., & Klopfer, L. E. (1979). Pioneers of elementary-school science: II. Anna Botsford Comstock. *Science Education*, *63*(3), 299–322.

Children & Nature Network. (2010). Retrieved May 15, 2010, from http://www.childrenandnature.org

Comstock, A. B. (1904). Suggestions for nature-study work. In State of New York – Department of Agriculture (Ed.), *Cornell nature-study leaflets: Being a selection, with revision, from the teachers' leaflets, home nature-study lessons, junior naturalist monthlies and other publications from the College of Agriculture, Cornell University, Ithaca, N.Y., 1896–1904* (pp. 55–79). Albany, NY: J. B. Lyon.

Comstock, A. B. (2010). *Handbook of nature-study* (24th ed.). Ithaca, NY: Comstock Publishing. (Original work published 1911)

Cornell University Library. (n.d.). Liberty Hyde Bailey: A man for all seasons. Retrieved October 23, 2007, from http://rme.library.cornell.edu/bailey/cornella/index.html

DeLay, R. (1996). Forming knowledge: Constructivist learning and experiential education. *The Journal of Experiential Education, 19*(2), 76–81.

Finkel, D. L., & Monk, S. (1995). The design of intellectual experience. In K. Warren, M. Sakofs, & J. S. Hunt, Jr. (Eds.), *The theory of experiential education* (pp. 259–274). Dubuque, IA: Kendall/Hunt.

Gordon, E. L. (Ed.). (1956, Fall). A chronology of Cornell nature-study leaflets, 1896 to 1956. *Cornell Nature-Study Leaflets 1896 to 1956, 50*(1), 4–8.

Herrick, G. W., & Smith, R. G. (Eds.). (1953). *The Comstocks of Cornell: John Henry Comstock and Anna Botsford Comstock. An autobiography by Anna Botsford Comstock.* Ithaca, NY: Comstock Publishing.

Hitt, J. E. (1961, Summer). The development of nature and science education at Cornell. *The Cornell Plantations, 17*(2), 19–24.

Kappa Alpha Theta Notables. (n.d.). Retrieved November 11, 2007, from http://kappaalphatheta.org/learnabouttheta/whatistheta/notablethetas

King, R. M. (2002, Spring). Managing teaching loads—and finding time for reflection and renewal. *Inquiry, 7*(1), 11–21.

Knapp, C. E. (2002). Outdoor and environmental education. *Encyclopedia of education* (2nd ed.) (pp. 1831–1835). New York: MacMillan.

Knapp, C. E., & Woodhouse, J. L. (2006). The nature study movement: A revolt to promote school reform. *Thresholds in Education, 32*(3), 20–25.

Kohlstedt, S. G. (2005). Nature, not books: Scientists and the origins of the nature-study movement in the 1890s. *Isis, 96*(3), 324–352.

Louv, R. (2005). *Last child in the woods: Saving our children from nature-deficit disorder.* Chapel Hill, NC: Algonquin Books of Chapel Hill.

Minton, T. G. (1980). *The history of the nature-study movement and its role in the development of environmental education.* Unpublished doctoral dissertation, University of Massachusetts, Amherst.

National Wildlife Federation. (n.d.). Conservation Hall of Fame. Retrieved November 11, 2007, from http://www.nwf.org/about/inductees/comstock/cfm

Needham, J. G. (1946a). The lengthened shadow of a man and his wife — I. *The Scientific Monthly, 62*(2), 140–150.

Needham, J. G. (1946b). The lengthened shadow of a man and his wife — II. *The Scientific Monthly, 62*(3), 219–229.

Ozman, H. A., & Craver, S. M. (1995). *Philosophical foundations of education* (5th ed.). Englewood Cliffs, NJ: Prentice-Hall.

Palmer, E. L. (1957). Fifty years of nature study and the American Nature Study Society. *Nature Magazine, 50*(11), 473–480.

Parlo, A. T., & Butler, M. B. (2007). Impediments to environmental education instruction in the classroom: A post-workshop inquiry. *Journal of Environmental & Science Education, 2*(1), 32–37.

Taylor, A. F., & Kuo, F. E. (2006). Is contact with nature important for healthy child development? State of the evidence. In C. Spencer & M. Blades (Eds.), *Children and their environments: Learning, using, and designing spaces* (pp. 124–140). Cambridge, UK: Cambridge University Press.

13 Charles A. Eastman and Luther Standing Bear

Two Early Indian Writers and Educators

Clifford E. Knapp

In selecting Charles A. Eastman (Ohiyesa) (1858–1939) and Luther Standing Bear (Ota Kte) (1868?–1939), I knew that these two men were influential forebears in the field of experiential education. Both were members of the Sioux Nation, but were from different bands. They both lived at the Pine Ridge Agency in the early 1890s and probably knew each other (R. Ellis as cited in Standing Bear, 1978). As authors, Eastman was assisted by his wife on nine books (Graber, 1978) and Standing Bear by E. A. Brininstool, author and historian, and Dr. Melvin R. Gilmore, University of Michigan Ethnology curator (R. Ellis in Standing Bear, 1978). Because these two men were contemporary lecturers and authors whose books are still in print and available, it was difficult to choose one as more important than the other. Both men wrote about similar topics and wanted to provide the dominant White culture with an accurate picture of Native Americans, as they knew them. During their lifetimes, they lectured widely and influenced various educational systems and non-formal, youth outdoor programs.

The fact that both men died in 1939, the year I was born, made my selection of them more personal as well as somewhat mystical, because although I am not Native American by birth, I consider myself an educational bridge builder between the Native and dominant cultures. I am dedicated to learning about Native ways through direct experiences and educating others about the importance of Indian contributions to the world. The purpose of this chapter is to illustrate how Eastman and Standing Bear influenced the theory and practice of what was later known as experiential education.

Charles A. Eastman (Ohiyesa)

Ohiyesa was a Santee Sioux, born in 1858 into an Eastern band that spoke the Dakota dialect of the Siouan language. Some people object to calling the tribe the "Sioux" because it was a derogatory name (Naduesiu means lesser snakes) given by their enemies, the Ojibway, and shortened by the French (Wilson, 1983). Others accept this historical name and are not troubled by how they were named.

On a cold February day in Redwood Falls, Minnesota, a fifth and last baby was born to Mary Nancy Eastman (Wakantankanwin) and Many Lightnings (Ite Wakanhdi Ota). Did the fact that Ohiyesa's mother and father had Indian names containing the word, "Wakan," meaning holy or sacred, bless this baby in a special way? First named, Hakadah (The Pitiful Last), the baby entered the world at a time when Indians were being chased from the Midwest by land hungry European settlers. At the age of four, during a midsummer feast in 1862 after a victorious game of lacrosse, a medicine man gave this boy a new name, Ohiyesa (The Winner)—a name he kept even after he obtained his English one (Wilson, 1983). The baby's mother was a Santee/European mixed-blood and his father was a Wahpeton Sioux. Both parents came from a long line of tribal leaders (Wilson, 1983). Shortly after Ohiyesa's birth, his mother died and his paternal grandmother, a Native traditionalist, raised him.

Growing up as a Santee Dakota in those days was difficult. Ohiyesa recalls: "It is wonderful that any children grew up through all the exposures and hardships that we suffered in those days" (1971, p. 16). When food was plentiful he ate well; when drought or other conditions were harsh, he went hungry. He told of his uncle bringing home two captive Ojibway women after a fight (Eastman, 1971). There were ample opportunities for him to learn many of the skills of living close to Nature. Ohiyesa writes: "It is commonly supposed that there is no systematic education of their children among the aborigines of this country. Nothing could be farther from the truth" (1971, p. 41). Some of his education came through sitting by the fire listening to stories that taught lessons of how to live and what to value. Other teachings came from playing games and doing wood-craft—activities that developed the physical and mental skills necessary to survive in a mostly hunting and gathering culture. "Our sports were molded by the life and customs of our people; indeed, we practiced only what we expected to do when grown" (Eastman, 1971, pp. 53–54).

Ohiyesa stated: "Religion was the basis of all Indian training" (1971, p. 49). At the age of eight he was formally introduced to the "Great Mystery" or Creator. It was the Santee custom to sacrifice something of great value to the Great Mystery. Ohiyesa's grandmother suggested that he sacrifice his beloved dog as his first offering. After considerable thought, preparation, and pain, the boy killed his dog and was initiated by a prayer into his first spiritual act as a young man. His grandmother asked the Great Mystery to "behold this little boy and bless him! Make him a warrior and a hunter as great as thou didst make his father and grandfather" (Eastman, 1971, pp. 95–96). Some would say that her prayer was answered as Ohiyesa grew to be a man, although he had to be a warrior and hunter in a different sense to survive in White society. He had been introduced to a spiritual path that he would never forget.

After the Sioux Uprising of 1862, the U. S. Government removed the Santee Sioux from Minnesota and sent them to Dakota Territory. Ohiyesa escaped to Canada and was separated from his immediate family. Believing that his father was hanged because of the uprising, Ohiyesa was adopted by his uncle. It was then discovered that his father was imprisoned. His father and brother later converted to Christianity and Ohiyesa rejoined his father after a 10-year absence and settled in Flandreau, South Dakota (Wilson, 1983).

Because of the influences of his father and brother, Ohiyesa also converted to the Christian faith, and for the first time, took the name of Charles Alexander Eastman, a name chosen from a book of names given to him by a minister. At the age of 15 his father enrolled him in a mission school at Flandreau, and he gradually was acculturated into the White world. He wore White men's clothing, had his long hair cut, and learned to speak English. This was a time of deep turmoil for Eastman because most of what he learned about the world from his grandmother and uncle appeared in conflict with what he learned at school and from his father and brother. He entered into what the dominant culture called "civilization" and in the process questioned his "savage" Indian upbringing. He wrote, "The subject occupied my thought more and more, doubtless owing to my father's decided position on the matter; while, on the other hand, my grandmother's view of this new life was not encouraging" (Wilson, 1983, p. 21).

After attending the Flandreau mission school for two years, he enrolled at the Santee Normal Training School in Nebraska where his brother, John, worked. There he improved his English and learned to read and translate his native tongue. He studied there for two years before attending Beloit College in Beloit, Wisconsin. During his three years there, Eastman experienced discrimination and great difficulty in dealing with a different way of thinking. Later, he was able to mesh these two worldviews. For example, he came to believe that there was no difference between the Christian God and Wakan Tanka, the Great Spirit of the Sioux. He also used his English and Santee names interchangeably. He said, "I believe ... that the spirit of Christianity and of our ancient religion is essentially the same" (Wilson, 1983, p. 87).

After leaving Beloit in 1879, he learned that a friend had arranged for him to attend Knox College in Galesburg, Illinois. There, Eastman regularly interacted with White women for the first time. He said that he found the "paleface maidens … very winning and companionable" (Wilson, 1983, p. 25). He later married a White woman. He was there from the fall of 1879 to the spring of 1881. While at Knox, he decided to become a physician and attend Dartmouth College in New Hampshire. Before attending, he enrolled at nearby Kimball Union Academy for a year and a half to improve some academic deficiencies. At Dartmouth, he took Latin, French, Greek, German, linguistics, and English over a four-year span. "Other subjects included zoology, botany, chemistry, physics, natural history, philosophy, geometry, political science, and history. He distinguished himself in all his studies and graduated with honors, but his successes went beyond the classroom" (Wilson, 1983, p. 32). He played football, baseball, and tennis, boxed, and was a distance runner. After receiving a BS degree, he entered Boston University School of Medicine. After a total of 17 years of schooling, he finally became a doctor in 1890 and then returned to Pine Ridge Agency in South Dakota to earn an annual salary of $1,200 (Wilson, 1983).

One of Dr. Eastman's first traumatic assignments was to care for injured Sioux, victims of a military clash at Wounded Knee Creek. Eastman was severely shaken by the incident and questioned the Christian ideals of the Whites. He and his future wife, Elaine Goodale, helped to care for the victims of this clash of cultures. Another disturbing event was Eastman's disagreements with the Pine Ridge acting Indian agent, George Brown. Over the course of more than a year, Eastman and his wife were in almost constant conflict with Brown. In the end Eastman was asked to resign in January 1893. He decided to take his wife and young daughter to St. Paul, Minnesota to set up a private practice. Charles and Elaine eventually had five daughters and one son (Wilson, 1983).

After only a year in private practice, Eastman accepted a job as Indian secretary of the International Committee from the Young Men's Christian Association (YMCA). After almost a year of travel studying Indian education in the United States and Canada, Eastman wrote a report recommending that the YMCA improve its Christian mission with Indians on reservations and in Indian schools. He advocated Bible studies in combination with exercise or participation in wholesome sports such as lacrosse and pony polo as ways to develop young Indian minds and bodies. After two years Eastman experienced a degree of success, but did not convince all Indian tribes that Christianity was the best religion to adopt. An old chief criticized the White man's disrespect for nature and God and decided: "We shall still follow the old trail" (Wilson, 1983, p. 86). After experiencing some success with the YMCA, Eastman decided to resign, and on April 1, 1898, he went to Washington, D.C. to pursue other ways of helping his people. He encountered financial and political difficulties there and in 1899 left for a brief job at Carlisle Indian School, a federal government residential school in Pennsylvania, as an outing agent. This job entailed arranging for Indian pupils to live with nearby Christian families and attend the public schools with the local children for short periods. He saw the value of experiential learning early in his career. In 1900 he became the government physician at Crow Creek Agency (Sioux) in South Dakota for nearly two and one-half years.

On March 5, 1903, after a series of intense conflicts with the Indian agent, Eastman moved back to Minnesota and accepted a position revising the Sioux allotment rolls. This involved changing Sioux names to names more closely resembling those given to Whites. After a short stay in Minnesota, Eastman moved his family to Amherst, Massachusetts, where he continued the project. He lived in Amherst until 1919. When he finished the project in 1909, he had revised about 25,000 Sioux names. After 1909 Eastman became an author and lecturer and devoted much of his time to these activities (Wilson, 1983).

Eastman's writings took three forms: autobiography, Indian culture, and Indian and White relations. *Indian Boyhood* (1902) covered his traditional Indian life up to the age of 15. His book, *From the Deep Woods to Civilization* (1916) covered his schooling and work until about 1915. In

The Soul of the Indian (1911) he described the "religious life of the typical American Indian as it was before he knew the white man" (Eastman, 1980, pp. ix–x). In all, he wrote 11 books and numerous articles (Wilson, 1983).

In 1910, Eastman began to work with the Boy Scouts of America and later the Campfire Girls of America. Ernest Thompson Seton, founder of another youth organization (The Woodcraft League), appointed Eastman (also Luther Standing Bear) to a committee of advisors consisting of Indians and Whites (Seton & Seton, 1966). Keller, one of Seton's biographers, described Eastman as "probably Seton's most effective instructor in the art of communal living [and] the Indian way of life" (1984, p. 164). In 1915 the Eastman family opened a girls' summer camp in New Hampshire. The next year, they expanded it to include boys and continued the camp until 1921.

In 1923 Eastman became a U. S. Indian inspector, largely because he was having financial problems. After that he worked for a private foundation dedicated to promoting better relations between America and Great Britain. He continued to lecture throughout most of the 1930s. On January 8, 1939, Eastman died from a heart attack in Detroit, Michigan (Wilson, 1983). His life mission of encouraging Whites and Indians to understand and appreciate each other had ended in one way, but still continues indirectly through his published works.

Luther Standing Bear (Ota Kte)

In his third book, *Land of the Spotted Eagle* (published in 1933), Ota Kte dedicated it to: "My Indian mother, Pretty Face, who, in her humble way, helped to make the history of her race. For it is the mothers, not the warriors, who create a people and guide their destiny" (Standing Bear. 1978, frontispiece). His mother gave birth to him in either 1863 or 1868 (the date is in question, but Ota Kte states it was 1868). Although he described himself as an Oglala (Lakota), a sub-tribe of the Teton or western Sioux, Richard Ellis in the foreword to this book believes he was a Brule. Nevertheless, Ota Kte received his allotments at Pine Ridge, where the Dakota Sioux lived. Plenty Kill (the English translation of his Indian name) was the son of a Brule chief on the Rosebud Reservation (N. Ellis, as cited in Standing Bear, 1978). Ota Kte describes his early years: "Wrapped in soft warm clothing made from buffalo calf skin I lay on a stiff rawhide board when not held in my mother's arms" (1978, p. 1). He was raised in a traditional Indian setting mostly by his mother for the first six years of his life. Later, other family members would take over the task of teaching him what he needed to know to survive. "A large portion of the care of a child fell to its grandmother, and in some respects she was as important in the child's life as the mother" (Standing Bear, 1978, p. 5). In this way Ota Kte's upbringing was similar to Ohiyesa's. The band lived in teepees and followed the buffalo when food was scarce. The buffalo was used for many things in this nomadic culture. His father assumed more of the parental responsibilities, as Ota Kte grew older. He wrote: "A lesson, in fact, did not imply much conversation on either side. But since I was to learn to do the things that he did, I watched my father closely" (1978, p. 11).

At the age of eight he was included in a deer hunting party. Later, he was to kill his first and last buffalo with five arrows; he never hunted buffalo again. When he was nine he participated in a Confirmation ceremony. Ota Kte described it:

> In nature it is social, religious, and ethical. It is social, for the life of the child … will be devoted as much as possible … to the service and welfare of other members of his band.… The ceremony is ethical in nature, for the practice of all virtues kindness, generosity, truthfulness and service are placed above gain and personal profit.… The religious import of the ceremony is profound, for the child is given into the guardianship of the invisible powers of goodness. (1978, p. 28)

At the age of 10, Ota Kte went on his first war party. He was disappointed when he returned home without seeing the enemy. He was learning the skills and values that accounted for the survival of the Sioux over many thousands of years. He explains: "Little children were taught to give and to give generously. A sparing giver was no giver at all" (1978, p. 14). In his book, *My Indian Boyhood*, Ota Kte wrote: "We observed everything of the outdoors, and in this way learned many things that were good and helpful for us to know" (1988, p. 7).

At the age of 11 in 1879, Ota Kte went to Carlisle Indian School in Pennsylvania; the school had opened that same year. In fact, he proudly states that he was the first Indian boy to enter the school: "The gate was locked, but after quite a long wait, it was unlocked and we marched in through it. I was the first boy inside" (Standing Bear, 1975, p. 133). Entering this school was quite a shock. "When I went East to Carlisle School, I thought I was going there to die; nevertheless, when father confronted me with the question, 'Son, do you want to go far away with these white people?,' I unhesitatingly said, 'yes'" (Standing Bear, 1978, p. 68). He also states: "I never knew embarrassment or humiliation of this character until I went to Carlisle School and was there put under the system of competition" (1978, p. 16). Like Eastman, when he entered the school he was exposed to a new way of academic learning centered primarily on reading:

We were to learn that according to standards of the white man those not learned in books are not educated. Books were the symbol of learning, and people were continually asking others how many books they had read. The Lakotas read and studied actions, movements, posture, intonation, expression, and gesture of both man and animal. (1978, p. 18)

Standing Bear was becoming aware of the cultural differences involved in how the White society and traditional Indian society learned. As a youth, he learned almost exclusively through direct experience in life situations; he was an experiential learner. Ota Kte was forced to give up speaking his language and learn a new one, have his long hair cut short, give up his native clothes and wear a uniform with a stiff collar and itchy underwear, conform to the clock and strict schedules, and learn new information and skills like reading and writing in a way foreign to him. He found himself living and learning with other students who spoke several languages because they came from various tribes. They had to forget about their traditional spiritual upbringing and choose a Christian religion: "All the boys and girls were given permission to choose the religious denomination which appealed to them best, so they were at liberty to go where they pleased to Sunday School. Most of us selected the Episcopal Church" (Standing Bear, 1978, p. 145).

Another example of how entering the White world confused Ota Kte is illustrated in the way Whites viewed "wild" nature:

We did not think of the great open plains, the beautiful rolling hills, and winding streams with tangled growth, as 'wild.' Only to the white man was nature a 'wilderness' and only to him was the land 'infested' with 'wild' animals and 'savage' people. To us it was tame. (Standing Bear, 1978, p. 38)

To summarize the Dakota philosophy of land and people, Ota Kte writes: "We are of the soil and the soil is of us. We love the birds and beasts that grew with us on this soil. They drank the same water we did and breathed the same air." (1978, p. 45). Ota Kte explains how he got his English name:

One day when we came to school there was a lot of writing on one of the blackboards. We did not know what it meant, but our interpreter came into the room and said, 'Do you see all these marks on the blackboard? Well, each word is a white man's name. They are going to give each one of you one of these names by which you will hereafter be known. (1975, pp. 136–137)

Ota Kte selected the name Luther and from that point on, he was known as Luther Standing Bear because his father was named Chief Standing Bear.

With his father's support, Luther stayed in school and did quite well academically once he became acclimated. He writes, "Toward the summer of 1881 we were doing splendidly in school" (1978, p. 153). Despite his success in the classroom, he was under constant stress: "That was one of the hard things about our education—we had to get used to so many things we had never known before that it worked on our nerves to such an extent that it told on our bodies" (1978, p. 159). Later, Luther was part of a group given the task of recruiting new students to the school. When they returned with 52 boys and girls, the head of Carlisle School asked Standing Bear to go alone to recruit more students (Standing Bear, 1978). Luther was given the responsibility to go to New York City and lead the school band during the dedication of the Brooklyn Bridge in 1883. He was also selected as one of two best Indian boys to work for a large department store in Philadelphia. He started in the invoice department and later was placed in the bookkeeping department as an entry clerk (Standing Bear, 1975). Through all of these accomplishments, Standing Bear's leadership skills were strengthened.

In 1884 Standing Bear finally decided to leave Carlisle and return to the Rosebud Agency in South Dakota to teach school. While there he was introduced to a woman teacher who taught Indian children. Standing Bear was not impressed with her ability to teach practical skills. He wrote: "We Indians wondered how the whites taught their girls only through books.... Book learning is very good, of course, but it strikes me that domestic science is the best thing for all girls to adopt, regardless of wealth or position in life" (1975, pp. 193–194). He once again considered the merits of experiential ways of learning compared to reading about ideas for which he had no direct application.

While teaching, Standing Bear met a young woman, Nellie De Cory, the daughter of a full-blood Indian woman and a White man. Nellie had been raised on the reservation as a "White" girl because of her father's wishes. Luther and Nellie married and had their first daughter in 1887 and a son the next year. Standing Bear moved closer to his family near the Pine Ridge Agency and managed a post office started in 1891. Then, a new school opened in Allen, South Dakota and Standing Bear was appointed as the teacher. While he was teaching, he began a general store and hired his brother Ellis to care for it. Later, Standing Bear bought a ranch and raised cattle. When financial difficulties arose, he went to work at the agency as a general store clerk. He also served as an interpreter and assistant preacher for a church and an assistant clerk in the Pine Ridge Agency office. In 1898 when his father died, Standing Bear moved to Allen, South Dakota, to manage a relative's store. There he heard about Buffalo Bill's Wild West Show and a job overseas as an interpreter, performer, and supervisor. He got the job and his career in show business was launched (Standing Bear, 1975).

As part of his duties with the Wild West Show, he supervised 75 Sioux performers on a trip to Europe. After nine days at sea, the ship docked in Liverpool, England. Following a performance in London, Standing Bear met King Edward the Seventh of England. Because of his dependability, Luther was respected by Buffalo Bill and the two engaged in many conversations. While on tour in England, another daughter was born to Luther and his wife. When mother and daughter were placed in the sideshow, people lined up to see them and gave gifts to the new baby. Standing Bear said, "before she was twenty-four hours old she was making more money than my wife and I together" (1975, p. 266). After 11 months in England, the performers triumphantly returned to the United States. The next season, Luther was again hired to supervise and interpret for the Sioux delegation. During a train trip to New York, a railroad accident in Illinois killed three and wounded 27 Indians. Luther was among the badly injured. To add to his difficulties, within the span of about a year around 1905, he lost his youngest daughter and only son. In 1905 Standing Bear was chosen as chief of the Oglala Sioux to take the place of his father.

When Chief Standing Bear gained his hard-earned U. S. citizenship in 1907, he purchased a home in Sioux City, Iowa, and went to work as a shipping clerk in a wholesale drygoods house. Later after becoming ill, he moved his family to Oklahoma and eventually to Los Angeles to seek a better climate. By 1912 he began to work in the movies with established stars such as Douglas Fairbanks, William S. Hart, and Charles Ray. Over the passing years, he also "lectured in high schools, churches, and grammar schools to show the white race what the Indian was capable of doing" (Standing Bear, 1975, p. 286). In 1925 he decided to become an author and began his first book, *My People the Sioux* (first published in 1928). He published three other books from 1931 to 1934. In *Land of the Spotted Eagle*, Standing Bear described traditional Sioux life. He considered this to be his most important book because he wanted White America to understand the traditional Indian and realize that they deserved humane treatment and equal rights (1978). Through his books, he was able to record his way of life and beliefs as a legacy to his people. He wanted to make an impact on the White culture during his lifetime and later. He wrote: "The white man does not understand the Indian for the reason that he does not understand America. He is too far removed from its formative processes" (Standing Bear, 1978, p. vii). Standing Bear died in California during a flu epidemic while making a Paramount film, Union Pacific, in 1939 (Raheja, n.d.).

Linking Charles Eastman and Luther Standing Bear to Experiential Education

Eastman and Standing Bear represented Indians who learned traditional indigenous ways during their youth at a time before the European invasion of their lands significantly changed their cultures. Later, they both were assimilated into the White culture. Although they successfully functioned as adults in the dominant society, they never forgot their early teachings. They believed that Whites could benefit from the lessons they learned about living close to the land and respecting the earth and the connections among humans, other animals, plants, soil, rocks, and other parts of the ecosystem. They served as educators and social activists through their lectures, demonstrations, writings, and in the case of Standing Bear, several popular movies. Their core indigenous philosophies formed a foundation for teaching about people and the land that is reflected today in the work of many experiential educators.

In 1994 the Association for Experiential Education approved a definition of experiential education that included 12 principles of practice (Proudman, 1995). Half of these principles relate directly to traditional Indian philosophy as taught by Eastman and Standing Bear and they are paraphrased below:

1. Learning occurs when experiences are supported by reflection, analysis, and synthesis. Eastman and Standing Bear valued spending time alone in nature to seek a vision for the future and to pray to the Creator for guidance. These times of solitude and fasting are often referred to as vision quests. Elders and medicine people prepared those going on vision quests and then upon completion, the questers were helped to understand the meaning of these experiences. Standing Bear explained the role of medicine-men: "They helped to make our lives joyful, to bring the rain so the grass would grow, to bring the buffalo near, and to get in closer touch with the forces of goodness" (1978, pp. 210–211). Vision quests, in one form or another, are still used by both Native Americans and by experiential educators who are involved in outdoor wilderness programs. Program leaders still have the responsibility to support learners by guiding their reflection, analysis, and synthesis of events.

2. Learners take the initiative for making decisions and are accountable for the results of their experiences.

   Traditional native ways are action oriented and based upon outdoor survival experiences that usually provide immediate feedback to the learner. After learning how to plant gardens, gather wild foods and hunt, protect the community, thank the Creator, prepare hides, and build shelters, young Indians were expected to share these skills with everyone. Some of these outdoor skills are incorporated into outdoor experiential programs today. Eastman describes a young boy's education: "Whatever there is for him to learn must be learned; whatever qualifications are necessary to a truly great man he must seek at any expense of danger and hardship" (1971, p. 43). Experiential educators often provide students with choices and hold them accountable for the results of their experiences.

3. Learners are engaged intellectually, socially, soulfully, and/or physically in authentic tasks.

   Traditional Indian cultures involve the whole person in coping with the challenges of surviving in a community. Human intellect, social behavior, spiritual belief, and physical challenge are not dealt with separately. They are integrated in ways that contribute to the completion of authentic tasks of living. Eastman believed that "to be in harmony with nature, one must be true in thought, free in action, and clean in body, mind, and spirit. This is the solid granite foundation of character" (1974, p. 1). Experiential educators honor all aspects of their students and recognize the interrelationships of all their human characteristics.

4. Relationships of all kinds are nurtured.

   Indian community life is based on developing and maintaining close relationships with people and nature. Survival is based on recognizing that all tribal members are connected and must be cared for. Standing Bear phrased the idea this way: "Strength was gained but from one source—nature—and until influenced, the Dakota mind was never blighted with the idea that strength was to be gained through the domination of other individuals" (1978, p. 125). Experiential educational programs are often based on a philosophy of group solidarity and cooperation among its members. The power of the group is recognized in many experiential activities.

5. As a result of experience, participants come to know success, failure, adventure, risk-taking, and uncertainty.

   Native ways of living close to the land involved all of these outcomes of experiential learning and they still do. Success is celebrated, failure is used to improve ways of solving problems, adventure and risk-taking are built in to all aspects of living through daily challenges. Standing Bear recognized that "the Dakota was industrious, his whole life's necessity tending to make him so; and in the natural, unhampered state of living he was, from his very needs, active" (1978, pp. 66–67). Experiential educators use these attributes of direct learning situations to meet program objectives.

6. Educators guide learners by structuring and supporting suitable experiences, posing problems, setting boundaries, insuring safety, and facilitating learning.

   Their parents and extended family used these methods of child and youth guidance to teach Eastman and Standing Bear how to live in traditional Indian ways. This early experiential foundation provided the stability to help them cope with the radical changes of assimilation into White society. Both of them never forgot their early teachings. Eastman remembers how his grandmother raised him during a ceremony dedicating a statue of an Indian: "While I have seen all that you have acquired in your enlightenment,… I have not once lost my head and forgotten that which was put into my very soul by an untutored woman, with the help of nature" (Lowden & Heckman, 1912, p. 12). These leadership roles are continued today in conducting many experiential programs.

Implications for EE Philosophy

In summary, Eastman and Standing Bear's philosophies, which resulted from their traditional lifestyle, have influenced the field of experiential education today. Both men described how the tribal elders encouraged reflection, analysis, and synthesis of their early life experiences, how they were held accountable for their actions, how they were treated as thinking, feeling, and spiritual beings when they performed practical survival tasks, how they came to understand the interrelationships among human and natural communities, how they came to know success, failure, adventuring, risk, and uncertainty as they contributed to the welfare of their people, and how their extended families provided the structure and support by posing problems, setting boundaries, insuring safety, and facilitating their learning. These indigenous lessons in living provided a foundational philosophy of experiential education and are reflected in many of the outdoor experiential programs offered now. Experiential educators can benefit from reading the writings of Eastman and Standing Bear in order to expand their personal philosophies.

References

Eastman, C. A. (1971). *Indian boyhood*. New York: Dover.

Eastman, C. A. (1974). *Indian scout craft and lore*. New York: Dover.

Eastman, C. A. (1980). *The soul of the Indian: An interpretation*. Lincoln: University of Nebraska.

Graber, K. (Ed.). (1978). *Sister to the Sioux: The memoirs of Elaine Goodale Eastman 1885–91*. Lincoln: University of Nebraska.

Keller, B. (1984). *Black Wolf: The life of Ernest Thompson Seton*. Vancouver, Canada: Douglas and McIntyre.

Lowden, F. O., & W. Heckman (Eds.). (1912). *Lorado Taft's Indian statue "Black Hawk": An account of the unveiling ceremonies at Eagles Nest Bluff, Oregon Illinois, July the first nineteen hundred and eleven Frank O. Lowden presiding*. Oregon, IL. (Unpublished, mimeographed version of the document)

Proudman, B. (1995, February). AEE adopts definition. *The AEE Horizon: Newsletter of the Association for Experiential Education, 15*, 1.

Raheja, M. (n.d). Luther Standing Bear (1868–1939). Retrieved May 1, 2007, from http:// www.litencyc. com/php/speople.php?rec=true&UID=4189

Seton, E. T., & Seton, J. M. (1966). *The gospel of the Redman: A way of life*. Santa Fe, NM: Seton Village.

Standing Bear, L. (1975). *My people the Sioux*. Lincoln: University of Nebraska.

Standing Bear, L. (1978). *Land of the spotted eagle*. Lincoln: University of Nebraska.

Wilson, R. (1983). *Ohiyesa: Charles Eastman, Santee Sioux*. Urbana: University of Illinois.

14 Aldo Leopold

Teaching in the Spirit of the Land Ethic

Steven Simpson

There are not many books that I have read more than once. *Walden* comes to mind. So do *Huckleberry Finn, Ishmael,* and *The Razor's Edge.* Of the books that I have read more than once, however, one stands out from the others. That book is Aldo Leopold's *A Sand County Almanac* (1966). It is the only book that I have literally worn out; the cover has broken away from the spine, and the glued binding is so cracked that, when I open the book, the pages flop out in four separate clumps. I keep two undamaged copies of *A Sand County Almanac* in my university office, but those are for loaning out or giving away. Each time I sit down to reread a particular section of *A Sand County Almanac,* I want to hold in my hands the ragged, barely functional copy that changed my thinking on education over 30 years ago.

The cornerstone of *A Sand County Almanac* is a chapter called "The Land Ethic," a concise synthesis of Leopold's environmental philosophy that asserts that a person's ethical decision-making must take into consideration not only family and community, but also the non-human elements of soil, water, air, animals, and plants. A land ethic is not simply the wise use of natural resources, although that would be a consequence; it is the inclusion of the natural environment as part of a person's value system. In Leopold's own words, "a land ethic changes the role of *Homo sapiens* from conqueror of the land-community to plain member and citizen of it" (1966, p. 240). In the first decade of the 21st century, this biocentric perspective may seem to be mainstream environmentalism, but it was a wholly new concept when articulated over a half century ago by the man who believed conservation was primarily about improving people and transforming culture (Newton, 2006).

I begin this chapter on education by defining the land ethic because Leopold's educational philosophy was inseparable from his commitment to the natural environment (Callicott, 1982; Orr, 1999). For him, a primary purpose of education was to connect students to nature.

> The question is, does the educated citizen know he is only a cog in an ecological mechanism? That if he will work with that mechanism his mental wealth and his material wealth can expand indefinitely? But that if he refuses to work with it, it will ultimately grind him to dust? If education does not teach us these things, then what is education for? (Leopold, 1966, p. 210)

Biography

Anyone who has read *A Sand County Almanac* already has glimpses of Aldo Leopold's life, his 15 years as a forester in the American Southwest and his later years as researcher and educator in Wisconsin. Born in Burlington, Iowa, in 1887, young Aldo learned about the outdoors from his father, then as a teenager attended boarding school in New Jersey. He moved on to Yale, earning a bachelor of science degree and a master's from the Yale Forest School. The Forest School was founded by Theodore Roosevelt's chief forester, Gifford Pinchot, partly as a training center for the newly established United States Forest Service, and upon graduation in 1909 Leopold accepted a Forest Service placement in New Mexico (Meine, 1988). It was in the Southwest that Leopold witnessed on a daily basis the ecological devastation of overgrazing, and it was there that he began conducting scientific research in game management, a sub-field of resource management that he would help to create (Newton, 2006).

Then in 1924, now married and with children, Leopold moved to Madison, Wisconsin, to assume an administrative position with the Forest Service's Forest Products Laboratory. Four years later he left the Forest Service to conduct wildlife research full-time, which led to a professorship of game management at the University of Wisconsin and to the authoring of *Game Management* (Leopold, 1933), a textbook that quickly became the standard on the subject (Newton, 2006).

In 1935, he and his family bought an abandoned farm near Baraboo, Wisconsin. This farm, known as "the shack," inspired many of the essays in *A Sand County Almanac* and today is a focal point of the Aldo Leopold Foundation, an environmental organization dedicated to regional land restoration and the teaching of Leopold's principles. On April 23, 1948, Aldo Leopold died of a heart attack while fighting a grass fire near the shack. *A Sand County Almanac* was published posthumously in 1949 (Flader & Callicott, 1991).

Teaching Toward the Land Ethic

On the topic of education, Leopold recognized that the technical training he received as a forestry student was not the kind of environmental and ecological education that most people needed. He urged universities to develop wildlife courses for a campus-wide audience (what we would now call general education courses in environmental literacy), but to make sure that they offered something more than watered down versions of their resource management professional preparation courses. Teaching to a general audience called for somewhat different teaching materials and sometimes even different teachers. The objective is to teach the student to see the land, to understand what he sees, and enjoy what he understands. Such teaching could well be called land ecology. Land ecology is putting the sciences and arts together for the purpose of understanding our environment (Leopold, 1991, pp. 301–302).

There, in a nutshell, is Leopold's philosophy of education—laced with some of the same elements espoused by Dewey and Hahn; i.e., facilitated experiences, preferably field experiences, taught with an interdisciplinary approach and with an element of fun. Where Leopold deviated from mainstream experiential education was his unvarying connection to a land ethic. In fact, an elaboration of Leopold's three-pronged objective of seeing, understanding, and enjoying the land offers experiential educators specific suggestions for incorporating environmentalism into their core teachings.

Seeing the Land

"Our ability to perceive quality in nature begins, as in art, with the pretty" (Leopold, 1966, p. 102). These words are hardly those most people would associate with a trained scientist, but Leopold worried that many educated people became so focused on their narrow areas of expertise that they lost the ability to see the holistic picture. He worked alongside scientists who were experts on the quantifiable phenomena of the natural world, but sometimes failed to appreciate nature's immeasurable essence. He wrote, "Education, I fear, is learning to see one thing by going blind to another" (Leopold, 1966, p. 168).

One group of people he believed could see the beauty and appreciate the essence of nature was children. Children approached nature with an open mind and had yet to undergo what Leopold called the educational "process of trading awareness for things of less worth." Of his own childhood, he wrote, "My earliest impressions of wildlife retain a vivid sharpness of form, color, and atmosphere that half a century of professional wildlife experience has failed to obliterate or improve upon" (Leopold, 1966, pp. 20, 128).

This early memory brings up an interesting point. Leopold's comments on childhood certainly represent a popular notion in American environmental literature. Many nature writers of the past have observed an innate awareness in children that often is lost in adulthood. Emerson (1950, p. 6), for example, wrote, "Few adults can see nature. The sun illuminates only the eye of the man, but shines into the eye and heart of the child." If Leopold and Emerson were correct, then seeing the land becomes, in part, the rejuvenating of childhood skills that wither over time. It includes slowing down and cleaning the mind of the clutter of everyday life, so that the beauty of nature is truly seen when people spend time in her.

Some contemporary writers, however, worry that these innate childhood abilities now wane prematurely because the modern child lacks unstructured and unsupervised experiences in nature. They wonder whether children today even spend enough time in the outdoors for Emerson's sun to shine upon them. Richard Louv (2005, p. 1), in *Last Child in the Woods*, noted, "Today, kids are aware of the global threats to the environment—but their physical contact, their intimacy with nature is fading. That's exactly the opposite of how it was when I was a child."

With that thought in mind, consider the following Leopold quote:

> It is the expansion of transport [roads into natural areas] without a corresponding growth of perception that threatens us with qualitative bankruptcy of the recreational process. Recreational development is a job not of building roads into lovely country, but of building receptivity into the still unlovely human mind. (1966, p. 295)

Leopold was addressing the outdoor recreation profession when he wrote these words, but in the 1930s and 1940s, it was primarily the recreation profession that was coaxing people to spend time in nature. Now that educators, including experiential educators, are assuming a greater role in exposing students to the natural world, a reasonable paraphrasing of the quote might read, "Taking field trips without a corresponding growth of perception threatens the quality of the educational process. Education is a job not of dragging students to the local nature reserve, but of building receptivity into students who need more opportunities to apply their innate skills of observation to the outdoors."

Understanding What is Seen

When I was working as a naturalist several years ago, there was an on-going debate within environmental education circles as to whether quality programs centered primarily on enjoyable encounters with nature (e.g., blind walks, hug-a-tree, snowshoe lessons) or on lessons in ecology. Should educators help people, mostly children, feel comfort and joy in nature or teach them the hard science of natural history? The argument, of course, was a false one; the best naturalists provided programming in both areas. Achieving this goal sometimes required additional on-the-job training on the part of the educator. Naturalists with a background in the sciences had to better their skills in communication and interactive leadership. Those already having the communication skills learned about the science, ecology, and natural history of the settings where they taught.

I mention this dichotomy because the two sides of the naturalist debate, along with the prerequisite skill sets, mirror Leopold's idea of *seeing* the land followed by *understanding* what is seen. Educators, according to Leopold, first help students see the land by making them comfortable in a natural setting, and then follow with lessons in ecology. Both are important. They complement each other, and the teaching of one does not excuse the absence of the other. In other words, experiential educators who bring people to natural places have an obligation to learn the natural history of those places and pass it on to their students when they get there. For Leopold, it was the first step to appreciating appropriate land use and sustainability (Newton, 2006). Most students want to know about natural places. Once in the outdoors, they ask questions for which educators should help them find answers. What is the name of that flower, and what is its role in this ecosystem? Why is this field called a restored prairie and that field just a meadow? Why are there so many dead fish here? Why is the trail eroded here, but not on the other side of the mountain? How come people can hunt here if it's a designated wildlife refuge? These are the kinds of questions Leopold expected his students to ask and find answers to. Today's experiential educators should encourage inquiry as well.

Aldo Leopold's message to the field of experiential education is clear: if educators bring students to natural areas, ecological education should not be an add-on, nor a subtopic only for those experiential educators who also are trained as professional naturalists. According to Leopold (1966, p. 261), "The most serious obstacle impeding the evolution of a land ethic is the fact that our educational and economic system is headed away from, rather than toward, an intense consciousness of land." From a Leopoldian perspective, experiential education is either part of the solution or part of the problem. It either confronts environmental indifference or is an extension of an educational system that contributes to its existence.

Enjoying What is Understood

Enjoyment, playfulness, and fun are integral parts of experiential education. John Dewey (1938, p. 27) claimed that they contributed to "an immediate aspect of agreeableness," which he linked directly to opening doors to new experiences. People who enjoy themselves in one experience are more likely to seek out other experiences in the future. Leopold voiced similar opinions about fun, but as might be expected, focused his comments specifically on enjoyable experiences in the outdoors. In a letter to a friend, he wrote, "What young people need most is not buildings or tracts to facilitate their contact with nature, but rather those inner qualities which enable them to enjoy nature wherever they go" (cited in Newton, 2006, p. 267). For Leopold, part of a complete education was instruction in outdoor recreation skills. He believed that outdoor recreation not only gave people a reason to be in natural settings, but was a first step to caring about wild things. Some of his insights concerning the teaching and promotion of outdoor recreation have application to experiential educators.

For example: Leopold felt that outdoor experiences should not be hand-fed to participants. The more educators do things for students, the more that they take away the mystery, the freedom, and the intensity of the experience. One of the Leopold essays most useful to experiential educators may be one called "Flambeau." In it, Leopold encounters two young men on a wilderness canoe trip just before they enlist in the Army. It is almost with envy that Leopold describes these men's freedom to encounter experiences with real-life consequences. If the men don't catch fish, they don't eat. If they pitch their tents poorly, they get wet. If they get lackadaisical with their paddling, they flip their boats.

The elemental simplicities of wilderness travel were thrills not only because of their novelty, but because they represented complete freedom to make mistakes. The wilderness gave [these young men] their first taste of those rewards and penalties for wise and foolish acts which every woodsman faces daily, but against which civilization has built a thousand buffers. Perhaps every youth needs an occasional wilderness trip, in order to learn the meaning of this particular freedom (Leopold, 1966).

Experiential educators frequently contrive group initiatives on a ropes and challenge course; untrammeled land provides comparable challenges by its very nature. According to Leopold (1966, p. 272), "Recreation is valuable in proportion to the intensity of its experiences, and to the degree that it differs from and contrasts with workaday life."

Leopold held great respect for hobbies. He delighted that amateur naturalists sometimes became experts on a particular bird or a particular geology, not because they sought notoriety, but because they loved their subject—and because they did not take themselves too seriously. "Becoming serious is a grievous fault in hobbyists. It is an axiom that no hobby should either seek or need rational justification. To wish to do it is reason enough" (Leopold, 1966, p. 182). One of the most valuable things an educator can do is to introduce another person to a hobby that engages him or her. From that point on, the learning and the experiencing is self-perpetuating. As Leopold (1966, p. 181) noted, "The man who does enjoy his leisure is to some extent educated, though he has never seen the inside of a school."

Implications for EE Philosophy

This may be an overstatement, but teaching in accord with Leopold's ideals comes down to taking into account the land ethic. Experiential educators have a choice. They can occasionally take their students into a natural setting and congratulate themselves for doing more than most other teachers—or they can embrace the land ethic and consider teaching toward that ethic in all of their offerings. This is not to say that every activity and every processing session have environmentalism as their primary theme. Teambuilding, cooperative learning, challenge, and all of the other goals common to experiential education obviously have great value. The land ethic simply suggests that consideration of the non-human receives equal weight in the educational thought process. Teaching in the spirit of the land ethic means that educational programming takes every reasonable opportunity to move both the individual and society toward an environmental consciousness. These educational programs calm students' minds and expose them to the art, literature, and philosophy of nature appreciation. They also provide ecological training so that students will understand the science of nature, and they teach students how to play in nature, so they will spend time in her on their own.

Teaching in the spirit of the land ethic also means that educators learn from nature themselves. I began this chapter by stating that *A Sand County Almanac* changed the way I think about education. I actually remember the incident that initiated that change. I was in my early 20s, just out of college, and I had a summer job as an interpretative naturalist in northeastern Wisconsin. One day in early July all nature center staff were ordered to report to work to help with a goose survey. In midsummer, the Canada geese were not able to fly. The adults were molting, and the goslings had yet to develop flight feathers. Therefore, about 15 staff members spread out across the nature center's small wildlife refuge and herded all the resident geese into a makeshift chicken wire pen for an annual goose count. To this day, my adventure in goose wrangling remains one of the most enjoyable work experiences I've ever had. I was cradling a goose under my arm and struggling to read the number on its bird band without getting pecked, I recalled a passage from *A Sand County Almanac*. I'd been introduced to the book two years earlier in an environmental education course, but at the time its impact on me was minimal. On goose banding day, however, some of Leopold's words came back to me. In the essay, "Conservation Esthetic" (1966), he wrote that environmental professionals hoard all of the best learning opportunities for themselves instead of sharing them with the people who they are supposed to be educating. Waist deep in 200 Canada geese, I wondered why I was having this glorious experience when its impact upon some lucky boy or girl would have been so great. Why, at least, couldn't a kid be alongside me to help read the bird bands? Not until that moment did I realize that good teaching was sharing my most spectacular experiences in nature with others.

That was the first time that the writings of Aldo Leopold stopped me short in the middle of an outdoor experience. It has not been the last. In fact, when I experience nature firsthand, I find it commonplace to discover that Leopold or Emerson or Thoreau or Muir had been there before me and had already written about it. This does not diminish the experience. It gently alerts me that something worthwhile may be happening and I should be open to the lesson that my encounter with nature has to offer.

References

Callicott, J. B. (1982). Aldo Leopold on education, as educator, and his land ethic in the context of environmental education. *Journal of Environmental Education, 14,* 34–41.

Dewey, J. (1938). *Experience and education.* New York: Simon and Schuster.

Emerson, R. W. (1950). The *complete essays and other writings of Ralph Waldo Emerson.* New York: Modern Library.

Flader, S. L., & Callicott, J. B. (Eds.). (1991). *The river of the mother of God and other essays by Aldo Leopold.* Madison: University of Wisconsin.

Leopold, A. (1933). *Game management.* New York: Charles Scribner's Sons.

Leopold, A. (1966). *A sand county almanac: With essays from Round River.* New York: Sierra Club/Ballantine.

Leopold, A. (1991). The role of wildlife in a liberal education. In S. L. Flader & J. B. Callicott (Eds.), *The river of the mother of God and other essays by Aldo Leopold* (pp. 301–305). Madison: University of Wisconsin.

Leopold, A. Letter to P. E. McNall (as cited in Newton, 2006).

Louv, R. (2005). *Last child in the woods: Saving our children from nature-deficit disorder.* Chapel Hill, NC: Algonquin Books.

Meine, C. (1988). *Aldo Leopold: His life and work.* Madison: University of Wisconsin Press.

Newton, J. L. (2006). *Aldo Leopold's odyssey: Rediscovering the author of A sand county almanac.* Washington, DC: Island Press.

Orr, D. 1999. What is education for? In C. Meine & R. L. Knight (Eds.), *The essential Aldo Leopold: Quotations and commentaries* (pp. 255–268). Madison: University of Wisconsin.

15 Lloyd B. Sharp
Trailblazer in Outdoor Education

Julie Carlson

He has to be counted among the key people who ever existed in outdoor education. He certainly has influenced many of us and has to be admired for that.

Hammerman (2002, p. 224)

Lloyd Burgess Sharp was a pioneer in the outdoor education movement in the United States during the early and mid-1900s. Throughout his long career, he taught and influenced countless educators who also became recognized leaders in outdoor environmental education—among them Reynold Carlson, Thomas Rillo, Clifford Knapp, Donald Hammerman, DeAlton Partridge, Robert Christie, Campbell Loughmiller, Elizabeth Roller, and Edward Ambry. Described by his associates as a unique and charismatic individual, Sharp changed people, careers, and society through his continual striving to integrate outdoor education into the lives of learners everywhere. Although he passed away before the term *experiential education* was commonly used, his work exemplified many of the tenets of this field.

Biography

L. B. Sharp was born on a Kansas farm in 1895, at the time the settling of the west was drawing to a close. Outdoor living on the frontier farm was an essential part of his upbringing, evidenced by several documented stories told by Sharp describing incidents and childhood pranks that took place outdoors on the farm (Sharp, 1960).

After high school, Sharp served as a grammar school principal, sans credentials, for one year before attending Emporia Normal School. He married Alice Whitney in 1918, the same year as his college graduation (Piercy, 1978). After a brief term in the U.S. Navy, he worked a few years for the Playground and Recreation Association of Michigan (Sharp, 1930). In February 1923, Sharp began graduate studies at Teachers College–Columbia University, majoring in Physical Education and taking courses in camp leadership. He studied under the pragmatists and progressivists at Columbia who were known as the New Educators. These included renowned scholars John Dewey, William Heard Kilpatrick, and E. L. Thorndike (Hammerman, Hammerman, & Hammerman, 1994). Sharp completed his Master's degree in 1924 and his doctoral studies in 1930. During his time at Columbia, an opportunity arose that launched a lifelong career for Sharp, and also began decades of experimental programming endeavors that came to be known as the *outdoor education movement* (Hammerman, 1980). His dissertation, *Education and the Summer Camp: An Experiment* (Sharp, 1930), was based on that initial opportunity that is described in the following section.

Formative Years in Outdoor Education

Through recommendations from some of Sharp's Columbia University professors, *Life Magazine* hired him in 1925 to reorganize its Fresh Air summer camps for children who received charity services in New York City (Secretary, 1925). Sharp successfully implemented the philosophies of the New Educators into the Fresh Air programs in New Jersey and Connecticut. He created small, decentralized, democratically oriented camping units where campers built their shelters, cooked their meals, and managed their food budgets. Sharp used the outdoors to teach self-reliance, spiritual uplift, and group relationships (Sharp, 1930). Many of the camp rituals and ceremonies were based on frontier and American Indian themes. The values and beliefs that Sharp instilled into the Fresh Air programs can be traced to impressionable learning experiences gleaned from his youth and early adulthood on the Kansas farm (Sharp, 1960).

Over time, Sharp became interested in expanding the educational possibilities of camping, and extending camping beyond the summer months into the regular school curriculum (*Extending Education*, 1948). In the early 1900s, as Sharp and others experimented, this type of programming was called camping education or school camping. Sharp used the term "outdoor education" in a 1943 article in *The Education Forum*, and, according to Knapp (2000), this was his first usage of the term. He adopted the following pragmatic statement that he referred to as his thesis of outdoor education:

> That which can best be learned inside the classroom should be learned there. That which can best be learned in the out-of-doors through direct experience, dealing with native materials and life situations, should there be learned. (Sharp, 1943, pp. 363–364)

Designed to work in conjunction with the Fresh Air Life Camps, Sharp opened National Camp in 1940 to provide outdoor leadership training (Partridge, 1943). The facility was located near the Girls Life Camp near High Point State Park in northern New Jersey. In 1951, *Life Magazine* officially closed its Life Camps, but Sharp continued the work of National Camp through the establishment of a national Outdoor Education Association (OEA). At that time, National Camp was relocated close to Pole Bridge, one of the children's camps that remained open, near Matamoras, Pennsylvania (Piercy, 1978). As a function of the OEA, and as the main funding source for National Camp, Sharp designed and served as a consultant for over 100 outdoor education centers, most of which are still operating.

In the late 1950s, complications arose with the land lease agreements for the National and Pole Bridge Camps and, in 1959, Sharp accepted an appointment at Southern Illinois University (SIU) at Carbondale. University president Delyte Morris wanted Sharp to design an outdoor environmental education center southeast of the campus that would serve as the pre-eminent headquarters for outdoor education nationally (Sharp, 1961). Soon after relocating to SIU, Sharp moved the OEA and equipment from Pole Bridge to Carbondale and officially closed National Camp in 1962. Unfortunately, before the new education center could be built, Sharp died suddenly of heart failure in 1963 (Brinley & Ambry, 1963) and the vision shared by Morris and Sharp was never fulfilled.

Contributions to Experiential Education

My research on the leadership of L. B. Sharp began as my dissertation study and has continued through the years since then. The original study entailed interviewing several people who knew him during the decades of his career. I will always be indebted to Clifford Knapp for connecting me with these special people. Their stories are real treasures in depicting who L. B. Sharp was as an inspirational person in their lives and in the lives of infinite numbers of adults and children. Robert Christie (2002) encapsulated what many of them shared:

[L. B.] was a very kind, gentle person. He was extremely thoughtful. He had a lot of patience in working with people and kids. He had a great deal of feeling and affection for people. Probably in terms of the world [of] ethics, he [had] one of the highest levels of any individual I have known. (pp. 226–227)

Interestingly, the narrative contributions of the people who were interviewed continue to be helpful at this juncture in drawing ties between Sharp's work and commonly accepted practices for experiential educators. These practices include promoting the importance of primary experiences, importance of appropriate learning environments, learner-centeredness, interpersonal relationships, real-life problem-solving, and reflection. Although an outdoor environment is not requisite for experiential education, that emphasis has been and is still quite prevalent. L. B. modeled and promoted environmental ethics and spiritual reverence for the outdoors in all that he did (Rillo, 2002). Following are a few snapshots of the original interviewees' contributions that depict these congruencies with experiential learning.

Learning Through Primary Experiences

[L. B.] encouraged learning through experience firsthand. He felt that you retain much more longer and more vividly than if you learned it by rote or by secondary sources. He was always in favor of direct experiences. (Rillo, 2002, p. 220)

We had to cook our own meals for part of the time. We had planned chicken. We got down to the dining room. One of the guys said, "Well, where are the chickens?" [L. B.] picked up a gunny sack. "Here they are." They were alive. You were put to the test at every opportunity. Whenever he could, he would challenge you and work you into a situation where you had to come through. (Emanuelson, 2002, p. 145)

Learning Matched with Appropriate Environment

He believed in education for what is real and had the ability to help others to understand that education is more than "Two by four: the four walls of a classroom, and the two covers of a book. He felt that children had been looking out of windows for a long time, and that outdoor education took them there. (Roller, 2002, p. 220)

He would say when he would lean back in his chair, "Some day, I'm going to watch and all the school buses will be going in the other direction". He would say that a lot of times at the end of a speech. That's what he was wishing for. (Ambry, 2002, pp. 214–215)

Learner-Centered

[L. B.] was talking to [our] whole group, and I heard a strange sound in the woods. I figured it was a bird, and I said, "L. B., what's that bird?" and he said, "Why don't you go and find out?" This was so typical of L. B. because he wouldn't easily give you answers when he thought you could find out yourself. Even if you couldn't easily find out yourself, he was opposed to giving you an answer. (Knapp, 2002, pp. 164–165)

Interpersonal Relationships

[L. B.] really invented what was called the "small camp concept". We lived out in the woods with the children. We had tepees or other kinds of structures, most of which the young people would build for themselves. We went to the dining room for one meal a day. Other times, we stayed in small camp and lived together like a family. (Ambry, 2002, p. 136)

Practical, Problem-Based Learning

We were given $.50 a day per person, so $5.00 a day to feed all ten of us. We had to submit our menu to the dietician to make sure it was nutritious and balanced. In the process of working out the menu, getting a good dessert or steak or something special that they all liked, they had to plan the menu with inexpensive foods. Those kids who didn't know arithmetic before they started, they knew arithmetic by the time we got done, because they had to do the calculations. The counselors did not. (Huntley, 2002, p. 136)

Reflection

[L. B.] encouraged us to be creative. I remember that we also did writing and especially poetry. I look back at my experience with L. B. as being an inspiration for poetry. I remember Joe True, a fellow camper, [who wrote] the poem, "What is the night? A dark and fearsome thing. Oh no, it's not. It's born of light and hope" and it goes on. This [was] a ten year old kid from Hell's Kitchen writing poetry and reading it to others. (Rillo, 2002, p. 178)

Every Sunday evening L. B. would lead a vesper service, and he led one at Clear Lake down by the lakeside. It was very inspirational, tying in the fire and the flame and the meaning of all this. (Hammerman, 2002, p. 158)

Reverence for the Out-of-Doors and Environmental Ethics

Each time [L. B.] wrote his report to accompany a master plan map [for outdoor centers], he would make sure that the text reflected the ethical and aesthetic treatment of the land. For example, he always recommended that buildings not be placed where they could be seen from the lake. He always wanted to preserve that aesthetic quality of being out in a canoe and looking on the shore and not seeing a structure. (Knapp, 2002, p. 229)

One of the things you had to look for was to see if you could find evidence of where any of the other groups had stayed while they were there and try to make it so that nobody can tell that you've been camped in the area. (Christie, 2002, p. 146)

He encouraged kinship with the earth in all his associations. (Morrison, 2002, p. 229)

Guided Discovery, Adventure, and Teachable Moments

[L. B.'s] philosophy [was] that the out-of-doors ought to be a constant source of discovery or exploration and the program ought to be planned so that happens. The essence of [L. B.'s] philosophy was "to explore an unknown area." (Knapp, 2002, p. 220)

He would stand erect as though he were the conductor and then he would try to time his hand movements to the start of a breeze that would come up the valley. That wind would shake the aspen leaves. So he would, in all the pomp and circumstance of an actor and a conductor, lead the symphony of the aspens. (Knapp, 2002, p. 234)

Challenges to Experiential Education

One of the hurdles that Sharp experienced was convincing school teachers and administrators to integrate outdoor education into the regular school curriculum. Commonly voiced obstacles such as time, effort, teacher training and motivation, cost, and equipment were similar to those facing experiential education today. The result then and now appears to be a type of *us against them* crusade between those who believe in the benefits of experiential education and those who are skeptical or resistant to it. Today, the national emphasis on high stakes testing has certainly played a part in educator reluctance to spend too much of the school day on things that aren't directly measurable or testable in relation to the school curriculum.

These challenges will continue to exist for experiential education. However, a bright spot on the horizon is that the research now being conducted and made available through electronic indexes is increasing. Additionally, research in experiential education arenas is being published in a greater variety of journals than ever before, a call that has been strongly promoted in past years as necessary to reach more publicly located audiences and heighten academic legitimacy for the field (Bunting, 2003; Ewert, 2005).

Although Sharp's programs served tens of thousands of children and adults, he did not see outdoor education embraced to the extent he had hoped for during his lifetime. Similar to Sharp, many experiential educators look forward to the day that experiential education will be merged with school curricula to the extent that it is not seen as something separate or different from regular education, and not viewed as extra-curricular. As public knowledge of experiential education has increased, this merger has begun, albeit slowly. There are lessons that can be gleaned from Sharp's lifework to help broaden the depth and accelerate the speed of acceptance into general educational settings.

Implications for EE Philosophy

Sharp was unwavering in his dedication to create the educational future in which he believed. In analyzing his leadership, and how he was able to extensively influence the outdoor education movement and inspire others to launch careers in outdoor experiential education, some key strategies emerge that are worthy of consideration by experiential educators today.

Succinct Philosophy: One of Sharp's strategies was to create a succinct philosophy of outdoor education that could be easily remembered, explained, and repeated by others (see thesis statement in *Formative Years* section above). For experiential educators, *learning-by-doing* fits the criteria of being easily repeated, but it is perhaps too simple to provide the credibility for the field that is desired. Accompanying explanations of when and how *learning-by-doing* should occur are not available. Educators continue to attempt to precisely define experiential education amidst disagreements as to whether it is a method or a philosophy or something else altogether (Itin, 1999, 2006). One argument against a universal definition is that it would be too limiting and exclude one or more of the numerous branches that now exist under the umbrella of experiential education (Gaddie, 2003). Sharp's philosophy was not a definition; it was more of a statement of beliefs—an educational stance of how he intended to proceed with his lifework. This approach may be a viable solution for those who are anxious to continue advancing experiential education, but are stalled by the perceived need to have a unified and agreed-upon definition.

Commitment to Spreading the Vision: Sharp was committed to integrating outdoor education into school classrooms across the country, and he spread this vision as widely as possible. He consistently used journals, newsletters, conferences, speeches, film, and radio to inform others about outdoor education. Elizabeth Roller (2002) described his work best when she explained,

[L. B. made a] pioneer effort to make the ideas acceptable to educators and showed through tests and studies that outdoor education can make a difference not only in science, but in other subjects in school. He inspired people to try this new approach to education and he helped many people to understand that this was a wonderful way to help some students learn and others to understand the out-of-doors. (p. 225)

Sharp's vision was focused on the big picture of a better education for children and a better life for all people by reconnecting them with the out-of-doors. He promoted the *approach to learning* he believed in, regardless of whether or not this resulted in more business for his camps. Widespread marketing of the overall benefits of experiential education, rather than marketing the benefits of individual companies and programs, will have a larger impact on advancing the public acceptance of experiential education (which, in turn, would eventually increase profitability). Admittedly, there has been a growing willingness among experiential educators to share their professional knowledge, an admirable shift from the proprietorship and paying-members-only mindsets prevalent in previous years. Joining together in the same direction will produce faster, more profound results than facing each other in competition.

Mindful Orchestration of Meaningful Learning Experiences: Years ago, an outdoor educator colleague of mine claimed success was achieved if participants ended their outdoor experience with the desire to stay or return some day. A simple idea, and easy to accept, yet complex in considering all that needs to happen mentally, emotionally, and physically for such a desire to be seeded. New experiences alone are not enough. L. B. Sharp was a master of mindfully orchestrating holistic learning experiences that resulted in campers and staff members returning year after year (Rillo, 2002). Traditions and rituals were regularly used to heighten meaning and a sense of belongingness. Camp newspapers with camper poetry and journal entries; songs and stories around campfires; steak-dinners cooked on coals; vesper services; and recognition ceremonies were all planned traditions at the Life and National Camps (Emanuelson, 2002; Knapp, 2002; Rillo, 2002; Roller, 2002). The adults and children who participated in his programs felt that they were a part of something special, and they were.

Granted, most of Sharp's programs operated in residential settings where campfires and special meals were easy to implement. However, rituals and ceremonies are just as effective in day programs or during single lessons, and should not be discounted. All learning experiences, including unplanned teachable moments, can offer something for the head, the heart, and the hands. If the creation of meaningful, holistic learning experiences is used as the main educational objective for programs and lessons, participants' desires for more or similar experiences would be optimized, and the demand for experiential education could become a perpetual process.

Summary

In summary, the career of L. B. Sharp was filled with correlations and lessons still useful in experiential education. This chapter overviews parallels between his work and experiential education such as the importance of primary experiences, appropriate environments, learner-centeredness, interpersonal relationships, problem-based learning, environmental ethics, and guided discovery. This chapter also provides lessons based on Sharp's work to further the public acceptance of experiential education. These recommendations were to promote a succinct philosophy rather than a precise definition, commit to the widespread acceptance of experiential education rather than emphasizing individual programs and companies, and to more mindfully orchestrate experiential education endeavors to ensure they are meaningful learning experiences.

I regret that I never met Lloyd Sharp, but am grateful that I have met those who knew him well. His lifework still holds valuable lessons for those in related fields today and can help us to find motivation to continue the work that is so paramount to the future of our children and planet. Sharp often repeated a phrase which aptly describes in many ways the various paths that experiential education has been navigating over the past three to four decades, and the work that is still to be done. It was simply, "Not finished, but just begun" (van Dien, 1965, n.p.).

References

Ambry, E. (2002). In J. A. Carlson, *Lloyd Burgess Sharp: An oral history of a career that shaped outdoor education.* Doctoral dissertation, Stephen F. Austin State University, TX. University Microfilms 3065515.

Brinley, A., & Ambry, E. (1963, December). Letter to friends and associates of L. B. Sharp. *The L. B. Sharp Papers,* Morris Library Special Collections, Southern Illinois University, Carbondale, Box 37.

Bunting, C. (2003). Scientific inquiry: A professional responsibility. *Journal of Experiential Education, 25*(3), 356–365.

Christie, R. (2002). In J. A. Carlson, *Lloyd Burgess Sharp: An oral history of a career that shaped outdoor education.* Doctoral dissertation, Stephen F. Austin State University, TX. University Microfilms 3065515.

Emanuelson, C. (2002). In J. A. Carlson, *Lloyd Burgess Sharp: An oral history of a career that shaped outdoor education.* Doctoral dissertation, Stephen F. Austin State University, TX. University Microfilms 3065515.

Ewert, A. (2005). Reflections on experiential education and the journal: Possible pathways to the future. *Journal of Experiential Education, 28*(2), viii–xi.

Extending education through camping. (1948). New York: Life Camps, Inc.

Gaddie, T. N. (2003). *The hidden wound: The fracture between the philosophy of education and the practice of education.* Unpublished alternate plan paper, Minnesota State University, Mankato, Minnesota.

Hammerman, D. (2002). In J. A. Carlson, *Lloyd Burgess Sharp: An oral history of a career that shaped outdoor education.* Doctoral dissertation, Stephen F. Austin State University, TX. University Microfilms 3065515.

Hammerman, D. R., Hammerman, W. M., & Hammerman, E. L. (Eds.). (1994). *Teaching in the outdoors* (4th ed.). Danville, IL: Interstate.

Hammerman, W. M. (Ed.). (1980). *Fifty years of resident outdoor education: 1930–1980.* Martinsville, IN: American Camping Association.

Huntley, L. (2002). In J. A. Carlson, *Lloyd Burgess Sharp: An oral history of a career that shaped outdoor education.* Doctoral dissertation, Stephen F. Austin State University, TX. University Microfilms 3065515.

Itin, C. M. (1999). Reasserting the philosophy of experiential education as a vehicle for change in the 21st century. *Journal of Experiential Education, 22*(2), 91–98.

Itin, C. (2006, November 3). *The definition of experiential education revisited.* Paper presented at the 34th annual Association of Experiential Education International Conference, St. Paul, MN.

Knapp, C. (2000). Learning from an outdoor education hero: Personal reflections about L. B. Sharp. *Taproot, 12*(2), 7–11.

Knapp, C. (2002). In J. A. Carlson, *Lloyd Burgess Sharp: An oral history of a career that shaped outdoor education.* Doctoral dissertation, Stephen F. Austin State University, TX. University Microfilms 3065515.

Morrison, E. (2002). In J. A. Carlson, *Lloyd Burgess Sharp: An oral history of a career that shaped outdoor education.* Doctoral dissertation, Stephen F. Austin State University, TX University Microfilms 3065515.

Partridge, E. D. (1943). National Camp: Reprint. *Nature Magazine, 36*(6), 322–332.

Piercy, I. (1978). *The extent of influence of Lloyd Burgess Sharp as identified in the lives and professional careers of selected educators and youth leaders.* Doctoral dissertation, University of Oregon, Eugene. University Microfilms International, 7907494.

Rillo, T. (2002). In J. A. Carlson, *Lloyd Burgess Sharp: An oral history of a career that shaped outdoor education.* Doctoral dissertation, Stephen F. Austin State University, TX. University Microfilms 3065515.

Roller, E. (2002). In J. A. Carlson, *Lloyd Burgess Sharp: An oral history of a career that shaped outdoor education.* Doctoral dissertation, Stephen F. Austin State University, TX. University Microfilms 3065515.

Secretary of Life's Fresh Air Fund. (1925, January 28). Letter to Rev. O. U. Mohr. *The L. B. Sharp Papers.* Morris Library Special Collections, Southern Illinois University, Carbondale, Box 1.

Sharp, L. B. (1930). *Education and the summer camp: An experiment.* Doctoral dissertation, Teachers College, Columbia University, New York, 1930.

Sharp, L. B. (1943). Outside the classroom. *The Educational Forum, 7*(4), 361–368.

Sharp, L. B. (1960, September). *Administrators, teachers and the out-of-doors.* Address presented at the first National Outdoor Teacher Education conference, Oregon, IL.

Sharp, L. B. (1961, October 6). Letter to Russ and Helena Rayner. *The L. B. Sharp Papers.* Morris Library Special Collections, Southern Illinois University, Carbondale, Box 13.

Van Dien, M. (1965). To his memory [Poem]. *The L. B. Sharp Papers.* Morris Library Special Collections, Southern Illinois University, Carbondale, Box 37.

16 Rachel Carson

Inspiring A Sense of Wonder

Karen Warren and Lorene Wapotich

With the publication of *Silent Spring* in 1962, Rachel Carson woke the nation from its naive and somnambulistic belief in "better living through chemistry." This was not the first time Carson wrote about the need to protect nature from the ravages of humankind, but by highlighting the dangers of widespread indiscriminant pesticide use, Carson helped launch the modern environmental movement. It was Carson's deep love of nature and her understanding of the interconnectedness of all life that motivated her to write *Silent Spring*. This same foundation shaped the course of her life and her contributions to the fields of environmental science, natural history literature, and ecology, as well as experiential education.

Biography

Born in 1907, Carson grew up at the height of the nature-study movement popularized by botanist Liberty Hyde Bailey and Anna Botsford Comstock. At that time, large numbers of agricultural families were moving to cities and nature-study advocates were concerned about urban children's increased alienation from the natural world. To remedy this they popularized hobbies such as bird watching and botanizing, with the hope that people would come to love nature and make an emotional commitment to protecting it (Lear, 1997). Rachel Carson's life echoes this commitment.

As a young child, Carson spent many hours wandering the forest along the Allegheny River near her Springdale, Pennsylvania, home with her mentor and mother, Maria Carson. Mrs. Carson was an avid amateur naturalist and wholeheartedly embraced the philosophy of the nature-study movement. Under her mother's tutelage, Carson developed an awe and appreciation for nature that lived at the core of her being and continued to grow throughout her lifetime.

From an early age Carson was determined to become a writer. She began college in 1925 intending to major in English and graduated four years later with a degree in biology. This unusual turn of events—as becoming a writer was a far more acceptable career for a woman at that time than becoming a scientist—was due to the influence of a brilliant new mentor in Carson's life. Professor Mary Scott Skinker inspired Carson with her own love of science and showed her new ways to explore the world of nature that she loved so dearly.

Following Skinker's guidance, Carson obtained a position as a beginning investigator at the Marine Biological Laboratory in Woods Hole, Massachusetts, during the summer of 1929, and in the fall headed to Johns Hopkins University, where she completed a master's degree in zoology in 1932. Carson completed a year and a half of doctoral work at Johns Hopkins before the economic strain of the Great Depression and the need to help support her parents and siblings led her to pursue full-time employment.

Carson's passion for the ocean, and her skills as a scientist and writer came together in 1935 when she was hired to write a series of scripts for an educational radio program on marine life. This opportunity led Carson into a 15-year career as a writer, editor, and aquatic biologist for the newly named U.S. Fish and Wildlife Service (FWS). The radio scripts also rekindled a spark in Carson for writing and she began selling articles on natural history topics to newspapers and magazines, often based on her research at the FWS.

While less known to today's audiences than Silent Spring, Carson's first three books *Under the Sea-Wind* (1941), *The Sea Around Us* (1951), and *The Edge of the Sea* (1955) were bestsellers, and reveal not only her attention to detail as a scientist and the lyrical quality of her writing, but also her incredible knowledge of natural history and the depth of experience she had with her subject. To write each of these books, Carson did extensive research and invested many hours of observation on the shores of the Atlantic Ocean.

Whether she was examining anemones during a spring tide in Maine or watching mole crabs on the Carolina shore, Carson embraced an intimate relationship with the natural world. She spent hours wading in tide pools, woke early to catch pre-dawn bird activity, and stayed up late searching by moonlight for ghost crabs and other nocturnal shore creatures. Through her experiences and her research Carson came to profoundly understand the interconnectedness of all life, as this passage from The Edge of the Sea illustrates.

> The shore is an ancient world, for as long as there has been an earth and sea there has been this place of the meeting of land and water. Yet it is a world that keeps alive the sense of continuing creation and of the relentless drive of life. Each time that I enter it, I gain some new awareness of its beauty and its deeper meanings, sensing that intricate fabric of life by which one creature is linked with another, and each with its surroundings. (1955, p. 2)

Educational Connections

Deeply touched by the majesty and eternal quality of life on Earth, Carson aimed, through her writing, to awaken in the reader an emotional response to the world of nature. She had a strong desire to help people develop a deeper appreciation for the natural world and crafted her writing to describe the wonders of nature in a manner that the average reader could understand. In this way, Carson was an educator, as well as a writer and a scientist.

Carson's views on education are most clearly expressed in her article, "Help Your Child to Wonder," originally published in *Woman's Home Companion* in 1956 and reprinted as a book, *The Sense of Wonder*, in 1965, after her death. The article encouraged parents to spend time exploring nature with their children and was based on Carson's experiences exploring the outdoor world with her grandnephew, Roger. From the time he was a baby, Roger and his mother, Carson's niece, regularly visited Carson at her summer cottage on Southport Island in Maine. By introducing Roger to the special places and wonders on her land, Carson passed on the mentoring she received as a child and refined her thoughts on nature education. Carson understood that children need adults as role models and companions on their journey of discovery and wrote, "If a child is to keep alive his [or her] inborn sense of wonder … he [or she] needs the companionship of at least one adult who can share it, rediscovering with him [or her] the joy, excitement and mystery of the world we live in" (1956/1965, p. 45).

Like Dewey, Carson believed that learning came from direct experience, which meant spending time outdoors discovering the mysteries and magic of the natural world. Carson felt that the most important aspect of these experiences was engaging the senses and developing an emotional connection with nature. "I sincerely believe that for the child, and for the parent seeking to guide him [or her], it is not half so important to *know* as to *feel*" (1956/1965, p. 45). Consistent with the manner and philosophy with which she was raised, Carson knew that hours and days playing in the woods or on the shore would instill a love of nature in children, which would spark a desire for more knowledge about the workings of the natural world. Carson explained, "If facts are the seeds that later produce knowledge and wisdom, then the emotions and the impressions of the senses are the fertile soil in which the seeds must grow" (1956/1965, p. 45).

In experiential education, a method of learning commonly referred to as "Letting the Mountains Speak for Themselves" would reflect many of the educational beliefs held by Carson. She knew that love of nature was the foundation of learning and the countless hours she spent alone, with friends, and with Roger on her beloved Maine coast exemplifies a philosophy of Letting Nature Speak for Itself. Suggesting that nature could be the teacher even without the scientific details and names, Carson gave the example of a night she spent watching the stars, "An experience like that, when one's thoughts are released to roam through the lonely spaces of the universe, can be shared with a child even if you don't know the name of single star. You can still drink in the beauty, and think and wonder at the meaning of what you see" (1956/1965, p. 55).

Our Experience

As writers, educators, and naturalists, the authors of this chapter have been profoundly influenced by Rachel Carson's life and work. We will each share a personal story as a living testimony to Carson's effect on our educational practice, a stirring example of Letting Nature Speak for Itself.

Karen's story: When my daughters were quite young we took them every year to a beautiful tide pool on the coast of Maine. This was the kind of experience Carson would recommend for children. As we waded in the chilly waters, looked under rocks for elusive crabs, and pulled aside rockweed, my children were consumed for hours by fascination with the world of the ocean. Later we stopped by the local library for books on this life of the sea and learned that brittle stars, green crabs, and knotted wrack were the names of some of our discoveries. But more importantly, this tide pool became a cherished spot that the girls begged to return to again and again. At various tides and over many summers we returned to this living classroom filled with adventure and delight, an experience that subtly instilled an understanding of the ecology of the ocean while flaming a love of the seashore in the children.

Lorene's story: A summer afternoon, while on one of our many wanders in the woods together, my niece and I came upon a set of animal tracks. Excited by our discovery, we dropped immediately to our knees and began looking more carefully at the tidy little impressions in the mud. Without ever suggesting who made the tracks, I guided our attention to the information we would need later to identify them. We estimated their size, counted toes, noticed the claw marks and gait pattern, and then turned our attention to the environment. The cool air brushed our skin, as our noses smelled the moisture still lingering in the empty streambed. A breeze rustled the maples high in the canopy and the birches on the bank. The tracks headed down the stream, and it appeared the animal felt at home in this environment and was searching for food. The tracks were relatively fresh, and we wondered if the animal had bounded through the area early this morning. Filled with anticipation, we abandoned our walk and headed back to her house. She quickly retrieved a field guide and we began referencing what we had seen against the images in the book. After 20 minutes of comparing tracks and debating, she shouted to the household, "There's a mink living on our land!" This led to a clamor of excitement from other family members wanting to see the tracks. Later, before I left, I mused out loud, "I wonder what they eat and where they sleep?" opening the door to the next adventure of discovery.

The Environmental Education Movement

At the same time as she was encouraging parents and educators to accompany and guide children on explorations in nature, Carson was working diligently to help preserve the beauty, health and integrity of that world. The publication of *Silent Spring* created a wake-up call about the environmental devastation occurring globally and spurred the development of environmental activism, one of the significant social movements of the 1960s and 70s.

Many activists realized that education was a necessary component in the strategies for protecting the environment, leading to a renewed interest in environmental education programs in schools and communities. While the idea of environmental education was not new, Carson's cry for environmental responsibility helped send many children out into the woods or schoolyard for experiential approaches to learning. With the rise of environmental education curricula came an imperative for a holistic, interdisciplinary study of the environment. This educational philosophy was congruent with the developing field of experiential education, as both advocated a rejection of the compartmentalized and conservative structures of traditional education (Koury, 2005).

The approach Carson used for learning can also be seen as a predecessor to the currently evolving place-based education field. Defined as an educational answer to the "landlessness" experienced in our society due to the destruction of wild places and the loss of awareness and admiration for the land, place-based education incorporates Carson's sense of wonder as a central theme (Baker, 2005). According to Baker, landlessness is particularly problematic in adventure education as "this disconnect has evolved to the point where participants in adventure-based programs may find themselves traveling through "Any Woods, USA", perceiving landscape as an interchangeable backdrop rather than developing a personal connection to it" (2005, p. 267). The cultivation of a sense of wonder by giving full attention to the immediate environment, supported by experiential learning principles, can be a powerful tool of reflection enhancing participants' development of a strong sense of place. Carson advocated that a love of the landscape and the resulting attachment to a place were the reasons to protect it.

Carson's influence in experiential education is rooted in her firm mandate that children and adults need to go outside and experience nature as the teacher. Yet, in an educational climate of high stakes testing, technologically induced ennui, and crammed schedules, it is precisely the experience in nature Carson called for that is lost. Instead children today are suffering from what Louv (2005) calls "nature-deficit disorder", an alienation from nature that has profound costs for today's youth and the future of our world. Carson would decry the diminished use of senses, dulled by being indoors and spending time in front of the computer and television. She urged parents, educators, and natural history writers to help children develop a sense of place in the environment and a spiritual connection to nature that would transcend the mundane distractions of everyday life.

Nature-Based Mentoring

If "nature-deficit disorder" (Louv, 2005) is the plague of our times, then nature-based mentoring, perhaps the modern reincarnation of the nature-study movement, may be the remedy. Nature-based mentoring works as an invisible school that invokes learning internally and externally. It engages the senses and draws students into the process, rather than focusing on the memorization or regurgitation of facts (Young, Haas, & McGowan, 2010). In essence, Young has described the educational process Carson used with her grandnephew. For example, one of the main objectives of nature-based mentoring is to help students engage all of their senses while exploring the world around them. Carson (1956/1965) expressed this by writing, "Exploring nature with your child is largely a matter of becoming receptive to what lies all around you. It is learning again to use your eyes, ears, nostrils and finger tips, opening up the disused channels of sensory impression" (p. 52).

In the stories of her adventures with Roger, Carson highlighted the importance of engaging children's innate curiosity about the natural world. This meant taking Roger out at night to watch ghost crabs scrambling along the shore, looking for fairies while walking in the woods, and guiding him on early morning adventures to listen to the birds. She wrote, "The sharing includes nature in storm as well as calm, by night as well as day, and is based on having fun together rather than on teaching" (1956/1965, p. 10). This echoes Young's philosophy of facilitated experiential learning (1998).

In the same vein Carson (1956/1965) wrote,

> I have made no conscious effort to name plants or animals nor to explain to him, but have just expressed my own pleasure in what we see, calling his attention to this or that. I am sure no amount of drill would have implanted the names so firmly as just going through the woods in the spirit of two friends on an expedition of exciting discovery. (p. 18)

This process of guiding a child's awareness to the wonders of nature, often through the use of questions designed to draw him or her into greater engagement with the natural world, and sharing one's own enthusiasm for the study of nature is at the heart of nature-based mentoring and Carson's own educational philosophy. This is no surprise as nature-based mentoring and Carson share a common goal—helping people develop deeper connections to the natural world, with the hope of instilling a sense of love and caring for all of creation. Carson's educational philosophy, which springs from her own childhood steeped in the teachings of the nature-study movement, offers abundant inspiration to anyone involved with the growing field of nature-based mentoring.

Parallels to Kurt Hahn

There is no evidence that Carson and Hahn ever met or knew of each other's work, but in a parallel universe way there are remarkable similarities in their philosophies as manifested in their life's work. The way Carson lived her life exemplifies the words of Kurt Hahn when he stated, "I regard it as the foremost task of education to insure the survival of these qualities: an enterprising curiosity, an undefeatable spirit, tenacity in pursuit, readiness for sensible self denial, and above all, compassion" (Hahn, n.d.).

Early in her life, Carson developed an insatiable curiosity about the natural world that grew throughout her lifetime and was the basis of all her actions. Hahn used the term "spectatoritis" to describe watching life rather than taking an active part in it. To Carson "spectatoritis" was reprehensible. She spent countless hours in nature, walking the rocky shore, listening to the trill of a woodland bird, or discovering the night sky.

Her tenacious courage led her to challenge the corporate chemical companies to insure the viability of the planet. As Terry Tempest Williams attests, "Rachel Carson's name is synonymous with courage. She dared to expose the underbelly of the chemical industry and how that industry was disrupting the balance of nature. In *Silent Spring* we see her signature strength as a writer who understands that a confluence of poetry and politics creates an ethics of place. But perhaps Carson's true courage lies in her willingness to align science with the sacred, to admit that her bond toward nature is a spiritual one" (2007, p. 145). Sensible self-denial was also evidenced in Carson's life. In the face of a propaganda campaign launched by the chemical industry to discredit her after the publication of *Silent Spring*, Carson, even though a private and reserved person, maintained a total commitment to defending the credibility of her research. For a woman who preferred the company of close friends, family, and nature, the public limelight was a form of sensible self-denial she was willing to endure in order to send her message to the world.

Above all, Carson's compassion for the sanctity of nature defined her advocacy work and was the source of her undefeatable spirit. Her view on nature not only inspired her work as a scientist and writer, but also her outlook on life. In *The Sense of Wonder*, in answer to the question of why study nature, Carson wrote:

Those who contemplate the beauty of the earth find reserves of strength that will endure as long as life lasts. There is symbolic as well as actual beauty in the migration of the birds, the ebb and flow of the tides, the folded bud ready for the spring. There is something infinitely healing in the repeated refrains of nature—the assurance that dawn comes after night, and spring after the winter. (1956/1965, pp. 88–89)

Carson's connection with nature fed her spirit and gave her the strength to face the many challenges life presented her—as a woman scientist, as the main breadwinner for an extended family, as a public figure trying to maintain her privacy, and as an advocate for the Earth battling a misinformation campaign against her, while at the same time fighting an aggressive form of breast cancer that ultimately took her life in 1964.

Spirituality In Nature

The strong spiritual connection to nature, evident throughout Carson's writings, was also part of her appeal to her audience. In her biography about Carson, Linda Lear suggested, "the fan mail revealed that *The Sea Around Us* had touched a deeper yearning for knowledge about the natural world as well as for a philosophical perspective on contemporary life" (1997, p. 205). Over and over again Carson offered a philosophical perspective that emphasized the beauty and wonder of the natural world, and the joy of having one's heart touched by intimate contact with that world. "The lasting pleasures of contact with the natural world are not reserved for scientists but are available to anyone who will place himself [or herself] under the influence of earth, sea and sky and their amazing life" (Carson, 1956/1965, p. 95).

In a speech given in 1954, Carson said, "I believe natural beauty has a necessary place in the spiritual development of any individual and society … I believe this affinity of the human spirit for the earth and its beauties is deeply and logically rooted" (p. 160). This belief, instilled in Carson as a child roaming free in the Allegheny woods and developed over a lifetime of contact with nature, guided Carson's life. Her words and example are a source of inspiration for those who embrace the belief that connection with spirit comes from and is an important component of nature-based education.

Implications for EE Philosophy

Rachel Carson's legacy to future generations certainly includes a healthier environment, a stronger conservation ethic, greater interest in environmental science and ecology, and a growing environmental education movement. She also left behind some of the most sublime and captivating articles on natural history and guides to the ocean and seashore ever written. Similarly, there is no doubt that Carson serves as a role model and source of inspiration for many women in science and other non-traditional fields.

Her most important legacy, however, may be her advocacy for nurturing children's inborn sense of wonder. Carson knew from personal experience that the curiosity and love of nature that is innately present in children is a doorway to the mystery and magic of life. In *The Sense of Wonder* she wrote,

If I had influence with the good fairy who is supposed to preside over the christening of all children I should ask that her gift to each child in the world be a sense of wonder so indestructible that it would last throughout life, as an unfailing antidote against the boredom and disenchantments of later years, the sterile preoccupation with things that are artificial, the alienation from the sources of our strength. (1956/1965, pp. 42–43)

She understood that nurturing children's connection to the natural world, would keep alive in them a connection to something greater than themselves. This deeper relationship with all of creation would lead to the development of adults and a society that valued the sanctity of life. For this to happen however, Carson knew children needed caring adults who also felt love and enthusiasm for the world of nature. Thus with every word she wrote, Carson sought to awaken in the reader a sense of wonder about the natural world. With her book, *The Sense of Wonder,* she left an inspirational and eloquent guide to cultivating that wonder in children through joining them on an exciting journey of discovery. Carson's willingness to embrace the magic of life and her ability and passion to share it with others are two of the most beautiful aspects of Carson's legacy to future generations.

References

Baker, M. (2005). Landfullness in adventure-based programming: Promoting reconnection to the land. *Journal of Experiential Education, 27*(3), 267–276.

Carson, R. (1941). *Under the sea-wind.* New York: Simon & Schuster.

Carson, R. (1951). *The sea around us.* New York: Oxford University Press.

Carson, R. (1954). The real world around us. In L. Lear (Ed.), *Lost woods: the discovered writing of Rachel Carson* (pp. 147–163). Boston: Beacon.

Carson, R. (1955). *The edge of the sea.* Boston: Houghton Mifflin.

Carson, R. (1962). *Silent spring.* Boston: Houghton Mifflin.

Carson, R. (1965). *The sense of wonder.* New York: Harper & Row. (Original work published 1956)

Hahn, K. (n.d.). Retrieved October 15, 2007, from http://www.kurthahn.org/quotes/quotes.html

Koury, D. M. M. (2005). A critical view of the history and perspectives in the field of environmental education: Study focusing on the Brazilian situation. *International Research in Geographical and Environmental Education, 14*(3), 160–171.

Lear, L. (1997). *Rachel Carson: Witness for nature.* New York: Henry Holt.

Louv, R. (2005). *Last child in the woods: Saving our children from nature-deficit disorder.* Chapel Hill, NC: Algonquin.

Williams, T. T. (2007). The moral courage of Rachel Carson. In P. Matthiessen (Ed.), *Courage for the earth* (pp. 129–146). New York: Houghton Mifflin.

Young, J., Haas, E., & McGowan, E. (2010). *Coyote's guide to connecting with nature.* Shelton, WA: OWLink Media.

17 Sigurd Olson and Paul Shepard
Experiential Education and Ancient Rhythms

Bob Henderson

What does perception mean to modern man, how can he nurture these desiccated nerve ends of his ancient knowing and make them flower again into a fuller life, with more appreciation of beauty and awareness and the potentialities of our relationships to others.

Sigurd Olson (1976, p. 24)

Like zoo born lions trying to bury their uneaten leftovers in the cement floor, we put bumper stickers on our cars reading, I'd rather be sailing.

Paul Shepard (1973, p. 211)

I had less than two months to make my submission to this book concerning philosophical foundations for experiential education. I was paddling alone one evening on Smoke Lake, in Algonquin Park, in Canada's canoe country. Hearing a loon call is not uncommon, but it is always special. Still, this evening, in the blackness of a moonless, starry night, I heard loon calls—many of them, all at once—and they sent a chill down my spine and swell of joy to my spirit. In such moments, I regularly turn to Sigurd Olson and Paul Shepard for guidance towards comprehension. Together they have helped acknowledge and advance the magic of such moments. Together they have helped me co-learn in such moments with students. I hope to share a sampling of their value to experiential education in this chapter.

My thoughts focused on that moment on that lake with the singing loons to the mystique of the north, the mystique of the canoe and all it knows.

There is magic in the feel of a paddle and the movement of a canoe, a magic compounded of distance, adventure, solitude and peace. The way of a canoe is the way of the wilderness and of a freedom almost forgotten. It is an antidote to insecurity, the open door to waterways of ages past and a way of life with profound and abiding satisfactions. When a man is part of his canoe, he is part of all that canoes have ever known. (Olson, 1956, p. 82)

My understanding and feelings for the north, the canoe and the aesthetic of gliding—all of these—are largely shaped by Sigurd Olson (1899–1981). He has been a powerful influence for me and for many others who teach experientially by canoe and campsite in the Northwoods. Olson uses language and expression that is vague and transient, but reflective of deep and sincere knowing. This is not the stuff of traditional school knowing. This is spiritual and, in our modern ways, may feel oddly both out of step with one reality while deeply embedded in another reality. Olson gives life to this mystic triad of north/canoe/gliding so that they are, oddly again, legitimized and totally engaging. The mystic is that quality beyond the norm. It is the spiritual impulse, the heightened senses, the aliveness in relationships, a love of being and the swell of this consciousness. Within the mystic, one is a part of a greater enterprise and complexity with nature and one is caring for the past and future.

From Olson I learned, both as a canoe traveler and as an educator in the wilds, how to communicate and how to guide others toward these mystiques in an unabasingly purposeful fashion. Without Sig, I might have been embarrassed to teach to the mystic, and to draw out—and distill the mystic in other new travelers/students in the wilds. Without Sig I might not have considered the stories of historical precursors as relevant to a traveler's present. With Sig, I teach students how to be part of the great long tradition of travel in the wild. Truly, in our Northwoods, *Every Trail Has a Story* (Henderson, 2005), and this is only part of the mystic. Is teaching to the mystic a hard or a soft skill? I think it is a warm skill (Henderson, 2001). The skill of the mystic for the north is akin to Sigurd's ancient knowing of ancient rhythms. This "knowing" is about ways of seeing, sensing, feeling, and being that are a departure from the central rhythms of people's urban working life. Wilderness travel is disorienting for many people, and Olson knew and taught that; he delivered a lesson of value for any educator/travel guide in the wild from one of the wild's finest spokespersons. Sigurd helps make sense of the spiritual meeting of nature, and *the* Other. Sigurd shows us how to make such a meeting possible and, for the travel guide, provides "the way." This is a warm skill: our way of meeting the land and dwelling with the land well. The canoe and campsite are good places to start. Sig Olson then helps us move beyond as an interpreter for our lofty feelings of connectedness.

Brief Biography of Sigurd Olson (1899–1981)

Sigurd Olson was born in 1899, the son of a Baptist minister in the Midwest. Then it seemed that there were three vocational choices for him: the ministry, teaching, or farming—all other options were deemed unessential (Olson, 1969, p. 63). In his own style, Sigurd fulfilled his calling as a preacher of the gospel of the wild and teacher for conservation and recreation. As a young man he fell in love with the Quetico-Superior country of Northern Minnesota, the southern edge of the Canadian Shield. His found his first employment there as Head of Biology of Ely Junior College, Minnesota. As he readied for his classes, Olson explored the natural world near the school. He explained: "I roamed the area, familiarizing myself with rock formations, ponds and woods within easy reach. By the time classes commenced, I had found enough possibilities within a mile or two to satisfy all needs for field trips" (Olson, 1969, p. 73).

Olson understood experiential education, as it unfolded in the school field trips for budding naturalists, and he carefully garnered ideas in his teaching and writings in keeping with his contemporary Aldo Leopold's avocation for the land ethic. Olson wrote: "unless we develop a feeling for the land and an understanding of it we cannot fully comprehend what conservation means" (1976, p. 120).

In these early years of his career, Olson worked during the summers as a canoe guide in the boundary waters. The lure of the far north followed. With growing experience and maturation, he soon broadened his range. He travelled north into Arctic watersheds and east and west into political activist arenas. He journaled accounts of his trips from his northern "Listening Point" cabin in the Minnesota woods. Publications followed, but Olson did note that the editors tended to want action stories more than his reflective thoughts (1969, p. 184). He battled for the infusion of philosophy and personal conviction when both were less than valorized. In his autobiography (1969) he wrote: "somehow the words would come if I were true and those who loved the wilderness would remember where they had been" (1969, p. 188). *The Singing Wilderness* (1956) considers Sigurd's guiding in the Quetico-Superior boundary waters. *The Lonely Land* (1961) chronicles a 1955 canoe trip down the Churchill River in Northern Saskatchewan. I most recommend his philosophical verse in *Reflections From the North Country* (1976).

For some, Sigurd Olson will be remembered as a formidable activist for wild lands. He was once the President of the American National Parks Association and Wilderness Society. I remember the day I read about Olson's Ely, Minnesota, home being stoned because of his negative commentary on motorboat use in the Quetico-Superior boundary waters. Others will remember Olson as a fine teacher. His legacy remains strong at Northland College in Ashland, Wisconsin, which is now the home of the Sigurd Olson Institute.

For most, particularly the northern canoeist, Olson will be remembered for words that ring true in simple, clear prose. Experiential educators with a focus on wild places would do well to consider the following gems from the Olson collection:

> When one finally arrives at the point where schedules are forgotten, and becomes immersed in ancient rhythms, one begins to live. (1976, p. 27)

> It is when we forget and divorce ourselves entirely from what man once knew that our lives may spin off without meaning. (1976, p. 31)

> This is the reason for the unrest and frustration of many people, their loss of contract, the root of their sense of fear and insecurity, through having abandoned the ancient state of oneness. (1976, p. 43)

The stars were bright on that special May night that I reflected on in the early pages of this chapter. The lake was calm and the loon calls beckoned in the distance. It was a grand invitation, an act of wild hospitality. No RSVP was needed. After an initial Olson muse, my thoughts turned to Paul Shepard. No wait, that's not true. My thoughts turned *to* Other, to place, to this ritual of encounter and engagement, and THEN to Paul Shepard.

Brief Biography of Paul Shepard (1925–1996)

Paul Shepard has been described as an intellectual maverick (Cayley, 1991, p. 14) and an iconoclastic provocateur (Shepard, 2003, XIII). He casts a wide net into historical, aesthetic, psychological, and anthropological dimensions of human ecology. He was a teacher at Pitzer College, Claremont, California, and a political activist. Shepard, like Olson, will be best remembered for his books and probing essays. And again, like Olson, his life is exemplary of his writings. For me, Olson and Shepard fit together like a well-seasoned paddle and that first stroke to commence a canoeing journey.

Paul Shepard, the academic, completed his PhD at Yale University in the 1950s. He studied the relationship between art and ecology and American attitudinal roots about nature. In 1958 an early research project prompted him to study the diaries of itinerant travelers along the Oregon Trail to explore cultural attitudes about nature. He retraced the travelers' routes, matching his photographs against their journal entries and sketching sites. He conducted similar work in New England and New Zealand (Shepard 2003, pp. 3–20, 89–154, 183–202). Reaction to landscape was a central early theme. Perhaps Shepard had read Olson's writings of retracing Canadian voyageur canoe routes (Olson, 1961). Around the same time, Olson had written: "History means the warmth of human association when one followed the trails of the past" (1969, p. 133).

From Shepard, I learned to avoid the words "landscape" and "scenery." Both words denote abstractions—nature as pictorial stage prop. Nature should never be reduced to visual representation as a habit of perception that separates rather than brings us into ongoing participation (Shepard, 2003, pp. 31–36).

By 1970, Shepard had been a seasonal park ranger (Olympic National Park); a dedicated teacher (he ran a field station for a biology program at Knox College); an environmental activist (he testified with Rachel Carson before Congress regarding the unrestricted use of pesticides and accompanied Sigurd Olson to meetings of the Nature Resources Council); and a promising author (see *Man of the Landscape* in 1967 and his seminal culture/ecology anthology, *The Subversive Science* with Daniel McKinley, 1969).

Shepard's books, through the 1970s until his death in 1996, involved jarring our complacency, bridging disciplines and exploring ideas that only now are becoming solid cultural themes. He certainly was considered an early figure in fields of study that are the now coming into acceptance—realms of nature/culture studies, ecopsychology, the root causes of environmental degradation, the wisdom of indigenous peoples, and our modern abuses in child rearing practices which result in conditions such as Nature-Deficit Disorder (Louv, 2005, 2008, p. 10). His last works concerned the importance of animals as the maturation and development of humankind. His rants over a 50-year career include; psycho-analytic literature's failings to consider the child's relationship with nature as place/as cosmos—juvenile imprinting on terrain (1980, pp. 23–24), and "the collapse of the adolescent karma" (1973, p. 227), and the putting of animals into slavery as "domesticated blobs" and what such a practice does to our psyche (in Cayley, 1991, pp. 17–18).

As an experiential educator working with groups in extended canoe travel experiences, I found all this writing informing. Of special note was Shepard's muse on the intellectuality of tribal peoples concerning their connection to the world via profound observation, story-telling, and their sophistication in relationship with animals. These educative qualities can be inherent in the wild travel experience and are not too readily found in a conventional school/university education. High status knowing such as the merits of economic and technological progress wins the day in most schools, while low status is given to knowing about the educative value of environment studies and outdoor travel. Shepard's work validates the work and convictions of the travel guide. The conventions of high and low status knowing are thrown asunder for the Shepard reader, and this is a good thing for the experiential educator (Bowers, 1997, pp. 4–11). Paul Shepard was a wide ranging scholar. He can help deepen one's search for profound knowing and enliven one's feelings for those starry nights filled with haunting loon calls. He unpacks the "haunting" and gives voice to a way of being that allows for places, nature, and animals to be loved and known. Indeed without such unpacking and voice we can all-to-easily slip away from our primal self in these all-to-easy, detached modern times.

From a wealth of rich epigrams, here are a few of Shepard's thoughts that the experiential educator would be wise to hold close to the surface for guidance.

> Without animals there will be no true otherness in the world to keep us both sane and small. (Shepard, In Jensen, 2002, p. 251) Culture, in racing ahead of our biological evolution, does not replace it, but is injured by its own folly. (1980, p. x)

> Bystanding is an illusion. Willy-nilly, everybody plays. This play contains has most intimate aspect of the mystery—our own identity—signified in finding ourselves in relationship to Others. (1996, p. 319)

Like Olson, the warnings for humanity come more often and stronger as life and wisdom advanced. Shepard started a university course for 35 years with the following question: "If the destruction of the natural world isn't making us happy, why are we doing it" (in Jensen, 2002, p. 248)? A related question critical to the educator follows: "What differences between civilized and tribal child rearing might predispose civilized children to be fearful and controlling of their world as adults" (in Jensen, 2002, p. 249). Shepard helps us explore what matters most—where our moral imperatives as educators lie. Olson's and Shepard's ideas and words have inspired me and given purpose and direction to my teaching. When I paddle quietly along Canadian waterways, I hear their music, and when I teach, I sing their songs. Sigurd Olson is the songwriter, and gives the educator an important "song" for the Northwoods. Paul Shepard is a "musician" offering individual "instruments." Olson's song is of ancient joy, ancient rhythms, and an angst for humanity's advancing disconnect from wild states and wild places. Might I, as guide, help people, even for fleeting moments, to hear the music? Might I help them paddle to more primal (closer to the earth) levels of consciousness?

Sigurd Olson sets the mood and gives an overview of thought and expression. Paul Shepard, as a younger colleague, teacher, activist, and writer fills out the details, and challenges us with probing and difficult cultural questioning. Together Olson and Shepard create a "grand symphony" for educators about the "out-there—in here" relationships of ancient rhythms. Their music is about the ancient joy of coming alive in our experience. On the strength of their foundations, the experiential educator can clarify otherwise vague notions of the mystic and respect and need for Other, for a place-based way of understanding and a consideration of ritual practice to work within. Olson and Shepard move us beyond the superficial aspects of personal growth for societal success, skill development, and fabricated outcomes-based research (Beames, 2006; Loynes 2002, 2007). It is not that there is anything wrong with these, but there is so much more. The "more" is the stuff of a joyous wild being with a spiritual aliveness that enables us to inform our life, our living, and our dwelling. Truth, beauty, and a profound warning dominate Olson and Shepard's writings.

Paul Shepard, like Olson, is a provider of language. Both give me ideas, ones that I would not come to on my own while traveling and guiding, yet are easy enough to grasp alongside paddle and tea pot. These ideas are not just ineffable, but also involve a big stretch of consciousness. Shepard gives expression to this complexity of our relationship to Other, the non-human, the beyond human. This knowing is found largely in animals, other sentient beings. It is found in the genius of place and the ritual practice we need to draw out and distil a knowing that adds deep meaning to our lives. Shepard studies these ideas from multiple disciplinary angles and often writes using difficult language. But the gems jump off the pages for the experiential educator who provides student experiences with Other, with place, and with rituals to advance the knowing of relationship with nature.

It isn't a question of whether one has a connected relationship or not. For Olson and Shepard, there is an affirmation that a connected presence with a greater enterprise of life is possible. It is indeed, a universal human, higher order quest. We dare not lose it. These men had it and serve as trail blazers for those teaching purposely in this realm. We must love the wild and know that the land teaches. You can hear this from the poet, songwriter, spiritual leader, environmental advocate and educator. Olson and Shepard are central among them. The mystical is not rendered as non-sense here. The mystical bond to nature is appreciated for its meaning and understood as a void to our Western world modern sensibilities.

For over 20 years, I have relied on Shepard to get me out of the name-calling associated with promoting outdoor education in hostile settings. When called a "back to nature freak," I retort in fine Shepard style, "how can you get back to something you have never left" (Shepard, 2002, p. 253). Colleague and fellow reader of Olson and Shepard, Bert Horwood has put the same thoughts this way: "we are born stone-age babies" (1988, p. 128).

Implications for EE Philosophy

One month following that starry night paddle filled with loon songs, I was back in Algonquin, intent on finishing this chapter. While hiking, I came upon a beaver at close range and a spruce grouse, beautiful animals. I paused in celebration. The swell of joy and wonder again aroused my spirit. So, Algonquin's northwoods had provided me an introduction and a conclusion for my writing. As I have worked on this chapter, Sigurd Olson and Paul Shepard came alive again in helping me appreciate, think deeply, and interpret for myself and my students as co-learners, the simple and profound gifts to be had in the wild. Canoe-trippers know and understand the wisdom inherent in Arne Naess' saying, "simple in means, rich in ends" (Devall, 1988).

My encounters with the northwoods, the canoe, the loons, and the words of Sigurd Olson and Paul Shepard, will certainly resurface in campfire stories shared with my students. I believe that experiential education can truly be about restoring ancient rhythms. Interpret this as you will, nonsense or filling a void, but please look into the ways and lives of Sigurd Olson and Paul Shepard for guidance. We should all be aware of Sigurd's warning:

> Could man in his new civilization afford to lose again and again to Progress? Did we have the right to deprive future generations of what we have known? What would the future bring? (1969, p. 210)

Author's Note

I would like to thank David Lang for first introducing me in 1972 to Sigurd Olson when I was a camper at Camp Ahmek, Algonquin Park, Ontario. In the late 70s Joss Haiblen reinforced the importance of Olson to canoe-trippers. I believe that it was Bert Horwood who did the same for Paul Shepard and me.

References

Beames, S. (2006, Spring). Losing my religion: *Pathways: The Ontario Journal of Outdoor Education,* 4–11.

Bowers, C. A. (1997) *The culture of denial: Why the environmental movement needs a strategy for reforming universities and public schools.* Albany, NY: State University of New York.

Cayley, D. (1991). *The age of ecology: The environment of CBC Radio's ideas.* Toronto, Canada: James Lorimer.

Devall, W. (1988). *Simple in means, rich in ends: Practicing deep ecology.* Salt Lake City, UT: Peregrine Smith.

Henderson, B. (2001). Skills and ways: Perceptions of people/nature guiding. *Journal of OBC Education, 71*(1), 12–17.

Henderson, B. (2005). *Every trail has a story: Heritage travel in Canada.* Toronto, Canada: Natural Heritage.

Horwood, B. (1988). Canoe trips: Doors to the primitive. In J. Raffan & B. Horwood (Eds.), *Canexus: The canoe in Canadian culture* (pp. 123–134). Toronto: Betelgeuse.

Louv, R. (2005, 2008). *Last child in the woods: Saving our children from nature-deficit disorder.* Chapel Hill, NC: Algonquin.

Loynes, C. (2002). The generative paradigm. *Journal of Adventure Education and Outdoor Learning, 2*(2), 113–126.

Loynes, C. (2007). Why outdoor learning should get real. In B. Henderson & N. Vikander (Eds.), *Nature first: Outdoor life the Friluftsliv way* (pp. 257–275). Toronto, Canada: Natural Heritage.

Olson, S. (1956). *The singing wilderness.* New York: Alfred A. Knopf.

Olson, S. (1961). *The lonely land.* New York: Alfred A. Knopf.

Olson, S. (1969). *Open horizons.* New York: Alfred A. Knopf.

Olson, S. (1976). *Reflections from the North country.* New York: Alfred A. Knopf.

Shepard, P. (1973). *The tender carnivore and the sacred game.* New York: Charles Scribners.

Shepard, P. (1996). *The others: How animals made us human.* Washington, DC: Island Press.

Shepard, P. (1980). *Nature and madness.* San Francisco: Sierra Club Books.

Shepard, P. (2003). *Where we belong: Beyond abstraction in perceiving nature* (F. R. Shepard, Ed.). Athens: University of Georgia.

Shepard, P. (2002). Paul Shepard. In D. Jensen (Ed.), *Listening to the land: Conversations about nature, culture and eros* (pp. 242–259). San Francisco: Sierra Club.

Shepard, P., & McKinley, D. (Eds.). (1969). *The subversive science: Essays toward an ecology of man.* Boston: Houghton Mifflin.

Part III

Psychologists and Sociologists

Nothing is more practical than a good theory.

Kurt Lewin (1951)

Although their roots extend far back in history, the sciences of psychology and sociology were essentially defined in the late 19th century. Leadership in the two fields developed theories of individual and group behavior and tested them by observing human behavior. Psychology grew to include professionals called clinical, counseling, educational, school, forensic, and industrial psychologists. In the latter years of the 20th century, in recognition of the importance of humans balancing their lives with the ecological systems of the earth, "ecopsychologists" were identified (Rozak, Kanner, & Brown, 1995). Sociology grew to include the fields of social work, psychiatric social work, and school social work. The two fields grew in parallel to the educational reform movements of the 20th century, and many of these professionals wrote about learning, teaching, educational theory and practice, and the purpose and organization of schools. The next group of chapters are about some of the psychologists and sociologists whose ideas should be carefully reviewed as experiential educators seek to refine their own theory and practice. A brief review of the historical development of the two fields may be of value in setting the stage for learning about these people.

Psychology

Although the development of the field of psychology is very complex, psychology in the 20th century was influenced primarily by four different theoretical foundations. These have been called "forces," and, although each is unique, all of them are concerned with understanding the human species. They might be considered as related to the philosophical questions of ontology—the science of being.

The history of modern psychology usually acknowledges beginnings in the research laboratories of William Wundt (1832–1920) in Germany and William James (1842–1910) in the United States, and on the couch of Sigmund Freud (1856–1939) in Vienna. William James produced the first textbook in psychology (James, 1890), and taught classes on the subject that included his student, John Dewey (1859–1952). Dewey later developed an educational philosophy that gave rise to the progressive education movement during the first half of the 20th century. Contemporary experiential education is related to that progressive movement and the literature recognizes John Dewey as one of the founding fathers.

Throughout the first half of the 20th century, there were two major fields of psychology—behaviorism and psychoanalysis. Psychologists interested in research studied the dynamics and principles of human behavior. Therapists and counselors applied those principles to the treatment of the emotionally and behaviorally distressed. Although both of these approaches appear in a number of variations, historians have discussed them as the two important forces of influence on psychology.

Behaviorism

This first force of psychology, the scientific approach to the study of behavior, was triggered by the laboratory methods of Wundt and the pragmatism of James. However, there were correct scientific approaches that differed with that tradition. The Wurtzburg school in Germany challenged Wundt's atomistic approach to the study of behavior and suggested that the "whole" took priority over the various "parts." As a result, the Gestalt School of Psychology was developed. In the United States, the approach called Behaviorism developed from the early work of John B. Watson (1878–1958), and the refinements of B. F. Skinner (1904–1990). It was in the 1950s that Noam Chomsky (1928–), a linguist, criticized Skinner and his behavioristic approach, arguing that language cannot be adequately explained by stimulus-response theory, and the field of Cognitive Psychology emerged (Chomsky, 2006). While there are theoretical differences in these various schools of thought, they all consider psychology as a science. Contemporary theorists of importance who developed from the behavioristic/research traditions of psychology include Howard Gardner and Albert Bandura.

Psychoanalysis

The second force driving psychology in the United States followed Freud, and involved the study of personality, development, and procedures for counseling. There were others who studied the psychodyanmics of personality but challenged Freud's ideas and methods, including Alfred Adler, Wilhelm Reich, Otto Rank, Harry Stack Sullivan, Carl Jung, and Karen Horney. Some of these "Aneo-Freudians" wrote about the process of learning as related to modifying behavior, and their ideas have relevance for experiential education. For example, Ira Progoff (1921–1998), one of Jung's students, became known for his methods of intensive journaling. The existentialist's approach to psychotherapy, which appeared after World War II, was also based on some disagreements with Freud. In any case, most historians recognize that until the 1950s American psychology was dominated by these two forces—behaviorism and psychoanalysis.

Later, two other forces of psychology came into being, humanistic psychology and transpersonal psychology.

Humanistic Psychology

What has been called "the third force"of influence had earlier roots in humanistic philosophy, but it emerged as a powerful influence on psychology in the late 1950s—partly as an alternative to the dominating influence of behaviorism and psychoanalysis. Major players in the development of humanistic psychology were Carl Rogers (1902–1987) and Abraham Maslow (1908–1970), however many others were also involved with this third force. These included Clark Moustakas, Gordon Allport, Arthur Combs, Earl Kelley, Henry Murray, Sidney Jourard and Rollo May. Philosophers Martin Buber and Paul Tillich, and psychoanalysts Eric Fromm and Victor Frankl, were also involved with this movement.

A *Journal of Humanistic Psychology* was published in 1961, and the Association for Humanistic Psychology (AHP) was founded in 1963. The Association for Supervision and Curriculum Development (ASCD) focused on the evolving field of humanistic psychology for their 1962 yearbook, with papers by Combs, Kelley, Rogers and Maslow (Combs, 1962). Thirty-seven years later, ASCD had classroom teachers and educational scholars review those earlier papers

(Freiberg, 1999). Contemporary educators considered that the ideas of those early humanistic psychologists were still of value.

The third force movement laid the groundwork for the human potential movement of the 1960s and 1970s, resulting in the development of T-groups, sensitivity groups, encounter groups, personal growth groups, and value clarification groups. When Rogers published his classic book *Freedom to Learn: A View of What Education Might Become* (1969), it soon became the foundation for the theory and practice of humanistic education.

The humanistic psychology movement had a 20-year head start on the experiential education movement, and yet there are parallels of success and failure. After reviewing the history of the humanistic psychology movement to the end of the 20th century, Fredrick Wertz concluded, "Humanistic psychology is in crisis" (1998, p. 42). He suggested that the movement had not succeeded because it had failed to sufficiently infuse into the traditional establishments of the academic world, and that many professional educators were still "unfamiliar with the nature of the movement" (p. 42). His recommendation was that leaders of the movement must "find more effective ways of infusing established institutions, upgrading its own institutions, and perhaps even creating new kinds of institutions" (p. 69). We find Wertz's comments and conclusions quite relevant for experiential education in the 21st century.

Transpersonal Psychology

At the point where psychology and spiritual experience intersect, a fourth force of American psychology begins. This movement is called "Transpersonal Psychology," and has roots in transcendental experiences and practices of the East, the West, and the esoteric practices of indigenous peoples about the world. Perhaps it was Abraham Maslow's attention to higher states of human consciousness, described in his last book, *Farther Reaches of Human Nature* (1973), which triggered this movement. A good overview of Transpersonal Education can be found in *The Education of the Heart* (Moore, 1997).

Sociology

Although psychology and sociology are different fields of study, holistic approaches to the study of human behavior require that both the individual and the group be considered in any attempt to make sense of the human experience. At the point where psychology and sociology intersect, humanistic psychologists and sociologists recognize that humans are continually looking inwardly (reflecting) but acting outwardly (behaving), and that understanding individuals involves attending to their needs, perceptions, growth, and functioning in relation to the other people and events in their environment.

The relationship of the individual to the group was noted by Rudyard Kipling in *The Second Jungle Book* (2004, p. 11).

> Now this is the Law of the jungle
> As old and as true as the sky;
> And the wolf that shall keep it may prosper,
> But the wolf that shall break it must die.
> As the creeper that girdles the tree-trunk,
> The Law runneth forward and back —
> For the strength of the pack is the wolf,
> And the strength of the wolf is the pack.

Humanistic psychologists and sociologists see the relationship between individuals and groups as similarly interdependent. The individual's growth process is strengthened by what he/she takes from the group, and the group is strengthened by what it takes from the individual. Individual growth does not unfold in a vacuum, and therefore, the writings of sociologists are important for experiential educators to review.

August Compte (1798–1857) coined the word "sociology" in 1838, and early textbooks on the subject were written by English philosopher Herbert Spencer (1820–1903) in 1874, and by American educator Lester Frank Ward (1841–1913) in 1883. Although his philosophy is more often considered political, some think of Karl Marx (1818–1883) as a sociologist. According to historians, the discipline of sociology was first taught under its own name in 1890, at the University of Kansas, by Frank Blackmar (1854–1931), and his notes for the course later became one of the early texts in the field (Blackmar, 1908). The first university department of sociology was established in 1895 at the University of Bordeau by Emile Durkheim (1858–1917). Durkheim and his contemporary, Max Weber (1864–1920), are usually considered as the fathers of modern sociology; some would include George Herbert Mead (1863–1931), a philosopher/sociologist/psychologist who was an example of a social theorist whose work didn't easily fit into conventional discipline categories.

Historically, the focus of sociology was on *macrosociology*, the general organizational structure and function of society. By the 1930s, microsociology approaches opened the door to the study of small groups, institutions within society, and individual development in relation to the group. This led to greater acceptance of Mead's theory of symbolic interaction, which he had developed when he was a colleague of John Dewey at the University of Chicago (Mead & Morgan, 1967). Talcott Parsons' (1902–1979) social action theory, showing the relationship between behavior and social structures, also became influential (Parsons & Turner, 1999). Kurt Lewin's (1890–1947) field theory opened the door to the study of group dynamics (Lewin & Gold, 1999), and led the field of sociology into greater study of the individual within the group.

This book could have included chapters on most of the people mentioned in this overview, but includes only a few. Appendix I does provide some information on many others, and includes suggested references for further research. We hope the chapters in this section motivate the reader to further study about the contributions of many others from the fields of psychology and sociology. There are six chapters in this section.

Chapter 18: Emile Durkheim: Socialization and Education
Chapter 19: Lev Vygotsky: Experiential Education—A View from the Future
Chapter 20: Fritz Perls: Gestalt Therapy and Experiential Education
Chapter 21: Kurt Lewin: Another Kurt for Experiential Education
Chapter 22: Earl C. Kelley: Education for What Is Real
Chapter 23: Carl Rogers: A Way of Being an Experiential Educator

References

Blackmar, F. (1908). *Elements of sociology.* New York: Macmillan.
Chomsky, N. (2006). *Language and mind* (3rd ed.). London: Cambridge University.
Combs, A. (Ed.). (1962). *Perceiving, behaving, becoming: New focus for education.* Washington, DC: Association for Supervision and Curriculum Development.
Freiberg, H. J. (1999). *Perceiving, behaving, becoming: Lessons learned.* Washington, DC: Association for Supervision and Curriculum Development.
James, W. (1890). *Principles of psychology.* New York: Henry Holt.
Kipling, R. (2004). *The second jungle book.* New York: Kessinger.
Lewin, K. (1951). *Field theory in social science: Selected theoretical papers.* New York: Harper & Row.

Lewin, K. & Gold, M. (Ed.) (1999). *The complete social scientist: A Kurt Lewin reader.* Washington, DC: American Psychological Association.

Maslow, A. (1973). *Farther reaches of human nature.* New York: Viking Press.

Mead, G. H.. & Morgan, C. W. (Ed.). (1967). *Mind, self, and society: From the standpoint of a social behaviorist.* Chicago: University of Chicago.

Moore, T. (1997). *The education of the heart.* New York: Harper.

Parsons, T., & Turner, B. (Eds.). (1999). *The Talcott Parsons reader.* New York: Blackwell.

Rogers, C. (1969). *Freedom to learn: A view of what education might become.* Columbus, OH: Charles E. Merrill.

Rozak, T., Kanner, D., & Brown, A. (1995). *Ecopsychology: Restoring the earth, healing the mind.* San Francisco: Sierra Club.

Spencer, H. (1874). *The study of sociology.* London: Kegan Paul.

Ward, L. F. (1883). *Dynamics of sociology.* New York: Appleton

Wertz, F. J. (1998). The role of the humanistic movement in the history of psychology. *Journal of Humanistic Psychology, 38*(1), 42–70.

18 Emile Durkheim
Socialization and Education

Thomas E. Smith

Emile Durkheim (1858–1917) is best known as one of the founding fathers of sociology. He developed the first European university department of sociology in 1888 and started one of the earliest journals devoted to the science of sociology in 1898. His major professional concern was how societies were organized and how they functioned. He wrote about how the different parts of a society operated independently and interdependently, and recognized that educational institutions were one of the most important parts of a society because they insured the passing of societal values from generation to generation.

His interest in education can be traced to his childhood. He was born in Epinal in the Lorraine province of France. He grew up in a Jewish community in a closely knit orthodox family, and had a traditional Jewish confirmation at the age of 13. Both his father and grandfather were rabbis, who were well read, conservative, and apolitical. As he grew up, the family assumed that he would also become a rabbi, but his intellectual curiosity took him in a different direction. He was in his adolescence during the Franco-German war, and when his community was occupied for a time by Prussian troops he observed and experienced some anti-Semitism. Historical reports suggest that he then turned his back on Judaism, briefly explored Catholicism, and eventually became an agnostic.

Durkheim was a brilliant student, and moved through the formal educational system rapidly. His early intention was to become a teacher. He finished his bachelor's degree in letters in 1874 when he was only 16 years old, and completed his bachelor's degree in science a year later. Despite his academic accomplishments, he had difficulty in getting accepted to the prestigious Ecoles College—because his interest in science was much stronger than his interest in classical studies. The system of Ecoles Normales (undergraduate studies) and Ecoles Normales Superieures (graduate studies) had been created under Napoleon to improve the preparation of teachers by emphasizing classical studies. Durkheim retreated for several years of preparatory study and he was finally accepted. One biographer notes that the class he joined was "a particularly brilliant one" (Jones, 1986, p. 15), for it included Henri Bergson, who was to become a prominent philosopher and influenced William James; Pierre Janet, who was to become a psychologist/analyst and influenced Sigmund Freud; and Jean Jaures, who later became one of most influential socialist leaders in France.

Durkheim finished his formal education and passed the examination required for teaching in 1882, and for the next few years he taught philosophy at several different schools. He arranged to go to Germany in 1885 to study with psychologist William Wundt, and this increased his interest in the scientific study of society and social problems. In 1887 he joined the Faculty of Letters at Bordeaux. A few years earlier, Bordeaux had established France's first course in pedagogy for prospective school teachers, and Durkheim was given the responsibility for lecturing on the theory, history, and practice of education. As a result, he became involved in the teaching of teachers for the rest of his life. He was a strong teacher, and one of his biographers suggested that he did not just teach students, but made disciples of them (Lukes, 1973).

In addition to his duties teaching, Durkheim also conducted research studies on the structure and function of groups and gave lectures on social problems. He thought that the French educational system needed to be more scientific. His research methodology was to observe groups and record the number of various types of interaction (Durkheim, 1982). Although most of his colleagues were more interested in classical studies of philosophy, history, law, and literature, his scholarly papers and lectures on developing a scientific approach to sociology brought him recognition. Five years later, before he was 30 years old, he was appointed as chair of a new Department of Social Science at Bordeaux.

Because of his notoriety as a sociologist, Durkheim's importance as an educational theorist has often been overlooked. In 1902, France's greatest university, the Sorbonne, appointed him a professor in a Department of the Science of Education. A decade later he assumed the chair of that department, and renamed it the Department of the Science of Education and Sociology.

When World War I erupted in Europe, the social-political right grew stronger. Durkheim's secular humanism was in keeping with the goals of France's Third Republic because it was reflective of the new humanistic religion that was replacing traditional Catholic and Protestant views. When that approach came under criticism, Durkheim was upset because he had always attempted to stay out of political controversies. He was also quite distressed when many of the students he had taught were drafted into the army, sent to the front, and perished in the bloody trench warfare. When his own son was killed in the war, he sank into a deep depression from which he never fully recovered. He did return to teaching for a short time a year later, but died of a stroke in 1917 at the age of 59.

Basic Philosophy

The foundations of Durkheim's philosophy may well have been his agnosticism. Like his contemporary philosophers Karl Marx and Max Weber, he believed that religion was based on an irrational illusion, and that was why the church could not provide the moral compass that people needed. The alternative guide for moral action was for society to come to a consensus about desirable values and behaviors. As a social scientist, he noted that the actual content of a society's morality is relative, for each society needs to have a system that fits its own needs. Like Marx, Durkheim had concerns about the problems created for a society by capitalism, but he advocated scientific study of those problems, not revolt against them. He truly believed that a rational-empirical understanding of the shortcomings of society would lead to change. What France needed, according to Durkheim, was a rational, humanistic, secular morality.

He argued that moral unity and consensus of values was necessary for any group or any society to survive, and it was the state—not religion and not the individual—that should stand as the authority on an appropriate moral code. He believed that once a society reaches consensus about appropriate morality and conduct, they can then socialize people into the patterns of behavior deemed important in that society (Durkheim, 2002). This was not a popular argument among the French people at that time, for there was considerable social-political conflict between modernism and the church about basic life values.

Although he tried to stay away from social/political arguments, Durkheim could not avoid being drawn in. The courses he taught at the Sorbonne were required for all students seeking degrees in the liberal arts, and he was responsible for the education of hundreds of future teachers. After he was appointed to the national Ministry of Public Instruction, he found himself in the middle of academic and social-political conflicts. His critics accused him of creating new positions and filling university chair positions with people who agreed with his moral philosophy and sociology of education. He was criticized by progressive educators who said that his ideas about education gave teachers domination over the minds of their students.

The Role of Education

Durkheim drew upon his studies of the structure and function of groups and societies, and argued that although communities and families are an important part of the socialization process, the most important force in that process is formal education. Society sets up schools primarily to impart societal values to students. He suggested that there was no difference between the processes of education and socialization.

He believed that, like society-at-large, the schools must maintain and model the values and morality that is to be transmitted to the children. Schools must be a microcosm of society, giving the students life experiences that will enable them to adjust in their adult lives. According to Durkheim, this meant that individuals must come to recognize their responsibilities to the group:

> Man is double. There are two beings in him: an individual being which has its foundation in the organism and the circle of whose activities is therefore strictly limited, and a social being which represents the highest reality in the intellectual and moral order that we can know by observation—I mean society. In so far as he belongs to society, the individual transcends himself, both when he thinks and when he acts. (Durkheim, 2006, p. 2)

He suggests that because humans are social beings, they must balance their personal needs and desires with attention to the greater good of the group. While autonomy and personal development is important, each person must accept their place in society and recognize that there is a higher authority in the group.

Durkheim suggested that societies also needed to recognize the importance of maintaining their vocational-industrial resources. This means there must be attention to the necessary division of labor for a smoothly functioning society, and thus education must play a role in teaching people the life skills for future occupations. The value of a division of labor must be recognized (Giddens, 1972). People must be educated to accept and find satisfaction in their vocational role within the group. Society and formal education should make no great distinction between the importance of the farm worker and the lawyer, or between the store clerk and the store manager.

What the Schools Should and Should Not Do

Durkheim suggested that the schools should serve society. Educators must consider how the schools function within society and recognize their responsibilities to society. Schools should prepare students for meaningful lives within their society. Educators should not have the goal of changing society. Although society's needs and values should continually change, as old standards outlive their usefulness, the necessary changes must be made by the larger society, not by the schools. Changes begin with societal re-definition, not with the educational process. In other words, he believed that the schools should follow society, not lead it.

He thought it important that schools imitate society. Educational systems usually do reflect societal systems because they are organized and funded by society, and society naturally seeks to "reproduce its collectively held values, beliefs, norms and conditions through its institutions" (Hoenisch, 2004, p. 1). Teachers should model the moral codes of their society. Like John Dewey, who believed that one of the purposes of education was to teach the values of democracy, Durkheim believed that all education should involve teaching people the values and behaviors needed for adjustment to their society. He noted that there must be congruence between the values of society and the methodology employed in schools. Just as there are always authority figures in society, so it is entirely appropriate that there are authorities (teachers) in the classroom who can direct the growth and development of each child toward discovery of their place in society.

When his critics argued that implementation of his recommendations would involve destroying the free-will of students, and treating them as puppets of the ideology of the state, Durkheim defended his belief by noting that each society must accomplish the socialization of youth in ways that correspond to their values and beliefs. If a society values rationality and trusts that knowledge will lead people to accept the common good, then students need not be indoctrinated with a state system of values because appropriate knowledge will lead them to understand the appropriate values.

Unlike Jean-Jacques Rousseau, educational theorist of the 18th century who did not trust the schools to cultivate good character in developing children, Durkheim had great faith in schools and teachers. Durkheim also disagreed with Rousseau's student, Johann Pestalozzi, who argued that teachers should guide students to counter-culture values and behaviors. Furthermore, he was skeptical that teachers educated within a society and usually employed by that society, could ever be a force in re-directing that society.

Durkheim offered suggestions for the actual process of education in the classroom. He admired Rousseau's ideas about learning by having experiences with objects and with nature, but thought that experiences with the group could facilitate learning about how people needed to balance their individual concerns with those of others. Education should be "a continuous effort to improve on the child's ways of seeing, feeling and acting at which he would not have arrived spontaneously" (Durkheim, 1982, p. 44).

Since formal education should focus on the development of knowledge and skills that prepared the individual for society, he was not in support of including much philosophy and history in the curriculum. However, he did advocate that it was important for students to study about the lives of historic figures who had done good things for their society, for they were ideal role models. He also approved of discussions about ethics, for learning about social morality was the most important part of a child's education. His book, *Moral Education* (Durkheim, 2002) presents 18 lectures that discuss the school as an appropriate setting for moral education (Durkheim, 2002). He saw a relativistic socially responsible ethic as most appropriate for schools.

Durkheim and Experiential Education

Durkheim's sociological philosophy of education should be explored by contemporary experiential educators for a number of reasons:

1. *Education vs. Socialization.* Although many people have made a distinction between the processes of education and socialization, Durkheim treats them as synonymous. It is appropriate for experiential educators to ask if Durkheim is right, or whether there is an important difference between them. Some of those who argue for a distinction usually see socialization as a process of preparing people to be effective members of society and education as a process to prepare people for critical reflection and a motivation to change society.

Durkheim argued, "society can survive only if there exists among its members a sufficient degree of homogeneity" (1956, p. 70). Furthermore, he thought that it is only within the collectivity of the group that individuality can develop appropriately. Humans are social beings, and cannot be whole without being connected to the group. While his critics seldom argue against socialization as a valuable process for society, they often suggest that educators should have different goals. Those who advocate that these two developmental processes are different, suggest that even though "we might expect all activities to have both socializing and educative aspects—the degree of which will vary from activity to activity" (Eagan, 2005, p. 4). Seeing the two processes as the same can lead to "the erosion of educational activities in schools in favor of increasing socialization" (Egan, 2005, p. 4).

In the context of this argument about distinguishing between education and socialization, it may be valuable for experiential educators to examine the intention of their programs and the desired goals of the various activities used in them. It may also be valuable to compare Durkheim's ideas with those of other educational philosophers who are considered important for experiential education.

2. *Durkheim and Dewey.* John Dewey, considered by many as the founding father of experiential education, did not make reference to Emile Durkheim, but his views on education paralleled Durkheim's in a number of ways. Dewey also saw education as a social process, beginning in the home and continuing in school. Dewey saw education as a two-sided process, having both psychological (personal development) and sociological (social development) goals, but the final goal was to prepare the child for adjustment to society. Dewey argued that schools would fail if they were not perceived as part of community life.

Reconstructionist educational philosophers criticized Dewey partly because of this parallel with Durkheim, suggesting that educators should cultivate individuality and critical thinking, and produce leaders who challenge society and reform the system (cf, Brameld, 1956; Counts, 1932/1978; Goodman, 1969, 1973).

Dewey recognized the problem. In his book *Democracy and Education* (1916/1966), he wrote about the importance of schools following the goals of broader society, but warned that the aims of society were ill-defined and thus poorly reflected in schools. He wrote about researching the problem and discovering that, "The aim of education and its national aim were identified, and the result was a marked obscuring of the meaning of the social aim" (p. 97). For Dewey, concrete application of Durkheim's abstract suggestion that schools reflect the goals of society proved difficult because in a democratic society there were many different opinions about what the moral code and the national goals should be. He concluded: "Conception of education as a social process and function has no definite meaning until we define the kind of society we have in mind" (p. 97).

Therefore, Dewey chose to emphasize the importance of individual growth and development, and the school as a model of democratic process. Like Durkheim, he saw the classroom as a microcosm of society, and for America that meant teaching children experientially about the democratic process. When the classroom focuses on the students' personal growth and development, and enhancing their understanding of small group and societal processes, there is less attention paid to traditional academics. Thus, Dewey's "progressive education," like Durkheim's "education as socialization," set the stage for criticism from traditional educators.

Conflict about educational philosophy and purpose continues to this day. "In North America there has prevailed a powerful reaction to seeing the schools merely as socializing institutions" (Egan, 2005, p. 5). "The traditionalists have not gone away, nor have the progressives conceded defeat with back-to-basics" (Egan, 2005, p. 7). Where do experiential educators stand on this issue?

3. *Durkheim and Freire.* The argument that the purpose of education is to teach people to hold the values of that society and to grow up and accept their place in society puts Durkheim in direct opposition to contemporary educational reconstructionists like Paulo Freire who believe that the purpose of education should be to teach people to rise up against the injustices of their society and change the social structure (Freire, 1970; Kincheloe, 2004). Freire's pedagogy has become increasingly popular with experiential educators during the past decade (Breunig, 2005; Itin, 1999). He advocates that the purpose of education should be to teach students to transform the social order; educational reform must precede societal reform. Students must be empowered with critical thinking and problem-solving skills. "Rather than feeling frustrated or powerless or depending on someone to advocate for them, individuals learn specific procedures for analyz-

ing problems, investigating alternative courses of action and carrying out these actions" (Sleeter, 1990, p. 8).

Implications for EE Philosophy

Experiential education is currently unfolding without a clear delineation of an underlying philosophy. Emile Durkheim's philosophy has been largely overlooked, but experiential educators should certainly ponder the questions raised by his views. Is it appropriate to see socialization and education as the same thing? Is the purpose of formal education to inculcate students with the values and beliefs of the society-at-large? If one makes a distinction between the two processes, should experiential education focus on education or socialization? Should experiential education be preparing students for society and the world as it is—or as it should be?

The Association for Experiential Education has a mission statement suggesting that experiential education should seek to educate students toward critical thinking and readiness for dealing with problems of justice in society. "The vision of the Association for Experiential Education is to contribute to making a more just and compassionate world by transforming education" (AEE, 2007, p. 2). Acceptance of this goal by many of those in the profession may account for the popularity of Paulo Freire's educational philosophy. However, this may not be the vision of many others in the profession, including the administrators who often bring EE programs to their schools.

There may even be inconsistency between AEE's statement of vision and their definition of experiential education. "Experiential education is a philosophy and methodology in which educators purposefully engage with learners in direct experiences and focused reflection in order to increase knowledge, develop skills and clarify values" (AEE, 2007, p. 1). Considering Durkheim's ideas one could ask, "personal values" or "societal values?"

Perhaps there is a continuum that runs from Durkheim's theory of education for social compliance on the right, and Freire's ideas about education for social change on the left. Dewey's philosophy of education falls somewhere between these two. Perhaps the experiential methodology can be used for both education (in the sense of developing critical thinking and motivations to change society) and socialization (in the sense of developing people who accept the values of society). I think it would be valuable for experiential educators to examine the intentions of their programs in relation to Durkheim's philosophy, as they seek to build a more comprehensive philosophy for use in their profession.

References

Association for Experiential Education (AEE). (2007). *What is experiential education?* Retrieved January, 2007, from http://www.AEE.org/about/whatisEE

Brameld, T. (1956). *Toward a reconstructed philosophy of education.* New York: Dryden.

Breunig, M. (2005). Turning experiential education and critical pedagogy theory into practice. *Journal of Experiential Education, 28*(2), 106–122.

Counts, G. (1978). *Dare the schools build a new social order?* (Reprinted from the 1932 edition). Carbondale: Southern Illinois University.

Dewey, J. (1966). *Democracy and education: An introduction to the philosophy of education.* New York: The Macmillian Company. (Original work published 1916)

Durkheim, E. (1956). *Education and sociology* (S. D. Fox Trans.). New York: Free Press.

Durkheim, E. (1982). *The rules of sociological method* (W. D. Halls Trans.). New York: Free Press.

Durkheim, E. (2002). *Moral education.* New York: Dover Publications.

Durkheim, E. (2006). Emile Durkheim quotes. Retrieved December, 2006, from http://www.emile-durk heim.com/emile_durkheim_quotes

Egan, K. (2005). Educating and socializing: A proper distinction? Retrieved July 10, 2006, from http://www.edu.sfu.ca/kegan/read823

Freire, P. (1970). *Pedagogy of the oppressed.* New York: Continuum Publishing.

Giddens, A. (Ed.). (1972). *Emile Durkheim: Selected writings.* Cambridge, UK: Cambridge University.

Goodman, J. (1969). *Growing up absurd.* New York: Random House.

Goodman, J. (1973). *Compulsory miseducation.* New York: Penguin Books.

Hoenisch, S. (2004). Durkheim and educational systems. Retrieved December, 2006, from http://www.criticism.com/philosophy/durkheim

Itin, C. (1999). Reasserting the philosophy of experiential education as a vehicle for change in the 21st century. *Journal of Experiential Education, 22*(2), 91–98.

Jones, R. A. (1986). *Emile Durkheim: An introduction to four major works.* Beverly Hills, CA: Sage.

Kincheloe, J. L. (2004). *Critical pedagogy.* New York: Peter Lang.

Lukes, S. (1973). *Emile Durkheim: His life and works.* New York: Harper & Row.

Sleeter, C. (1990). *Empowerment through multicultural education.* Albany: State University of New York.

19 Lev Vygotsky

Experiential Education—A View From the Future

Jayson Seaman and Matthew Gingo

Regarding soccer's halting popularity in the United States, Uruguayan author Eduardo Galeano quipped: "It is the sport of the future, and it always will be" (2002, p. 191). One might make a similar statement about experiential education in the United States: it is the reform movement of the future, and it might always be. This challenge is relevant to the question raised by this collection of biographies and philosophies: What is the future of experiential education philosophical foundations beyond those of John Dewey and Kurt Hahn?

One answer to this provocative question may paradoxically come from the past, by studying a contemporary of Dewey who is only starting to gain recognition in the experiential education fields. Like Dewey, Russian scholar Lev Vygotsky was ahead of his time, and may be ahead of ours. As one writer asks: "who was this man of blue eyes and mellow voice who speaks to us from the future?" (Blanck, 1990, p. 32). Although occasional references have been made to Vygotsky's writing (e.g., Carver, 1996; Kraft, 1990; Quay, 2003), his ideas have had little impact on the theories and research approaches used in experiential education.

This chapter reflects our effort to listen more closely to this voice from the future.

Who Is this Voice from the Future?

Lev Semenovich Vygotsky, born November 17, 1896, into a well-off Jewish family in Belorussia, was intellectually encouraged as a child. He benefitted from supportive teachers who felt he could excel in any area he chose. He studied literature, drama, history, and philosophy, and spoke several languages including Russian, Greek, Hebrew, English, French, and Esperanto. Despite his intellectual ability, Vygotsky faced discriminatory admissions policies when applying to Moscow University, which only allocated 3% of its seats for Jews. His superior performance on his qualifying tests earned him a place in the admissions lottery and luck won him one of these seats. At the University, Vygotsky studied medicine, law, linguistics, psychology, and philosophy before defending his dissertation at age 20 (Gielen & Jeshmaridian, 1999).

Vygotsky's turn to psychology was particularly influenced by three diverse fields, as well as by his early religious and intellectual training. First, his background in literature and poetics prompted an interest in the relationship among language, thinking, and creativity. Second, Darwin's On the Origins of Species by Natural Selection, published in 1859, opened to Vygotsky an evolutionary, or developmental, way of thinking about human functioning (Bruner, 1987). Finally, and perhaps most importantly, Vygotsky was drawn to Marxist philosophy: "Having as a Jew endured all the fears of pogroms and oppressions in Gomel, his hometown, he looked at Marxian ideology and at Bolshevik promises of proletarian freedom as representing rational, humanistic, and European promises of salvation and redemption" (Gielen & Jeshmaridian, 1999, p. 279). Marxism gave Vygotsky a comprehensive social, cultural, and historical framework for his grand psychological theory, yet his commitment to individual intellectual development enabled him to think beyond the strict determinism common at the time (Elhammoumi,

2002). These conditions would be both a defining feature of his approach and a political problem that would contribute to his death.

As a young man, Vygotsky openly critiqued the behaviorist masters of his era. Their focus on stimulus and response, he argued, denied human consciousness and neglected the role of culture in development (Cole & Scribner, 1978). He sought a psychology that would account for humans' active purposes while also recognizing the influence of culture and history on development. Because of his challenge to behaviorism, then dominating Russian psychology, Vygotsky's work was both intellectually and socially revolutionary.

Central to his challenge was the desire to create a psychology rooted in social interaction, uniting what happens "in the head" with what happens "out in the world"—key tenets of Marxist philosophy. Educational anthropologist Jean Lave (1988) describes the essence of Vygotsky's theory:

> What we call cognition is in fact a complex social phenomenon… The point is not so much that arrangements of knowledge in the head correspond in a complicated way to the social world outside the head, but that they are socially organized in such a fashion as to be indivisible. "Cognition" observed in everyday practice is distributed stretched over-not divided among-mind, body, activity and culturally organized settings. (p. 1)

In this view, people learn and develop not just by responding to behavioral stimuli. They are shaped by and actively shape the activities in which they participate, relying on tools such as language, art, maps, writing, and mathematical symbols to do their thinking and accomplish their goals (Vygotsky, 1981).

As his perspective became more widespread in the early 1930s, Vygotsky emerged as a major figure in Soviet psychology. However, the Vygotskyan school would soon face political pressure. Since Vygotsky synthesized European ideas regarding intellectual development with Marxism, he was labeled a "bourgeois psychologist" and was blacklisted when Stalin rose to power. His work was banned from 1936 to 1956 as Stalin revived a reductionistic strain of behaviorism to support his political ideology. Sadly, Vygotsky died a lonely and desperate death at the age of 37, finally succumbing to tuberculosis after being ousted from the Communist Party—a blow that crushed his spirit (Gielen & Jeshmaridian, 1999).

Uniting his personal upbringing, his wide-ranging intellectual interests, and the social fervor of the Russian revolution, Vygotsky developed what has become known as a cultural-historical perspective on human development (Cole, 1995). In this view, humans weave webs of culturally meaningful thought, action, and understanding in which they are also embedded. Vygotsky's ideas have had a profound influence on psychology in Russia and increasingly in the West, as scholars such as Michael Cole began importing his ideas in the 1960s (Roth & Lee, 2007). His ideas are highly compatible with the pragmatism of Dewey and Mead (Engestrom & Miettinen, 2003), creating a possible point of connection with experiential education at a philosophical level. However, many of the models of contemporary experiential education practice obscure this connection. For instance, despite Kolb's (1984) brief reference to both Vygotsky and Cole, his model emphasizes structured settings, time-frames, and instructional techniques for experiential learning to occur. These should be contrasted with a Vygotskyan framework, which would see experiential learning as the natural way we learn through collaborative participation in everyday community practices.

This distinction is sharpest in two key areas. First, Vygotskyans downplay the role of reflection as a basic condition for learning, focusing instead on people's changing participation in various activities. Second, institutionalized schooling would not be viewed as "non-experiential" (cf. Lindsay & Ewert, 1999). A helpful way to understand this distinction is to view classroom learning as experiential, the question being what and how students learn through classroom experiences, many of which segregate them from adult activity, are deskbound, and take for granted Western middle-class ways of knowing as a developmental endpoint. This stance helps Vygotskyans separate "assembly line" and "scientific" learning in formal settings from "everyday" learning while maintaining theoretical coherence (Hedegaard & Lompscher, 1999; Rogoff, 2003). This distinction can also help overcome the problematic "theory" versus "practice" dichotomy found in popular experiential education texts (Coleman, 1995; Wurdinger & Priest, 1999).

While not described as an educator per se, Vygotsky was involved in the field of education. In his experiments, "Vygotsky's special focus was on children's development and education within their historically and culturally constituted environments" (Gielen & Jeshmaridian, 1999, p. 274). He helped found pedology, which was "a kind of action-oriented educational psychology emphasizing a psychological approach to child development, testing, and certain kinds of intervention by educators" (Gielen & Jeshmaridian, p. 283). Pedology was similar to the child-centered psychology influencing early 20th century Progressive educators in the United States. However, in contrast to Western developmental psychology, Vygotsky did not think children's interests and developmental trajectories were solely internal to the child; they were interpreted through the dual lenses of history and culture. This led to consideration of social interaction with peers and adults as a central feature of Vygotsky's approach. Although not "experiential" as we now understand it, it was through their interactions with mature others that children would "grow into the intellectual life of those around them" (Vygotsky, 1978, p. 88), internalizing social attitudes and ways of thinking. In Vygotsky's terms:

> We are conscious of ourselves because we are conscious of others; and in an analogous manner, we are conscious of others because in our relationship to ourselves we are the same as others in their relationship to us. I am aware of myself only to the extent that I am as another for myself.... The individual aspect of consciousness is constructed as derived and secondary, based on the social and exactly according to its model. (Vygotsky, 1925, p. 174)

Habits of mind (e.g., thinking flexibly, posing problems, using judgment), in Vygotsky's framework, are profoundly social from the very start, rooted in longstanding cultural traditions passed on through our interactions with caregivers, peers, texts, and other artifacts. These emphases continue to guide research in the Vygotskyan tradition.

Although there are several different interpretations of Vygotsky's ideas, three major principles guide most current scholarship:

Mental/social functioning is shaped by culturally provided tools and goals.
"Mediation" is key to this process.
Researchers should study co-development, or the ways individuals, situations, and institutions evolve together. (cf. John-Steiner & Mahn, 1996)

Researchers will often focus on one principle in any given study, yet the integration of these points is what makes Vygotsky's theoretical framework most influential. Broadly speaking, complex mental processes begin as social activities; as children develop, they gradually internalize processes they use in social contexts and begin to use them independently as tools for thinking and self-regulation. This theory rests on the proposition that higher psychological functioning—"self-directed attention, categorical perception, logical memory, and conceptual thinking" (Gredler, 2007, p. 235)—originates in social interactions, which are themselves influenced by broader historical, cultural, and economic patterns such as capitalism. Vygotsky wrote: "every function in the child's cultural development appears twice: first, on the social level, and later, on the individual level" (Vygotsky, 1978, p. 57). It is by collaborating with others in long-standing cultural practices that meaning, knowledge, and habits of mind are constructed. People learn as they participate in socially valued activities, gaining dexterity with the goals, practices, and tools common to the activities of which they are a part. Three examples help illustrate these principles.

The Rogoff Study: Girl Scout cookie sales. Rogoff and her colleagues (Baker-Sennett, Lacasa, & Goldsmith, 1995) studied the ways children learn habits of memorization and organization when involved in the sale of Girl Scout cookies. The planning and management of orders, sales routes, and exchange of money, organized in collaboration with parents, peers, customers, and scout leaders all contributed to the girls' complex problem-solving skills. In addition to the negotiation of these social factors, the girls' experience was guided by tools provided by the national organization and adapted from the experience of previous scout troops (e.g., mathematical and memory aids added to the order forms, such as color-coded columns). As the girls participated in and gained experience with these culturally constituted activities, they began to develop and reorganize their mental habits to help them solve future problems.

Rogoff et al.'s (1995) study illustrates how a culturally valued activity—selling Girl Scout cookies—is imbued with artifacts, roles, and objectives that powerfully shape the paths taken by its participants, and are also shaped by the participants over time. This longstanding economic activity forms an important "social situation of development" (Vygotsky, in Bodrova, 2003) in which its participants collaboratively develop new skills such as mathematical reasoning, memorization, and logical organization.

The Seaman Study: In an empirical study of challenge course programs, Seaman (2007) argues that experiential learning in an adventure context is a process of "kinaesthetically mediated collaboration." In the workshops he studied, leaders skillfully used different artifacts—ropes course elements, flipchart diagrams, small hand-held "props"—to achieve the institutional goal of personal development in a group setting. In other words, the challenge course served as a set of tools requiring bodily, spatial, and verbal coordination among people as they solved problems together.

Seaman's work builds on the three central Vygotskyan principles: (a) In addition to helping people develop as adventure educators, the programs he studied fit within a larger cultural framework of individual autonomy, instrumental reasoning, and social role taking—key values of Western adventure practice and education. (b) Many events on the challenge course were structured to promote mutual interconnection as an integral element of people's knowing about their experiences. This awareness arose as relative strangers touched one another, disclosed personal information, stood in close proximity, and adjusted their perspectives with others who held differing values, beliefs, and behaviors. (c) People's deeper conceptual achievements seemed to occur during these moments of joint negotiation, when people used these newly developed, shared tools to restructure their relations. These achievements may be considered complex forms of subjectivity, which "is the ability to show by coordinated acts that purposes are being consciously regulated" and intersubjectivity, which "is the ability to adapt one's practical activities to the subjectivity of others" (Elhammoumi, 2002, p. 95). These concepts, which blur the line between cognitive, social, and emotional development, may open up new ways of researching learning in experiential settings.

The Emo Study: Science Learning in 4-H. Using the same methodological approach as Seaman, Emo (2006) studied the way children learned scientific habits of mind through participation in 4-H agricultural fairs. The children studied—along with adult volunteers—raised a large animal to bring to market. Emo posited that "what [children] learn is shaped by the activity in which they are involved and how they participate in that activity" (p. 1).

Emo found the 4-H activity to have explicit and implicit rules for conduct that shaped children's learning. These rules included deadlines, weight restrictions, guidelines for animal care, methods for data recording, and financial restrictions. These rules affected both the children's and their supportive adults' approach to raising their animal and preparing it for the market. Although the primary goal of the activity was to raise, exhibit, and sell an animal, not to teach them about science, by engaging as apprentices in this activity, children practiced scientific habits of mind: causal thinking, logical reasoning, and methodical data interpretation. These findings illustrate the ways complex forms of thinking are embedded within informal work practices and are not limited to schooling (cf. Lave, 1988; Scribner, 1984).

These examples represent an exciting new wave of interest and research into experiential learning as it occurs in and out of schools, with children and adults alike. What we have presented here is just the tip of the iceberg. We want to emphasize that learning through experience is a central topic in classical and neo-Vygotskyan research, and we want to encourage the exploration of further links with experiential education practices. There are, however, several implications worth noting.

The studies reviewed above reinforce the value of social interaction, joint problem solving, and real-world practice in learning. These themes will resonate with experiential educators. Yet the theory behind the examples also challenges some basic assumptions descendant from the humanist legacy of the 1970s. First, the examples suggest that learning has much to do with the ways people coordinate their actions around historically established tools, rules, and goals, and the ways they adapt them to new uses. This realization challenges the belief that individual learners are "free to chart the course of our own destiny" (Kolb, 1984, p. 109) and that instructors are somehow not "mediators between students and the world" (Chapman, 1995, p. 239). Our examples show how people's actions and learning are mutually embedded within historical and cultural worlds, aspects that are downplayed in many learner-centered models. However, adopting a more explicit social perspective does not mean that experiential educators should ignore individual contributions.

> Clearly, for collaboration to occur, there must be a degree of overlap in goals and a willingness to attempt to understand the perspectives of others. Without the contribution of new and even antithetical ideas and suggestions, there would be no way of going beyond ways of acting and thinking repeated from the past; and although well-tried solutions are often a good starting point, they may have to be challenged and transformed if they are to become adequate responses to novel predicament. (Wells & Claxton, 2002, p. 5)

Adopting this principle will require experiential educators to identify the social knowledge traditions emphasized in the activities they organize, in addition to supporting individuals' learning.

As Vygotsky challenged establishment thinking in Russia, Dewey wrestled with the problem of education in post-industrial American education. During the early years of the 20th century, many individual teachers adopted Dewey's ideas, but the school system in general was more influenced by curricular politics when agrarian schoolhouses consolidated into a bureaucratic school system (Kliebard, 1995; Seaman, 2008, 2010). The 1970s saw a resurgence of some of the principles of progressive education when humanistic educators championed experiential learning as a promising reform in higher education, adult development, and informal settings such as outdoor adventure programs (Chickering, 1977; Keeton, 1976; Miner, 1996).

Guided in part by Dewey, experiential educators since the 1970s have promoted reflective thinking and have established the legitimacy of hands-on approaches to learning in and out of schools. Their learner-centered philosophy has provided an important check to the depersonalized, industrial-era educational system, and their inventiveness has contributed to many exciting practices to schools and communities. However, in today's era characterized by cultural diversity, interactive media, interdisciplinary research, and rapidly changing knowledge, experiential education may be constrained by these very philosophies and ideologies. In particular, the notion that "learning happens through cognitive reflection, experience can be considered like a bounded object, and an individual learner can be separated from his or her experience to process knowledge from that experience" (Fenwick, 2001, pp. 7–8) is increasingly recognized as a narrow interpretation of Dewey and a limited view of experiential learning (Miettinen, 2000; Wilson & Hayes, 2002).

The assumptions noted above, which appear widely in popular definitions of experiential education (e.g., AEE, n.d.; Itin, 1999), ironically downplay the role of human interrelationships, culture, and materiality in people's learning. Instead, they emphasize the individualized, abstract, and overly cognitive knowledge systems prioritized within Western society (Fenwick, 2001). In contrast, sociocultural theories of learning and mental development, such as Vygotsky's, retain a focus on hands-on learning and cognitive development while systematically taking social interaction and cultural context into account. In other words, they open up deeper ways of thinking about the relationship between experience and learning. Vygotsky's perspective may better support experiential educators' central claims as we look to the future: namely that individual learners benefit from collaboration with others, that problems are better solved jointly, that we learn by interacting with the physical world, and that social change and individual change are interrelated. At the very least, it is becoming more and more apparent that experiential educators should consider "the interrelatedness of education and culture" (Wichmann, 1980, p. 12) at a deeper level in their theories and practices. While for experiential educators this is an underexplored topic, it defined Vygotsky's career over 80 years ago.

From a practical point of view, Vygotskyan concepts have implications for the role of the instructor and peers in joint problem solving. It has long been suggested that instructors should be "intentional" in the ways they orchestrate the social and physical conditions of experience, yet this raises a question: What principles guide intentionality? Presently, these principles seem largely to be "gut instinct, past experience, and borrowed or untested philosophical understanding or belief" (Sibthorp, 2003, p. 81). Two ideas come to mind within a Vygotskyan framework. On the activity side, educators might ask: What activity do I hope learners can perform skillfully after receiving instruction? And, on the learner side: What can they do now, on their own? These questions then lead to: What kinds of experience would help learners (a) adopt the goals of the activity, and (b) gain dexterity with its tools and interpersonal relationships? According to Rogoff and Wertsch, "It was in the course of applying [his] theoretical concepts to practical problems in cognitive and educational psychology that Vygotsky introduced the notion of the zone of proximal development" (ZPD; 1984, p. 2). Vygotsky (1978) defined the ZPD as "the distance between the actual developmental level as determined by independent problem solving and the level of potential development as determined through problem solving under adult guidance or in collaboration with more capable peers" (p. 86). In the ZPD, children, aided by more expert partners, appropriate the skills needed for a participation in activity that is slightly beyond their competence. This helps children further participate in mature activities, along with mastering cultural tools they can use elsewhere (e.g., language or arithmetic). In the "zone," mentors provide verbal cues, arrange physical spaces, and introduce challenging problems, each ripe with cultural meaning and ways of knowing, in order to help children take on more responsibility and become self, rather than other, regulated. In this process, "learning awakens a variety of internal developmental processes that are able to operate only when the child is interacting with people in his environment and in cooperation with his peers" (p. 90). One useful metaphor for this process of guided instruction is "scaffolding" (Bruner, 1975). Like the construction of a building, a mentor's assistance provides temporary support for the learner as skills develop—a new way to think of being intentional with one's instructional moves. By using this scaffolding, learners can rehearse practices they will be required to perform independently in the future. Taking this view, however, may require instructors to play a larger role than they ordinarily would in "discovery learning" as it is defined by many constructivist educators (Kirschner, Schweller, & Clark, 2006).

While the concept of the ZPD is helpful to instruction, much remains to be known about it in group settings where no clear expert exists. Here, experiential educators have a unique opportunity to study the concept of ZPD in a group setting; if collaboration with a mentor extends a child's individual capacities, how do multiple peer contributions expand a group's zone of proximal development, resulting in a whole that is greater than the sum of its parts? Researchers are starting to examine this question. Rogoff (2003) notes that in such group work "it is impossible to say 'whose' an object of joint focus is, or 'whose' a collaborative idea is" (p. 195). These principles should resonate with experiential educators interested in promoting active learning in groups, and researchers might find the Vygotskyan toolkit useful for taking up this important theme. This is a research area in which experiential educators can make an enormous contribution.

Vygotsky's ideas have further implications for research in experiential education. It has become commonplace for experiential education researchers to focus on individual variables and measure program outcomes. New research from a Vygotskyan perspective might adopt broader "units of analysis" than individual change on specific variables:

> When looking at both individual and social activity, we need to look beyond solitary actors to the communities to which they belong, and to the inherited resources of artifacts and practices that serve as 'tools' for achieving the goals to which their activities are directed. (Wells & Claxton, 2002, p. 3)

Adopting such an approach may also help experiential educators better understand and explain the powerful connections forged between people's experiences in different settings, helping them understand the phenomenon now known as "transfer" (cf. Beach, 1999).

Implications for EE Philosophy

Though developed across the globe from one another, Vygotsky's cultural-historical theory of development and Dewey's theory of social learning through experience share many similarities. There is some evidence suggesting that Dewey and Vygotsky met in 1928 when Dewey visited Russia to study their educational system and to speak with educational leaders (Prawat, 2000). Whether or not they met or knew each other's educational philosophies, their compatibility can be seen in Dewey's ideas on knowledge: "If the living, experiencing being is an intimate participant in the activities of the world to which it belongs, then knowledge is a mode of participation, valuable in the degree in which it is effective. It cannot be the idle view of an unconcerned spectator" (p. 393). Central to both perspectives is the shift from the individual actor to social activity as the key unit of analysis. By focusing on learning and development as social processes, both perspectives integrate the individual and the culture as mutually constitutive. Comparing and combining both perspectives may also provide deeper theoretical insight into Kurt Hahn's desire to promote human compassion and feelings of interconnectedness. In fact, we see great promise in exploring the possible connections among Dewey, Hahn, and Vygotsky, rather than using Vygotsky to speed beyond these important figures too quickly.

This shift from looking at the group as a collection of individual learners to a focus on active participants mutually engaged in one another's development stands at edge of our zone of proximal development as experiential educators. We see Vygotskyan theory as a lens through which our models, practices, and central assumptions can be viewed, challenged, and ultimately improved. Given the recent rise in popularity of Vygotsky's theory in Western scholarship, and given its inherent emphasis on learning through experience, we are again poised to stress the importance of experience in education in the 21st century. The question now is: Will we listen to this voice from the future?

References

Association for Experiential Education (AEE). (n.d.). AEE definition of experiential education. Retrieved November, 2005, from http://www.aee.org/faq/nfaq

Beach, K. (1999). Consequential transitions: A sociocultural expedition beyond transfer in education. *Review of Educational Research, 24*, 101–139.

Blanck, G. (1990). Vygotsky: The man and his cause. In L. C. Moll (Ed.), *Vygotsky and education: Instructional implications and applications of sociohistorical psychology* (pp. 31–58). Cambridge, UK: Cambridge University.

Bodrova, E. (2003). Vygotsky and Montessori: One dream, two visions. *Montessori Life, 15*(1), 30–33.

Bruner, J. S. (1975). The ontogenesis of speech acts. *Journal of Child Language, 2*, 1–40.

Bruner, J. (1987). Prologue to the English edition. In R. W. Reiber & A. S. Carton (Eds.), *The collected works of L. S. Vygotsky* (Vol. 1, pp. 1–36). New York: Plenum.

Carver, R. (1996). Theory for practice: A framework for thinking about experiential education. *Journal of Experiential Education, 19*(1), 8–13.

Chapman, S. (1995). What is the question? In K. Warren, M. Sakofs, & J. Hunt (Eds.), *The theory of experiential education* (pp. 236–239). Dubuque, IA: Kendall Hunt.

Chickering, A. (1977). *Experience and learning: An introduction to experiential learning.* New Rochelle, NY: Change Magazine.

Cole, M. (1995). Socio-cultural-historical psychology: Some general remarks and a proposal for a new kind of cultural-genetic methodology. In J. Wertsch, P. del Rio, & A. Alvarez (Eds.), *Sociocultural studies of mind* (pp. 187–214). New York: Cambridge University.

Cole, M., & Scribner, S. (1978). *Introduction to L. S. Vygotsky's mind in society.* Cambridge, MA: Harvard University.

Coleman, J. (1995). Experiential learning and information processing: Toward an appropriate mix. In K. Warren, M. Sakofs, & J. Hunt (Eds.), *The theory of experiential education* (pp. 123–130). Dubuque, IA: Kendall Hunt.

Elhammoumi, M. (2002). To create psychology's own capital. *Journal for the Theory of Social Behavior, 32*(1), 89–104.

Emo, K. (2006). *It's in the rulebook!: How rules shape children's use of science as they raise market animals in 4-H.* Paper presented at the SEER Symposium, 34th Annual Association for Experiential Education Conference.

Engestrom, Y., & Miettinen, R. (2003). Introduction. In Y. Engestrom, R. Miettinen, & R.-L. Punamaki (Eds.), *Perspectives on activity theory* (pp. 1–16). Cambridge, UK: Cambridge University.

Fenwick, T. (2001). *Experiential learning: A theoretical critique from five perspectives.* Ohio State University: ERIC Clearinghouse on Adult, Career, and Vocational Education.

Galeano, E. (2002). *Soccer in sun and shadow.* New York: Verso.

Gielen, U., & Jeshmaridian, S. S. (1999). Lev S. Vygotsky: The man and the era. *International Journal of Group Tensions, 28*(3/4), 273–301.

Gredler, M. E. (2007). Of cabbages and kings: Concepts and inferences curiously attributed to Lev Vygotsky (Commentary on McVee, Dunsmore, and Gavalek, 2005). *Review of Educational Resarch, 77*(2), 233–238.

Hedegaard, M., & Lompscher, J. (1999). *Learning activity and development.* Aarhus, Denmark: Aarhus University.

Itin, C. (1999). Reasserting the philosophy of experiential education as a vehicle for change in the 21st century. *Journal of Experiential Education, 22*(2), 91–98.

John-Steiner, V., & Mahn, H. (1996). Sociocultural approaches to learning and development: A Vygotskyan approach. *Educational Psychologist, 31*(3/4), 191–206.

Keeton, M. (Ed.). (1976). *Experiential learning: Rationale, characteristics and assessment.* San Francisco: Jossey-Bass.

Kirschner, P. A., Schweller, J., & Clark, R. E. (2006). Why minimal guidance does not work: An analysis of the failure of constructivist, discovery, problem-based, experiential, and inquiry-based teaching. *Educational Psychologist, 41*(2), 75–86.

Kliebard, H. M. (1995). *The struggle for the American curriculum, 1893–1958* (2nd ed.). New York: Routledge.

Kolb, D. (1984). *Experiential learning: Experience as the source of learning and development*. Englewood Cliffs, NJ: Prentice-Hall.

Kraft, R. (1990). Experiential learning. In J. C. Miles & S. Priest (Eds.), *Adventure education* (pp. 175–183). State College, PA: Venture.

Lave, J. (1988). *Cognition in practice: Mind, mathematics and culture in everyday life*. Cambridge, UK: Cambridge University.

Lindsay, A., & Ewert, A. (1999). Learning at the edge: Can experiential education contribute to educational reform? *Journal of Experiential Education, 22*(1), 12–19.

Miner, J. (1996). The creation of Outward Bound. In J. C. Miles & S. Priest (Eds.), *Adventure Education* (pp. 55–66). State College, PA: Venture.

Prawat, R. S. (2000). Dewey meets the "Mozart of psychology" in Moscow: The untold story. *American Educational Research Journal, 37*(3), 663–696.

Quay, J. (2003). Experience and participation: Relating theories of learning. *Journal of Experiential Education, 26*(2), 105–116.

Rogoff, B., & Wertsch, J. (1984). *Children's learning in the zone of proximal development*. San Francisco: Josey-Bass.

Rogoff, B. (2003). *The cultural nature of human development*. New York: Oxford University Press.

Rogoff, B., Baker-Sennett, J., Lacasa, P., & Goldsmith, D. (1995). Development through participation in sociocultural activity. In J. Goodnow, P. Miller, & F. Kessel (Eds.), *Cultural practices as context for development* (pp. 45–65). San Francisco: Jossey-Bass.

Roth, W. M., & Lee, Y. J. (2007). Vygotsky's neglected legacy: Cultural-historical activity theory. *Review of Educational Research, 77*(2), 186–232.

Scribner, S. (1984). Studying working intelligence. In B. Rogoff & J. Lave (Eds.), *Everyday cognition: Its development in social context* (pp. 9–40). Cambridge, MA: Harvard University.

Seaman, J. (2007). Taking things into account: Learning as kinaesthetically mediated collaboration. *Journal of Adventure Education and Outdoor Learning, 7*(1), 3–20.

Seaman, J. (2008). Experience, reflect, critique: The end of the 'learning cycle' era. *Journal of Experiential Education, 31*(1), 3–18.

Seaman, J. (2010). *A fresh look at a master's ideas: Reengaging Dewey's concept of 'experience' as curriculum theory*. Paper presented at the New England Educational Research Conference: Annual Meeting, Portsmouth, NH, April 9, 2010.

Sibthorp, J. (2003). An empirical look at Walsh and Golins' adventure education process model: Relationships between antecedent factors, perceptions of characteristics of adventure education experience, and changes in self-efficacy. *Journal of Leisure Research, 35*(1), 80–106.

Vygotsky, L. (1925). Consciousness as a problem in the psychology of behavior (N. Veresov, Trans.). In *Undiscovered Vygotsky: Etudes on the pre-history of cultural-historical psychology* (pp. 251–281). New York: Peter Lang.

Vygotsky, L. S. (1978). *Mind in society*. Cambridge, MA: Harvard University.

Vygotsky, L. S. (1981). The genesis of higher mental functions. In J. V. Wertsch (Ed.), *The Concept of activity in Soviet psychology* (pp. 144–188). Armonk, NY: M. E. Sharpe.

Wells, G., & Claxton, G. (2002). Introduction: Sociocultural perspectives on the future of education. In G. Wells & G. Claxton (Eds.), *Learning for life in the 21st century* (pp. 1–18). Oxford, UK: Blackwell.

Wichmann, T. F. (1980). Babies and bath water: Two experiential heresies. *Journal of Experiential Education, 3*(1), 6-12.

Wilson, A. L., & Hayes, E. R. (2002). From the editors: The problem of (learning in-from-to) experience. *Adult Education Quarterly, 52*(3), 173–175.

Wurdinger, S., & Priest, S. (1999). Integrating theory and application in experiential learning. In J. C. Miles & S. Priest (Eds.), *Adventure programming* (pp. 187–192). State College, PA: Venture.

20 Fritz Perls
Gestalt Therapy and Experiential Education

Thomas Lindblade

Personal Retrospective

The decades of the 1960s and 1970s were the seed-bed years in which experiential education germinated. At that time, much formal education consisted of a process in which a teacher lectured to students who memorized what was said and then regurgitated it on a test. The civil rights movement and the anti-war protests of this period launched an era in which that traditional authoritarian education model was questioned, and much of this debate focused on higher education. Educational critics and reformists like Paul Goodman (1960), James Coleman (1961), John Holt (1964), Neil Postman and Charles Weingartner (1969), and Ivan Illich (1971), questioned the relevance of an education that did not deal directly with the life issues facing students, and the value of memorizing material that was usually not used and forgotten in a short time. These issues were not always raised politely; sometimes they were discussed as part of student sit-ins, demonstrations, and campus take-overs. Not knowing how to deal with protesting students who sat in administrative offices, took over campus buildings, and even burned down a building or two, college administrators and faculty began a frantic search for a solution, and new "experimental" educational programs were born. Although some were little more than attempts to co-opt and pacify the protesters, others were legitimate attempts to re-think teaching and learning strategies.

This search for new approaches benefitted outdoor experiential education programs like Outward Bound, National Outdoor Leadership School, and Project Adventure, which were then developing their innovative strategies for facilitating personal growth in the outdoors. Young academics, like myself, who shared some serious concerns about traditional education, found that this demand for experimentation and innovation was tailor made for them. It was an exciting time to begin a career in education.

In 1970 I was hired as a counselor at the College of DuPage, a new two-year community college in suburban Chicago. The college had a solid financial base, a new young faculty, and a relatively inexperienced administration. Community colleges were different from traditional four-year higher education institutions with their political "publish or perish" expectations. We were, so to speak, the "new kids on the block," and we had the freedom to innovate and demonstrate effective alternatives to the old ways of teaching. Like most of my colleagues, after working at traditional institutions, I was ready for challenge and change.

I had been trained in a Rogerian counseling program. Carl Rogers' (1961) emphasis on compassion and humanism appealed to me. While I had become a passable Rogerian, I had begun to feel that the approach was too passive, and it did not seem that my clients grew very much. During a summer workshop to train Rogerian encounter group leaders, I was exposed to a two-film series called "Fritz Perls and Gestalt Therapy" (Perls, 1970). Perls wore an embroidered dashiki shirt, and looked like a somewhat balding Santa Claus, but it quickly became clear that he was no passive elf! In the films, he confronted clients, took risks, and structured the therapy sessions to help clients work through their own fantasies, issues and dreams. He had his clients make up their own metaphors and use them to work out unfinished emotional business and arrive at new awareness in the "here-and-now" of the present. The films showed accomplished performances by a master therapist and teacher, and I was quite inspired.

Biography

Frederick Saloman Perls (1893–1970) was born into an educated Jewish family in Berlin, Germany. He was a good student and chose to study medicine. His education was interrupted while he served in the army during World War I. After the war, he resumed his studies in medicine and began to concentrate on psychiatry. He was influenced by Freud and stimulated by the thoughts of a young psychoanalyst who became his friend, Wilhelm Reich.

Fritz, as he had come to be known, was in his mid-30s when he finished his studies, and 37 years old when he married. His wife, Laura, was to become his partner in life and in his professional work. As Hitler's influence expanded, they left Germany for the Netherlands, and then, in 1934, they moved to South Africa. Perls practiced psychiatry, growing progressively distant from Freud's ideas. With assistance from Laura, he completed his first book, *Ego, Hunger and Aggression: A Revision of Freud's Theory and Method* (Perls, 1942). The seeds of his therapeutic method of Gestalt Therapy appear in that book, and after a decade, reprints were subtitled, *The Beginnings of Gestalt Therapy* (Perls, 1969a).

During World War II, Perls served as a psychiatrist in the South African army, and after the war ended he immigrated to America, settling in New York. He worked with neo-Freudians Karen Horney and Otto Rank, and befriended a young writer, Paul Goodman. With the help of Goodman and Ralph Hefferline, an ex-patient who had become a psychologist, Perls published an overview to his ideas, *Gestalt Therapy: Excitement and Growth in Human Personality* (1951). The book was moderately successful, but because he was a dynamic personality and an effective showman, Fritz Perls and Gestalt Therapy became much better known through the series of films that showed him conducting therapy sessions.

In 1964 Perls moved to the Esalen Institute in California, the think tank and spiritual home of many leaders of the human potential movement. He quickly became a favorite speaker and presenter of workshops, and was one of the primary "gurus" at Esalen. There he worked with George Brown who was developing an educational approach based on Gestalt ideology which he later called "Confluent Education" (Brown, 1971). The literature on Gestalt Therapy expanded, but Perls recognized that the methodology could not be learned effectively from books. Throughout the 70s and 80s, he and his followers established Gestalt institutes and training centers around the country and the world. Although Perls always took primary credit for developing Gestalt Therapy, many others, including his wife Laura and his friend Paul Goodman, were involved in the expansion of the theory and practice through the years (Stoehr, 1997). After a long and successful career, Frederick Perls, colorful and beloved Fritz, died in Chicago at the age of 77 (Shepherd, 1975).

Brief Overview of Gestalt Therapy

Gestalt Therapy takes its name from the German school of Gestalt Psychology, but expands basic concepts of the perceptual field to a broader theory about human needs and behaviors. Perls' wife, Laura, had also trained as a psychoanalyst, and had worked with brain-injured soldiers after World War I under the guidance of Kurt Goldstein. She and Fritz were impressed with his "Organismic Theory," which viewed people and their experiences as a unified whole (Goldstein, 1939). This idea became the foundational theory of Gestalt Therapy. Goldstein also had an influence on Kurt Lewin, whose "Field Theory" became important to the theory and practice of Gestalt Therapy (Lewin, 1951).

Laura Perls also had a background in dance and movement exercise, and as young intellectuals in Berlin, she and Fritz became quite involved in the world of art, drama, and dance. This interest led them to an appreciation of psychoanalyst William Reich's ideas about "Character Armor" and "Orgonomy" (Reich, 1961). This focus contributed to the development of a number of innovative strategies for helping people break through their ego defenses in therapy. Perls was also interested in psychoanalyst Otto Rank's ideas about the implications of focus on the present as opposed to the past (Rank, 1978). Some of the classic Gestalt Therapy exercises were also developed from the Perls' appreciation of Jacob Moreno's techniques of "Psychodrama" (Moreno, 1946).

The influences of Goldstein, Lewin, Reich, and Rank can be seen in an overview to Gestalt Therapy from the institute in Philadelphia:

> In Gestalt Therapy, the whole and the integrity of the whole are crucially important. A core Gestalt concept is that we are born whole and full of possibilities and that we create adjustments as a way to cope with adversity. Gestalt Therapy seeks to resolve these "creative adjustments," which have become rigid, in order to enhance people's creativity, liveliness, and presence in the world. (Gestalt Therapy, n.d)

A singular comprehensive philosophy of Gestalt Therapy does not exist. It is a practice that involves using techniques that have roots in a variety of philosophies. A course on contemporary approaches to Gestalt Therapy offers this as a general description:

> The Gestalt approach has its roots in psychoanalysis, existentialism, Gestalt psychology, phenomenology, Field Theory, the philosophy of Martin Buber, some of the theories of William Reich, psychodrama and Zen Buddhism. In a remarkable synthesis borrowing from these and other approaches, Fritz and Laura Perls developed Gestalt Therapy in the 1940s and refined it in the 50s… They sought to look beyond the orthodoxy of psychoanalysis and behaviorism, seeking a model of human experience which valued authenticity and choice living. (Gunther, 2007, p. 1)

Gestalt Therapy was developed primarily as a set of strategies for effective counseling, and what might be considered as underlying theory grew out of practice. The conglomeration of valuable therapeutic strategies was complex from the start, and has become increasingly more complex through the years as professionals with diverse backgrounds and goals became involved. As a result, any attempt to offer a brief summary of Gestalt risks omissions and oversimplifications. However, Gestalt Therapy may be viewed as focusing on two important cornerstones, awareness and relationship.

Awareness: Gestalt Therapy is about heightened awareness, which is both the process and the goal. The process of becoming aware is an experience that involves mind, body and spirit. It involves more than just current thoughts and past memories; it includes feelings, perceptions, sensory and somatic stimulations, and social interactions. One of Perls' early students published a book, *Awareness: Exploring, Experimenting, Experiencing* (Stevens, 1973), which provided an overview to the process of awareness and suggested a repertoire of activities for facilitators.

Drawing on the ideas of Otto Rank about "here-and-now" therapy, Perls suggested that the role of a therapist is to facilitate experiences that will enhance present-centered awareness, because new awareness can only occur in the "here-and-now." According to his theory, talking about life in the past tense should be avoided, and in therapy sessions, when patients referenced the past, Perls would respond with a comment about them clenching their fist or wiggling their foot, activating the process of awareness of the here-and-now (Perls, 1970).

Achieving awareness as a goal implies that the facilitated experiences will lead the client to fuller cognitive and emotional understanding of self, others, environment, and their unity. The result of improved awareness is a more realistic appraisal of personal power and personal responsibility. Appropriate experiences in therapy result in the client becoming aware of how present behaviors, some of which may be dysfunctional, are the result of previous defensive adjustments to threatening situations which no longer exist. The ultimate goal of Gestalt Therapy is to help the client become more authentic, self-accepting, and aware of his/her higher possibilities.

Relationship: Gestaltists write about the importance of contact and dialogue because that creates relationship, and all experience is based on relationship. In other words, contact brings awareness of the boundaries between "me" and "not-me," and all experience is the result of interaction between self and non-self. There are strong parallels here with Martin Buber's ideas about "I-thou" and "I-it" interactions (Buber, 1970). Buber said, "all real life is meeting" (p. 15).

According to Perls, all experience is co-created. One of the key aspects of awareness is knowing the importance and value of relationships, and that means that the contact, the dialogue, the relationship between client and therapist is of great importance. The Gestalt therapist thus provides the client with an authentic, honest, direct, here-and-now relationship, which not only models desirable human interaction, but also guides the client to greater awareness of self in relation to others. The client can also begin to use self-to-self dialogue more effectively, as with the Gestalt activity of "empty chair," in which the client role-plays both self and a significant other in conversation.

One important aspect of the therapist-client relationship is related to questions about responsibility. Both therapist and client are fully self-directed and self-responsible, and there is no place for authoritarian advice in Gestalt Therapy. "However, it is not enough for the therapist to be responsible for self and for the patient to be responsible for self—there is also an alliance of patient and therapist that must be carefully, constantly, and competently attended to" (Youtef, 1993, p. 2). This implies that what is going on for both the therapist and the client—somatically, emotionally, cognitively—in the here-and-now— is an important focus in the therapeutic interaction.

Personal Retrospective, Continued

As a beginning counselor I was interested in Perls' therapeutic procedures, because I was then developing my personal educational pedagogy, I was also fascinated by the implications of Gestalt ideology for teaching and learning. My personal and professional development was to unfold in three ways:

First, after being inspired by those Fritz Perls' films, I started reading about Gestalt Therapy and attending Gestalt workshops; and I entered a post-graduate training program offered by the Gestalt Institute of Chicago. In that program I honed my skills as a counselor and an educator. I learned that Fritz Perls and his collaborators were among the first therapists to emphasize that real learning must involve immediacy, experiment, emotional involvement, and risk (Perls, 1969b).

When I read *Gestalt Therapy Integrated* (Polster & Polster, 1974), I learned that:… one cannot be either a teacher or a therapist unless one has learned how to effectively deal with personal emotional agendas,… you cannot ask another to do something you are unwilling to do,… personal conflicts are related to unfinished emotional situations, and … it is only in the existential here-and-now that we can resolve emotional issues and truly learn.

Second, at the college where I worked, I became involved in an experimental program called Alpha One, or simply Alpha. That program involved a "small college" within the larger college, designed as a laboratory to try out new approaches to teaching and learning. The college hired 10 full-time, interdisciplinary faculty for the experimental program. They were indeed a diverse group. The original Alpha staff included a New York lawyer, a data processing instructor, an alcoholic ex-priest, a Cuban-born Spanish instructor, a field naturalist, a psychologist, two English instructors, and a dyslectic PhD as the director. Everyone had different ideas about what programs should be developed and explored, how to structure the learning process, and how to evaluate students' progress. A classic philosophical and pedagogical struggle ensued.

Alpha offered great freedom and very little structure, so individual faculty could do just about anything they wanted with the students and give them academic credit. Several innovative programs were developed, including an urban field center in Chicago, travel studies courses, field biology courses, and interdisciplinary approaches to academics. The programs were successful for many years, but as the voices of conservative educators grew louder at the end of the 70s, the days of experimentation were drawing to a close.

I had taught some courses for Alpha, and was impressed by the experiential and interdisciplinary approach to field studies. My goal was to salvage those aspects of Alpha, so I took over as coordinator of the program in 1980. Within a few months we changed the name to "Field and Interdisciplinary Studies," and required that all of our courses meet the same academic standards as other courses at the college. Fortunately, a great deal of flexibility still existed, and I was excited about the possibilities of creating an experiential education program that offered comprehensive academic studies. I was guided by the words of Fritz Perls:

> To me, learning is discovery ... There is another idea of learning which is the drill, the routine, the repetition, which is an artifact produced in the person which makes them into an automation until he discovers the meaning of the drill. If you learn concepts, if you work for information, you don't understand, you only explain. (Perls, 1969b, p. 25)

I worked with that "Field Studies" program for over 20 years, and it became one of the most popular programs at the college. As the century ended, the program offered over 200 courses every year, and student interest and involvement had progressively increased.

The third part of my personal and professional growth involved becoming active in the unfolding experiential education movement, and the new organization called the Association for Experiential Education (AEE). The AEE was organized by outdoor leaders and educators who believed that true learning results from direct experience. During the late 60s and early 70s, programs like Outward Bound and the National Outdoor Leadership School operated with what Steven Bacon called "The Mountains are the Message" (Bacon, 1983), an educational approach that many outdoor leaders interpreted as meaning they should "Let the mountains speak for themselves." This was essentially a method in which the instructor/teacher planned a small group experience, managed the logistics, insured the safety of participants, and then took a fairly passive role, letting participants draw their own conclusions (Gass, 1995). Other leaders raised the question of whether the mountains can speak for themselves, thereby suggesting that leaders take more active role in guiding the learning processes of their students (James, 2003).

Gestalt Therapy emphasized that the therapist should become active and involved in the therapeutic process (Polster & Polster, 1974), and I thought this approach could be applied to teachers or outdoor leaders. Although the debate continues, most AEE professionals now recognize the responsibility of the leader to be more involved in the whole learning experience, especially in helping students through the sometimes difficult phase of processing their experiences. The teacher as active participant has now become a defining characteristic of most experiential education programs. AEE (2007) puts it this way:

> The educator's primary roles include setting suitable experiences, posing problems, setting boundaries, supporting learners, insuring physical and emotional safety, and facilitating the learning process ... The educator recognizes and encourages spontaneous opportunities for learning ... Educators strive to be aware of their biases, judgments and preconceptions, and how these influence the learner.

My experiences with Gestalt Therapy, the College of DuPage's Field Program, and AEE have led me to think that Fritz Perls and his colleagues have much to offer to the theoretical foundations of experiential education.

Implications for EE Philosophy

Historically, there is an intervening link between Perls' ideas about the therapeutic process and experiential education theory and practice. George Brown, a student and associate of Perls in the 1960s at Esalen, became director of an educational research project at the institute. Out of that project came his ideas about "Confluent Education," which, like Gestalt Therapy, is a blend of holistic, humanistic, and affective processes. Confluent education was an attempt to transmute Gestalt Therapy into an educational context. In his book, *Human Teaching for Human Learning: An Introduction to Confluent Education* (1971), Brown defined confluent education as "a process of teaching and learning in which the affective domain and the cognitive domain flow together" (p. 4). He acknowledged his debt to Perls: "Gestalt theory revolves around this integration of the affective and the cognitive" (1975, p. 101).

Confluent education recognizes the importance of emotionally-based and experience-based learning in recommending that teachers focus on: "Subject matter which is closely related to the significant personal needs and feelings of the students … and experience-based learning. This means learning that is closely tied to the direct contemporary experiences of students" (Shapiro, 1983, p. 113).

Both experiential education and confluent education recognize the importance of the teacher-student relationship, and the role of the teacher as facilitator of both experiential activities and the important follow-up step of reflection. By the mid-1970s, ideas from Gestalt Therapy as summarized by Confluent Education were recognized as valuable guidelines for outdoor adventure leaders. Experiential educator Reldan Nadler wrote a manual titled, *Instructors Guide to Confluent Education Curriculum: Outdoor Adventure Program* (Nadler, 1977). Nadler suggested that the Gestalt-Brown ideas about facilitating processing were important, and he later co-authored a book on processing in experiential education (Nadler & Luckner, 1992).

Several other aspects of Confluent Education theory have become standard features of many experiential programs. Brown talked about the need to have "participants involved as much as possible in decisions relating to their training," and the idea that "no one has to do anything he does not want to do" (Brown, 1975, pp. 106–107). These principles have since become embodied in Project Adventure's well known concepts of the Full Value Contract and Challenge by Choice in which participants take responsibility for how they respond during the group experiences (Project Adventure, 2007).

Fritz Perls believed that in order to grow holistically as human beings, peoples' learning had to be experienced and integrated. Today, we see many of his ideas at work in experiential education programs, although few recognize that Perls and the early Gestalt practitioners were among the first to explore and articulate them. There are now Gestalt institutes around the world, and, because it is still a very diversified theory of counseling and education, many people have been positively influenced. There are numerous books that provide an introduction to Gestalt Therapy. Perls' books, *In and Out of the Garbage Pail* (1969b) and *Gestalt Therapy Verbatim* (1992); and his films, would be excellent places to start. The book by Polster and Polster (1974) is still a good secondary resource.

Those who want a deeper exposure to this therapy should know that books and films can only provide a cognitive understanding of the Gestalt process and its implications for education. The best way to understand the potential of the process for experiential education is to engage in that process by attending workshops at one of the Gestalt training centers. Because it happened for me, I believe that experiences with the legacy of Fritz Perls and Gestalt Therapy can guide other experiential educators to discover some theoretical foundations and effective program strategies for the 21st century.

References

Association for Experiential Education. (2007). What is experiential education? Retrieved July, 2007, from http://www. AEE.org

Bacon. S. (1983). *The conscious use of metaphor in Outward Bound.* Denver, CO: Colorado Outward Bound School.

Brown, G. (1971). *An introduction to confluent education.* New York: Viking.

Brown, G. (Ed.). (1975). Human is as confluent does. *The live classroom.* New York: Viking.

Buber, M. (1970). *I and thou* (W. Kaufmann, Trans.). New York: Scribner's.

Coleman, J. (1961). *The adolescent society: The social life of the teenager and its impact on education.* New York: Free Press.

Gass, M. (1995). *Book of metaphors (Vol II).* Boulder, CO: Association for Experiential Education.

Gestalt Therapy: An Overview (n.d.). Retrieved July, 2007, from http://www.gestaltphila.org

Goldstein, K. (1939). *The organism: A holistic approach to biology derived from pathological data in man.* New York: Zone Books.

Goodman, P. (1960). *Growing up absurd.* New York: Random House.

Gunther, S. (2007). Contemporary approaches to Gestalt Therapy: Course description. Retrieved July, 2007, from www.drzur.com/gestaltcourse.html

Holt, J. (1964). *How children fail.* New York: Pitman.

Illich, I. (1971). *Deschooling society.* New York: Harper & Row.

James, T. (2003). Can the mountains speak for themselves? Retrieved March, 2003, from http://www.wilderdom.com/facilitation/mountains

Lewin, K. (1951). *Field theory as social science: Selected theoretical papers* (D. Cartwright, Ed.). New York: Harper & Row.

Moreno, J. T. (1946). *Psychodrama: Foundations of psychotherapy.* New York: Mental Health Resources.

Nadler, R. (1977). *Instructor's guide to confluent education: Outdoor adventure program.* Santa Barbara, CA: Santa Barbara Middle School.

Nadler, R., & Luckner, J. (1992). *Processing the adventure experience: Theory and practice.* Dubuque, IA: Kendall/Hunt.

Perls, F. (1942). *Ego, hunger, and aggression: A revision of Freud's theory and method.* London: G. Allen & Unwin, Ltd.

Perls, F. (1969a). *Ego, hunger and aggression: The beginnings of Gestalt therapy.* New York: Random House.

Perls, F. (1969b). *In and out of the garbage pail.* Moab, UT: Real People Press.

Perls, F. (1970). *Frederick Perls and Gestalt therapy* [Video]. New York: Psychological & Educational Films.

Perls, F. (1992). *Gestalt therapy verbatim* (rev. ed.). New York: Gestalt Journal Press.

Perls, F., Hefferline, R., & Goodman, P. (1951). *Gestalt therapy: Excitement and growth in human personality.* New York: Julian.

Polster, E., & Polster, M. (1974). *Gestalt Therapy integrated.* New York: Vintage.

Postman, N., & Weingartner, C. (1969). *Teaching as a subversive activity.* New York: Delacorte.

Project Adventure. (n.d.). Retrieved July, 2007, from http://www.pa.org/glossary

Rank, O. (1978). *Will therapy.* New York: W. W. Norton.

Reich, W. (1961). *Selected readings: An introduction to Orgonomy* (M. Higgins Ed.). New York: Farrar Straus Giroux.

Rogers, C. (1961). *On becoming a person.* Boston: Houghton Mifflin.

Shephard, M. (1975). *Fritz, an intimate portrait of Fritz Perls and Gestalt therapy.* Boston: Dutton.

Stevens, J. (1973). *Awareness: Exploring, experimenting, experiencing.* New York: Bantam.

Stoehr, T. (1997). *Here, now, next: Paul Goodman and the origins of Gestalt therapy.* Cleveland, OH: Gestalt Institute, Book Series, TF-ANYLYTC.

Youtef, G. (1993). *Awareness, dialog, and process: Essays on Gestalt therapy.* New York: Gestalt Journal.

21 Kurt Lewin

Another Kurt for Experiential Educators to Know

Thomas E. Smith and Christopher S. Leeming

For experiential educators, the most known and quoted "Kurt" is Kurt Hahn, organizer of the Outward Bound programs. Another "Kurt" of significance is Kurt Lewin, a psychologist whose theory and research on group dynamics and group processes has much to offer those in the field of experiential education. The lives of these two Kurt's were surprisingly similar. Both were raised Jewish in pre-Nazi Germany during the early years of the 20th century, and both were afforded an opportunity for a university education. With Hitler's rise to power in the 1930s, both men came to disagree with the social system that was developing throughout Germany. Kurt Hahn left his native land to immigrate to England where he became a prominent educator. His attitude about the politics in Germany was recorded when he told the parents and colleagues of his Salem School that they would either have to side with Hitler or with him (Miner, 1990). Kurt Lewin was also discouraged about the rise of Hitler, and left Germany in the 1930s to immigrate to America.

"Kurt Lewin was a seminal theorist who deepened our understanding of groups, experiential learning, and action research" (Smith, 2001, p. 1). That is the opening statement of a paper by M. K. Smith summarizing Kurt Lewin's influence on the theory and practice of experiential education. Still, within the field of experiential education there has been relatively little conscious attention to his work. This chapter provides a brief overview of the life and work of Kurt Lewin, and suggests that the ideology of this other "Kurt" should be reviewed by contemporary experiential education theorists—and by leaders who facilitate experiential education groups.

Biography

Kurt Lewin (1890–1947) was born at Mogilno, Prussia, in Germany in 1890, the second of four children of a middle-class Jewish family. They lived above a small store operated by his mother and father. They also owned a small farm just outside the town, and Kurt spent time there enjoying nature as he grew up. His parents sought better educational opportunities for their children, so they moved to Berlin when Kurt was an adolescent. In the more advanced schools of the city, Kurt learned about the ancient Greek philosophers, and he remained interested in them for the rest of his life.

When he graduated from secondary school in 1909, he immediately enrolled at the University of Frieberg to study medicine. His goal was to become a country doctor, but his interest in science resulted in a change of schools and goals; he transferred to the University of Munich to study biology. At Munich, as he and his friends watched the anti-Semitic movement grow in Germany, he became involved with activities sponsored by the socialist movement. He helped organize adult education programs for working class women and men (Marrow, 1969). At Munich, Lewin was introduced to the new field of psychology, and then transferred to the University of Berlin to study with the early Gestalt psychologists. At the age of 26 in 1916, he obtained his PhD in psychology, and shortly thereafter joined the Kaiser's army for a four-year enlistment.

He married in 1917, just before his unit was sent to war. He was wounded in combat, and later awarded the prestigious German Iron Cross. His first child of four, a daughter, was born in 1919, while Lewin was still in the army.

After his time in the service, Lewin returned to academia taking a position at the Psychological Institute in Berlin, where he taught philosophy and psychology for 12 years. The war had taken a toll on his marital relationship, and even though his second child, a son, was born in 1922, the marriage ended in divorce. He remarried in 1929, and had two more children.

At the Psychological Institute, Lewin began a lifelong friendship with Fritz Heider, who was also to become a prominent social psychologist. (Heider was responsible for developing "balance theory" and "attribution theory" in the 1950s). Heider immigrated to America in 1930, and helped arrange a 1932 visiting professorship at Stanford University for his friend Lewin. When Lewin returned to the Psychological Institute, he found increasing political pressure against his colleagues, a leftist, socialist faculty. The following year the government closed the institute, and Lewin accepted an invitation to teach at Cornell University. In 1935, shortly after Lewin published his first book, *A Dynamic Theory of Personality*, he took a professorship at the University of Iowa, where he taught for almost a decade. He began to gain notoriety with social psychologists all over the world, although most of his early papers and books were written in German and required translation. Many years later, Fritz Heider and his wife translated Lewin's 1936 book, *Principles of Topological Psychology* (Lewin, Heider, & Heider, 1966).

Lewin became an American citizen in 1940. He had escaped the holocaust, but his parents did not. His father died in hiding in the early 1940s, and his mother was killed at a German extermination center in 1944.

During World War II, Lewin became involved with applied research on small group functioning and social processes. He worked on some government research projects dealing with the morale of the troops, psychological warfare, and rehabilitative programs for the disabled. His reputation was well established by 1944, and, when a government grant led to the founding of the Research Center for Group Dynamics at the Massachusetts Institute of Technology, Lewin was appointed director. This led to work with community leaders who wanted to develop strategies for changing people with prejudice and intolerance, and that led to the development of the methodology of training groups called "the laboratory method" or "T-groups." In 1946, Lewin and his colleagues received funding from the U.S. Office of Naval Research to set up the National Training Laboratories (NTL) in Bethel, Maine, but Lewin died of a heart attack before that center opened.

Philosophy

Lewin is often considered the founder of modern social psychology, because throughout his life he was interested in both the theory and its application to real world problems. His "field theory" has roots in Gestalt philosophy's postulates about the significance of the whole as more than the sum of the parts, and suggests that understanding human behavior must involve attention to the total "life space" of the person. He defined a "field" as all the interacting aspects of a person's perceptions, behaviors and dynamics in any situation. "A group is therefore not basically a collection of individuals; it is the interdependence found in all the relationships of the individuals and their environment" (Schellenberg, 1978, p. 79). Lewin believed the dynamics of the group have impact on each individual's consciousness and behavior; and, conversely, the way each individual behaves in the group changes those dynamics.

Lewin also believed that "the creation of an empirically verifiable theory was the essence of science" (Morrow, 1969, p. 18). In his desire to develop a theoretical system for understanding the dynamic interrelatedness of the individual and the group, he created special vocabulary and complex schematic conceptualizations for studying the whole field of phenomenological existence. "For this he turned to topology, a non-quantitative mathematics of spacial relations," and that led him to develop schematic diagrams using "an egg-like oval or Jordan curve to identify the psychological field or life space" (Schellenberg, 1978, p. 69). Valences and vectors pointed out various forces of influence, and he had a formula for the process, $B = f(P,E)$, which suggested that behavior is a function of the person and the environment (Coghlan & Jacobs, 2005). The implications of this formula for the study of individuals and groups by the social sciences parallels what Einstein's formula, $E = MC^2$, is for the physical sciences.

Lewin coined many terms that became a part of the vocabulary of social psychologists, and some that were re-named and researched by others. Some of his terms seem to have been set aside through time; for example, he used the term "foreign hull" to describe the region that lies just beyond the life space of an individual. He wrote about "barriers," "positive valences," "re-education," "tension systems," "gateways," "awakened needs," "locomotion," "freezing and unfreezing," and "feedback," in relation to group dynamics. His commitment to applying psychological theory to the many problems of society led him to conduct research studies and develop theoretical explanations of personality development, brainwashing, organizational change, conflicts within an individual's perceptual field, race relations, and marriage.

The broad scope and complexity of Lewin's philosophy makes it impossible to summarize in a few words, and interested readers should look to other sources (e.g., Lewin, 1951; Marrow, 1969; Schellenberg, 1978; Ritzer & Goodson, 2003). The intention here is simply to view his work in terms of a few concepts and applications, and to identify some of the points of importance to experiential education theory and practice.

Group Dynamics. Throughout his lifetime, Kurt Lewin worked with groups in an attempt to understand how they developed and functioned. His writing on group dynamics had a profound affect on succeeding generations of social psychologists and group workers. Those ideas have been applied in education, counseling, and the corporate world.

In Education. The experiential education movement has much in common with the movement for promoting "cooperative learning." Cooperative learning involves individuals working together to maximize their learning. It is based on Lewin's ideas about social interdependence, and has historical roots in the work of Lewin's colleague at the M.I.T. Research Center for Group Dynamics, Morton Deutsch. Books by the Johnsons, who are recognized as early advocates of cooperative learning (Johnson & Johnson, 1987; Johnson, Johnson, & Holubec, 1994), are found on the shelves of many experiential educators. Lewin's ideas about trust, communication, cooperation, and processing found their way into the early publications about cooperative learning (Brown, 1988).

David Kolb's (1984) learning cycle model (experience, reflection, conceptualization, experimentation … experience, reflection, etc.) has been considered as basic theory in experiential education. Kolb's theory was inspired by Kurt Lewin, and his graphic representation of it reflects back to the complex geometric schemas of Lewin's topology. Kolb's diagrams of the learning cycle are reminiscent of Lewin's, as are explanations of how the cycle unfolds. (Note: Recent philosophical discussions have raised some questions about the value and application of Kolb's model to the experiential education process.)

Like John Dewey, Lewin examined the role of education in guiding people toward an understanding of democracy. Perhaps, echoing his own personal experiences, Lewin "saw democracy, and the spread of democratic values throughout society, as the central bastion against authoritarianism and despotism" (Burnes, 2004, p. 980). In the introduction to Lewin's book on resolving social conflicts (1948), Gordon Allport summarized the similarities of Dewey and Lewin. "Both see the intimate dependence of democracy upon social science. Both agree that democracy must be learned anew in each generation, and that it is a far more difficult form of social structure to attain and to maintain than is autocracy" (1948, p. 3). Both Dewey and Lewin believed that the appropriate place to learn about democratic values was in small group interaction.

In Counseling. There is a significant connection between Lewin and Gestalt Therapy, whose founder was Fritz Perls. Perls was trained as a psychoanalyst, but later studied with the Frankfurt group in Germany when Perls was there. Gestalt Therapy's approach to personality involves seeing the individual as part of a dynamic field, and the process often begins with a "life space" interview, one of Lewin's coined terms. In the introduction to a reprinted edition of one of his earlier books, *Ego, Hunger and Aggression* (1942/1969), Perls admits that he "admired a lot of the work of the Gestalt psychologists, especially the early work of Kurt Lewin" (Perls, 1969, p. 5). Students of Gestalt therapy find many traces of Kurt Lewin there. For example, Perls took Lewin's ideas about "tension systems," which result from conflicting vectors in the individual's experiential field, and called it "unfinished business," that had to be dealt with. While the healthy person has resolved most of these tensions along the way, a less healthy person may move through life with a mass of conflicts that have to be dealt with in the counseling process.

The innovative practice called adventure, outdoor, or wilderness therapy, which has developed under the umbrella of experiential education for the past 30 years, usually emphasizes a group counseling approach. "Adventure therapy theory draws from a mixture of learning, personality, and developmental theories, including Albert Bandura, John Dewey, Kurt Hahn, and Kurt Lewin. These theorists also have been credited with contributing to main theories comprising experiential education" (Itin, 2007).

In the Corporate World. Starting in the 1980s, experiential educators took their developing methodology into the corporate world. They consulted with companies to promote leadership development and goals of team building. This brought them into contact with other corporate consultants who drew upon the work of a generation of theorists (e.g., Bradford, Argyris, Gibb, Senge), most of whom had been influenced by Lewin's theory. Working with other consultants would have been much easier if the experiential educators had more understanding of Lewin's work.

Edgar Schein, who first designed corporate programs for "planned change" at the National Training Laboratory, summarized:

> Few people have had as profound an impact on the theory and practice of social and organizational psychology as Kurt Lewin.... The power of his theorizing lay not in a formal propositional kind of theory but in his ability to build 'models' of processes that drew attention to the right kind of variables that needed to be conceptualized and observed. In my opinion, the most powerful of these was his model of the change process in human systems. (2007, p. 1)

Lewin's Theories Influenced Many Others. One of the time tests of any psychological theory is to examine its influence on other theorists. Kurt Lewin's theories would certainly pass that test. Beyond those already mentioned (Fritz Heider, Fritz Perls, Edgar Schein, David Kolb, and Johnson & Johnson), many others were influenced by Lewin and later developed theoretical constructs that are valuable for the field of experiential education. Four of importance were: Jack Gibb was a young professor of psychology at the University of Colorado when he traveled to the National Training Laboratories where Lewin's colleagues were applying his principles to leadership development. Gibb was to become one of the first NTL trainers, and co-authored the classic book on the T-group methodology (Bradford, Gibb, & Benne, 1964). He later developed the TORI (trust, openness, realization, interdependence) system for group and organizational development (Gibb, 1972, 1978). His work on trust has been suggested as very important in working with small groups in experiential education (Smith, Roland, Havens, & Hoyt, 1992).

William Schutz was trained at UCLA in the late 1950s as a social psychologist, when the developing field was filled with people influenced by Lewin's philosophy. His fascination with groups led him to research on group dynamics, to the NTL, and on to development of his own theory of group work. He called his system "FIRO," an acronym for "fundamental interpersonal relationships orientation" (Schutz, 1958). In the tradition of Lewin, he formulated schematic overviews of his three-dimensional theory of interpersonal behavior—inclusion, control, and affection.

Irvin Janis developed his theory of "groupthink" out of Lewin's earlier work on groups and consensus decision making. His model defined groupthink as "a mode of thinking that people engage in when they are deeply involved in a cohesive in-group, when the members' strivings for unanimity override their motivation to realistically appraise alternative courses of action" (Janis, 1972, p. 9). When experiential educators emphasize the importance of decision-making by consensus, they should be aware of the dangers of groupthink, because the highly cohesive group can lead individuals to set aside their personal opinions.

B. W. Tuckman finished his PhD in 1963 and went to work as a research social psychologist at the U.S. Office of Naval Research, which had originally funded the NTL program where Lewin's ideas were so influential. In 1965, after reviewing numerous studies of group process, he created his model for team development. He postulated that the growth of any group passes through four stages—forming, storming, norming, and performing. This model has become the basis of many subsequent models of team development, and has taken a firm hold in the field of experiential education where teambuilding and leadership development are key goals (Tuckman, 1965; Tuckman & Jensen, 1977).

Lewin and the T-Group. As indicated earlier, Kurt Lewin's interest in group dynamics and training others to apply the principles of social psychology to their interrelationships led him to plan and implement the National Training Laboratories. As they worked together in the planning stages for NTL, the Lewin team developed what they called a "Basic Skills Training Group," a method for working together more effectively. When NTL opened the model was called "Training Groups," or, simply "T-Groups" (Potter, 2005).

In his autobiographic book, *The Passionate Path* (1995), Jack Gibb wrote about his learning from the Lewinian group at NTL:

> Learning to see small groups as a transcending environment in an organic situation very different from a dyadic relationship, we tried small groups in team building, therapy, education, social planning, organizational development, political action—almost any relationship could be improved by creating intense, organic, intimate, transcending small groups. (p. 44)

As NTL unfolded, divergent thoughts about goals emerged. Some thought that the lab should focus on personal growth and more traditional clinical practices, while others were more interested in corporate training. Through the years, those who saw the importance of small group participation as important for individuals tended to leave NTL and become involved in the human potential movement. T-groups for personal growth paved the way for the sensitivity groups, encounter groups, and personal growth groups of the 1960s. Carl Rogers, in his book on encounter groups, suggested that the whole movement of developing small groups for changing individuals and organizations may be the most significant social invention of the 20th century (Rogers, 1970).

A decade later, the groupwork strategies first explored at NTL influenced the early leaders of the outdoor/adventure experiential education movement. As at NTL, some leaders were more interested in experiential groups for personal growth, learning, and individual development, and others were more interested in working with corporations to change the corporate environment. In both cases, while the methodologies used were based, in part, on Lewin's ideas, the leaders were more concerned with adapting and utilizing the strategies than with the underlying the theoretical constructs. We might conclude that while many of Lewin's strategies were adopted, their theoretical foundations were not well understood.

Implications for EE Philosophy

Many of the concepts that follow from Kurt Lewin's theories about group development and group dynamics provide a rationale for experiential education practices or help to clarify the processes involved. Three examples are:

1. When a facilitator readies a group for experiential activities on a ropes course, one of the basic points of orientation is "challenge by choice" (Schoel, Prouty, & Radcliffe, 1988). Lewin's theory suggests that the choices an individual makes are not just the result of personal inside forces, but are affected by everyone in the group and the circumstances of the environment. Different choices will be made depending on the level of group development and the individual's positive and negative valences with various members. For example, Charlie's choice may well be affected by whether Susan or Mike is on the other end of the belay line. When Bob is asked to do a trust fall, his choice may be affected by where Jim is standing in the line.

2. Experiential education facilitators often define themselves as change agents. Lewin noted that "people change when they experience the need for change (unfreezing), move to a new standard of behavior and values (moving), and then stabilize the change in normative behavior (refreezing)" (as cited in Coghlan & Jacobs, 2005, p. 444). Leaders can provide the need for change in many ways—by adjusting the parameters of an activity, imposing time limits, allowing or disallowing certain activities, and placing limits on members of the group. Any of these modifications change the dynamics of the whole field of play, and the individuals have to find new ways of achieving their goals.

3. Group leaders have to move their groups into activities that are most appropriate for the group at that stage of development. This leadership skill has been called "sequencing," and has been recognized as extremely important in experiential education. Lewin's theory guides leaders to understanding that groups are like snowflakes—none of them are the same. There is no standardized sequence for offering groups activities, and leaders have to sequence the activities offered each group in terms of the time, place, and readiness of that group. This has been summarized in the following instruction to facilitators, "you must sequence, but there is no sequence" (Smith, 1985, p. 23). Lewin would also point out that groups have self-esteem and self-esteem needs, just as individuals do. By carefully choosing activities that are most appropriate for the group, leaders can ensure that the group members develop positive self-esteem and are ready for more complex activities for growth and learning.

Lewin's philosophy and recommendations for small group education can help in the development of a more comprehensive theoretical framework for the practices of experiential educators. Not only should he be recognized as "another important Kurt" for experiential educators to know, his philosophy should be explored by all those interested in EE theory and practice.

References

Bradford, L. P., Gibb, J. R., & Benne, K. D. (1964). *T-group theory and laboratory method*. New York: Wiley.

Brown, R. (1988). *Group processes: Dynamics within and between groups*. Oxford, UK: Blackwell.

Burnes, B. (2004). Kurt Lewin and the planned approach to change: A re-appraisal. *Journal of Management Studies*, 41(6), 977–1002.

Coghlan, D., & Jacobs, C. (2005). Kurt Lewin on re-education: Foundations for action research. *Journal of Applied Behavioral Science*, 41(4), 444–457.

Gibb, J. (1972). TORI theory and practice. In J. W. Pfeiffer & J. E. Jones (Eds.), *1972 annual handbook for group facilitators*. San Francisco: University Associates & Jossey-Bass.

Gibb, J. (1978). *Trust: A new view of personal and organizational development.* New York: Guild of Tutors.

Gibb, J. (1995). *The passionate path.* Los Angeles: Omicron.

Itin, C. (2007). Experiential practice in social work: Adventure therapy. Retrieved March, 2007, from http://www.wikipedia.org/wiki/adventure-therapy

Janis, I. (1972). *Victims of groupthink.* Boston: Houghton-Mifflin.

Johnson, D., & Johnson, R. (1987). *Joining together: Group theory and group practice.* Englewood Cliffs, NJ: Prentice-Hall.

Johnson, D., Johnson, R., & Holubec, E. (1994). *New circles of learning.* Washington, D.C.: Association of Supervision and Curriculum Development.

Kolb, D. A. (1984). *Experiential learning: Experience as the source of learning and development.* Englewood Cliffs, NJ: Prentice-Hall.

Lewin, K. (1935). *A dynamic theory of personality.* New York: McGraw-Hill.

Lewin, K. (1936). *Principles of topological psychology.* New York: McGraw-Hill.

Lewin, K. (1948). *Resolving social conflicts: selected papers on group dynamics.* New York: Harper & Row.

Lewin, K. (1951). *Field theory in social sciences.* New York: Harper.

Lewin, K., Heider, F., & Heider, G. (1966). *Principles of topological psychology.* New York: McGraw-Hill.

Marrow, A. J. (1969). *The practical theorist: the life and work of Kurt Lewin.* New York: Basic Books.

Miner, J. (1990). The creation of outward bound. In J. Miles & S. Priest (Eds.), *Adventure education* (pp. 55–66). State College, PA: Venture.

Perls, F. (1969). *Ego, hunger and aggression.* New York: Vintage. (Original work published 1942)

Potter, S. (2005). A social history of the T-group. Retrieved November, 2005, from http://www.psicopolis.com/Kurt/groupstory

Ritzer, G., & Goodson, D. J. (2003). *Modern sociological theories, 6th edition.* New York: McGraw-Hill.

Rogers, C. (1970). *Carl Rogers on encounter groups.* New York: Harper & Row.

Schein, E. H. (2007). Kurt Lewin's change theory in field and in the classroom: Notes toward a model for managed learning. Retrieved January, 2007, from http://www.psicopolis.com/KurtLewin

Schellenberg, J. A. (1978). *Masters of social psychology.* New York: Oxford University.

Schoel, J., Prouty, D., & Radcliffe, P. (1988). *Islands of healing.* Hamilton, MA: Project Adventure.

Smith, M. K. (2001). Kurt Lewin: Groups, experiential learning and action research. Retrieved March, 2007, from http://www.infed.org/thinkers/et-lewin

Smith, T. (1985). Issues of challenge education. In G. Robb & E. Hamilton (Eds.), *The Bradford papers: Special edition* (pp. 75–87). Bloomington: Indiana University.

Smith, T., Roland, C., Havens, M., & Hoyt, J. (1992). *The theory and practice of challenge education.* Dubuque, IA: Kendall/Hunt.

Tuckman, B. W. (1965). Developmental sequence in small groups. *Psychological Bulletin, 63,* 384–399.

Tuckman, B. W., & Jensen, M. (1977). Stages of small group development. *Organizational Studies, 2,* 419–427.

22 Earl C. Kelley
Education for What Is Real

Edward O. Raiola

Most writing on theory in the field of experiential education has come from widely known educators and researchers such as Dewey (1938), Hahn (1960), Lewin (1951), Kolb (1984), and Piaget (1970). Critics of the limited framework of conventional classroom educational experiences have explored the rich history of progressive thinking and writing from the field of experiential education. One significant influence on progressive thinkers has been Dr. Earl C. Kelley. Kelley explored far-reaching perspectives on how we learn and the role of the educator in the learning process. This chapter will explore his work to help broaden our understanding of the role of experience in learning, which is especially relevant to those who have struggled as teachers in experimenting and expanding a repertoire of teaching approaches.

Biography

Kelley was born on February 16, 1895, in Hay Springs, Nebraska. He received his BS degree from University of Chicago in 1920, his MA from Northwestern University in 1936, and his PhD from Northwestern University in 1940. In 1966 Dr. Kelley was awarded an honorary EdD from Western Michigan University.

His rich professional career included positions as a teacher in a one-room rural school; a high school teacher of chemistry and natural science in Oak Pak, Illinois, from 1921 to 1927; principal and superintendent of Milwaukee Vocational School in Milwaukee, Wisconsin, from 1929 to 1938; an education psychology instructor at Northwestern University from 1938 to 1940; a supervisor of secondary schools for the Detroit Board of Education, Detroit, Michigan, from 1940 to 1945; a professor of education at Wayne State University from 1940 to 1965; and finally a distinguished professor of education at Eastern Michigan University from 1965 to 1967. He was the founder of the youth bureau of the Detroit Police Department, founder of Detroit commission on children and youth, and he served for years in a variety of roles in the Michigan Department of Public Instruction.

His main writings included *Education for What is Real* (1947), *The Workshop Way of Learning* (1951), *Education and the Nature of Man* (Kelley & Rasey, 1952), In *Defense of Youth* (1962) and *Humanizing the Education of Children: A Philosophical Statement* (1969). Earl Kelley died on April 19, 1970 in San Francisco, California.

John Dewey, the great American philosopher and theorist, respected and admired throughout the world for his contributions to progressive thought and democratic values as they apply to education, developed a close personal and professional relationship with Earl Kelley late in his career. Jerry Wyett, a former student and then colleague of Earl Kelley, reports that "A shared interest in perception first brought Dewey and Kelley together" (1998, p. 157). After seeing and reading Kelley's book, Dewey wrote the foreword to *Education for What is Real* (1947). Wyett reports that "Dewey reportedly told Kelley, 'My work is not finished, it is your job to complete'"

(p. 157). Dewey believed that Kelley's work would extend and complement his own: "I am especially grateful to Dr. Kelley for permitting me to have a part in calling attention to a work whose significance will prove virtually inexhaustible" (Dewey, in Kelley, 1947 p. vi).

Kelley's Vision

To understand Kelley's vision of experiential education, one must first examine some of his basic beliefs about the nature of learning and perception. In *Education for What is Real* (1947), Kelley suggests that many of the ills of our educational system and its product (people) come from two major areas:

> (1) That we present knowledge as absolute and existing before learning can begin, instead of something to be lived;
> (2) That we disregard and often work counter to the learner's purpose or needs. (1947, p. 73)

Kelley holds that learning must begin before knowledge can exist; that learning is not a matter of acquisition and acceptance, but is a result of process, subject to continuous modification. Learning is made possible through memory and is uniquely held and uniquely used.

Kelley asserts that the formal educational system disregards and therefore impedes the learner's purpose. From this perspective, the traditional classroom has two important components: the teacher and the subject matter. The student gets his or her purpose from the teacher and then learns, perhaps, the subject matter presented by the teacher. The subject matter is objectively and independently extant, and most of the modification necessary to bring the student and subject matter together takes place on the part of the student. The student should find suitable meaning within the framework of the subject matter, but if she or he does not do so, then the student should be coerced. While educators may not think of grades as a form of coercion, the threat posed by this judgment upon the student's worth, according to the criteria set by the teacher, is not subtle.

What Kelley proposes is that students learn in accordance with their own purposes (or needs) and prior experiences. Therefore one must look to a modification of the role and usefulness of the subject matter, the role of the teacher, and conditions of the learning environment. In order for learning to take place, the learner must be capable of receiving in a particular situation. For Kelley and Rasey (1952), an individual's experiential learning process begins with perception and purpose, moves toward experience, then to thought and value which results in knowledge acquisition or learning. This capacity to learn is thus a function of purpose/need and readiness.

Perception is the person's construct of his or her external world, an interpretation made by the learner that comes into consciousness, originating within the learner and not from without. Purpose, as Kelley and Rasey (1952) use the term, means a conscious or unconscious urge to satisfy a perceived need. "Purpose is a driving force which gives expression for, or points a path to, the expenditure of the energy which we constitute" (p. 56).

Conscious purpose is that which comes into our awareness; unconscious purpose is the biological "... driving force of tissue purpose that shows the path through which energy may be spent with compliance and satisfaction. It is the force through which the plant, the animal, the human being become more perfectly that which it already is" (Kelley & Rasey, 1952, p. 61). Purpose influences what can come into awareness and become part of one's construct about reality. Learning occurs as one interacts with the environment, and the way in which the accumulation of knowledge is used depends upon the person's purpose. Kelley and Rasey also suggest that the learner must be ready to learn:

When the organism lacks experience and purpose to receive, it lacks readiness. Now we can see more clearly how crucial to education the matter of readiness is. The force of this idea is much greater when we realize that readiness is basic to the nature of the perceptual process, and lack of readiness is not a matter of unwillingness to learn. (p. 73)

Many contemporary social science researchers (Elkind, 1989; Schunk, 1991; Larsen, 2000; Wigfield & Eccles, 2000) support the notion that learners must be both developmentally and socially ready for learning. Readiness can influence what, when and how we learn. If the energy spent by teachers in ignoring (or defying) the factor of readiness can be turned to constructive use, enormous progress in intellectual growth can be made and readiness itself could in many cases be acquired. For example, teachers can emphasize active, experiential learning for elementary and middle school age students who are at a developmental point where they interact with and learn from their environment kinesthetically. This honors students' readiness to learn through their entire sensory repertoire, instead of simply sitting in a classroom, passively giving back what has been presented to them. Such flexibility of approach to teaching could mitigate many of the "behavior problems" we find in schools today. "We do not have to continue to waste our educational strength going counter to the powerful tide of the learner's purpose. We do not always have to paddle upstream" (Kelley, 1947, p. 73).

Kelley and Rasey (1952) state that "Experience, then, is the process of undergoing the contact with the concrete, the working out of the project circumstances" (p. 34). Humans are bundles of experiences, in flux and in process, continually being modified. We acquire knowledge through experience. In the learning process it is not the event alone which constitutes an experience, but the perceptual interaction between the event and the learner. Knowledge, or memory, is thus the product of experience-perception. It is a result of process, and is subject to continuous modification as the learner goes forward in a changing world. Kelley and Rasey describe what remains in memory as knowledge, subjective in nature and unique to each learner.

The final step in the experiential learning process for Kelley and Rasey (1952) is the attribution of value. After one has had an experience, one thinks about it, interprets it, evaluates its effect, and judges it. One usually makes some generalizations based upon the experience and codifies it in thought, remembering it.

This thinking/attributing phase in Kelley and Rasey's experiential learning process involves the organization and integration of experience. For Kelley and Rasey (1952), we all consist of accumulated experience: "… man is a bundle of experience, influx or process, being continually modified or rebuilt as he makes his way in a changing world, or a world of new circumstances" (p. 34). In other words, one perceives only what one has the experience and purpose to perceive. Perceptions grow and mature with the learner, and thus shape future perception/experience. "Since experience is essential to perception, or to a new experience, we must say that man is built by where he has been and what he done. He is continually building himself by a combination of his past and his new surroundings or circumstances" (p. 34). Kelley's (1947) view of this interrelationship between the individual, with all of his/her history, and the environment, is "… growth in its widest meaning; growth which enables the whole organism to become more competent to cope with life" (p. 72)—this comprises education.

Thus, the uniqueness of every individual is basic to Kelley's educational proposals. For Kelley, readiness influences what, when and how one learns. His notion about the nature of learning is that people only learn and acquire knowledge in accordance with their own purpose (need). In order for learning to take place the learner must see purpose or meaning in the subject matter at hand. The capacity to learn is therefore a function of purpose/need and readiness. If educators accept this notion of the learning process, then it should shape all of teaching practice, from the design of the curriculum to the environment in which teaching occurs.

Implications for EE Philosophy

Earl Kelley assumes that reality is different for each of us, because of our individualized perceptions of whatever is out there and also because of our unique purposes as individuals, which shape our perceptions. He argues that, for each person, any given object will be experienced somewhat, or even radically, differently. Therefore, although an educator may assume some consensus among students about "what the ocean is like," one cannot anticipate the effects of a marine biology expedition on any two individuals.

Kelley challenges us to think and practice in some radical ways if we want to grow as educators and make a difference in people's lives:

> Much of the baggage of pedagogy inherited from the dim past will have to be abandoned. For example, we will have to stop foisting subject matter upon learners because we think it is good for them. We will need to begin consultation with learners as to what is to be done, in order to take advantage of the individual paths of energy pointed out by individual purpose. We will have to abandon animism in our attitudes toward what is to be taught, and cease to use certain items of subject matter for magical reasons. We will need to cease using repudiated faculty psychology as explanation for doing what we want to do for other reasons. (Kelley & Rasey, 1952, p. 74)

Kelley would have the educator leave behind many common and erroneous assumptions about the learning process:

1. The idea that working on tasks devoid of purpose or interest is good for learners.
2. The answer to the problem is more important than the process of solving it.
3. It is more important to measure what has been learned than to ask a student what has been learned.

Kelly suggests that we must look to a modification of the role and usefulness of the subject matter. The curriculum should grow out of the needs of the learner and emphasize the concrete before the abstract. Details of the curriculum should be derived from the learner, where planning would be an essential part of the day's work. Learning environments should be places of activity where the learners are involved in planning, executing and evaluating activities. Kelley states: "The particulars of subject matter must be those for which the learner can find functional use in his own concrete world" (1947, p. 101).

Earl Kelley also informs an ongoing exploration of education and suggests how best to engage in that process. He points out that education is about communication and that one of the primary concerns for educators is how best to communicate. He reminds us about the limitations or inadequacy of words (lectures), discussions and readings to communicate knowledge and skills. "Teachers have long labored under the false impression that to have spoken is to have been heard, and that to have read is to know" (Kelley, 1952, p. 74). He reminds us that to increase the probability of understanding, students should express ideas in a number of ways and be provided opportunities for two-way communication.

For Kelley, experiential education or learning-by-doing involves a unique relationship between the event and the experiencing person(s). He recognizes that the key to learning is how the individual interacts with his or her experience and the meanings gleaned by that individual. For example, one could be given carefully detailed verbal instructions on how to ride a bicycle, but it is not until one actually gets on and begins to experience the motion and gravity of the bicycle that learning really can occur. A group of college students can read extensively about Scotland's geography and culture, but it is the experience of traveling in Scotland that will remain longer and more vividly in their memories.

Kelley's concepts about the problems of evaluation are also useful today. He suggests that we especially look at evaluative techniques that will measure progress in growth, and that we need to provide more opportunities to cause learners to ask themselves how they are doing, rather than cause educators to ask how the learner is doing. This "directs the learner's attention to his own learning and places responsibility on the learner, where it belongs" (Kelley, 1952, p.103).

Finally, Kelley stresses the importance of cooperation and problem solving in the curriculum. He holds that through cooperation "we can teach responsibility and states that of all the skills we teach, problem solving is the one thing that we can be sure the learner will need as he becomes an adult" (Kelley, 1969, p. 10).

Providing opportunities for people to become motivated to learn helps to encourage readiness in the learner. Listening to their students' helps educators shape experience to meet expressed needs and create a meaningful framework around subject matter. Following Kelley's recommendations of integrating the needs of the student, the demands of the environment, and the capacity of the educator is a lifelong process of development. For example, in the field of outdoor adventure education, there are certain areas of knowledge in which students should demonstrate competence—such mastery is expected by the faculty, the college administration, and employing agencies for which students want to work. These competencies can include knowing the history and philosophy of adventure education, understanding developmental characteristics of clients/participants, legal considerations, environment and natural history, and group process skills. Presuppositions about what constitutes "minimum competencies" could be seen as conflicting with the notion of learner-directed education, but the balance is dynamic between the need to ensure that students are minimally competent and letting them choose what they want to learn about.

For educators who wish a deeper understanding about the philosophy and pedagogy of Earl C. Kelley, *Education for What is Real* (1947) provides the best overview of his methods and suggestions for practice.

References

Dewey, J. (1938). *Experience and education.* New York: Macmillan.

Elkind, D. (1989, October). Developmentally appropriate practice: Philosophical and practical implications. *Phi Delta Kappan, 71*(2), 113–117.

Hahn, K. (1960). Education and changes in our social structure. *BACIE Journal, 14*(1), 5–9.

Kelley, E. C. (1947). *Education for what is real.* New York: Harper.

Kelley, E. C. (1951). *The workshop way of learning.* New York: Harper.

Kelley, E. C. (1962). *In defense of youth.* Englewood Cliffs, NJ: Prentice Hall.

Kelley, E. C. (1969). *Humanizing the education of children: A philosophical statement* (NEA Stock Number 281-00872). Washington, DC: National Education Association of the United States.

Kelley, E. C., & Rasey, M. (1952). *Education and the nature of man.* New York: Harper.

Kolb, D. A. (1984). *Experiential learning: Experience as a source of learning and development.* Englewood Cliffs, NJ: Prentice Hall.

Larsen, R. W. (2000). Toward a psychology of positive youth development. *American Psychologist, 55,* 170–183.

Lewin, K. (1951). *Field theory in social science.* New York: Harper and Row.

Piaget, J. (1970). Piaget's theory. In P. H. Mussen (Ed.), *Carmichael's manual of child psychology* (3rd ed.). New York: Wiley.

Schunk, D. H. (1991). Self-efficacy and academic motivation. *Education Psychologist, 26,* 207–231

Wigfield, A., & Eccles, J. (2000). Expectancy-value theory of achievement motivation. *Contemporary Educational Psychology, 25,* 68–81.

Wyett, J. L. (1998, Fall). John Dewey & Earl Kelley: Giants in democratic education. *Education, 119*(1), 151–175.

23 Carl Rogers

A Way of Being an Experiential Educator

Thomas E. Smith

Carl Rogers' essential message, what he called the "basic hypothesis" on which most of his theoretical perspectives were based, has been described as deceptively simple.

> All individuals have within themselves the ability to guide their own lives in a manner that is both personally satisfying and socially constructive. In a particular type of helping relationship, we free individuals to find their inner wisdom and confidence, and they will then make increasingly healthier and more constructive choices. (Kirschenbaum & Henderson, 1989a, p. xiv)

Carl Ransom Rogers (1902–1987) is most remembered for his theory and practice of Client Centered Therapy (CCT), and is considered by many as the most influential psychotherapist of the 20th century. He also had a long career as an educator, advocating student-centered classrooms, and many educational theorists and practitioners were deeply affected by his courses and his writings. He was a wonderful teacher, and I was fortunate to have been one of his students during his years at the University of Wisconsin (1957–1963). His ideas have been recognized by many leaders in the field of experiential education (EE), and there is value in reviewing his thinking in search of implications of his work for the field.

Rogers was a prolific writer, authoring 16 books and over 200 professional articles. There are even more writings about his thinking, some filled with praise, others with criticism. There are also several excellent biographies and summaries of his life and works (Evans, 1975; Kirschenbaum, 1979, 2007; Thorne, 1992; Barrett-Leonard, 1998).

About Carl Rogers

Rogers' book, *Client-Centered Therapy*, which defined his approach to counseling, was published in 1951, although his ideas had been developing for many years. During his adolescence, growing up on a farm in Wisconsin, he was interested in the great moths that flew at night, and that may have been a starting point for his belief in the possibilities of human transformation. He enjoyed the outdoors, and tells about how he and his two brothers had special "hidden spots in the woods" (Rogers & Russell, 2002, p. 31). He also noted, "I was much affected by Emerson—I think all the writings of the transcendental school had a deep influence on me" (Rogers & Russell, 2002, p. 44).

He enrolled at the University of Wisconsin in 1920, majoring in Agriculture, and at the end of his sophomore year he was selected as a student delegate to a World Christian Federation Conference in China. The conference involved small group interactions which may have been the start of Rogers' desire to understand the common denominators of the human experience. After graduating in 1924, he enrolled at Union Theological Seminary. He soon found that he was not comfortable with a profession that required him to narrow his thinking to a specific dogma, nor with the teachers who seemed to just feed ideas to the students. Rogers and his fellow students began to gather together for their own interactive discussions, and that was probably his introduction to the value of small group processes for learning and personal growth.

He transferred to Columbia University, seeking a profession where "freedom of thought would not be limited," and began his doctoral program in education (Kirschenbaum, 1979, p. 52). He held various fellowships and field jobs during the next few years, including work as a counselor at a summer camp for troubled boys. Although he started out majoring in education, he moved to psychology after a course with noted progressive educator, William Kilpatrick. By the time he received his PhD in 1931, he was working as a counselor.

Throughout the 1930s, he worked in a child guidance clinic, and began developing his thoughts about the nature of the effective therapeutic relationship. In his first book, *The Clinical Treatment of the Problem Child* (1939), there were traces of his developing theory and practice. He suggested that the success of counseling was partially dependent on the qualifications of the therapist. He did not mean the academic or professional training preparation, but the characteristics and qualities of the therapist as perceived by the client. He suggested that therapists should have an accepting, non-judgmental respect for the individual, a characteristic he would later call "unconditional positive regard" (p. 282). He also wrote about the importance of helping professionals having a good understanding of themselves, an important theme throughout his life (pp. 283–284).

Rogers joined the faculty of Ohio State University in 1940. Soon after, he published his second book, *Counseling and Psychotherapy: Newer Concepts in* Practice (1942). In that book he began to write of "the client" instead of "the patient," reflecting his developing attitude about the nature of the counseling relationship. In 1945, he relocated to the University of Chicago with responsibility for establishing and overseeing the university-based counseling center. Rogers credited the dynamic staff meetings at the counseling center with creating considerable personal growth for everyone.

The 1950s were a time of developing his theory of personality to parallel his ideas on counseling and personal growth, and this involved him as a major player in the development of the field of Humanistic Psychology as a "third force" in American psychology. He joined other prominent psychologists, including Gordon Allport, Clark Moustakas, Rollo May, Henry Murray, Gardner Murphy, Arthur Combs, and Abraham Maslow in calling for a psychological theory that was an alternative to Behaviorism and Psychoanalysis. At the end of the decade, he published his next major work, *On Becoming A Person* (1961).

In the 1960s he began to see the possibilities of applying his person-centered approach to the field of education and to the rapidly developing personal growth group movement. At the end of that decade, he published two very important works: *Freedom to Learn: A View of What Education Might Become* (1969) and *Carl Rogers on Encounter Groups* (1970). Rogers was a key leader in expanding the fields of application for his ideology. This expansion continued throughout the 1970s, as he turned to issues of politics, power, and the future of humankind. He traveled internationally, offering seminars and workshops to bring people with conflicting values—economic, religious, cultural, and political—together. He began to think about the political and social implications of his theories, and about how his ideas might affect the future. He published *Carl Rogers on Personal Power: Inner Strength and Its Revolutionary Impact* (1977).

To summarize Rogers' professional interests throughout the years: The 1930s were the formative years for the development of his ideas about human relations; in the 1940s he became interested in what individual and small group counseling might become; he began to consider what the person might become in the 1950s; the next decade led him to consider what education might become; and in the last decades of his life he focused on what the world might become.

Rogers on Counseling and Psychotherapy

At the core of his person-centered orientation to counseling is the belief that certain attitudes and characteristics of the therapist will result in therapeutic effectiveness. The attitudes that must be communicated to, and perceived by, the client are: (a) congruence or genuineness, (b) unconditional positive regard, and (c) accurate empathic understanding (Rogers, 1961).

Rogers never intended that his thoughts about how a therapist should behave would become a "school" of psychotherapy. In one of my classes with him, he talked about being uncomfortable when the client-centered approach was listed as a "technique" of psychotherapy alongside Freud's Psychoanalysis, Fritz Perl's Gestalt Therapy, John Rosen's Direct Analysis, and Albert Ellis's Rational-Emotive Therapy. He said that his approach was not a "technique," and shortly thereafter he wrote, "It has never been my intention to inaugurate a 'school' of psychotherapy" (Rogers, as cited in Arieti, 1959, p. 183). He told us that the person-centered approach was not a format for counseling that one could learn and practice. He said it was simply "a way of being," and he was to use those words to title a book 20 years later (1980).

According to Rogers, one could not learn the techniques of CCT, one could only become a real, congruent, sensitive, caring, and empathic human being. Critics who thought of Rogers' approach as a technique, often missed his whole point. Rogers knew that by considering the approach as a technique people might want to learn the protocol rather than take the risk to engage in the struggle of their own personal growth.

Rogers truly believed in his basic hypothesis: Individuals have within themselves the necessary resources for fully understanding and altering their own self-concept, attitudes, values, and behaviors. If the therapist provides the desired climate, these resources within the client will surface. Clients are the experts on themselves; therapists have expertise in creating a relationship and a climate which gives the "therapist" within each person a chance to go to work. When the therapist creates that climate, the individual has both the freedom to be, and the motivation/desire to become. The important question for the therapist is not "What should I do?" but "How should I be?"

Rogers on Personality and Development

As Rogers thought about the nature of psychotherapy, he began to develop his thinking on the nature of the human being. He titled one chapter in his first book on Client-Centered Therapy "A Theory of Personality and Behavior" (1951), but the most formal presentation of this theory, titled, "A Theory of Therapy, Personality, and Interpersonal Relationships, As Developed in the Client-Centered Framework," was published in the third volume of a series overviewing the whole field of psychology (Koch, 1959). His theory rests on two hypotheses. The first revolved around his belief that the core of the human mind and self-concept was essentially positive. The second was an elaboration of his basic hypothesis about the human tendency towards growth, which he later described as "the formative tendency" (Rogers, 1978, p. 23).

Because of my personal studies of nature with Native American elders, I was interested in the fact that some of Rogers' early examples of this formative tendency involved seaweed and mushrooms. He also applied this idea to forest ecosystems, and recalled his early life on the farm. For Rogers, like the indigenous Americans, all life was inspirited, growing, and becoming. In a 1972 interview, he spoke of his love of gardening. "I love nurturing plants and have often thought about the parallels between growing plants and growing people. It's like providing a climate and conditions where they can best grow" (Rogers, as cited in Wood, 1972, p. 17).

Rogers' theory of personality and development focuses on the self-concept. He saw the self as an organized conceptual whole that is fluid and changing. He used the term "gestalt" to suggest that small changes in a part of the individual's phenomenological self-concept can subsequently influence the whole field of self-perception and create a new person. He identified two aspects of the self-concept—the "real self-image" and the "ideal self-image." The real self is the self as perceived and the self as experienced is the self as one really is. The ideal self is not real, but is a projected image based on values and life lessons about how one ought to be.

Rogers on Small Groups

Near the end of the 1950s, Rogers began to recognize that his ideas were applicable to anyone who was interested in providing others with what he called a "helping relationship," and he wrote one of my favorite papers, "The Characteristics of the Helping Relationship"(1958). At that time, Americans were becoming fascinated by the small group process, and there were "T-groups," "encounter groups," "sensitivity groups," "sharing groups," "sensory awareness groups," "gestalt groups," and "values clarification groups," being offered in the corporate world, counseling centers, and schools. In one of his books about group processes, he wrote:

> One of the most fascinating aspects of any intensive group experience is to observe the manner in which a number of the group members show a natural and spontaneous capacity for dealing in a helpful, facilitating, and therapeutic fashion with the pain and suffering of others … This kind of ability shows up so commonly in groups that it has led me to feel that the ability to be healing or therapeutic is far more common in human life than we suppose. Often it needs only the permission granted or the freedom made possible by the climate of a free-flowing group experience to become evident. (Rogers, 1970, p. 3)

Although the public fascination with personal growth groups began to decline during the 1970s, there was a rising interest in this approach to personal growth in the outdoor adventure groups organized by the Outward Bound Schools, the National Outdoor Leadership School, and Project Adventure. By the end of that decade, outdoor leaders were discovering the power of their small groups as personal growth experiences.

When Rogers discussed the role of the facilitator/leader in the small group, he returned again to his basic hypothesis. The first task for the leader is that of "climate-setting," which involves creating the stage for the group members to make the experience what they want it to be, and establishing feelings of comfort, safety, and trust by being genuine and non-threatening. The facilitator must show acceptance and empathic understanding of the individuals in the group. As in any effective therapeutic process, the facilitator must be perceived as genuine, accepting, and empathic.

Rogers on Education

In the introductory lines of this chapter, I wrote that Carl Rogers was "a wonderful teacher." In retrospect, he might not have liked that description, for he argued that people can't really teach anything to anyone, they can only facilitate the learning of others. I remember his comments about observing classrooms in which the teacher appeared to be doing "lots of teaching," but the students did not appear to be doing "lots of learning" (personal communication, 1957).

His basic hypothesis applied to education was that all people have a natural tendency to learn. He was certainly not the first to suggest that the natural development of the child involves self-discovery and learning; Rousseau, Pestalozzi, and John Dewey, among others, had also argued that point. For Rogers, the most important part of the learning climate is the interpersonal relationship between teacher and students, and among the students themselves. Patterson summarized the three characteristics of the teacher-student relationship that Rogers deemed important.

Learning is enhanced when the teacher is not playing a role prescribed by the system but rather is himself or herself, genuine, authentic, honest ...

The learner is accepted as a person of worth, a unique individual, and is respected, his or her feelings, opinions, and person are prized ...

Empathic understanding comes from putting oneself in the place of the student to understand his or her reactions from the inside, to experience the student's perceptions and feelings ... (Patterson, 2000, pp. 23–24)

Rogers' belief in the importance of the human relationships is reflected in a paper titled, "The Interpersonal Relationship in the Facilitation of Learning" (Leeper, 1967). Two years later, in his first major book on education, *Freedom to Learn: A View of What Education Might Become,* Rogers re-edited that paper and wrote:

When a facilitator creates, even to a modest degree, a classroom climate characterized by all that he can achieve of realness, prizing, and empathy; when he trusts the constructive tendency of the individual and the group; then he discovers that he has inaugurated an educational revolution. Learning of a different quality, proceeding at a different pace, with a greater degree of pervasiveness, occurs. Feelings—positive, negative, confused—then become part of the classroom experience. (1969, p. 115)

Carl Rogers was clearly an experiential educator! Not only did he believe that the interactional classroom would provide significant learning experiences for students, he believed in experience as the best teacher.

Experience is, for me, the highest authority. The touchstone of validity is my own experience. No other person's ideas, and none of my own ideas, are as authentic as my experience. It is to experience that I must return again and again, to discover a closer approximation to truth as it is in the process of becoming in me. (Rogers, cited in Kirschenbaum, 1979, p. 25)

He also believed that didactic instruction had little impact on students, and felt that there was a clear distinction between the terms teaching and facilitating. Teaching involves passing on purported wisdom from the outside to the students, while facilitation involves releasing the wisdom of the students from within themselves. I have often summarized this distinction by suggesting that we don't need teachers, we need "releasers" (of wisdom and knowledge that students already have based on their own experiences and learning).

Rogers On The Future of Humankind

In the last decade of his life, Carl Rogers suggested that his model for personal growth and learning had two long-term implications: (a) The person-centered approach was the appropriate educational strategy for the worldwide movement of global, unicultural, and peace education. (b) The desirable characteristics for all humankind in the future world would be like those he described in the "fully functioning person." Rogers' vision of the "person of tomorrow" would be a person having understanding of his/her existence as a person in the process of becoming, and who would meet others who were also appreciated as persons in the process of becoming. Such meetings would involve tolerance and total positive regard for others, and would encourage people to tap into their own goodness and wisdom. Such relationships would, to borrow a phrase from theologian Martin Buber, serve to "confirm the other." "Confirming means ...

accepting the whole potentiality of the other ... recognize in him, know in him, more or less, the person he has been. I can say it only in this word—*created* to become" (Buber-Rogers dialogue, as cited in Kirschenbaum & Henderson, 1989b, p. 60).

In one of his later books, *Carl Rogers on Personal Power: Inner Strength and Its Revolutionary Impact* (1977), he wrote about the person-centered approach as useful in resolving inter-cultural tensions. In that book he discussed the similarities he saw between his own work and that of Paulo Freire's, who sought to help illiterate peasants become empowered to take control of their own lives.

It is prophetic that it was a trip to an international conference in China in 1922 that turned him in new directions he would follow for the next 60 years of professional work. In his later years, Rogers traveled to many foreign countries to participate in group meetings concerned with peace and the future of humankind. In the last decade of his life, he became a virtual globetrotter, facilitating groups in Japan, Mexico, Austria, Hungary, Spain, Italy, England, Ireland, South Africa, the Soviet Union, and China. Many of these seminars and conferences were sponsored by the Carl Rogers Institute for Peace which he had founded in 1984. Rogers died early in 1987, not knowing that he would be nominated for the prestigious Nobel Peace Prize later that year (Rogers & Russell, 2002).

Implications for EE Philosophy

1. Goals and the process of personal growth: A major goal for many experiential education programs is to facilitate the personal growth of participants, and Carl Rogers' analysis of personal growth can help leaders understand that process. His ideas about how to facilitate personal growth process are important, and every experiential education leader should be aware them. His theoretical perspectives, especially as related to the small group process, have direct application to EE, especially the facilitation of processing/debriefing discussions.

2. Leadership development: Rogers' basic belief in developing counselors, teachers, and lay leaders to become more facilitative under the guidelines of his basic hypothesis has significant implications for the training of experiential education leaders. After he left the University of Wisconsin in 1963, he joined the staff of the Program of the Center for Studies of the Persons in La Jolla, California. Thousands of professionals, with backgrounds in counseling, education, philosophy, psychology, sociology, theology, and business went to La Jolla for their professional development. Awareness of the expanding group movement led him to be concerned with training professionals to become effective facilitators of the personal growth and psychological healing of others, and this was to become a major concern for the rest of his life.

There were three parts to the program at La Jolla that had relevance to experiential philosophy. The first component was what Rogers preferred to call "building facilitative skills"—as opposed to "training." He thought that the concept of training implied making a person more proficient in some trade or art or work, but that it was quite impossible to train an individual to be a person. The program at the Center involved future facilitators joining small groups not to observe and take notes on the procedures, but to attend to their own personal growth—to become more genuine, congruent, and empathic.

The second component of the La Jolla experience was what Rogers called "cognitive sessions." While these were shaped in part by the needs and desires of participants, the choices were to study with the available permanent and visiting staff. These were not courses, per se, but lectures, or a series of lectures, covering such topics as group dynamics, personal growth and the drug scene, psychodrama, movement and art, or spirituality in the modern world. Students were encouraged to read in original sources, and to form small discussion groups to exchange ideas and interpretations.

The third component, for the more advanced participants, was the opportunity to actually co-facilitate groups in process. Rogers thought that the La Jolla program was quite different from leadership development programs about the country:

> It de-emphasizes the manipulative, interpretative, highly specialized expertise which appears to be more and more prominent in the training of group leaders. It does not stress the 'exercises' which have become such a large bag of tricks for many group leaders. Instead, it concentrates on the development of persons who are more effective in interpersonal relationships. (1970, p. 171)

3. Risk-taking: Most experiential educators would support the notion that personal growth often involves the taking of risks. Scott Wurdinger identified the issue of taking risks in experiential education as one of the core "philosophical issues," and noted that there were psychological risks as well as physical risks (1994). Rogers made frequent comments about taking psychological risks, and these may be helpful in understanding the relationship between risk and personal growth. This relationship is important and should be explored by EE leaders and their clients.

Rogers wrote about the risks that clients and students face when opening themselves to emotions, and in sharing those feelings and the associated values with others. "When a person expresses something personal, he or she is exposed and vulnerable, and that is a very risky experience" (Kirschenbaum & Henderson, 1989a, p. 168). In teaching and counseling, this is true for both teachers and counselor as well as for the student/client. Rogers suggests that "We are deeply helpful only when we relate as persons, when we risk ourselves as persons in the relationship" (1980, p. 170). He speaks of the risks that teachers must take to create a student-centered classroom. "Who knows whether students can be trusted and whether a process can be trusted? One can only take the risk; and risk is frightening" (1977, p. 4). Rogers often spoke of his own willingness to take risks.

> It seems to me that the experiences I value most in my recent life all entail considerable risk ... Perhaps the major reason I am willing to take chances is that I have found that in doing so, whether I succeed or fail, I learn ... Such learning helps me to expand, so I continue to risk. (1980, pp. 74–75)

4. Silence and Patience: I close with a personal lesson learned from working with Rogers that is important for all EE facilitators to think about. As my supervisor in cultivating skills for counseling and psychotherapy, he and I were listening to a taped session in which I was counseling an underachieving student. We listened to the interaction for a few minutes, and then he asked me to stop the tape. His first observation was, "You seem uncomfortable with the silence. Is that the case?" "I don't think so," I replied, but he replied, "I think I heard you break the silence more often than the client." We listened again, and I had to admit that his observation was correct. "There's nothing wrong with silence," he told me, "sometimes the client just needs that time to process her own feelings." We listened to more of the interview, and the next time we stopped it he commented, "I call it sitting-on-your-hands, and I have found that very difficult to do sometimes, too. It is difficult to be patient and wait for the client to take charge of the session. We just seem to think that there is something we are supposed to be doing, some direction we are supposed to be taking the counseling" (personal communication, 1958).

Many years later, as a facilitator of experiential adventure groups, I recalled that lesson when I read Bill Proudman's comment: "If a teacher truly believes in the experiential process, the teacher will create safe working boundaries for the student and then get right out of the way" (1995, p. 44). It may be difficult for facilitators of personal growth to "sit-on-their-hands," to let the silence be a time of importance, and to allow our students and clients to learn at their own pace, in their own way.

I often think of my beloved mentor working in the garden. I am sure he did not stand there and tell the flowers to grow, or how to grow. He just made sure they had sunshine and water, and then "got right out of the way." He trusted the growth potential and actualizing tendency of each flower, and that is what we should do with our students in experiential education.

References

Arieti, S. (Ed.). (1959). *American handbook of psychiatry, Vol. 3*. New York: Basic Books.

Barrett-Leonard, G. (1998). *Carl Rogers' helping system: Journey and substance*. London: Sage.

Evans, R. (Ed.). (1975). *Carl Rogers: The man and his ideas*. New York: E.P. Dutton.

Kirschenbaum, H. (1979). *On becoming Carl Rogers*. New York: Dell/Delta.

Kirschenbaum, H. (2007). *The life and work of Carl Rogers*. New York: PCCS Books.

Kirschenbaum, H., & Henderson, V. (Eds.). (1989a). *The Carl Rogers reader*. Boston: Houghton Mifflin.

Kirschenbaum, H., & Henderson, V. (Eds.). (1989b). *Carl Rogers: Dialogues*. Boston: Houghton Mifflin.

Leeper, T. (Ed.). (1967). *Humanizing education*. Washington, DC: National Education Association and Association for Supervision and Curriculum Development.

Patterson, C. H. (2000). *Understanding psychotherapy: Fifty years of client-centered theory and practice*. Ross-on-Wye, UK: PCCS Books.

Proudman, B. (1995). Experiential education as emotionally engaged learning. In K. Warren, M. Sakofs, & J. Hunt (Eds.), *The theory and practice of experiential education* (pp. 240–247). Boulder, CO: Association for Experiential Education.

Rogers, C. (1939). *The clinical treatment of the problem child*. Boston: Houghton Mifflin.

Rogers, C. (1942). *Counseling and psychotherapy*. Boston: Houghton Mifflin.

Rogers, C. (1951). *Client-centered therapy: Its current practice, implications, and theory*. Boston: Houghton Mifflin.

Rogers, C. (1958). The characteristics of the helping relationship. *Personal and Guidance Journal, 37*(1), 6–16.

Rogers, C. (1959). A theory of therapy, personality, and interpersonal relationships, as developed in the client-centered framework. In S. Koch (Ed.), *Psychology: A study of a science, Vol. III* (pp. 184–256), New York: McGraw-Hill.

Rogers, C. (1961). *On becoming a person: A therapist's view of psychotherapy*. Boston: Houghton Mifflin.

Rogers, C. (1969). *Freedom to learn: A view of what education might become*. Columbus, OH: Charles E. Merrill.

Rogers, C. (1970). *Carl Rogers on encounter groups*. New York: Harper and Row.

Rogers, C. (1977). *Carl Rogers on personal power: Inner strength and its revolutionary impact*. New York: Delacorte.

Rogers, C. (1978). The formative tendency. *Journal of Humanistic Psychology, 18*(1), 23–26.

Rogers, C. (1980). *A way of being*. Boston: Houghton Mifflin.

Rogers, C., & Russell, D. (2002). *Carl Rogers: The quiet revolutionary*. Roseville, CA: Penmaren.

Thorne, B. J. (1992). *Carl Rogers*. London: Sage.

Wood, J. (1972, November–December). Carl Rogers, gardener. *Human Behavior*, 17–22.

Wurdinger, S. (1994). *Philosophical issues in adventure education*. Dubuque, IA: Kendall/Hunt.

Part IV

School and Program Founders

Theory to Practice, Practice to Theory

> Before a thing can be learned, it has first to be lived … I learn only and exactly what I live.
>
> W. H. Kilpatrick (1942)

Interdependence is a complex concept which implies a mutual interactive relationship. Two things are said to be interdependent when they are necessary and beneficial to each other. In biology and ecology we speak of the interdependence of various species. This relationship can be illustrated by an indigenous folk tale. An Inuit story tells about the wolves and the caribou being brothers because they make each other strong. The wolf pack is strengthened by the flesh of the caribou they kill and eat, and the caribou herd is strengthened because the wolves take the old, sick, and weak.

The concept of interdependence can be applied to experiential education (EE) to clarify the relationship between philosophy (theory) and methodology (practice). As with the wolves and the caribou who strengthen each other, EE theory can strengthen the practice and EE practice can contribute to building the underlying philosophy. As we seek to expand our personal philosophy, it is important to attend to both theory and practice. When young leaders learn program practices without knowing the underlying theoretical foundations, they are simply being trained, not educated. When ivory tower philosophical systems are taught without attention to applications in the real world, they cannot be fully understood by the student.

It has been said that EE is experience rich but theory poor, noting that program development and methodology have progressed much more rapidly than the written theoretical foundations of the field. If this is true, there are a number of possible reasons for this:

1. There is continuing controversy about the definition of EE, whether it is a philosophy or methodology.
2. The field of EE involves people of diverse educational backgrounds and professional affiliations, and these people and professions have different philosophical orientations and audiences.
3. A wide range of educational and therapeutic programs with variable goals have gathered under the EE umbrella.
4. Some EE practitioners tend to be more concerned with applying the methodology than with the developing of theoretical foundations.

It is important that the field of EE develop a deeper philosophical understanding. This is not to imply that every field practitioner should be a philosopher, but they should appreciate and explored the interdependence between theory and practice. There is a parallel in other fields. For example, some social workers tend toward dealing more with human problems, leaving the development of theory to the sociologists. Of course, field applications should be based on sound philosophy (good philosophy informs practice), and experiments in the field should continually influence philosophy (good practice informs philosophy).

The chapters in this section are about people who have started programs to facilitate the growth and learning of children and adults. Some of them based their programs on a formalized theory, but others simply followed their personal ideas about best practices. Some of them developed a program philosophy before, during, and after implementing the practices; but many of them were field practitioners who did not spend a lot of time outlining and writing about their philosophies. Certainly, most of them did not write about the implications of their programs for experiential education, and yet these programs and their creators can make significant contributions to contemporary EE theory and practice.

In many cases, although those developing programs did not yield comprehensive written philosophies, nor even provide information to create a broad theoretical foundation for EE, some of them did offer a rationale for their various program practices and goals. There are many examples of this: Paul Petzoldt (1908–1999), founder of the National Outdoor Leadership School, who was not known previously as an educational theorist, often spoke and wrote about the importance of sound leadership development in outdoor adventure programs. Kurt Hahn (1886–1974), founder of the Outward Bound schools, did not base his program on a comprehensive learning theory, but his ideas about the goals of education and training (challenge and character development) are very important to any philosophy of experiential education.

Life is experience; living is experiencing. The very process of growth and development involves increasing one's repertoire of behavior by experiential learning. From early infancy humans experience the joy of accumulating new behaviors. White (1959) suggested that one of the most basic human motivations is that of mastering new skills, solving new problems, and having feelings of achievement or competence. There may be a natural inclination for human beings to introduce others to activities that they have found enjoyable or meaningful, behaviors that have led them to feelings of joyful competence.

Healthy humans are social beings, and much of their life experience, their life learning, is related to becoming socially competent and achieving good adjustment within the group. Through time, the group norms and expectations become important lessons for the individual, and social institutions and programs are formed to pass along customs, values, behaviors, ideologies, and qualities of personality and character that are deemed important.

In any case, whether because of individuals' desires to share personal experiences of joyful competence, or because they have become involved in the process of passing on cultural norms and expectancies, people develop programs to facilitate the experiential learning of others. School camps, community programs, treatment interventions, festivals and games are some of the ways that people organize their efforts to facilitate the growth and learning of others. Most of the people involved in building and operating such programs exemplify the often-stated mandate of experiential education—Just Do It. They go about their business without giving a great deal of thought to any comprehensive philosophical foundations, but most of them certainly do have a rationale for implementing their programs and practices. Experiential education theorists might find much of value in reviewing the many programs created by the doers.

Consider, for example, people like Robert Baden-Powell (1857–1941) who was the founding father of the Boy Scout movement in Great Britain, or Juliette Gordon Low (1860–1927) who started the Girl Scout movement in the United States. Many experiential education practitioners became involved in the field because of their early experience with scouting. Luther Gulick (1865–1918) was a physical fitness advocate, and helped bring the Boy Scouts to America; and his wife, Charlotte Gulick (1866–1928) founded the Camp Fire Girls organization. It may be valuable for experiential educators to look to the Gulicks and ask, why did they do what they did. Campbell Loughmiller (1965), therapeutic camp leader, developed a wilderness camping program for troubled youth that is still referred to in the adventure education literature. He wrote very little about his philosophy, but did explain some of his practices of wilderness survival and group work assignments. Steve Van Matre (1972) developed programs to enhance environmental awareness and teach students earth friendly behaviors. He based his programs on an earth education philosophy, but does not give a lot of attention to experiential education theory. Still, many of the activities created and recommended by Van Matre are part of the bag of tricks of many experiential education leaders.

The developmental schools of Maria Montessori (1870–1952) and Rudolph Steiner (1861–1925), are based on theories of child development and age appropriate teaching, and they have strong experiential components. Examples include the New School programs developed in the early years of the 20th century. Cecile Reddie (1858–1932), Herman Letiz (1868–1919), Homer Lane (1875–1925), and A. S. Neill (1883–1973) are others who warrant the attention of experiential education theorists.

Programs emphasizing the value of movement, dance, folk music and drama are all examples of experiential learning. For example, Myles Horton (1905–1990), developed the Highlander Folk School in Tennessee and emphasized the importance of communication and interaction between teachers and students.

A number of community-based programs that have had impact on experiential education can be described as involving "Play Education" (Smith, Roland, Havens, & Hoyt, 1992, pp. 30–36). The creative play movement began in the late 1960s in the San Francisco counterculture with festivals of peaceful, cooperative play which gave rise to the concepts of New Games. The New Games Foundation was established in the early 1970s, and the *New Games Book* was published a few years later (Fluegelman, 1976). This book, along with a number of other cooperative play books that followed (e.g., Weinstein & Goodman, 1980), was one of the earliest to find a place on the book shelves of young outdoor experiential leaders—next to Karl Rohnke's classic *Cowstails and Cobras* (1977).

All of these field practitioners offer some rationale for their practices that should be carefully considered by EE professionals. There have been thousands of doers through the years, people who were not educational theorists or philosophers, but were interested in offering particular experiential opportunities for others. Most of them did not focus on theory, but simply went about facilitating growth and learning experiences for others. However, in recognition of the interdependence of philosophy and methodology, these programs and their founders should be studied. Most of these leaders thought deeply about what they were doing and why they were doing it. It would be valuable for contemporary EE professionals to think about what they do and why they do it. Their practices can inform the theory of experiential education.

This book could have included chapters on all of the people mentioned above—and many others. Appendix I does offer a list of some of those who deserve a closer look as the field of EE expands and refines its philosophical foundations. There are 10 chapters in this section.

Chapter 24: Maria Montessori: Founding Mother of Experiential Education?
Chapter 25: Cecil Reddie: Pioneer Headmaster
Chapter 26: Fridtjof Nansen: Adventure and *Friluftsliv*
Chapter 27: Juliette Gordon Low: Scouting and Experiential Education
Chapter 28: Paul Petzoldt: Man of the Mountains
Chapter 29: Sylvia Ashton-Warner: Teacher and Reflective Practitioner
Chapter 30: Campbell Loughmiller: The Father of Therapeutic Camping
Chapter 31: Sidney B. Simon: Values Clarification Pioneer
Chapter 32: Eliot Wigginton: Foxfire—No Inert Ideas Allowed Here
Chapter 33: Tricia Yu: The Tao of Experience

References

Fluegelman, A. (1976). *New games book*. New York: Doubleday.

Loughmiller, C. (1965). *Wilderness Road*. Austin: Hogg Foundation/University of Texas.

Rohnke, K. (1977). *Cowstails and cobras*. Hamilton, MA: Project Adventure.

Smith, T., Roland, C., Havens, M., & Hoyt, J. (1992). *The theory and practice of challenge education*. Dubuque, IA: Kendall/Hunt.

Van Matre, S. (1972). *Acclimatization*. Martinsville, IN: American Camping Association.

White, R. W. (1959). Motivation re-considered: The concept of competence. *Psychological Review, 66*(5), 299–331.

Weinstein, M., & Goodman, J. (1980). *Playfair: Everybody's guide to non-competitive play*. San Luis Obispo, CA: Impact Press.

24 Maria Montessori
Founding Mother of Experiential Education?

Michael J. Swiderski

In every age there are certain people who are recognized for their significant contributions. These individuals fall into Emerson's phrase of a "Representative Man." This group of select people is what the Germans call the spirit of their age, or *Zeitgeist*. In such personalities, a clear expression of their aspirations stirs the hearts of thousands.

One such representative person, who started an educational reform movement, has an eternal flame, brightly focused and beaming on the historical chalk board of education. It takes little thought to compare the distance between traditional methods of teaching and the experiential pedagogy of Dr. Maria Montessori. Just who was this polymathic woman who began an educational revolution that changed the way we think about children more than anyone before or since?

Biography

The Early Years

In 1870, the same year that Italy became a unified, free nation, one of the world's greatest educators was born in the provincial town of Chiaravalle, Italy. Maria's father, Alessandro, a successful government official and member of the bourgeois civil service was married to Renide Stoppani, a well-educated, wealthy, and patriotic woman who was devoted to the ideals of liberation and the unity of Italy. At the age of five, the family moved to a more sophisticated and cosmopolitan Rome, which enabled Maria to have a better education and the use of museums and libraries (Flaherty, n.d.).

Maria was considered to be optimistic, self-confident, and greatly interested in change. As a child it was not uncommon for her to interfere in arguments her parents would have. During that time, elementary education was a local concern, with the schools usually dirty and crowded. However, Maria learned very easily and did exceptionally well on her exams. With her mother's support and encouragement she made the first move in her educational career by entering a technical school, usually considered off-limits to females, at the age of 13.

Technical Studies

She began her technical studies at the Regia Scuola Tecnica Michelangelo Buonarroti where she began developing a mental model of what a school should not be like. She graduated from technical school in 1886, and then went on to study engineering at the Regio Instituto Tecnico Leonardo da Vinci. Her favorite studies were math, but by the time she was ready to graduate, she had decided she wanted to study the biological sciences. Her father was shocked and disapproved, for it was considered impossible for a woman to be accepted into a medical school ("Maria Montessori," n.d.).

Medical School

Maria first investigated the University of Rome, but they did not admit women into the medical program. Undaunted, she decided to try a back door approach; she enrolled at the University of Rome to study physics, math, and natural sciences. In 1892 she passed her exams and received a *Diploma di Licenza* making her eligible to study medicine. Maria persisted until she was accepted into the medical program. It was shocking and unprecedented that a woman be accepted to study medicine during this time ("Maria Montessori," n.d.).

In 1896, before a board of 10 men, she presented her thesis. They were highly impressed with her brilliant work and granted her the degree of doctor of medicine, making Maria Montessori the first woman to graduate from medical school in Italy (Kramer, 1976). She quickly jumped into her work, securing a surgical assistant position, while at the same time continuing research and joining the staff at the University of Rome as an assistant doctor. In her work at the University Psychiatric Clinic, Dr. Montessori developed an interest in the treatment of special needs children. For several years, she worked, wrote, and spoke on their behalf.

The Significance of Heartfelt Observation

As part of her duties at the Psychiatric Clinic, she visited the asylums for the insane in Rome in order to select suitable subjects for the clinic. It was in this way she was led to take an interest in "idiot children," as they were referred to at the time. Dr. Montessori looked around the room and saw that the children had no toys or materials of any kind. The room was void of objects and absolutely bare with nothing to hold and manipulate in their fingers.

Montessori saw in the children's behavior a craving of a very different and higher kind than for mere food. There existed for these poor creatures, she realized, one path and one only towards intelligence, and that was through their hands (Standing, 1957, p. 28). The more she came in contact with these children, observing and studying them, meditating over their condition, and longing to help them, the more strongly she came to differ with the generally accepted views with regard to teaching them. It became increasingly apparent to her that their mental deficiency was a pedagogical problem rather than a medical one.

Thoughts on Education

This fundamental revelation of special needs children in 1897 gave Dr. Montessori new insight. As she continued to study the children she was working with, a number of beliefs, educational theories, and learning principles were developed. She based most of her approach to teaching on truths about human nature ("Maria Montessori," n.d.).

As an astute scientist and focused observer of child behavior, she discovered revolutionary principles about children and their process of learning. Among these was the concept that children have an inherent desire to learn, and that on their own they are capable of accumulating an incredible amount of information and wisdom about their natural surroundings. Dr. Montessori further revealed that children's natural capacity for learning worked best when they were turned loose in a safe, hands-on learning environment. She felt her most significant discovery was the recognition that it was teachers who must pay detailed attention to their students, not the other way around—a notion contrary to the educational expectations of her time. Dr. Montessori continued to transfer energy between the medical profession, and perfecting her thoughts, concepts and principles of education (Standing, 1957).

Contributions of Educational Theories, Principles, Concepts, and Methods

Dr. Montessori was able to evolve her educational theories by drawing on her academic training, professional background and experience in medicine, clinical psychology, and anthropology. She was, therefore, well poised to tackle the reforms needed in the education system.

She developed her educational theory, combining the ideas of Friedrich Froebel, who laid the foundation for modern education based on the recognition that children have unique capabilities and needs; French physician Jean Marc Gaspard Itard, the patriarch of special education; Itard's pupil, Dr. Edouard Seguin, who worked with mentally handicapped children in France and the United States and wrote the earliest known treatises about the special needs of children with mental disabilities; and Giuseppe Sergi, an influential Italian anthropologist of the early 20th century.

In 1900 Dr. Montessori was given an opportunity to apply her theories when she began to direct a small school in Rome for "challenged" youth. The teaching methods she employed were both experimental and miraculous. Aside from a new pedagogy, among the premier observations and contributions to educational thought by Dr. Montessori were:

Belief that each child was born with a unique potential which needed to be revealed, rather than waiting for the "blank slate" to be written upon. ("Maria Montessori, MD," n.d.)

Theories of the "sensitive periods" in the development of a child were new at the time, however, they now seem to correspond with what is considered to be the "needs" of a child at different stages in their development. ("Maria Montessori," n.d.)

The observation of the child in the learning environment was the basis for ongoing curriculum development, sequencing of exercises for skill development and information accumulation. ("Maria Montessori," 2007)

Small, child sized furniture and the creation of a small, child-sized environment (microcosm) helped produce a self-running, small children's learning world. ("Maria Montessori," 2007)

The creation of a scale of sensitive periods of development provided a focus for class work that was appropriate and uniquely stimulating and motivating to the child (including sensitive periods for language development, sensorial experimentation and refinement, and various levels of social interaction). ("Maria Montessori," 2007)

The importance of the "absorbent mind," the limitless motivation of the young child to achieve competence over his or her environment and to perfect his or her skills and understandings as they occurred within each sensitive period. (Montessori, 1995)

The duty of the teacher (directress) was to help and facilitate development, rather than judge. (Standing, 1957)

True mental work, when the child was truly engaged and uninterrupted, did not exhaust but rather gave nourishing food for the spirit. (Standing, 1957)

The mainspring of the child's work and motivation was the reliance on the painstakingly designed schoolroom environment and the spontaneous interests of the children. (Standing, 1957)

Children have natural learning tendencies. ("Maria Montessori," 2007)

The instruction of children in 3-year age groups, corresponded to the sensitive periods of development (Ex.: Birth–3, 3–6, 6–9 and 9–12 years old). ("Maria Montessori," 2007)

Children, as competent beings were encouraged to make maximal decisions. ("Maria Montessori," 2007)

The self-correcting, "auto-didactic" materials and hands-on manipulatives created learning avenues from the hands to the brain (based on the work of Itard and Seguin). ("Maria Montessori," 2007)

The Montessori method prepared the most natural and life-supporting environments for the child. ("Maria Montessori, MD," n.d.)

The Montessori pedagogy continually adapted the learning environment in order that the children fulfill his or her greatest potential in all five realms: social, physical, mental (intellectual), emotional, and spiritual. ("Maria Montessori, MD," n.d.)

The Montessori method focused on development rather than mere learning. (Standing, 1957)

The school environment included the use of nature in the classroom in order to meet the real needs of the children. (Montessori, 1912)

Thoughts on Learning & Teaching

In Dr. Montessori's mind, one of the main ingredients in the success of her teaching methods was the careful and meticulously designed learning environment.

The Learning Environment

The Montessori learning environment was much different than the traditional model. Instead of information being passed from the teacher to the student, the teacher was skilled in putting the child in touch with the educational environment and helped them learn to make intelligent choices. The teacher then protected the student's concentration from interruption. This fostered a love of lifetime learning in the student ("Montessori Materials," n.d.).

Work Centers

The Montessori school environment was arranged according to subject areas, e.g., cooking, cleaning, gardening, art, caring for animals, library corner. The children were always free to move around the room instead of staying at desks. There was no limit to how long children could work on something they had chosen. At any one time in the day all subjects such as practical work, math, language, science, history, geography, art, music, would be studied, at all levels, by children of mixed ages. Children learned from each other, although guided by careful observation and individual lessons, record keeping, and the facilitative assistance of the teacher ("Montessori Materials," n.d.; "Teaching Montessori," 2007).

An Educational Environment Conducive to Spontaneous Learning

Dr. Montessori believed that the learning environment was just as important as the learning itself ("Maria Montessori," 2007). Through giving children some freedom in a specially prepared environment that was rich in activities, children aged four to six years old learned to read on their own, chose to work rather than play most of the time, loved order and silence, and developed a real social life in which they worked together instead of competing against one another. In Dr. Montessori's book, *The Montessori Method* (1912), a typical room found in the Montessori school system is described. The classroom and learning environment became a miniature-sized home for learning and personal development. There was usually a central room for intellectual work with some small rooms off to the side and a lot of outside space to work. She was the first in education to have child-sized tables and chairs made for the students. The furniture in the room was light enough so the children could rearrange it for comfort. Cabinets containing items the children could use were set low so they could reach them. When it was time for their meals, they would help prepare their place at a table, wash their hands, and also clean up after a meal ("Maria Montessori," n.d.). A visitor to the school would see a Lilliputian world with small children scurrying about in some rooms, reflecting in total absorption in other rooms and what looked like play in yet another room, all being "guided" by the teacher (directress).

Facilitative Learning and the Decentralization of the Teacher

Another related element of the Montessori method was the "decentering" of the teacher. The teacher was the "keeper of the environment." When children got on with their activities, the task of the teacher was to keenly observe and to intervene from the periphery. The focus was on self-realization through independent activities, and the diligence of the teacher to unobtrusively orchestrate the integrity of the environment.

Multi-Aged Grouping

Children were grouped in mixed ages and abilities in three-year spans: 0–3, 3–6, 6–9, 9–12, etc. There was constant interaction, problem solving, child-to-child teaching, and socialization. Children were challenged according to their ability and never became bored. Montessori teachers ideally had taken all of Dr. Montessori's training courses plus graduate work in a specialized academic area or areas ("Teaching Montessori," 2007).

Teaching Method: Teach by Teaching, Not by Correcting

No papers were turned back with red marks and corrections. Instead the child's effort and work was respected as it was. The teacher, through extensive observation and record-keeping, planned individual projects to enable each child to learn what was needed in order to improve and develop ("Teaching Montessori," 2007).

Learning Styles

All kinds of intelligences and styles of learning were nurtured: musical, bodily-kinesthetic, spatial, interpersonal, intrapersonal, intuitive, and the traditional linguistic and logical-mathematical (reading, writing, and math). Today, this particular model is backed up by Harvard psychologist Howard Gardner's theory of multiple intelligences (1983).

Color and Multi-Sensory

Standing (1957), describes the colorful environment of a typical Montessori classroom:

> There are some twenty or so gaily painted little tables with chairs to match, dotted around the room as in a restaurant ... All round the room are long, low brightly colored cupboards. These house an immense variety of fascinating occupations, the teaching materials, many of which are brightly colored also.

> Everywhere there is color—even the dainty little dusters hanging in a row are all of different shades, as are the children's smocks. On most of the tables are placed vases of flowers. All these things together—as the sun comes shining in through the large and low windows—make a most beautiful and attractive picture. (p. 185)

Activity & Hands-On-Learn-By-Doing

Activity was the key word of the life inside this "new world." Nearly all the children were busy doing something with their hands as well as their brains. Knowledge was finding its way into those little heads via their hands, eyes, ears, and feet. This was obviously a school where "children learned by doing." But what were they doing? "Here are some forty different children, scattered in different parts of the room, and nearly all of them doing different things... Even the teacher does not know" (Standing, 1957, p. 186).

According to Standing (1957), who worked with Montessori in the learning environment, "[The teacher] is quite content if she knows that they are working; for then she knows that they are teaching themselves [through the materials] better than she herself could do" (p. 186).

Stages of Learning and the Importance of Movement

In the Montessori system there were two distinct stages of learning. First, in the short "introduction stage," the child was initiated into the use of a new learning manipulative. Second, a much longer and more important stage, the child worked with the materials, day after day, and often week after week at chosen intervals. As the second stage was the longer of the two, it appeared to the infrequent visitor that the children were not being taught at all by the teacher. This was not true. This second stage of spontaneously working with the materials always involved movement. Movement was in fact a sine qua non of the Montessori method—bodily moving to and from the cupboards, manipulating objects of some kind, all engaged in activities which involved definite and precise movement. It was the teacher's primary aim to set the children in motion towards this second stage in which they entered into a partnership with the materials, lived with them, and worked with them. Dr. Montessori maintained that a more profound impression was gained through movement than merely by any visual or auditory aids. Interest needed to be aroused between the child and the object, an interest which brought about a prolonged and repeated activity. When the child's interest and repeated actions had been established, the directress would go away and leave the child in the company of the materials (Standing, 1957).

The significance of the children's actions was greater than just supporting their achievements in learning. Movement and activities were in fact the basis for the development of their personality. The child was always moving, not just in large movements, such as sweeping a room or laying a table but also when the child merely saw, thought or reasoned. This concept of movement was strategic in shining a light on the children's development and functioned as a guide to pointing out their developmental path to follow (Standing, 1957).

Visual aids were not enough, and telling was the least important part of the Montessori learning process. A lesson was always followed by creative movement. For example, if that teacher wanted to get across the idea of shapes and the color grading of these objects, it was of little value merely to show students diagrams of objects of various sizes. They were required to manipulate the materials (cylinders, towers, cones) with all having different shades. Whether it be multiplication tables, operations in math, letters of the alphabet, parts of speech, or theories of Pythagoras, there was always movement with manipulatives (Standing, 1957).

There was no substitute for movement. Montessori, in her books, lectures, and conversations incessantly returned to this great theme of the importance of movement. "The fundamental technique in education is this—that the child should always be active, and allowed to choose his occupations; and thus give form to his actions." She continued, "This principle of movement should be carried right through education... The organization of movement is not simply the completion of the psychological construction; it is the foundation" (Standing, 1957, p. 231). Moreover, says Dr. Montessori, children deprived of any of their senses, tend to be retarded in their mental development. She purported that children deprived of movement would also be arrested in their development. She went as far as saying that "The man who has developed without practical activity in life is in a worse condition than he who has been deprived of one of his senses" (Standing, 1957, p. 232).

The Difference Between Traditional Education and the Montessori Method

What is the difference between the Montessori method and traditional education? Dr. Montessori emphasized learning through all five senses, not just through listening, watching, or reading. Children in the Montessori classes learned at their own, individual pace, and according to their own choice of activities (from hundreds of possibilities). Learning was natural and an exciting process of discovery, which naturally lead to concentration, motivation, self-discipline, and a love of learning. Dr. Montessori formed learning communities in which the older children spontaneously shared their knowledge with the younger ones. Her revolutionary practices represented an entirely different approach to education ("Frequently Asked Questions," 2007). In addition, as her programs grew, she argued for the development of training for teachers and developed the principle that was also to inform her general education program: First the education of the senses, then the education of the intellect (Smith, 1997).

Thoughts on Growth and Development

Dr. Montessori gave the world a scientific method, practical and tested, for bringing forth the very best in young human beings. She instructed her teachers how to respect individual differences, and to emphasize social interaction and the education of the whole personality rather than the teaching of a specific body of knowledge ("The Montessori Method," 2007). Her approach to education incorporated the belief that simply imparting knowledge was not good teaching. She was convinced that her method released the human potential of children.

Referring to Dr. Montessori's far-reaching comprehension of the child's needs and her tireless attention to developing the potential of the whole child, Standing (as cited in "Maria Montessori," n.d.) notes, "No one has so completely understood the soul of the child in its depth and greatness, in its immense potentialities, and in the mysterious law of its development." It is this innovative attention to developing the whole child—body, mind, and spirit—that sets the Montessori method apart from other forms of education.

Developing the Mind, Body, and Spirit

Standing (1957) later writes of Dr. Montessori's views of the unity of the body and soul:

> [I]n the case of us human beings the soul and the body are inextricably woven together in an indissoluble unity. This fact profoundly affects all our manner of thinking, and is a dominant factor in the child's development … [M]ore than in any other system of education, her whole method is based on a deep understanding of the relationship between these two elements—mind and body …[H]e possesses a material body with inherited instincts. It is this material body, with its five senses, that connects his inner life—even his highest spiritual experiences—with the physical outside world. (p. 159)

Standing goes on to write:

> In the growing child there are, according to Montessori, two streams of energy whose balanced interplay is of the utmost importance. One is the physical energy of the body—especially the muscular energy expended in voluntary movement; and the other is the mental energy of intelligence and will—which in the last analysis is an immaterial spiritual force. (1957, p. 170)

In Dr. Montessori's view, these energies never operate in complete separation. Indeed, if anything should stand out clearly in Montessori's view of the child it is just this; these two aspects of the psyche, mind and body, should never be thought of as separate.

Teaching Is "Heart-Work"

The discipline and art of teaching comes from both the head and the heart. Is it any wonder why teaching is often referred to as "heart-work"? From the onset, Dr. Montessori, with her significant observations of the poor and deprived children, demonstrated heart-felt compassion and a focused understanding of human nature. It was the "medium of the methodology" that influenced the intrapersonal and interpersonal development in her children. Dr. Montessori's methods focused on development rather than merely teaching for academic learning. Therefore, the aim of the Montessori method was not designed as a system for academic studies as much as it was for the natural development of the whole child. Dr. Montessori continually adapted a carefully designed learning environment, crafted an experiential learning methodology, and decentralized the teacher's role into a facilitative guide. Thus, the Montessori method was deliberate in its design to fulfill the greatest potential in the child's development and growth in all five realms, physical, social, emotional, intellectual and spiritual.

Holistic Development through the Classroom Environment

The Montessori classroom environment promoted social development through multi-age groups and life support lessons and activities. Social interaction was encouraged amongst the children; the older students often taught the younger children. A round table discussion was often facilitated by rearranging the easily moved child sized tables and chairs. Personal hygiene, cleanliness, order and organization were evidenced by low lying classroom sinks for washing hands and dishes, child-sized brooms, small cloakrooms and cupboards for storage of their lessons and manipulatives. Classroom emphasis was placed on the children's self-determination in the learning of their lessons, the practice of independent problem solving and self-realization. As a result of the Montessori method and the classroom environment, the child naturally developed initiative, independence, self-disciplined behavior and concern for others.

Character Development

Montessori education was never to be a system for training children in academic studies, nor a label to be put on educational materials. It is a revolutionary method of observing and supporting the natural development of children. Dr. Montessori's educational practices helped children develop creativity, problem-solving, social, and time-management skills. The aim was for the child to eventually contribute to society and the environment, and to become a fulfilled person. The basis of the Montessori method in the classroom was to respect individual choice of research and work, and provide uninterrupted concentration rather than group lessons led by an adult ("Montessori," 2007).

Developing character is considered equally with an academic education—children learning to take care of themselves, their environment and each other through cooking, cleaning, building, gardening, moving gracefully, speaking politely, being considerate and helpful, and doing social work in the community ("Teaching Montessori," 2007).

Growth Though Movement

In the Montessori method, "The value of movement goes deeper than just helping in the acquisition of knowledge. It is in fact the basis for the development of personality" (Standing, 1957, p. 230). Movement was the key to unlocking the secret of the child's development and the foundation of the child's psychological construction. According to Dr. Montessori, the potential of the child was not just mental. The child's potential was revealed only when the complete Montessori method was understood and followed.

> The child's choice, practical work, care of others and the environment, and above all the high levels of concentration reached when work is respected and not interrupted, reveal a human being that is superior not only academically, but emotionally and spiritually, a child who cares deeply about other people and the world, and who works to discover a unique and individual way to contribute. ("Maria Montessori, MD," n.d.)

This sums up the essence of real Montessori work today.

Implications for EE Philosophy

Dr. Montessori's theories, concepts, and teaching methods were instrumental in reforming education in the early 1900s. With her academic training, professional background, and experiences in medicine, clinical psychology, and anthropology, she pioneered the recognition of the child's developmental stages, the comprehension of learning capabilities and the observation of personal growth potential. Mix this background and experience with a strategic blend of innovative approaches to hands-on learning, a meticulously designed classroom environment and a learn-by-doing philosophy, and we have an applied pedagogy which is the precursor to today's field of experiential education. Impactful?... absolutely. Influential?... no question. Legendary?... without a doubt.

It does not take much insight to recognize the disparity between the long-established traditional educational practices of today and those of the Montessori method and her pedagogy of experiential learning. Dr. Montessori's understanding of human nature and the inherent developmental capabilities of the child were the underlying foundations that supported her revolutionary theories and educational concepts. In the late 1800s and early 1900s, she was given an opportunity to re-engineer the way children could learn by being one of the first educators to holistically facilitate emotional growth, intellectual learning, spiritual awareness, physical exercise and social development through the use of hands, feet and all five senses. Dr. Montessori was one of the first to practice a learn-by-doing methodology using movement and strategically designed learning activities.

The Montessori method required the skilled teacher to put children in touch with the learning environment, encourage them to explore their own learning, challenge them to step beyond their self-perceived limitations, inspire them to make intelligent choices, and then closely observe them so as to facilitate their development using unconventional educational practices of the time. Is this not unlike today where the ropes course facilitator encourages the student to immerse themselves in an unconventional learning environment, where emotional challenge, personal development and self exploration abounds? Was Dr. Montessori ahead of her time? Before Dewey was publishing his theory of the experience," the Montessori teacher was already the keeper of the learning environment. Dr. Montessori was applying her own theories on how the child could best learn and develop, long before the educational theorists, and her focus was on development of the child rather than merely learning.

The depth and breadth of Dr. Montessori's influence may never be fully known. But her theories, concepts, and educational practices in the early 1900s are evident in today's practices and writings. Her writings and educational techniques indicate an early understanding of Gardner's theories on multiple intelligences (1983) and Goleman's ideas about emotional intelligence (1995). The fact that she divided her students into selected age groups of sensitive periods indicated her early understanding of the stages of child development.

Dr. Montessori argued that traditional education was based on the dualisms of mind and body, the assumed ignorance of the child and the wisdom and authority of the teacher. She believed that the concept of mind, body and spirit were interconnected and that hands-on experience, learning and personal development were interconnected as well. Is not this interconnecting concept the jumping off point for various forms of experiential education today? Would this early application of theory and practice not make Dr. Montessori one of the first experiential practitioners and educators?

Could her philosophy of education have influenced the founding fathers of experiential education? Could her writings have been a point of reference for Dewey (1963) who suggested that we learn how to transform experience into knowledge and that we use this knowledge for our personal development? Is it by coincidence that Goleman's *Emotional Intelligence* (1995) documents the ways in which prior experience conditions our responses to current experiences, offering physiological evidence that we learn from experience and must pay attention to the design of experiences of our students. And could have Kolb been influenced by Dr. Montessori in his ground breaking *Experiential Learning* (1984), when he suggests that learning is the "process" whereby knowledge is created through the transformation of experience?

Her writings were impactful, her methodologies influential, and her learning environment legendary. As she sits alongside our founding fathers on the settee of experiential education is it not time we consider Dr. Montessori one of our founding mothers of experiential education?

References

Dewey, J. (1963). *Experience and education* (rev. ed.). New York: MacMillan.

Flaherty, T. (n.d.). Maria Montessori (1870–1952). Retrieved June 27, 2007, from http://www.webster.edu/~woolflm/montessori.html

Frequently asked questions (FAQs). (2007). Retrieved June 27, 2007, from The International Montessori Index, http://www.montessori.edu/FAQ.html#QUESTIONS

Gardner, H. (1983). *Frames of mind: The theory of multiple intelligences.* New York: Basic Books.

Goleman, D. (1995). *Emotional intelligence.* New York: Bantam Books.

Kolb, D. (1984). *Experiential learning: Experience as the source of learning and development.* Englewood Cliffs, NJ: Prentice-Hall.

Kramer, R. (1976). *Maria Montessori: A biography.* New York: G. P Putnam & Sons.

Maria Montessori. (2007). Retrieved June 23, 2007, from http://en.wikipedia.org/wiki/Maria_Montessori

Maria Montessori. (n.d.). Retrieved June 27, 2007, from http://www.webster.edu/~woolflm/montessori2.html"

Maria Montessori, MD (1870–1952). (n.d.). Retrieved June 27, 2007, from The International Montessori Index, http://www.montessori.edu/maria.html

Montessori, M. (1912). The Montessori method: Scientific pedagogy as applied to child education in 'The Children's Houses' (chap. X). Retrieved June 27, 2007, from http://digital.library.upenn.edu/women/montessori/method/method-X.html

Montessori, M. (1995). *The absorbent mind* (rev. ed.). New York: Henry Holt.

Montessori, M. (2007). Retrieved June 27, 2007 from The International Montessori Index, http://www.montessori.edu/

Montessori materials and learning environments for the home and the school. (n.d.). Retrieved June 27, 2007, from The International Montessori Index, http://www.montessori.edu/prod.html

The Montessori method of bringing up and educating children. (2007). Retrieved June 27, 2007, from The International Montessori Index, http://www.montessori.edu/method.html

Smith, M. (1997). Maria Montessori. Retrieved June 27, 2007, from http://www.infed.org/thinkers/et-mont.htm

Standing, E. M. (1957). *Maria Montessori: Her life and work.* New York: New American Library

Teaching Montessori. (2007). Retrieved June 27, 2007, from The International Montessori Index, http://montessori.edu/info.html

25 Cecil Reddie
Pioneering Headmaster

Robbie Nicol and Peter Higgins

Cecil Reddie was an educational pioneer who founded Abbotsholme School in England. He was thought of as the father of the international "New School" movement and railed against the limits of the classical education provided by Victorian Public Schools. He was also a radical intellectual who had a direct influence on the educational thinking of Kurt Hahn, Hermann Lietz, and many others. For all this he remains an enigma, a man described as an indefatigable fighter against the very powerful social and educational influences of the public school and the wider society (Giesbers, 1970), yet someone who could be an authoritarian who ruled his class with a rod of iron. He was a man who believed in liberty, yet was obsessed with rules. In order to understand Reddie's legacy and Giesbers' (1970) assertion that he was the father of the "New School" movement and progenitor of the progressive education movement, some thought needs to be given to Reddie the man, who was described by Searby as a "volcanic personality" (1989, p. 1).

Biography

Cecil Reddie (1858–1932) was born October 10, 1858, in London. He lost both parents at an early age and went to live with relatives. He finished his schooling at Fettes School, Edinburgh, a Public School in Scotland. He was educated in three public schools involving a classical education. Of this he said:

> I left school ignorant as regards the conditions and developments of my country, and knowing nothing of foreign lands, our Colonies, America, and the world generally. I knew nothing about my own body, my mind, nor their stages of development; my mind was in a whirl as regards religion, ethics (and) philosophy. (Giesbers, 1970, p. 23)

Although he admitted the ancient classics of Latin, Greek, and theology provided wonderful opportunities for discussion, he also found his study of them to be unconnected to each other and of little relevance to real life problems. Indeed he stated that education should aim at unity; if it leaves the mind chaotic, it can hardly be recommended (Giesbers, 1970). This is in keeping with Reddie's contemporary John Dewey (1859–1952), who thought that experiences should be part of a joined pattern where one experience has an influence on later experiences so as they are linked and not isolated (Dewey, 1963).

Reddie went to Edinburgh University and studied chemistry, physics, and mathematics to gain a BSc degree and then went to study for a chemistry PhD in Germany. In addition to his formal studies, he liked to read about philosophy and religion. It was in Germany that Giesbers says he acquired his notorious and excessive devotion to rules, management, and organization (1970). His experiences in the German educational system, which he viewed as superior to that of his homeland, convinced him not to remain an academic in the world of academia. His interests in the practice of education were best served though a career as a schoolmaster.

As a product of the late Victorian period, one of the main ideological debates of the time was between science and religion. The developing theory of evolution was challenging the central orthodoxy and supremacy of the church as the main or only source of truth. The intensity of this debate can be observed throughout many countries of the world and in its wake there was an inevitable void of confusion, alienation, and uncertainty for those whose fundamental Christian convictions were challenged by the findings of science. It is a condition of society that Durkheim (1984) termed "anomie" (where the rules of society were changing and leaving people not knowing what to expect from each other and eventually to a state of little societal consensus). However the developing Darwinian theory of evolution also appeared to Reddie to begin to fill this void because of its stress on the importance of the cooperative instinct in life (Searby, 1989), and it was the idea of cooperation in school that was central to his own ideas on educational philosophy.

Within this lack of moral framework it is easy to see how, as an educationalist, Reddie became preoccupied with the role of values. Indeed he came to see morality as the focus of all educational processes (Giesbers, 1970, p. 57). At the same time the influential educationalist and inspector of schools Mathew Arnold was highly critical of the system of education in England. As Darling observed: "Like Arnold, Reddie had clear ideas about what was wrong with society and (like) Arnold he aimed for nothing less than society's regeneration through the boys he taught" (1981, p. 17). Taken together, this observation regarding the state of society and a school system that was generally considered as poor and in need of reform, it is easy to see how Reddie's solution was to create a new type of school with a new philosophy to deal with the social issues of the day. Searby suggests that Reddie saw the problem as follows:

> [The] existing schools were microcosms of the competitive capitalist society, whose replacement by the co-operative commonwealth he looked forward to. The classrooms were factories in miniature, where boys worked at repetitive mechanical tasks, cramming Latin and Greek without understanding them, for the sake of competitive examinations that were the keys to scholarships and success in the commercial rat-race. (1989, p. 1)

The solution therefore, was that the school had to break the mold and be unlike any other school. Given Reddie's enthusiasm for Germany's development as an industrial nation, he wanted a school run on the basis of orderliness. This was important to Reddie's developing pedagogy which stressed "the need for ordered, planned, structured learning" (Searby, 1989, p. 3). Reddie recognized the importance of the boarding school as it offered a challenge to the "ghastly selfishness and laissez faire of our towns and trades" (1900, p. 19). Not only did Reddie want to develop a new form of education, but the purpose of it was to address the moral inadequacies he saw in society. In order to achieve this vision he felt the need to "step outside" of society to develop his ideas. To achieve this he chose a boarding-school, because of its "ready-made community," to develop his educational philosophy and also because it "provided more scope for controlling the pupils' life-style than a day-school could offer (Darling, 1981, p. 16). It was here that theory and practice could come together and provide the springboard for Reddie's radical ideas.

In 1889, with the financial help of associates, Reddie leased and later bought Abbotsholme, a country house in Derbyshire. His intentions were to:

> ... challenge the restricted academic curriculum, its neglect of the emotional and physical aspects of the pupil's lives, its glorification of competition instead of cooperation, its old-fashioned teaching methods, its ineffective religious teaching, sexual instruction and

physical education, its lack of spontaneous personal relationships, and its exaggerated concerns with examinations. (Giesbers, 1970, p. 28)

Furthermore, Reddie believed that rural conditions were essential to his educational ideals, hence the location of Abbotsholme. Indeed the first attempt in modern times to formalize the outdoors into an educative medium in the United Kingdom can probably be attributed to Reddie (Parker & Meldrum, 1973). Reddie was particularly concerned about exercise for both mind and body through mediums such as community work, with a view to engendering social responsibility:

> [We] aimed definitely at making work indoors and out of doors a unity, interrelated and interlocked, as far as the abilities of each master could carry it. In particular, in all that concerned Mathematics and Natural Science, Hygiene and Economics, we had freely used the school surroundings and the school community as our fundamental object lessons. (Reddie, 1900, p. 114)

Educational Philosophy

Central to this philosophy was that educational objectives were more readily achieved in pleasant surroundings. It was a philosophy inspired by the Romantic movement of which one of the chief characteristics was a passionate concern regarding the relationship between human beings and the natural environment. Sederman reports that Abbotsholme is in a delightful situation "providing contacts with natural beauty and every opportunity for observing agricultural methods and learning respect for the farmer whose work the town dweller simply takes for granted" (1989, p. 58). This clearly links Reddie to the ideas of Ruskin, Thoreau, and Whitman, all of whom embrace the power, spirituality, and interconnectedness of nature. The sources of these ideas as Searby (1989) observes is the belief that rural life is more "natural" and more truthful, than urban.

The importance of the outdoors to Reddie's own educational philosophy is clear in the following statement:

> In order to avoid the ill effects of modern town life, with its unwholesome physical surroundings, with the distractions (sic) of its intellectual activity, and the dangers of its moral atmosphere, a school should be remote from towns, and placed amid the wholesome, beautiful, simple and fundamentally instructive surroundings of the country. (Reddie quoted in Darling, 1981, p. 16)

Indeed, rather than passively observing, pupils were required to undertake a range of building and agricultural tasks as part of their curriculum. Reddie's plan was to work with the sons of wealthy leaders of industry whose lives had been blighted, as he saw it, by being bound up with industrial city activities and who had little concept of how the vital production of food for the nation took place.

Yet, even at this stage, Reddie acknowledged that his ideas lacked a "clear systematic, philosophic theory to render our concrete, practical, instinctive work a really intellectual power" (Reddie, 1900, p. 114). This is in keeping with the embryonic thinking of the progressive education movement at that time. Punch (1973) suggested that this educational ideology "never approximated to a readily identifiable doctrine but more a philosophical flag of convenience that tenuously united a diverse group of thinkers and practitioners" (Darling, 1981, p. 13).

Darling (1981) suggests that some of the key features of the progressive education movement's philosophy were:

1. an emphasis on the cultivation of the soul and things of the spirit;
2. a belief in the improving effect of outdoor physical activity;
3. a desire for a simpler, healthier lifestyle;
4. a commitment to community or promotion of the common good.

It is perhaps Reddie's recognition that there was a lack of theoretical overview that begins to indicate his true legacy, for within a very short period of time Reddie's ideas did take shape in terms of both theory and practice. For example, it was clear even at this stage that his educational philosophy was clearly located within the realms of what is now termed experiential learning. Talking of his staff at Abbotsholme, Reddie states:

> We all knew vaguely that all correct instruction begins with simple, concrete facts, and proceeds inductively to abstract principles, and that from these one passes deductively to apply the doctrines reached to the fresh problems of practical life. (1900, p. 114)

This process was important to Reddie because facts on their own did not provide an adequate understanding as they can be got by any fool from an encyclopedia and works of reference; what matters is that you should learn to think (Reddie in Searby, 1989, p. 17).

Reddie was influenced by Herbartian psychology which he learned about from his masters (teachers) while visiting Germany. Since the central theme of this theory is morality and the development of character, it seems that Reddie found theoretical explanation for the practical work he was already engaged in. He describes it thus: "As if by magic, the fog lifted, and we saw a new instructional heaven and earth" (Reddie, 1900, p. 115). He returned to Abbotsholme "feeling we had behind our aims the arguments of an entire philosophy" (Reddie, 1900, p. 116).

Reddie thought that the masters at his New School Abbotsholme were strong in the teaching of the sciences. This is hardly surprising given the strong connections with the teachings of Professor Sir Patrick Geddes. Reddie had worked for Geddes in Edinburgh and later sent his own staff to work as part of a summer school to provide new opportunities for pedagogic study. The effect of Geddes' philosophy may be seen in the Abbotsholme program, in particular its stress on cooperation, practical tasks and the education of the emotions, and its sense that a restructured education would help to fashion a better world (Searby, 1989). Reddie was also influenced by Geddes' idea that the three R's—Reading, wRiting, and aRithmetic—were an incomplete model of learning, relying as it did on so much rote learning. Instead the three R's should be transformed into a holistic philosophy embracing the three H's, Heart, Hand, and Head, respectively symbolic of emotional, physical and intellectual learning. Importantly those who posited this idea shared Geddes' view that the order was important. This is understandable since it was a challenge to the dominance of both rote learning and book learning (Head). By emphasizing the importance of Heart, Reddie, like Geddes, identified what was absent in the way in which people in Britain were being educated. It is also Reddie's way of challenging his own classical education in order to come up with something new and fit for preparing pupils for life.

For Abbotsholme this meant that although a little Latin and Greek were still to be taught there was greater emphasis given to English, modern languages, history and geography, and science. These were to be taught vividly, from the modern, concrete, and particular, to the older, more abstract, and general (Nearby, 1989, p. 2). The curriculum also included programs of physical exercise, manual labor, recreation and the arts. Noting these curricular inclusions is important as they help to show the changes that Reddie thought necessary to reform the school curriculum. An intriguing aspect of this developing philosophy was the way that it was developed through the conscious use of the concepts of space and time. The purpose of the curriculum was to provide a culture conducive to learning where the school should be a home (space). For example Reddie states:

The educative influence of Dormitory becomes one of the most valuable in the daily life of school; and it is most important that every Boy should realize that the friendly intimacy naturally arising from the grouping of a small number together in Dormitory, affords valuable opportunities for mutual help. (Reddie quoted in Sederman 1989, p. 23)

This concept of space was characterized by its immediacy, involving self and others and a focus on the present, and attending to the physical landscape immediately surrounding the school. However, in keeping with his concern of the state of society, Reddie believed that educational influences should extend beyond the local context.

The concept of time provided the key to this because the curriculum embraced the idea of lived experience and the pupils were generally encouraged to have an outward outlook on life. In this way space centered on the school as a hub, the common home of all (and time involved) traveling (metaphorically) from the school as a starting point, to England, France, Germany and the World of today, and finally to Rome and the origins of culture (Reddie, 1900).

These ideas show Reddie to be a reformist in terms of the content of the curriculum. However he also believed that the school was only one part of a lifelong process of learning. He states:

And even if in school we could follow always a logical or historical sequence, out of school the impressions will come without order of any sort, especially in our modern life, and the boy must learn to connect his impressions and pigeon-hole them for himself. (Reddie, 1900, p. 117)

In this statement it is apparent that Reddie was concerned not just with the content of the curriculum, but the process of thinking. His was a philosophy that focused on the importance of the individual and the teaching relationship in the learning process where success may be judged by the extent to which learners are able to think for themselves. This was clearly a challenge to conventional thought which celebrated the superiority of the role of the teacher (although Reddie did believe this) whose prime function was to fill their "empty vessels" (pupils) with knowledge. There was a clear role for individuals to be active (physically and mentally) rather than passive in their own learning. Here we clearly see Reddie's contribution to the development of experiential learning and also to what is now commonly called lifelong learning.

The early development of Abbotsholme under Reddie is a checkered one. It opened in 1889 with 16 boys and school numbers continued to grow to their peak in 1900 when there were 61 boys and 6 masters (Searby, 1989). Reddie's temper was legendary and his fallouts with staff and pupils are two features of his temperament that are well documented. A pupil at the time said:

Always a complex combination of devil and saint, the devil now took command. His temper was ungovernable. He shouted, stormed and raged. He seldom came into class without a cane. Teaching, what there was of it, was thrown to the winds. (Giesbers, 1970, p. 39)

Searby (1989, p. 9) talks of the "Great Row" that "poisoned relationships between Reddie and his staff and led to a loss of pupils" so that by 1908 the school had only 30 pupils. Numbers continued to fall with the First World War and Reddie, who had suffered nervous breakdowns before, continued to be plagued by emotional unrest.

Despite his temper, Reddie had a gentle side characterized by a teaching ability that was said to be "magnetic and compelling" (Searby, 1989, p. 17). His pastoral care for pupils was important to him. He believed in the value of personal hygiene and taught this as a theoretical discipline (e.g., physiology), but also through the monitoring of pupil illnesses and the offering of vegetarian diets (something quite unusual at that time). When practiced alongside his insistence that the curriculum included healthy outdoor activities, this twin concern with health and hygiene can be seen as a precursor to the modern concern of health and well being as a curricular subject. His gentler side was shown in his relationships with pupils and parents. One pupil described him as "intensely spiritual … the softest and gentlest man I've ever met" (Searby, 1989, p. 13). As Searby observes, Reddie was "always energetic and commanding, he may be glimpsed radiating charm at a parents" gathering, laughing uproariously at a schoolboy skit on their teachers (1989, p. 12).

This is the same person who bullied some masters into resigning, and it is these relationships that were a great source of conflict because without their subservience Reddie saw them as a potential threat. Despite this, quite a few of those masters who left went on to set up their own independent schools based on Abbotsholme principles, thereby, paradoxically, ensuring Reddie's legacy. Abbotsholme was his personal property and his only means of income, so it is understandable that he was under pressure to keep the program successful throughout the 37 years of his life's work.

Scholarly success among pupils was mixed. For example, an inspection in 1904 by Patrick Geddes found that some subjects could have been better taught, but he nevertheless complimented the school on its "out-of-door activities, the spirit of co-operation, and the great attention paid to moral education" (Giesbers, 1970, p. 139). Since seeking outstanding academic success does not appear to be part of Reddie's philosophy, it remains unclear whether these minor criticisms would have bothered him, although as he clearly held Geddes in high esteem it seems likely to have done so. Interestingly, Reddie's obsession with rules was vindicated by Geddes who "had feared over-regulation but that he eventually realised the educational value of all these rules because they were a codification of the practical experience of boys and masters" (Giesbers, 1970, p. 121).

Abbotsholme continued to develop its practical curricular activity, which involved farming animals and vegetables, haymaking, growing flowers, swimming and beekeeping, in addition to those activities that nowadays are more commonly called outdoor pursuits (canoeing, rambling, and walking). A lot of these tasks were conducted with the older pupils supervising the younger ones and this responsibility extended throughout the curriculum, including classes and in the dormitory. When viewed within a contemporary context, this form of outdoor education is much more expansive than the modern and narrower conception of adventurous outdoor activities practiced in most countries.

Implications for EE Philosophy

While Reddie's legacy in progressive education is extensive, it is not at first apparent. Part of the reason for this is because he did not believe in writing about such things. However, there were those who worked at Abbotsholme and knew Reddie who went on to set up their own schools. Examples of this include: J. H. Badley who set up Bedales also in England; Kurt Hahn who set up Gordonstoun in Scotland; Edmond Demolins who established L'Ecole des Roches in France and Herman Lietz's three schools in Germany.

So Searby is perhaps correct to suggest that "Reddie was more successful in inspiring others than in building up an enduring institution" (1989, p. 20). However, Searby does point out that "the school has risen to higher things since his time" (p. 21).

An indication of Reddie's standing in society during his own life was the company he kept. He belonged to a group of influential thinkers and social innovators and members of the progressive movement which included Edward Carpenter (socialist, writer, and poet), Nobel Prize winning author George Bernard Shaw, philosopher and social reformer Bertrand Russell, and the prolific author D. H. Lawrence.

Giesbers suggests that Reddie was the pioneer of the progressive education movements both in Europe (France and Germany) and the United States (1970, p. 49). Kurt Hahn acknowledges Reddie as one of his own main influences when as a 16-year-old he was given a book about

214 Robbie Nicol and Peter Higgins

Abbotsholme by two of Reddie's students (Darling, 1981). Reddie did a lecture tour in the United States between 1906–1908 (Searby, 1989). He does not appear to have used the term "experiential education," but his views on it are apparent in what he did and what he said, for example, by introducing farming to the school, and going outdoors for the study of mathematics, natural science, hygiene and economics. This shows that direct experience with phenomena was important to his methods and so the object of study and the medium by which it was studied became part of the same process.

His main contribution to the 21st century is not so much the theory he developed, but the educational practices that he pioneered which later came to be associated with what is now called "experiential learning." As Giesbers points out:

> It would be an irresponsible exaggeration to depict Reddie as a systematic thinker in education, philosophy and psychology. He was a practical reformer, headmaster of a New School, an eclectic who picked up notions and suggestions wherever he found them. (1970, p. 70)

Perhaps Giesbers' comments are a little unkind. Anyone who was able to integrate the separate theoretical bodies of literature relating to education, philosophy and psychology, liberally spice it with theosophy, and then use this heady mix of ideas to provide a commentary on society, would in other circumstances be called a polymath. What is particularly impressive was the way in which Reddie was able to apply this developing ontology to challenge an existing ontology. It is not surprising that he suffered nervous breakdowns, perhaps because the gap between the vision he aspired to and the position he was starting from was too great for one person to achieve in a lifetime. His work was, no doubt, further hampered by the effects of The Great War and, towards its end the loss of a former pupil and "head boy" at Abbotsholme, Roderick Bemrose, who he had set his heart on becoming his successor.

Perhaps also it was his ungovernable temper, his unwillingness to trust in colleagues, his resistance to co-educational schools and adherence to the contemporary belief in the inferiority of women, and his general stubbornness that made him an easy person to dislike. If this is true, then Giesbers' suggestion that Reddie was "the wrong man with the right ideas" may in part explain why his ideas flourished whilst Reddie, the man, became all but forgotten (1970, p. 10).

Acknowledgment

The authors would like to express their gratitude to Mr. Derek Sederman, formerly Head of Physical Education at Abbotsholme School from 1960 until 1998 whose responsibilities included Outdoor Education. In writing this chapter, we relied exclusively on secondary sources. Although these sources are biographically rich, they do not portray Reddie's work in a contemporary context particularly in relation to experiential learning (the task of this chapter). Whilst the views expressed in this chapter are our own, we would like to thank Derek for his contribution, which included identification of material and commenting on drafts.

References

Darling, J. (1981). New life and new education: The philosophies of Davidson, Reddie and Hahn. *Scottish Educational Review, 13*, 12–24.
Dewey, J. (1963). *Experience and education*. London: Collier-Macmillan.
Durkheim, E. (1984). *The division of labor in society*. Macmillan: Basingstoke.
Giesbers, J. (1970). *Cecil Reddie and Abbotsholme*. Nijmegan, The Netherlands: Centrale Drukkerij NV.
Parker, T., & Meldrum, K. (1973) *Outdoor education*. London: J. M. Dent & Sons.

Punch, M. (1973). Darlington Hall School doctoral disertation. University of Essex, Colchester, Essex, UK.

Reddie, C. (1900). *Abbotsholme*. George Allen: London.

Searby, P. (1989). The new school and the life of Cecil Reddie (1858–1932) and the early years of Abbotsholme school. *History of Education*, *18*(1), 1–21.

Sederman, D. (1989). *The history of Abbotsholme School 1889–1989*. Staffordshire, UK: Abbotsholme School.

26 Fridtjof Nansen
Adventure and *Friluftsliv*

Gunnar Repp

Friluftsliv is a Norwegian word, loosely translated as "open air living," which descibes a lifestyle that involves balance and harmony between people and their environment. The term, and the associated philosophy of living, has a long cultural tradition in Norway. By the 21st century, the concept of friluftsliv had become part of the philosophical foundation of the environmental education and ethics movement, and had also become an important concept in Norway's philosophy of education. This chapter discusses the appropriate interpretation of friluftsliv and touches on the question of passive versus active interactions between people and nature, as exemplified by the life and ideas of Fridtjof Nansen, famous Norwegian explorer, scientist, statesman, humanitarian, and sometimes educational philosopher.

Fridtjof Nansen has been described as a man in the limelight almost all his life, a man of legend. He had qualities that led to biographers describing him as a great hero, and the first among sportsmen, explorers, statesmen, humanitarians, and scientists. In 1882, when he was 21 years old, and working on a seal hunting boat off Greenland's eastern coast, he began his scientific and arctic exploration career by going ashore to hike about the ice fields. Some years later (1888/1889) with a group of five men, Nansen made a successful land crossing of Greenland from the east, through the ice fields and over the ice cap, to Godthab on the west coast. He then felt he was ready for realizing his next and more ambitious project, heading for the North Pole.

A few years later, his ship, Fram, was stuck in the ice, adrift across the northern seas of our globe. The meaning of Fram is "forwards," and the boat and crew were successful in coming through the unknown arctic seas and returning to the mainland after three years of adventure. During their time frozen in the drift, Nansen and the crew attempted a daring adventure; they left the Fram with skis and kayaks and tried to be the first human beings to reach the North Pole. Although that expedition failed, and they had to turn southwards at 82 degrees 14 minutes north, Nansen's fire for adventure was surely reinforced.

As a determined young man, Nansen noted that an explorer's deepest personal yearnings had to be paralleled by the ability to overcome hardships and dangers. Throughout his life, he met the problems that the world brought him head on, always willing to try harder to overcome adversity. He was a man who learned as much from experiences of failure as from experiences of success. His interest in learning by experience was an important factor in his work as a scientist, politician, diplomat, humanitarian, sportsman, and world renowned explorer. In his life, he tried to walk a balanced line between theory and practice, between laboratory scientist and field explorer, and between his own private family life and his personal relationship with nature. As we examine his life, it should be understood that the spectacular expeditions were in no way his only interest and experiential background.

Adventure and *Friluftsliv*

The concepts of adventure and friluftsliv were of importance in the thinking, speeches, and life of Fridtjof Nansen. He thought of friluftsliv as a time for silence, reflection, simplicity, art, and communing with nature, but he also saw the outdoors as a source of adventure. His simultaneous belief in both a passive, simple, peaceful interaction with nature, and an active, sport, and adventure involvement with nature, might be interpreted as reflecting conflicts and inconsistencies in his life and his words.

Nansen's ideas about the importance of humankind finding balance with the earth closely parallel the contemporary rhetoric of Norwegian philosopher Arne Naess, as presented in his comments about friluftsliv in *Ecology: Community and Lifestyle* (1995).

> Friluftsliv: exuberance in nature … A way of life in free nature that is highly efficient in stimulating the sense of oneness, wholeness and in deepening identification … We should see true friluftsliv as a route towards paradigm change… And with our future in mind, it is important to stake out guidelines for ethical and ecologically responsible friluftsliv. (pp. 177–179)

At the same time, Nansen saw the spirit of adventure as an obvious ally of friluftsliv, and did not see any conflict between passive and active interactions with nature. Nansen was an ideologist and paragon for the Norwegian way of outdoor life with nature. He was also an artist and author, a model for new generations of young people. According to Huntford (1997), Nansen, who was considered the father of modern polar exploration, inspired youth in many countries. One year after his death a memorial article in The American-Scandinavian Review portrayed him as "the idol of Norwegian youth" (Rygg, 1931, p. 267). Who was this man who was considered a legend in his own lifetime?

Biography

Fridtjof Nansen was born near Oslo (then called Christiana), the capital of Norway, in 1861. "His father was a lawyer in private practice, a religious man with a clear conception of personal duty and moral principle; his mother was a strong minded, athletic woman who introduced her children to outdoor life and encouraged them to develop physical skills" (Nobelprize.org., n.d.). It was from his father that Fridtjof developed his personal values about service to community, country, and the cause of world peace. It was from his mother, and time spent with his half-brothers, that he developed his love of the outdoors and adventure.

His exposure to friluftsliv started on the family's own doorstep between Oslo and Nordmarka, a remarkably natural environment. As a very young boy he was allowed to start the experiential training and personal development that would lead to becoming an explorer of nature and a scientist in nature. From early childhood Nansen loved personal experiences of learning. While still an adolescent, he would stay alone in the wilderness for weeks at a time.

The wilderness of Nordmarka is an expansive area of forests, small rivers, and good fishing lakes. Moreover, it is a natural environment of great importance to many people working and living in Oslo. At the age of 17 Nansen, with his elder half-brothers, set off for exciting adventures in the distant wilds and the highest mountain ranges of Norway. The unanimous opinion among biographers is that his friluftsliv—his "nature life"—was most important in forming his character and individuality. Bain (1897) asserts that the argument "the boy makes the man" is quite relevant to understanding Nansen.

He was a studious youth; given, in his schoolmaster's eyes, to finding out the what, how, why, and wherefore of things. His brothers and sisters were frequently provoked at his everlasting questions of "What's that?" or "How can that be?" (Bain, 1897, pp. 11–12). Bain suggests that from early childhood his thoughts were more important to him than his meals; and when he was absorbed in anything he was oblivious to the surroundings.

As Nansen grew, he became skilled in skating, tumbling, and swimming, but it was his expertise in skiing that paved the way for his life of adventure. In school he excelled in the sciences, and, when he entered the University of Oslo in 1881, he decided to major in zoology. For the next 15 years, Fridtjof sought ways to unite his interests in science with his desire for outdoor adventure. Perhaps the synthesis had first begun in 1882 when he shipped out on that sealing vessel to Greenland and spent over four months there. While there he made observations of seals and bears (which he reported in a book years later), and became enchanted with hiking and skiing in the world of sea and ice. That first trip led to the trek across Greenland six years later, and by the age of 30, Fridtjof Nansen had set the stage for becoming a polar explorer.

According to Freuchen (1928), great scientists seldom undertook polar explorations in Nansen's day. The explorer had to be a resolute man, inured to hardships. But given a theodolite and a sextant, the man accustomed to outdoor life and driving a dog sled could uncover important scientific information, perhaps more important than the scientist who by his indoor life had been unfitted to endure hardships and to solve the practical problems of survival in the wilderness. Freuchen (1928) maintains that Nansen understood the requirements of the new age and assumed leadership of the new polar exploration because his intellect spanned over the various natural sciences, and because he had the physical skills psychological qualities required.

It was Nansen's love of adventure, his curiosity about nature, and his interest in the physical requirements of expeditionary pursuits, that led him to the natural sciences. He wrote a thesis entitled, "The Structure and Combination of the Histological Elements of the Central Nervous System." Huntford (1997) concluded that Nansen's studies and academic dissertation confirmed his place among the originators of neurology. By 1897, Nansen was a professor of zoology at the University in Oslo. He also became a professor of oceanography. He was politically active in the movement for the separation of Norway and Sweden, and in 1906, following Norway's independence, he was appointed as ambassador to England. After World War I, he became involved in the League of Nations, and was active in helping refugees find settlement. In 1922 he was honored with the Nobel Peace Prize (Nobelprize.org n.d.). He died in 1930, and was buried on Norway's Independence Day.

Nansen and Experiential Learning: The Call of the Unknown

As an educator Nansen urged his audience to develop their abilities "to see the hidden things," to be open to "the call of the unknown," and indulge themselves in "the longing for the Land of Beyond" (Nansen, 1927, p. 20). Put differently, his message to our generation is: Develop the faculty to see the simple, elemental things, try new trails, run the risks, and dare the unknown. He told young people to have at least one hour daily of solo time with nature to concentrate and fully realize their capabilities. Such a recommendation parallels that of Kurt Hahn, founder of the Outward Bound Schools, who knew the value of solo time. Fifty years after Nansen, Hahn insisted that "true learning required periods of silence and solitude as well as directed activity, and each day his students took a silent walk to commune with nature and revitalize their power of reflection" (James, 2000, p. 3).

Many stories could be told about Nansen's personal reliance on experience for learning. The wintering forced upon him and his men at Godthaab after their crossing of Greenland is an example of him practicing his own principles and ideals. The last vessel back to Europe that autumn could not wait for them, so the six men had to winter at Godthaab. This made more exploring possible. Nansen reportedly "spent much of his time wandering among the natives, talking with them, dwelling in their huts, taking part in their dangerous hunting excursions on land and sea, and becoming a proficient kayaker and sledge driver" (Bain 1897, p. 40). After his interview with Nansen in 1896, Bain's concluded that Nansen had actually "lived their [the Eskimo's] life in his endeavour to obtain an accurate knowledge of their habits," and that he had concluded that the Eskimos "were highly adapted to their environment, and therefore must have lessons to teach" (p. 40). According to Bain, Nansen felt that their vital kayak was "a formidable piece of design," and concluded, "if you want to know the Eskimo in his element, you must follow him in a kayak" (Huntford, 1997, pp. 124–125).

Nansen's speech "Adventure," delivered to the young people at St. Andrews University in Scotland on November, 3, 1926, showed his interest in the general educational challenges of young people, and the importance of their interest in both adventure and friluftsliv in relation to the natural world. His interest in personal growth and development, and the challenges of pedagogy and education of future generations should be underlined.

> It is our personal yearning to overcome difficulties and dangers, to see the hidden things, to penetrate into the regions outside our beaten track—it is the call of the unknown—the longing for the Land of Beyond, the divine force deeply rooted in the soul of man which drove the first hunters out into new regions—the mainspring perhaps of our greatest actions—of winged human thought knowing no bounds to its freedom. (Nansen, 1927, p. 20)

In that famous speech he talks about three deities of importance for reaching one's goals in life—courage, independence, and the spirit of adventure. As noted, Fram, the name of Nansen's ship, means "forwards." This seems appropriate in accordance with one of his greatest recommendations for young people, which I translate and paraphrase as follows: Burn the boats and blow up the bridges behind you, concentrate only on the road ahead. Don't look back, look forward, and meet the challenges you find. One of Nansen's main messages to youth was to develop the ability to stand alone and to have confidence in their own plans and judgments. At the same time they were told to beware of obstinacy and foolhardiness. Throughout his life, those dictums of courage, independence, and the spirit of adventure occasionally led him to charge forward in a manner that increased the risk. He was sometimes criticized by national and international authorities for his irresponsibility and risk-taking. His response was that people always have to take risks to attain achievements and to gain their ends, but he did believe that there should definitely be some proportion between what is ventured and what can be attained within reason (Nansen, 1927).

Experiential learning had convinced Nansen that to be successful in reaching his goals, he had to regard nature with respect, meet her with an open mind and with love, and live and work with her, not against her. Cooperation is an essential element if we are to live with nature without courting danger and accidents. Indeed, he was fairly successful in his interactions with nature, but he admitted that sometimes he had difficulty deciding whether success was because of high personal proficiency or because he had strokes of good luck. Nansen was a very experienced friluftsliv-man as far as basic skills for survival were concerned, but his adventure skills were limited. He was an accomplished skier and certainly had endurance like few others, both physically and mentally. On the other hand, he had little or no climbing experience, and he and his men had some narrow escapes in the ice falls on the east coast of Greenland because they lacked knowledge about dealing with glaciers and crevasses. On the trip to the North Pole, when Fram became stuck in the ice on the north of the New Siberian Islands, the men took to their dog sleds for survival. As it turned out, Nansen was not an accomplished dog driver, and he was reportedly humiliated when making his first attempt at driving the dog team solo (Nansen, 1897; Shackleton, 1959).

On many different occasions Nansen voiced his criticism of modern civilization; he showed great foresight in writing about ecological dilemmas, questions, tasks, and ventures. He was also one of the first to present and discuss friluftsliv as special and valuable encounters with nature.

Learning from Friluftsliv and Adventure

Over a century ago Nansen urged that an appropriate upbringing of youth should emphasize passing on traditional knowledge, and also cultivating a sense of joy about being in nature. Later generations suggested that the Norwegian traditions of friluftsliv make an excellent supplement to the standard academic curriculum. Only first-hand encounters with nature can guide people to love nature and feel strong identification with the whole of nature.

Nansen recognized that people's friluftsliv practices were quite variable. Some sought what are now considered "slow experiences" (Gelter, 2007, p. 43), involving a quiet, contemplative, and reflective interaction with nature; others used the outdoors for active adventure and sport. Nansen advocated the former, although his personal preference for skiing crossed some lines into active adventure. Perhaps Nansen did not see the conflicts that were to develop between these two patterns of meeting with nature because he personally enjoyed both quiet solo time in the wild and other more adventurous experiences with nature. Indeed, it may be in the wisdom of Nansen that one can find appropriate balance between interacting with nature to cultivate ecological awareness (environmentalism) and seeking the excitement and rewards of sporting and outdoor recreation (adventure). Friluftsliv can involve both quiet and exciting contacts with nature (Repp, 1995). Nansen's advice to the young was to venture independently, and not be diverted on to other trails, because "... the great events in the world depend on the spirit of adventure shown by certain individuals in grasping opportunities when they occur" (Nansen, 1927, p. 24).

Because of his own joyful experiences with nature, Nansen engaged enthusiastically in the promotion of cross country skiing, an activity strongly influenced by the friluftsliv traditions. He and his collaborators suggested that people take to the wilderness on their skis to contemplate their relationship to nature and learn lessons about balance with the environment, wholesome living, peace within oneself, and about the world. They were destined, however, to fight a losing battle with many people. Under the influence of British ideologies of sport, a lot of Norwegians chose competitions and sport for the sake of the activity itself, rather than as a way of finding inner peace and balance with nature (Breivik, 1989).

Nansen was critical of the tendency among people to come together in crowds to follow the traditional and trodden paths or ski tracks. He was conscious of the historical traditions of his ancestors living in nature. For most people, this historic heritage, the experiences of our grandfathers and grandmothers, and their know-how and tacit knowledge about survival in nature has been keenly appreciated and considered valuable—until our time. Perhaps our generation is at a crossroads? The third green wave in the second half of the 20th century brought many people to a closer understanding of the environmental discussion about ecopedagogy and the necessity of changing attitudes about the use and consumption of nature. Teachers, instructors, and guides now have to ask themselves many questions about humankind's relationship with nature. Why not consider nature herself as a value in our education or instruction—in our thinking and our practicing? When we talk about valuing nature, are we talking about nature's intrinsic value, or as nature being important as a resource or an arena where we can search for adventures and recreations in our leisure time? I am here considering the tensions between nature and culture, and between theory and practice. How do we change our ecological consciousness? Who are the good models? And, finally, what is the contextual role of history and tradition?

A scientific approach to friluftsliv, adventure, personal growth and learning, and experiential education from a perspective of the sociology of knowledge is one gateway to answering these questions. Nansen's reflections on adventure, courage, running risks, and facing challenges can be important for discussions about the relationship between adventure education, risk recreation, outdoor education, environmental education, and experiential education. His life and thoughts may help in our attempts to understand apparent conflicts between the orientations of friluftsliv and outdoor adventure. Nansen had both a scientific and sociological perspective on knowledge which can help us clarify our beliefs and values.

For many years there have been intense debates about these things in Norway. There is a lot of adventure thinking and adventure practicing in the name of friluftsliv. The two phenomena adventure and friluftsliv do have some aims in common. As suggested earlier in this chapter, Nansen felt that the spirit of adventure was the obvious ally of friluftsliv. Still, he sometimes spoke of taking aggressive actions toward the natural environment. He was usually suspicious of what he called "the much-praised 'line of retreat'—a snare for people who wish to reach their goal." His advice to the young listeners was to always look ahead because "there is no choice for you or your men but forward. You have to do or die!" (Nansen, 1927, p. 27). Is this a desirable ideal or example for our time for our young people? Nansen's concept of adventure can be problematic because it easily relates to risk-taking and hazardous activities in the rapids, on steep mountain walls, or in deep winter snow.

Perspectives

Gradually, since the beginning of the 1970s, friluftsliv has gained more public status in Norway's government, schools, organizations, and media as a concept and process. The same period has seen a competitive struggle between groups of people with different orientations to friluftsliv. The problem has been broad and complex. In order to avoid being misunderstood or misinterpreted, one needs to explain their preference and understanding of the concept. My personal belief is that friluftsliv is about good meetings with nature, ecological thinking, environmental responsibility, and social commitment. Friluftsliv as a tool for political and educational undertakings can also be considered. The worlds of the theoretical and the practical have often been bound together through deep ecology, environmental activism, and, sometimes, civil disobedience because of local and global environmental threats. At other times friluftsliv guides, instructors, and teachers have had to lean on knowledge and theory from the natural sciences, whether it be glaciology, snow, avalanches, weather, foodstuffs, or high-tech equipment for many different friluftsliv activities. It has to be emphasized, however, that the historic cultural phenomenon of friluftsliv focused on a simple and practical nearness to nature, primarily of an emotional and physical character. A central educational goal for today should be rediscovery of nature and the promoting of a genuine willingness to take care of nature. We may start asking for our generation's thinking about values. What have we really seen as valuable in our meetings with nature? What will the message to our descendants be?

A few comments on a social and historical aspect of the problem may be in order. Only a few generations ago, thinking about nature and culture in the world had an antagonistic character. Culture meant civilization, cultivation, individuality, control, refinement, rational thinking, and moral superiority. Nature was associated with primitivism, irrationality, the wild, chaos, and vulgarity. Opinions and attitudes have now changed a little, but there are still serious discussions about the place of nature in our modern society. Is nature only a frame or scenery for our daily life and our spare time activities, a resource for our production of things? What about nature's unquestionable values and meaningfulness—its colors, its sounds, its scents, the snow, rain, cold, animals, the organization, the patterns, the variety, and silence? Good relations with nature involve emotions and feelings, impressions, joy, friendship, knowledge, and finding an identity. To be more precise, we are talking about feeling at home in nature, to find peace and comfortable survival in "open air living." To be able to do that it is necessary to know nature from experience, to be happy there and feel safe there. It begins with basic contact with nature; the hope being that the consequences of this contact will be eagerness to defend and take care of nature.

From a friluftsliv perspective the essential thing is a rediscovery of nature, with adventures and challenges to the whole person. Friluftsliv may involve both passive and active interactions between people and nature. Fridtjof Nansen's legacy can teach us that. The challenge is to cultivate respectful and care-taking attitudes toward nature. Friluftsliv can lay the groundwork for ecological understanding and responsibility. The ecology movement has played an important role for decades. In the years to come its importance can be expected to increase because of the continuing evidence of impending environmental crisis. We now know a lot more about the serious environmental consequences of modern technological development and the past and present generation's greediness for resources. Fridtjof Nansen once expressed doubt as to whether or not humankind is making progress, although he admitted that "it is such a nice comforting idea" (Nansen, 1927, p. 10). Have we made progress? Are we turning our lifestyles and our society toward harmony with nature and concern for nature's diversity? If we can answer those questions positively, it would indeed be comforting, but can we do so?

Implications for EE Philosophy

In the early paragraphs of this chapter, I asked the question "Who was this man?" There is certainly no simple answer to that question. Fridtjof Nansen recognized that friluftsliv not only helped us discover their place in nature, but in society as well. He believed that experiences that teach us to understand all of nature can also help us to understand all of human nature. He seemed to understand that the 20th century was a time for a developing crisis of both nature and human nature, and he saw those two problems as interdependent. His friluftsliv practices led him to voice skepticism about increasing urbanization. He warned his own generation, and the future ones as well, against a uniform education, feeling uneasy himself about vanishing "characteristic differences between peoples, nations, and cultures which have made life interesting and beautiful, and acted as an important stimulus to new thought" (Nansen, 1927, p. 17).

Nansen devoted many years of his life to humanitarian labors, negotiating repatriation of prisoners of war, aiding huge numbers of refugees, and other starving and distressed people needing protection and other help to survive. The Nobel Peace Prize award for his international humanitarian work in 1922 made it possible for him to increase his aid to starving and suffering fellow human beings. Rygg concluded: "Great as an explorer, a scientist, and a patriot, he was, in the opinion of the world, to appear even greater as a humanitarian" (1931, p. 276). One might certainly ask if his life's devotion to humanitarian causes and advocacy for world peace was not related to his practices of friluftsliv.

What are the basic values and ideals of our present-day notions of friluftsliv compared to those of Nansen? In contemporary times the debate between those who advocate friluftsliv as simple, gentle engagement with nature, and those who go to nature for sport and high adventure continues. One of the paradoxes of Nansen's life was that he can be seen as supportive of both sides of this issue. His recommendation for students was a type of friluftsliv marked by simplicity, responsibility, curiosity, hands-on experiences, and firsthand encounters with nature. He believed in developing the love of silence, the loneliness and the magnificence of nature. At the same time, he lived a life filled with outdoor adventure. Still, his major emphasis for friluftsliv as a supplement to youth educational programs would be for "soft," simple, and solo contact with nature. This recommendation can be easily implemented in educational programs (see Knapp & Smith, 2006).

Because Fridtjof Nansen lived a life that intertwined traditional friluftsliv and high adventure, and because he recognized the importance of friluftsliv for healthy growth and development, any discussion about either of these concepts should certainly include attention to the man and his life. Of course, his concept of friluftsliv is anything but simple; it is certainly not an easy task to discover and decipher Nansen's character and value orientation. There are many questions that might be asked about Fridtjof Nansen and his ideas. Are our notions about Nansen as the "archaic" ancestor of our generation's friluftsliv-people correct? Do we perhaps overemphasize his significance? Which are the values implied by his life and ideas (Repp, 2001)? Most importantly: To what extent does our thinking and formulations about friluftsliv, and our practicing of it, reflect the values, the ideals, and the inconsistencies of Fridtjof Nansen?

References

Bain, J. A. (1897). *Life of Fridtjof Nansen: Scientist and explorer.* London: Simkin, Marshall, Hamilton, Kent & Co.

Breivik, G. (1989). F. Nansen and the Norwegian outdoor life tradition. *Scandinavian Journal of Sports Sciences, 11*(1), 9–14.

Freuchen, P. (1928). *Arctic explorations in the future.* New York: The American-Scandinavian Foundation.

Gelter, H. (2007). Friluftsliv as slow experience in a post-modern 'experience' society. In B. Henderson & N. Vikander (Eds.), *Nature first: Outdoor life the friluftsliv way.* Toronto, Canada: Natural Heritage Books.

Huntford, R. (1997). *Nansen.* London: Duckworth.

James, T. (2000). *Kurt Hahn and the aims of education.* Retrieved December, 2003, from http://www.tj@kurthahn.org.html

Knapp, C., & Smith, T. (2006). *Exploring the power of solo, silence, and solitude.* Boulder, CO: Association for Experiential Education.

Nansen, F. (1897). *Farthest north: Being the record of exploration of the ship Fram 1893–96 and of fifteen months' sleigh journey.* Westminster, UK: Constable.

Nansen, F. (1927). *Adventure.* London: Leonard & Virginia Woolf at The Hogarth Press.

Naess. A. (1995). *Ecology, community and lifestyle.* New York: Cambridge University Press.

Nobleprize.org (n.d.). Fridtjof Nansen: The Nobel Peace Prize 1922. Retrieved November, 2007, from http://nobelprize.org/nobel_prizes/peace/laureates/1922/nansen-bio.html

Repp, G. (1995, November 9–12). *Living inside or outside nature?* Presentation at AEE's 23rd Annual International Conference, Lake Geneva, Wisconsin.

Repp, G. (2001). *Verdiar og ideal for dagens friluftsliv: Nansen som føredøme* [Values and ideals of our generation's outdoor life friluftsliv: Nansen as a model? Thinking and formulations about friluftsliv today reflecting the values and ideals of Nansen? A comparative study] (Summary in English, pp. 407–416). Oslo: The Norwegian University of Sports and Physical Education.

Rygg, A. N. (1931). Fridtjof Nansen. *The American-Scandinavian Review, 19*(5), 265–285.

Shackleton, E. (1959). *Nansen the explorer.* London: Witherby Ltd.

27 Juliette Gordon Low
Scouting and Experiential Education

Thomas E. Smith

Outdoor and experiential education professionals are a diverse group, but most of them share some common childhood experiences. If one were to survey 100 educators of outdoor adventure and experiential learning, chances are quite good that a very high percentage of them had experiences between the ages of 8 and 18 with summer camps, 4-H programs, Campfire Girls, or scouting. Those early experiences of individual accomplishment and small group adventure are typically remembered quite fondly and vividly. Camp counselors and scouting leaders are mainly practitioners, and not known as theorists; yet their emphasis on learning by experience can certainly be seen as supporting and enriching experiential educational theory.

This chapter provides an overview of the life and ideas of Juliette Gordon Low, founder of the worldwide Girl Scout movement in America. Although she did not publish much, her influence on the organization and implementation of Girl Scout programs is noteworthy. A closer look at Low and the scouting movement may be helpful in expanding and refining the theoretical foundations of experiential education.

Biography

Juliette Magill Kinzie Gordon was born in Savannah, Georgia, in 1860. She was the second of six children born into a prominent and wealthy family. Her paternal grandfather had a cotton plantation, and this established the Gordon's as Southern aristocracy. Her father became a Confederate Captain during the Civil War. Because he was away from home during the war, little Juliette lived with her maternal grandparents where she was exposed to the outdoors and to a lifestyle quite different from that of the sophisticated Southern society.

John Kinzie, her maternal grandfather, was the son of a woman who had been captured by the Seneca Indians in early life and later became the adopted daughter of the Seneca chief, Cornplanter. Years later, he granted her wish to return to her own people. John Kinzie served for a time as a government Indian agent, and Juliette's mother, Eleanor Kinzie Gordon, wrote a book about her father's adventures on the western frontier. After his years in the west, John Kinzie had maintained friendships with Native Americans, and Juliette therefore had interaction with Native children—who knew of the connectedness of all things and living in the outdoors.

These two worlds of influence molded Juliette through her developmental years. The influence of the Savannah Gordon's meant attending private boarding and finishing schools, where she was taught proper social skills and cultivated her interests in poetry, painting, sculpting, dance, and drama. The influence of the Kinzie's meant playing with Native children, learning to enjoy the outdoors, and getting involved in what were then considered as "tomboyish" activities. These childhood experiences kept her from fitting the conventional image of the aristocratic Southern belle. Biographers seem to disagree about her personality and adjustment during childhood. Some say that she was a sensitive and talented youngster and had a happy childhood ("Juliette Gordon Low biography," n.d.a), while others suggest that she was unhappy with the superficialities of upper-class society and the continual expectations for her to be "ladylike," resulting in her being considered as rebellious ("Juliette Gordon Low," n.d.a).

In her early 20s Juliette developed an ear infection which was treated with silver nitrate. Either the infection or the medical treatment imposed damage, and she lost most of hearing in that ear. At the age of 26, Juliette married William Mackay Low, the son of a wealthy cotton merchant who traded with England. The joy of the wedding was short-lived.

> A grain of rice thrown at the wedding became lodged in Juliette's good ear. When it was removed, her ear drum was punctured and became infected, causing her to become completely deaf in that ear. Her hearing was severely limited for the rest of her life. ("Juliette Gordon Low biography," n.d.a)

After this ominous beginning, the marriage did not go well, and William soon began to have extra-marital affairs. When his business required that they move to England, Juliette went along reluctantly, but she soon resumed the world travel she had begun before the marriage. She found happiness in riding elephants in India, hiking in the Alps, and climbing the Great Pyramid in Egypt. She also spent time in the United States, especially in Florida during the Spanish-American War where she helped her mother organize a convalescent hospital for wounded soldiers returning from Cuba.

Ten years of childless marriage to an unfaithful husband led Juliette to contemplate a divorce, but William became ill so she stayed on until he died in 1905. She was shocked to find out that he had willed his money to his mistress, leaving her only their home in England and a small pension. However, she had personal wealth from her family so she was still able to live comfortably.

When she turned 50 years old, Juliette Low was still seeking her mission in life, still wanting to find happiness and purpose. It is ironic that her involvement with the higher society of England (the continuing influence of Southern aristocracy) brought her into contact with Robert Baden-Powell, a hero of the Boer War, who had founded the Boy Scouts in England. Those two worlds of influence that had been prominent since early childhood ultimately gave direction to Juliette's life. Her interest in sculpture had evolved into working with iron (she molded decorative iron gates), which was also Baden-Powell's passion, so they became friends.

Shortly after Baden-Powell founded the Boys Scouts in 1910, his wife, Olave, and his sister, Agnes, prompted him to start a similar program for girls. Lord Baden-Powell resisted their suggestion because, like others of the time, he did not see value in girls learning to live outside and developing skills for an out-of-the-home career. Lady Olave persisted, and when Baden-Powell relented and started the Girl Guides program, Juliette Low became one of the early troop leaders. While she was excited about the broader goals of the program—to provide healthy activities for girls leading to good character and citizenship—Juliette found Baden-Powell's vision for the Girl Guides to be somewhat restricting. She began to think about returning home to Georgia and starting her own program for girls.

It was 1912 when she returned to Savannah, and on the night of her arrival she reportedly called an old friend: "I've got something for the girls of Savannah, and all America, and all the world, and we're going to start it tonight" ("Juliette Gordon Low," n.d.c, p. 1). She organized the first troop of 18 girls, and developed a Girl Guides program that involved physical fitness, hiking, camping, and community service. The next year the program's name was changed to Girl Scouts, and the movement spread rapidly throughout America. The organization, Girl Scouts of United States of America (GSUSA), was formally chartered in 1915, with Juliette serving as president for the first five years.

In 1922, Juliette Low developed breast cancer at the age of 62, but she continued her work with the Girl Scouts until her death in 1927. She had spent her entire fortune to establish the

Girl Scout program, and years later she was honored by being the first inductee into the Georgia Women of Achievement Organization. She was buried in her Girl Scout uniform, and in her breast pocket was a note from the current head of the Girl Scouts of America (GSUSA), which read: "You are not only the first Girl Scout but the best Girl Scout of them all" ("Juliette Gordon Low," n.d.a, p. 2).

Juliette Low and the Philosophy of the Girl Scouts

Although Juliette Low did not write her complete philosophy and vision for the Girl Scouts, her ideas are clearly reflected in the literature on the movement. She oversaw the composition and publication of the first *Girl Scout Handbook* (1917), and although that handbook was revised many times, some of her basic principles are still apparent. By the end of the 20th century, there were five different handbooks paralleling the five levels (age brackets) of the Girl Scouts (Daisies, age 5–7; Brownies, age 7–9; Juniors, age 9–11; Cadets, age 11–14; Seniors, age 14–17).

Juliette Low was involved in the production and direction of a publicity film about the Girl Scouts, titled *The Golden Eaglet*, which was shown in movie theaters in 1918. She also authored a U. S. Government Department of Education paper titled "Girl Scouts as an educational force" (Low, 1919). In the early 1920s she helped establish the foundations for the Girl Scout sponsored magazine, American Girl, which was to be published for over 50 years.

In 1919, Low's GSUSA joined with Lord and Lady Baden-Powell to form a World Association of Girl Guides and Girl Scouts (n.d.; WAGGGS). Low and many women like her, worked closely with Powell to adapt the movement to local conditions and cultures around the world. She attended the first international convention of WAGGGS, an organization that has grown to include representatives from over a hundred countries. The ideas of Baden-Powell and Low are reflected in the mission statement of WAGGGS.

> WAGGGS offers a dynamic educational program to girls and young women to develop their full potential as individuals, through concern for others. WAGGGS strives for excellence by providing opportunities to enable girls and other young women to make informed decisions in a changing world. ("World Association of Girl Guides and Girl Scouts," n.d.)

In parallel with Baden-Powell's Boy Scout movement, Low saw her Girl Scout movement as providing girls with experiential opportunities for small group interaction, outdoor adventure, community service, and development of individual skills. The Baden-Powell and Low goals are similar to those advocated by Kurt Hahn, founder of the Outward Bound Schools. Although there was some emphasis on the traditional female values of homemaking and service to others, Low's disagreement with Baden-Powell revolved around her advocacy for teaching young women outdoor skills and preparing them for community leadership. Her ideas predominated, and experiences of camping and adventure for girls became a major focus of the Girl Scouts.

Juliette Low was a forerunner of the feminist movement, and her emphasis on developing leadership in young women has prevailed. In fact, as the 21st century unfolds, leadership development has become a major focus of the Girl Scouts:

> Girl Scouting is undergoing a historic transformation to modernize the iconic organization and focus on leadership development for girls in the 21st century. The monumental changes have been designed to deliver a program that focuses on Girl Scouts' core strength of leadership development. Girl Scouting has identified some core tenets of its' leadership philosophy—discover, connect, and take action—which will form the basis of all Girl Scout activities beginning in October 2008. ("Girl Scouting undergoes historic transformation," n.d.)

Juliette Low believed in involving every young women in the decision-making process, and advocated a fully democratic approach to decision making. She would likely agree with this statement in the Venture Leader Manual of the Boy Scouts:

> Leadership is not power over others. It is not making decisions for others, and it is not telling others what to do. Rather, it is about empowering others through service. Leadership is about creating an environment where everyone feels a sense of self-worth, where people grow. ("Leader Training in Scouting," n.d.)

Scouting and Experiential Education

Experiential educators generally recognize three patterns of experiential learning. First, there is learning that results from life experiences, unstructured and unguided. Some of these experiences may be self-chosen and self-directed, but many of them result from random acts of interacting with the environment. Second, there are learning experiences that are facilitated by significant adults—such as parents, grandparents, camp counselors, clergy, recreation specialists, and organizational leaders. These adults are teachers, but they are not school teachers. Third, there are learning experiences guided by institutionalized curricula and facilitated by professional school teachers. Teachers may educate in more structured and teacher-centered formats, but there are many who recognize the value of student-centered experiential education theory and practice.

Scouting brings boys and girls of all backgrounds into the outdoors, and gives them opportunities to develop self-reliance and leadership, experience the joys and necessities of cooperative work and play, and learn the skills of good citizenship. Scout leaders must surely be recognized as experiential educators.

An overview of various Girl Scout programs illustrates the importance of experiential learning in a number of ways.

> Girl Scout camping gives you an opportunity to grow, explore, and have fun—always under the guidance of caring, trained adults. It is experiential learning through which girls develop their outdoor recreation interests and skills. Every girl should have a chance to go to camp. ("Linking Girls to the Land," n.d.)

> Sample a variety of activities, with a focus on fun and trying new things. Go on out-of-camp expeditions, such as hikes or canoe trips … Build an understanding of our natural surroundings, acquire confidence in yourself, and become comfortable working in groups to solve every-day problems." ("Camp Juliette Low," n.d.)

Girl Scout programs stress the importance of experiential learning in the training of leaders for facilitating outdoor programs. One training program offers the following overview:

> This training is a hands-on way to introduce you to living outdoors. You will also learn to play and teach outdoor games, lead nature activities, and learn to live and work cooperatively in the out-of-doors. You will be introduced to the philosophy of low-impact camping and responsible behavior habits toward our natural environment. ("Outdoor Training," n.d.)

The new emphasis on leadership development emphasizes the importance of experiential learning, and a schematic overview from the Denver Girl Scouts suggests six important factors in cultivating leadership in young women. Leadership development programs should be:

1) By girls, for girls—meaning that the program should involve girl-choices and be girl driven.

2) Co-operative learning—meaning that there should be experiences of the girls working together in small groups.

3) Girl-adult partnership—recommends the importance of shared responsibility and good role modeling for the girls.

4) All girl—pointing out that there is greater emotional safety when the girls are working with same-sex peers.

5) Non-formal education—recognition that learning which involves the girls directing their own learning is more effective.

6) Experiential learning—through the experiential learning process, participants hare ideas and gain a fuller meaning from each experience and apply that learning to future experiences. Sharing observations, reflecting, and evaluating are as important to the participants' growth as the planning and experiencing of the actual activity. (Girl Scouts of the USA, 2006)

The Girl Scouts have had historic confrontations with social-political issues that are now faced and frequently discussed in experiential education programs. From the beginning, the Girl Scout movement has faced challenges reflective of societal attitudes:

1. Juliette Low's disagreements with Robert Baden-Powell involved problems of gender role differentiation. (He tended to think that a woman's place was in the home, not in the outdoors and on expeditionary adventures.)
2. The Girl Scouts have always dealt with the needs of special populations, and as early as 1917, under Juliette Low's direction, troops existed for physically disabled and sensory impaired girls. A Girl Scout camp near Kansas City, Missouri, now known as Camp Juliette Low, offers programs for children with special needs.
3. In the early years there were special programs for racially diverse groups, including Black Americans, Asian Americans, and Native Americans. As the 20th century unfolded, GSUSA has had to deal with the issues and problems of segregation and integration, and the history of the ensuing debates and decisions can be valuable for contemporary experiential education.
4. During World Wars I and II, Girl Scout troops across America offered service learning experiences by having the girls collect scrap paper and scrap iron, planting "victory gardens," and selling war bonds door-to-door. Between those two wars, the Girl Scouts had begun their annual fund raising program of selling Girl Scout Cookies.
5. GSUSA also has a long history of teaching girls to care for the environment and deal with issues of conservation and ecology. The earliest handbooks had information on conserving materials and protecting nature, and there have always been badges to earn by studying endangered species. More recently, the Girl Scouts have adopted the principles of low impact camping.
6. Since the rise of the feminist movement, the issue of co-educational scouting has been debated, and the GSUSA has had to continually defend its "girls only" philosophy.
7. GSUSA currently has a "don't ask, don't tell" policy on sexual orientation, but this issue continues to be controversial. Reflecting general society attitudes, there are some who feel

that this policy does not prevent scout troops from discriminating against homosexuals, and others who question the inclusion of homosexuals in Girl Scout programs.

The historical precedents of the Girl Scout movement and the discussions and decisions about social issues that they have been faced through the years offer considerable food for thought for experiential educators.

An Educator's Story

Girl Scouting in the United States today is educative as Dewey defines education. "It is experience within an experiential continuum" (Hettinger, 1997, p. 1).

Beth Hettinger had experience as a Girl Scout troop leader, camp counselor, and trainer of other leaders when she returned to college to become a teacher. As she was exposed to the philosophy of experiential education, she recognized that her own school experiences were rooted in a more traditional—and less desirable—methodology. Like many developing educators, she found herself "between educational systems" (Hettinger, 1997, p. 6). Her experience with Girl Scouting had taught her the value of student-centered, process-oriented educational groups. She realized that Girl Scout programs, like those of many 20th-century outdoor and experiential educators "developed from the concerns of the progressive movement" (Girl Scouts of the USA, n.d., p. 6).

Hettinger concluded that the Girl Scout goals of character and leadership development, environmental stewardship, and compassionate concern for others were supported by Dewey's philosophy. When she discovered that Dewey had argued that growth and learning was enhanced by having students face challenging experiences (Dewey, 1963), she realized why the challenges she had faced in Girl Scouting were of great value. "In Girl Scouts we call this difficulty a challenge. I remember the topic being extremely important during my Cadette years when I was learning to rock-climb, sail, and work on badges (one in particular called 'a challenge')" (Hettinger, 1997, p. 2).

Hettinger found support in Dewey's philosophy for her personal ideas about education being more than a process of cognitive development, but that insight led her to more confusion. In her scouting work, there were always goals for holistic development of the children, and she wondered how she could pursue those goals as a teacher. As she gained more experience with formal education, she realized that many teachers, like most Girl Scout leaders, did have broader goals for their students. She wrote, "I think, like Eleanor Duckworth, that educators set more goals than knowledge and skill acquisition, but that these goals are not as highly valued and thus not evaluated" (Hettinger, 1997, p. 5). I suspect that Hettinger is now a "certified" experiential educator, working in classrooms toward the same goals that she worked for in scouting.

Implications for EE Philosophy

Perhaps, if experiential educators are interested in expanding their theory and practice, there may be value in looking to the theory and practices of Girl Scouting. As the National Board of Directors of Girl Scouts USA endorsed renewed focus on leadership development, they offered a mission statement: "Girl Scouting builds girls of courage, confidence, and character, who make the world a better place" ("Mission Statement," n.d.). Such a mission statement is quite like that of many experiential education programs, and that points to the potential value of comparing experiential education and scouting theory. The foundations of the scout movement, worldwide, have relevance to the contemporary theory and practice of EE in a number of ways: (a) the emphasis on outdoor activities; (b) the concerns about the cultivation of leadership in the young people involved; (c) the development of moral values and good character traits; and (e) the promotion of civic responsibilities and community service.

References

Camp Juliette Low. (n.d.). Retrieved August 2007, from www.//cjl.org/history/html

Dewey, J. (1963). *Education and experience*. New York: Collier Macmillan.

Girl Scout History. (n.d.). Retrieved August 2007, from http://www.qas-church.org/gas.gs

Girl Scouts of the USA. (n.d.). Mission statement. Retrieved August 2007, from http://www/wikipedia. org/wiki/girlscouts

Girl Scouts of the USA. (2006).What are the approaches for the unique Girl Scout experience. Retrieved April, 2006, from http://www.girlscoutsofcolorado.org./index/girlscoutleadership

Girl Scouting Undergoes Historic Transformation. (n.d.). Retrieved August 2007, from http://www. girlscouts.org/news/news_releases/2006

Hettinger, B. (1997). John Dewey's principles embodied in Girl Scout programs. Retrieved August 2007, from http://homepage.mac.com/mhettinger/hettingr/KERA/JohnDewey.html

Juliette Gordon Low. (n.d.a). Retrieved August 2007, from http://www.wikipedia.org/wiki/Juliette_Low

Juliette Gordon Low. (n.d.b). Retrieved August 2007, from http://www.lkwdpl. org/wihohio/low-jul

Juliette Gordon Low. (n.d.c). Retrieved August 2007, from http://www/gawp,em.org/honorees/long/low

Juliette Gordon Low biography (n.d.). Retrieved August 2007, from http://www.girlscouts.org/whoweare/ history/lowbiography

Leader Training in Scouting. (n.d.). Retrieved August, 2007, from http://www/dscpitomg.org/ leadertraininginscouting

Linking Girls to the Land. (n.d.). Retrieved September 2007, from http://www.girlscouts milehi.org/index. cfm?fuseaction

Low, J. (1917). *How girls can help their country* [the Girl Scout handbook]. Author & D.A. Byck Company.

Low, J. (1919). *Girl Scouts as an educational force: Bulletin/Department of the Interior, Bureau of Education*. Washington, DC: U. S. Government Printing.

Outdoor Training. (n.d.). Retrieved August 2007, from http://www.girlscouts-chicago.org/ outdoortraining

World Association of Girl Guides and Girl Scouts. (n.d.). Retrieved August 2007, from http://www.gsa-church.org/gas_gs

28 Paul Petzoldt
Man of the Mountains

Tim O'Connell

Mention the Grand Tetons, National Outdoor Leadership School, or the Wilderness Education Association and the name, Paul Petzoldt, immediately springs to mind. Considered by many as the pioneer of outdoor adventure education in North America, Paul Petzoldt has left an enduring impression on outdoor adventure educators around the world. Petzoldt's many first ascents, establishment of the American School of Mountaineering in the Grand Tetons in 1929, and his educational practices have certainly shaped contemporary outdoor adventure education and experiential education.

Biography

Paul Petzoldt (1908–1999) was born on a small farm in Iowa to parents of German and Slavic decent. Paul's father, Charles, passed away when he was only three years old, leaving his mother, Emma, and eight siblings to manage the family farm. As the youngest of the nine children, Petzoldt was often assigned the farm chores that none of his siblings wanted to do. His thirst for learning began at an early age; he started school before his fifth birthday and eventually ended up being taught by Lily, one of his older sisters. Lily recognized Paul's appetite for learning and encouraged him to read classic literature, poetry, and adventure stories. Paul was especially fascinated by the accounts of mountaineers, and tales of life in the western United States, and the mountains of Europe (Ringholz, 1997).

Life was hard for the Petzoldt family during the years of World War I, especially since their German name caused neighbors to look upon them with suspicion. After the war, the family moved to Twin Falls, Idaho, where Paul first experienced the mountains of the American West. It was the Sawtooth Range, a spur of the mighty Rocky Mountains, which first afforded him opportunities for mountain climbing. Although his first "climb" did not seem like the summits of the Swiss Alps he had read about, his disappointment only served to increase his burgeoning passion for reaching the top of unclimbed mountains.

In 1924, in the summer of his 16th year, Petzoldt and a friend, Ralph Herron, hitchhiked to Jackson Hole, Wyoming, with the intent of climbing the Grand Teton. As word of their plans spread through Jackson Hole, many of the local folks laughed at the idea of two teenaged, untried mountaineers reaching the summit. However, the boys located Billy Owen, who had led the first successful summit bid on the Grand Teton, and he supplied them with maps and advice on climbing the mountain. On July 25, 1924, after spending two nights camped high on the mountain, Petzoldt and Herron stood on the summit. They had climbed the mountain in their cowboy boots, having cut steps into the icy sections of the climb with a pocketknife (Ringholz, 1997). After returning to Jackson Hole and getting Owen's confirmation they had indeed reached the summit, Paul Petzoldt's life would never be the same.

Petzolt became fast friends with Billy Owen, then 65 years old, and agreed to guide him to the top of the Grand Teton. Word spread quickly and several local people joined the climbing party. Paul quickly took on the guise of mountain guide, and realized that climbing with groups of people required planning, communication, and proper equipment in order to be successful. Soon people from the cities who were visiting the ranches around Jackson Hole began approaching the young Paul Petzoldt to guide them to the summit. When the Grand Teton National Park was established in 1929, 21-year-old Paul Petzolt was awarded the guiding concession for mountain climbing (Ringholz, 1997).

Paul realized that the mountain environment called for a guide to take on an aggressive leadership role, making decisions regarding such things as route, group dynamics, and when to retreat in case of bad weather or adverse conditions. He invented the popular climbing commands based on the number of syllables in each word. First, the belayer (the person tending the rope so the climber wouldn't fall) would say, "On belay" (three syllables). The climber would reply, "Climbing!" (two syllables). Finally, the belayer would confirm everything was okay with the instruction to, "Climb!" This series of commands could be understood in harsh mountain environments where the noise of wind, the height of a climb, or other obstructions could obscure long verbal exchanges between members of a climbing party.

The mountaineering concession in the Grand Tetons enabled Petzoldt to save some money to attend college. After Petzoldt guided the dean of the chapel at Windsor Castle on some hiking trails in the Tetons, the dean offered him a chance to spend a year in England, studying and traveling. At the end of that year, Petzoldt traveled by bicycle through Europe, and managed to fulfill his dream of climbing in the Alps, where his reputation as a mountain guide preceded him. Paul's observations of the style of climbing in vogue in Europe in those days influenced how he worked with his own clients in the future. In his experience, the guides in Europe pressed on without regard to the condition of the people who they were leading. Petzoldt recognized that the safety of every member of the climbing party should be of utmost concern for the guide. He took these lessons with him back to the United States. When the freighter that brought him back from Europe docked in New Orleans, Petzoldt enrolled for a time at Louisiana State University. He went on to spend time at the universities of Idaho, Wyoming, and Utah (Howard, 1969). He never did get a college degree, substituting a wealth of experiential learning as he traveled the world as a mountaineer.

As Petzoldt's reputation as a premier mountaineer grew, he gained international attention and was invited to join the first American attempt to summit K2 (the second highest mountain on earth, after Mount Everest, in the Karakoram range). This expedition reinforced his understanding of the importance of proper planning and equipment for the success of any group. In one instance, Petzoldt and his climbing partner, Charles Houston, discovered that matches had not been packed for their climbs high on the flanks of K2. Much to Petzoldt's dismay, the ascent had to be abandoned because not enough food and equipment had been ferried high enough up the mountain. Ultimately, the expedition was abandoned without reaching the summit.

The experience of organizing the multitude of logistics of the K2 expedition paid dividends to Petzoldt during World War II. He worked in the Department Agriculture organizing supplies for governmental programs (Ringholz, 1997), including the Lend-Lease Program. However, his experience and passion for mountaineering led him to transfer to the 10th Mountain Division (ski troops). He was promoted to sergeant, and put in charge of developing operating procedures for mountain evacuations (Ringholz, 1997). His involvement changed the way the army trained personnel and developed proper equipment for missions in mountain environments. After spending time in post-war Germany, Petzoldt was ready to return to the mountains of Jackson Hole.

Taking advantage of a federal government program that was giving away land, Petzoldt acquired a parcel near Riverton, Wyoming, and settled down to become a wheat farmer. He had given up the climbing school concession in the Tetons in order to devote his time to farming, and when the land proved inadequate, he moved to California and became a used-car salesman.

He made enough money to pay off his debts, but when his relationship with his wife soured, he returned to his beloved mountains in Lander, Wyoming.

During the spring of 1961, Petzoldt was hiking and came across a group of kids rock climbing. He went to the city council and obtained permission to instruct the kids in proper and safe climbing and mountaineering skills. A year later, when he read about the opening of an Outward Bound (OB) school in Colorado, Petzoldt contacted a friend, Tap Tapley, who was involved with the school. Petzoldt was invited to become the school's mountaineering advisor, and in the summer of 1963 he met OB director, Josh Miner. The immediate need was to train OB instructors. Petzoldt summarized the problem:

> We had school teachers who were probably good leaders in their environment, but they didn't have leadership ability in Colorado—to plan and execute trips in wild country where an accident would mean walking out ten miles for help. We had steep snow slopes, rock cliffs, loose boulders that dropped down from the mountains, big streams to ford, and severe thunderstorms to endure. (cited in Ringholz, 1997, pp. 179–180)

By joining the OB school, Paul Petzoldt became an educator and became involved in disputes methods and goals of educational programs. He believed that outdoor leaders should not only have the physical skills to work with students during the challenges of an outdoor adventure course, but they should also have leadership skills for dealing with students and a heartfelt environmental awareness that would lead to ethical environmental practices (Ringholz, 1997). After he travelled to Washington, DC to speak in support of the Wilderness Preservation Act of 1964, a vision for his own school developed, and Petzoldt resigned from OB to start the National Outdoor Leadership School (NOLS).

Petzoldt worked furiously on acquiring the necessary equipment and recruiting students for the initial NOLS course. On June 8, 1965, the first NOLS course started in Lander, Wyoming. Petzoldt and Tap Tapley spent much of the first summer in the field ensuring that things were running smoothly, and that strict minimum impact camping methods were observed. These standards were the ancestors of the Leave No Trace movement (Ringholz, 1997). During the next decade, NOLS grew rapidly, with Petzoldt as the driving force behind much of that expansion. However, NOLS never achieved financial security. Philosophical and programmatic disagreements developed between Petzoldt and the NOLS Board of Directors, and he was re-assigned from the day-to-day operations to a position as "Senior Advisor in Outdoor Education." That was the beginning of the end, and over the next couple of years all ties between Petzoldt and NOLS were terminated (Ringholz, 1997). During his time with NOLS, Petzoldt's training notes were prepared and *The Wilderness Handbook* (Petzoldt, 1974) was published and revised and expanded a decade later (Petzoldt, 1984). A revised publication of that book came out a few years ago (Harvey, 1999). The next summer, an all-women's course was conducted as well. As time passed, NOLS courses became increasingly popular, and they expanded locations to meet the needs of greater numbers of courses.

Paul Petzoldt was 70 years old, but he was still interested in training leaders for the developing field of outdoor adventure and experiential education. It became apparent to him that outdoor leaders needed additional training if the environment was to be protected from abuse and overuse. Petzoldt worked with a group of university professors and developed an 18-point university-level curriculum on wilderness leadership, and that became the foundation of the Wilderness Education Association (WEA), which was founded in 1977. Petzoldt was involved with the WEA for the next decade. In 1994, at the age of 86, Petzoldt attempted to climb the Grand Teton to celebrate the 70th anniversary of his first ascent; he made it to 11,000 feet before exhaustion set in (Ringholz, 1997). He then drifted into retirement, and passed away in 1999 at age 91.

Educational Practices

Paul Petzoldt was not an educational philosopher, but he certainly had a philosophy of teaching and learning. He was an outdoor and experiential educator. Through his own experiences as a boy, he realized the potential of experiential learning. In commenting on his first climb of the Grand Teton, Petzoldt remarked, "The experience set the direction of my life" (cited in Absolon, 1995, p. 2). An avid reader, Petzoldt would spend time as a child reading about the adventures of mountaineers and explorers from around the world. As he grew older and travelled from place to place by hopping free rides on railroad cars like the hobos, he would "hide out" in libraries and read as a way to escape being caught by railroad detectives (Ringholz, 1997). Whenever he had the chance he would reach out to experience the things he had read about. After he went to school in England, he bicycled and hiked around Europe, visiting many of the places he had read about. After he climbed on K2, he chose to spend a year in India. He commented, "Hell, I was over there and I probably would never get back. So why leave a place that was of such great interest to me. I didn't believe in mysticism or reincarnation, but I wanted to see what made these people tick. I wanted to find out about India" (cited in Absolon, 1995, p. 4).

One of the fascinating stories Petzoldt told about his own experiential learning involves meeting an elderly American doctor when in India, and becoming his assistant. "I even started to use the knife," Paul said. "The doctor would say, your hands are probably steadier than mine cut here, cut here" (cited in Absolon, 1995, p. 4). That would certainly be called experiential learning.

His focus on learning by doing is emphasized as he described the typical student experience on a NOLS expedition. "Divided into patrols of 12, they carry everything they need in back-packs that can weigh more than 40 pounds. There is no weaving of lanyards, no compulsory sings of jolly songs around campfires. The students eat what they carry and find and catch, sleep in tents, and read topographical maps so they can plot their own 100-mile itineraries learning as they travel to recognize mushrooms, wildflowers, and trees" (Petzoldt, as quoted in Absolon, 1995, p. 2).

Petzoldt and Experiential Education

Paul Petzoldt's contributions to experiential education are vast, and his thinking should be reviewed by all experiential educators.

Environmental Ethics

Although Paul Petzoldt is not often considered as one of the champions of environmental ethics, his contribution to teaching people safe and sensitive environmental practices should not be overlooked. Early in his life he developed a deep appreciation for the natural beauty of the mountain wilderness, and his experiences at OB generated some feelings of dissatisfaction: "Here we were at OB taking people out and devastating the wilderness. Bad camping, crapping all over. I was dismayed at the ideas kids were getting about how to treat the wilderness" (Petzoldt, as quoted in Absolon, 1995, p. 6).

The standards he developed at NOLS for wilderness adventure groups were the ancestors of the Leave No Trace movement (Ringholz, 1997). When he helped organize the WEA courses, Petzoldt recommended inclusion of training about low-impact camping. A 1969 *Life* magazine story about Petzoldt titled "Last Mountain Man? Not If He Can Help It," is subtitled, "Don't Destroy the Outdoors, Learn How to Enjoy It" (Howard, 1969). In that article the author reports that Petzoldt once made two boys walk back 12 miles to pick up a couple of pieces of tinfoil. Such an action is a reflection of his concern for environmental stewardship.

Expedition Behavior

Petzoldt is also known for his development of the concept of expedition behavior (Absolon, 1995). In essence, expedition behavior is the notion that the individual wilderness traveler is in an interconnected web with others in the group, with local people, with governmental and non-governmental land managers, and with the wilderness. He encouraged individuals to focus on these interrelationships, and to figure out how their actions and behaviors might influence all the others during the course of a wilderness expedition. The notion of expedition behavior is now used by a number of groups throughout the world, and some of the underlying principles have been adopted for use in settings other than that of outdoor adventure education. Expedition behavior has also served as the foundation for other group dynamics models in the field of experiential education and outdoor adventure education.

Equipment

In early climbing expeditions, Petzoldt learned the value of proper equipment, and throughout his life he created, innovated, and recommended many best practices. He conducted experiments with cotton and wool sock combinations when with the 10th Mountain Division during World War II. Through these experiments, he concluded, for example, that a combination of two pairs of wool socks performed better than other combinations of socks (Ringholz, 1997). Petzoldt (n.d.a) once said, "There is no such thing as bad weather, just unprepared people." When he was at NOLS, he organized an equipment manufacturing business and this allowed him to experiment with different fabrics and materials, and to create equipment specific to the rigors of wilderness travel. *The Wilderness Handbook* (Petzoldt, 1984) he prepared while at NOLS is filled with tips on appropriate clothing, equipment, supplies, and procedures.

Leadership Training

Petzoldt recognized the importance of leadership training for outdoor adventure. From the time he instructed Teton climbers about safe and successful procedures, he began to polish his own instructional skills. He realized the need for professional demeanor that required practical experience to acquire. When he went to work with OB he saw the importance of appropriate leadership training, and that was to lead him to the creation of NOLS, and later the WEA. NOLS was not just a program of outdoor adventure; it was a program of training for future leaders of outdoor adventure groups.

> His school would give young people authentic adventure to replace the antisocial activities that teenagers often pursued in the name of adventure. It would provide leadership training along with opportunities to practice and master the outdoor skills they learned in the basic course. It would prepare leaders to take their friends, families, Boy Scout troops, or church youth clubs into the wilds safely and enjoyably and lay the groundwork for those wishing to become forest or park rangers or other professionals in the field. Most importantly, it would do away with the teacher who was inept at outdoorsmanship, the skilled outdoorsman who couldn't teach, the mountain climber who cared more about showing off than motivating others. (Ringholz, 1997, p. 182)

In Petzoldt's opinion, the outdoor guide needed to have the technical skills to move a group safely in the outdoors, but also needed leadership skills, environmental awareness, and interpersonal skills to insure a quality experience for all. Petzoldt responded to the needs of the fledgling outdoor adventure industry before the industry even recognized those needs. He was thinking about leadership training having to focus on both the technical skills and interpersonal skills of future leaders.

The Grasshopper Method

Petzoldt is also known for his "grasshopper method," the name he gave the teaching process used by outdoor leaders because leaders are always moving from teaching opportunity to teaching opportunity, just as grasshoppers hop from place to place looking for shelter or food (Martin, Cashel, Wagstaff, & Breunig, 2006). Petzoldt had concerns with the grasshopper approach, thinking that new leaders might not always be able to adequately help participants connect these distinct experiences into a whole, coherent package of understanding by the end of a wilderness trip. He suggested that being familiar with the material by planning teaching ahead and by systematically linking individual topics together will allow for the effective use of the grasshopper method. When used properly, this method allows for the use of many different types of teaching techniques and addresses a variety of learning styles. Importantly, it allows outdoor leaders to choose situations to convey pertinent information in circumstances in which the material is relevant. The grasshopper method avoids the problems of a rigid schedule in that it allows the instructor to read the group and sequence their learning experiences in relation to how prepared they are to learn at that moment. The outdoor leader may choose to move on to another topic or to abandon a lesson altogether if the group doesn't appear ready to learn.

Judgment

Perhaps the greatest of Paul Petzoldt's contributions to the field of experiential education is how to teach judgment. He suggested that judgment is knowing what you know, as well as what you don't know (Petzoldt, 1984). Guiding wilderness trips without proper judgment can be dangerous, therefore it is essential that leadership training programs cultivate good judgment by providing students with knowledge, practical situations which require different judgments to be made, and opportunities to get feedback on one's leadership style. Petzoldt (n.d.a) once said, "A challenge … to lead instead of being led, to participate instead of watching, to act instead of waiting with idle hands."

Petzoldt realized that some structure was necessary for outdoor leaders to implement judgment and for decision making. However, he also stated that "Rules are for fools!" suggesting that rules could actually bind outdoor leaders to a certain course of action that would not make sense for a particular group in a particular situation. By training outdoor leaders to use good judgment, rules wouldn't be necessary.

Tom Smith tells the story of being on a discussion panel with Paul Petzoldt in the early 1980s, where the group was trying to list and prioritize the essential qualities of good outdoor leadership. There was a lot of discussion, but little progress was being made; and then Paul commented, with that big smile that matched his size, "Just give me a person with good judgment, and everything else will fall into place" (Smith, 2006, p. 26).

Implications for EE Philosophy

It is difficult to capture the extent of the impact Paul Petzoldt has on the field of experiential education. How he lived his life, the things he accomplished, and the people he touched are the best examples of his influence on the field. His devotion to using the outdoors as a medium for teaching individuals that they can succeed, his innovations in the practice of outdoor leadership and outdoor travel techniques, and his enduring legacy of NOLS and the WEA are a testament to the depth and breadth of his contribution to experiential education.

All my life, people have asked the question, directly or indirectly, "Why the hell do you climb mountains?" I can't explain this to other people. I love the physical exertion. I love the wind, I love the storms: I love the fresh air. I love the companionship in the outdoors. I love the reality. I love the change. I love the oneness with nature: I'm hungry; I enjoy clear water. I enjoy being warm at night when it's cold outside. All those simple things are extremely enjoyable because, gosh, you're feeling them, you're living them, you're senses are really feeling, I can't explain it. (Petzoldt, n.d.b)

Paul Petzoldt was not a man of letters. He was a man of action, a man of adventure, a man of the mountains, a man of experience.

References

Absolon, M. (1995, Fall). Paul tells his story. *The Leader*. Lander, WY: National Outdoor Leadership School.

Harvey, M. (1999). *The National Outdoor Leadership School's wilderness guide: The classic handbook, revised and updated*. Bloomington, IL: WEA/Fireside.

Howard, J. (1969, December 19). Last mountain man? Not if he can help it. *Life*. Retrieved April 2007, from http://www.nols.edu/news/articles/life69

Martin, B., Cashel, C., Wagstaff, M., & Breunig, M. (2006). *Outdoor leadership: Theory and practice*. Champaign, IL: Human Kinetics.

Petzoldt, P. (n.d.a). Retrieved May 2007, from http://cs.earlham.edu/~outdoor/wiki/Gear_Advice

Petzoldt, P. (n.d.b). Retrieved May 2007, from http://wilderdom.com/Petzoldt.htm

Petzoldt, P. (1974). *The wilderness handbook*. New York: Norton.

Petzoldt, P. (1984). *The new wilderness handbook* (2nd ed.). New York: Norton.

Ringholz, R. (1997). *On belay! The life of legendary mountaineer Paul Petzoldt*. Seattle, WA: The Mountaineers.

Smith, T. (2006). *100 Books: Recommended reading for experiential education*. Lake Geneva, WI: Raccoon Institute.

29 Sylvia Ashton-Warner
Teacher and Reflective Practitioner

Maureen Zarrella

As I sit here, in the shadow of Mt. Rainier, I am thinking about a quote by Sylvia Ashton-Warner from the book *Spinster* (1958). In describing her approach to teaching Maori children in New Zealand, in the 1930s and 1940s, she said that she pictured her students as little volcanoes. Each volcano had two vents. Out of one vent came anger, violence, and negative thoughts. Out of the other vent arose creativity, kindness, joy, and learning. She considered it her mission as a teacher to widen and expand the vent of creativity and joy, and, in doing so, to lessen the size of the explosive and destructive vent. Just as the live volcano that was only 30 minutes away from my home can cause destruction and calamity in an instant, Mt. Rainier is also a creative force that has transformed the valley into an agricultural paradise. In fact, the Nisqually name for Mt. Rainier is Tahoma, which means "the mother of all waters." The dual nature of the volcano was not lost by the local tribes, who realized and appreciated both the bounty and the destructive power of Tahoma. All of the stories of the people indigenous to this region reflect this creative/destructive potential, and they teach the wisdom of finding the balance between the two opposing forces in their own lives.

Sylvia Ashton-Warner was a teacher and reflective practitioner. Early in her life she valued time alone for finding balance in her own life. Throughout her life, wherever she lived, she found a special place for thinking and writing. She called it Selah, a place of rest. She practiced the art of teaching experientially. She also met the challenge of bridging the gap between two very different cultures. When she taught in New Zealand, almost all of her students were Maori and they were used to a very different approach to learning than the traditional British form. Sylvia approached her task with the idea that allowing children to develop naturally, according to their own proclivities and rhythms, would go a long way toward avoiding the inherent resistance that comes with the rote method of teaching so popular at the time. After many trials, and frequent run-ins with the authorities, Sylvia Ashton-Warner not only succeeded in her small classroom in New Zealand, but went on to influence educational practices in other parts of the world. Many teachers, especially when working with cross cultural populations, continue to explore her experiential methods of introducing children to reading.

Biography

Sylvia Ashton-Warner (1908–1984) was born near Stratford, New Zealand. She was the sixth of ten surviving children of Margaret Maxwell and Francis Ashton-Warner and named after another daughter who had died in infancy. Her parents were very poor. Her father was an invalid and remained at home, an early version of what is now called a house husband. The entire family was supported by the meager wages of Margaret, who taught Maori children. The entire clan was frequently uprooted when she would be posted to yet another school in far-flung regions of New Zealand. Because of the peripatetic habits of the family, Sylvia attended no less than 11 primary and 3 secondary schools.

Sylvia's mother was not only the main breadwinner of the family, but the principal educator, disciplinarian, and task-master for the children. Her mother was her primary teacher until Sylvia was 11, and thus her control over the young girl was almost complete. To break away from her mother's domination, Sylvia escaped into a world of fantasy and story whenever she could. She was aided and supported in this effort by her father. According to Clemens, her father was "a poet-parent who gave form and legitimacy to Sylvia's life" (1996, p. 16).

This unusual domestic partnership, the rural isolation of the indigenous tribes, the frequent moves, and the oddity of being both raised and taught by an all-powerful mother and a weakened father, caused the young Sylvia to be socially backward, full of fears and imaginings, and prone to develop a rich fantasy life. These attributes come out clearly in her two books, *Spinster* (1958) and *Teacher* (1963), and also set the stage for her remarkable approach to teaching.

In the 1920s, as Sylvia was coming of age and deciding her career path, few options were open to women. Most women, if they worked outside the home at all, became teachers or nurses. Although Sylvia wanted to be an artist, practicality pushed her towards a teaching life. She attended Auckland Teacher Training College, and while attending there she also enrolled at the Elam School of Art. At this time she also met her future husband, Keith Dawson Henderson. Upon completion of her teacher training in 1931, Sylvia was unable to secure a teaching position and tried her hand at commercial arts. This was unsuccessful, and "in poor physical and emotional condition, near starvation, she goes home to her mother" (Clemens, 1996, Appendix 1).

She later had an unsatisfying teaching stint at East Hutt School, but she then married Keith Henderson and followed him to Whareorino School where he was teaching in a remote, forested region of the North Island of New Zealand. For nearly two decades, Sylvia taught in several rural schools, learned the Maori language and culture, had three children of her own, and had a nervous breakdown—most likely caused by the continual conflict between her passion for writing and painting and the demands of being a wife and mother. She ultimately arrived at Fernhill School in a rural area near Hastings, New Zealand, where she developed the "key vocabulary" procedure that is the linchpin of her ingenious method of teaching reading to the very young.

In 1970, Ashton-Warner accepted an invitation to move to North America and teach her "organic teaching methods" at the Aspen Community School in Colorado. In 1971 she took a position at Simon Fraser University in Vancouver, British Columbia, Canada. Eventually, she was more recognized and honored in America than she had ever been in her own New Zealand. "Many in New Zealand education still speak of her as if she was not special. In the rest of the world her influence is felt, although usually not in mainstream" (Clemens, 2007, p. 3). She continued to teach and reflect on educational practices until her death in 1984.

Educational Theory and Practice

Gleanings from Spinster *(1958)*

When I decided to investigate Sylvia Ashton-Warner's educational philosophy, I first read her novel *Spinster* in an attempt to understand the woman who has influenced the whole field of education and yet remained virtually unknown to most teachers. As I read this fictionalized account of her years teaching at Fernhill and the creation of the "key vocabulary" approach, I saw more of the artist in the teacher than the pedagogue. I believe that it was the creative artist in Sylvia that was free and inventive enough to come up with a method for bringing out the reading skills in her young Maori students. In reading *Spinster*, I came to know Sylvia Ashton-Warner in a more personal way. By creating a fictional persona for herself, she was able to reveal much about her life, her teaching, her relationships, and her fears and triumphs. I could see the struggles of a woman who was at odds with the educational establishment and their recommended methods of teaching the unique population she faced in the classroom. Her need for creative outlet, both in and out of the classroom, shines through in this engaging, semi-autobiographical account of her years at Fernhill School. She describes in lovely prose the trials and fears that many teachers experience when trying to impact the lives of their students:

> Day by day as the spring days beat by, this one in sun and frost, and this one in wet, I sink deeper into my infant room. Never do I hear again or feel again, in here among the children, the voice and the hand of the Reverend as I do over a meal in my house. Indeed the only male presence in the prefab with the power to disturb me is the shadow of an inspector. But is there anything new in that? (Ashton-Warner, 1958, p. 40)

Gleanings from Teacher (1963)

In the book *Teacher*, Ashton-Warner spells out how she developed and implemented her creative teaching techniques with five- to seven-year-old Maori children. She explains how she used "organic reading" as the vehicle to reach these native learners in a way they could understand. She had observed the folly of trying to use standards that applied to European students with the Maori children. She expressed particular disdain for the Janet and John books, which were the primers used in New Zealand at the time. (They seemed very much like the Dick and Jane books that several generations of American children, including this writer, were subjected to.) According to Ashton-Warner, these books were mind numbing and soul crushing when foisted upon young Maori children. She also thought these books did little to foster a love of reading in her European students. In the case of the Maori, Sylvia sought to teach in a way honored by the Maori culture rather than attempt to obliterate that culture and replace it with a European world view. "The method of teaching any subject in a Maori infant room may be seen as a plank in a bridge from one culture to another, and to the extent that this bridge is strengthened may a Maori in later life succeed" (1963, p. 31).

Key Vocabulary

Ashton-Warner believed that "children have two visions, the inner and the outer. Of the two the inner vision is brighter" (1963, p. 32). This duality is constantly revisited in both *Spinster* and *Teacher*. She often speaks poetically of "the world behind our eyes" (1963, p. 32). Like any good teacher, she wanted to enter that world of her students' minds, and set them free to learn and grow.

Through time, she developed a method for teaching beginning reading that she dubbed the "key vocabulary." The strategy begins with gathering words during individual interviews with each child—words that have special meaning for that child. Once it is decided, by the child, that a particular word is wanted, the teacher writes it down on a piece of tag board and gives it to the child. That word is then to be recited, repeated, traced, and spoken until the children feel that they know it. It is then practiced with a partner, and the boards are collected at the end of the lesson. The next day the children find all of their words mixed together on the floor and they are asked to find their words. Any words that are not remembered or picked-up are discarded, since they were not "key words" for any child. There is no negative attachment to the discarding of a word; it simply was not important enough to the child to remember. In this organic way, a beginning vocabulary is born. After this, the progression proceeds to sentences and eventually books, all made by the children themselves.

Social critic and educational reformer Paul Goodman wrote:

> Consider … the method employed by Sylvia Ashton-Warner in teaching little Maoris. She gets them to ask for their own words, the particular gut-word of fear, lust, or despair that is

obsessing the child that day; this is written for him on strong cardboard; he learns it instantaneously and never forgets it, and soon he has an exciting, if odd, vocabulary. From the beginning, writing is by demand, practical, magical; and of course it is simply an extension of speech—it is the best and strongest speech, as writing should be. What is read is what somebody is importantly trying to tell. (1964, p. 26)

The Reflective Instructional Approach

Sylvia was an artist, and had an artist's need to structure into her students' day plenty of time for music, painting, physical activity and reflection. She encouraged students to do as she had done in her own childhood: find a special place to think and create. She encouraged her students to express strong feelings via all the mediums: speech, writing, song, poetry, dance, and even sport. Clemens (2007) states:

> Ashton-Warner was motivated by the artist's urge to express strong feelings and saw the same urge in the children. This observation led her to develop her reflective instructional method. She also orchestrated the school day so that it would alternate between expressive activities chosen by the children and activities in which the teacher imparts new information. She called this alternation 'breathing in and out'. She wrote about the relationship of early education to world peace, believing that if children have a peaceful means of expression they will not be aggressive or vicious. (p. 2)

In the preface to *Teacher* (1963), Sir Herbert Read encapsulates Ashton-Warner's philosophy of teaching and learning. He suggests that Sylvia believed that she had discovered a method of teaching that "can make the human being naturally and spontaneously peaceable" (p. 11). He notes that she believed there are two main drives of human beings—self-preservation and sexual gratification, drives that are virtually ignored in most educational settings. "By recognizing and even welcoming their presence in the child and making them the foundation of an organic method of teaching, these instincts can be allowed expression and be at the same time molded into patterns of constructive delight" (p. 11). Her belief is that destructiveness and creativity cannot exist simultaneously in the mind. "To create is to construct and to construct cooperatively is to lay the foundations of a peaceful community" (p. 11). Read's words lead us back to Ashton-Warner's metaphor of the volcano with two vents. Letting off steam in the creative vent reduces the need for release of the destructive forces within each child.

Ashton-Warner and Experiential Education

The Association for Experiential Education (AEE) has had continuing conversation about what experiential education is. The most recent definition offered on the website is: "Experiential education is a philosophy and methodology in which educators purposefully engage with learners in direct experience and focused reflection in order to increase knowledge, develop skills and clarify values" (Association for Experiential Education, 2007). AEE's list of the basic principles of experiential education includes a number of points that were important for Sylvia Ashton-Warner:

> Experiences are structured to require the learner(s) to take initiative, make decisions and be accountable for results.
> Learners are engaged intellectually, emotionally, socially, soulfully, and/or physically.
> This involvement produces a perception that the learning task is authentic.

The results of the learning are personal and form the basis for future experience and
    learning.
The educator's primary roles include setting suitable experiences, posing problems, setting
    boundaries, supporting learners, insuring physical and emotional safety, and facilitat-
    ing the learning process.
The design of the learning experience includes the possibility to learn from natural conse-
    quences, mistakes, and successes.

Sylvia Ashton-Warner's theoretical and programmatic ideas can help us understand the experiential education process in a number of ways. Here are two examples in which her thoughts
can clarify it:

> Example 1: Ashton-Warner's metaphor of the two-vented volcano can help us understand
> the dynamics of the small group facing a typical problem solving initiative as facilitated by
> challenge course leaders. Problem-solving initiatives are creativity in action. In an activ-
> ity such as "Nitro-Crossing," which involves the group having to move everyone across an
> open space (e.g., "the Swamp of Despair"), the creativity of individuals and the entire group
> is evidenced in the many novel attempts that are tried, discarded or accepted, and finally
> implemented.

The creative vent of the volcano is wide open and any destructive impulse displayed is quickly
squelched by either failure to help in the task or by pressure from the group to find a better
solution. The fear of individual and group failure may certainly be there, but it is controlled by
the process of solving the problem creatively within the group. To paraphrase Ashton-Warner,
the creative, positive vent overcomes the destructive, negative vent because the will to solve the
problem is stronger than the fears of individual group members.

> Example 2: In her book *Teacher*, Ashton-Warner suggests that any child's key vocabulary
> centers around fear and sex. As I reflected on that statement, I clarified what I think she
> meant by broadening the definitions of fear and sex; I came to think she was writing about
> the importance of general emotional arousal in learning. Imagine an outdoor adventure
> group outing to learn basic canoe skills on a weekend trip, or hiking and climbing in the
> mountains on a day trip. In the broadest sense of the term, such new experiences are emo-
> tionally charged, both in terms of fear and arousal.

Ashton-Warner's perspective seems to parallel a thought held by Bill Proudman, who
answered the question about definitions of experiential education as follows: "Maybe we should
think of experiential education as emotionally engaged learning." (1995, p. 241)

Implications for EE Philosophy

Having taught for five years in a Native American school in the state of Washington, I can attest
to the wisdom of teaching native students in a child-centered, culturally focused, emotionally
engaging, and experience-based manner. The school where I taught had a student body which
represented 62 different Native American and Native Alaskan tribes. How can a teacher and
the lessons remain relevant to this diverse group without honoring and using the diversity of
experience that comes through the door of the classroom each morning? The answer is, "you
can't, and they don't." That is why the experiential methodology works so well in that setting.
Whether you call it creative or organic teaching, the language experience approach, a child
and culture-centered classroom, or experiential education, focusing the learning process on the

experiences of children and their culture makes sense. Sylvia Ashton-Warner not only created a meaningful way to teach reading to children, she also left us with a roadmap to teaching anything to anyone.

As William Butler Yeats so aptly said, "Education is not filling a bucket, but lighting a fire" (n.d., p. 1). Sylvia Ashton-Warner truly "lit a fire" that still warms and illuminates me and other educators to the present day.

References

Ashton-Warner, S. (1958). *Spinster*. New York: Simon and Schuster.

Ashton-Warner, S. (1963). *Teacher*. New York: Simon and Schuster.

Association for Experiential Education. (2007). What is experiential education? Retrieved May 28, 2007, from http://www.aee.org/customer/pages.php?pageid=47

Clemens, S. G. (1996). *Paying attention to the children: Lessons for teachers and parents from Sylvia Ashton-Warner*. Napa, CA: Rattle OK Publications.

Clemens, S. G. (2007). Sylvia Ashton-Warner, 1908–1984. Retrieved May 28, 2007, from http://ecceteacher.org/articles/warner.html

Goodman, P. (1964). *Compulsory education*. New York: Vantage.

Proudman, B. (1995). Experiential education as emotionally engaged learning. In K. Warren, M Sakofs, & J. Hunt (Eds.), *The theory of experiential education* (3rd ed., pp. 240–247). Boulder, CO: Association for Experiential Education.

Yeats, W. B. (n.d.). Retrieved, May, 2007, from Brainyquote.com/quotes/authors/w/william_butler_yeats.html

30 Campbell Loughmiller
The Father of Therapeutic Camping

James Doncaster

Anyone who has spent time in Re-ED (the Project for the Re-Education of Emotionally Disturbed Children)[1] during the late 60s and 70s knew of Campbell Loughmiller. His book, *Wilderness Road* (1965), was the first book handed me when I became a teacher-counselor in Tennessee in 1970. *Wilderness Road* is the remarkable story of the first 20 years of the Dallas Salesmanship Club Boys Camp, a unique treatment program for troubled boys established in the piney woods of East Texas in 1946. Loughmiller had been the director and prime mover of the program which, by the time of the book's publication, had helped hundreds of boys overcome significant emotional, behavioral, and learning difficulties to gain new leases on life. The book was unlike any professional book I had ever encountered. Simple, straightforward and devoid of technical jargon, *Wilderness Road* was more a narrative than a treatise or text. The accounts of the boys, the staff, and the woods that served as their home and classroom cast therapeutic work in a whole new light for me. The book stirred my imagination, and as I prepared to face my first group of troubled boys, my mind danced to the possibilities.

Three years were to pass before I made my first of several trips to the Salesmanship Club Camp. I arrived to find it just as Loughmiller had described. The boys looked like any other boys their age, a sure sign that the program was working. They were excited by the daily challenges of camp life and proud of their many accomplishments. The live-in staff were young, energetic, committed, and equally proud. The only disappointment of the trip was that I did not get to meet Loughmiller. He had retired a few years before and his trips to the camp were now sporadic. I had missed him by a day or two; it would be another two years before our paths would cross.

In January of 1975 I signed on with Pressley Ridge, a Pittsburgh-based organization serving troubled kids and families. My charge was to direct the start-up of a new therapeutic camping program in the mountains of Western Pennsylvania, the first such program north of the Mason-Dixon Line. Pressley Ridge was committed to Re-ED and to the Loughmiller model of therapeutic camping. To underscore that commitment, the organization formed a national advisory group and invited both Campbell Loughmiller and Nicholas Hobbs, who had been the architect of Project Re-ED, to serve on it. To our delight, both accepted.

Over the next six years, Campbell Loughmiller was much in evidence at Pressley Ridge. He would come, at minimum, a week in the spring and another in the fall, and on each visit he would immerse himself in camp life. He blended in perfectly. Without fanfare, he would attach himself to a group, eat with the kids, join whatever activity they were engaged in, and sit in on family meetings if any were being held. By virtue of sampling all aspects of camp life, he would take the pulse of the program and ascertain where we were developmentally. Later, in a quiet moment, he would sit with us, and, in his modest and unassuming way, share his gleanings. He could talk for hours, and we never grew tired of listening to him. During that period, Campbell

Loughmiller was our polestar, and our discussions with him became the means by which we took our bearings, modified our course, and charted the way ahead.

I left Pressley Ridge in 1980, about the time Loughmiller began winding down his consultation to the program and to others like it. I had other fish to fry, and so did he. However, we stayed in touch. I would visit him in Texas; he would visit me in Tennessee. My daughter and I joined Campbell and his wife Lynn on an extended camping trip that stretched from the Texas Hill County to the Davis Mountains as they shot photographs of flora that would later become part of their classic *Texas Wildflowers: A Field Guide* (Loughmiller, 1984). They reciprocated by coming East and allowing me to be their guide in the Great Smokies and on a number of Civil War battlefields. Our relationship remained close until his death at his home outside of Tyler, Texas in 1993.

Biography

Born October 19, 1906, Campbell Loughmiller grew up in a large family in the small, east Texas town of Canton. While his family was not wealthy, neither were they poor, as Loughmiller's father owned and operated five cotton farms and several cotton warehouses in the region. Year after year as Loughmiller grew to maturity, the family's business flourished. Then one harvest season the rains came, heavy and protracted, destroying the cotton crop and ruining the family business. The elder Loughmiller, ignoring the counsel of his bankers, refused to declare bankruptcy. Instead he sold off all his holdings except the family farm; this land he continued to work in order to settle his debts. The family remained close, but things had changed. Prior to the reversal, Loughmiller's parents had taken great pride in dispatching each child in succession off to college. Now that it was Campbell's turn, they lacked the means to send him. Undaunted, Loughmiller put himself through his first year of college by picking cotton. When his resources were exhausted, he left college and took to the road in search of work. Walking, hitching rides, and occasionally hopping freights, he wandered across the South and Southwest doing odd jobs to feed himself and to save money for college. When the work ran out on land, he went to sea. Initially, he shipped out of Galveston on short trips to other ports in the Gulf of Mexico. Later he sailed to more exotic ports-of-call in the Caribbean and Europe. Eventually he settled on the west coast and embarked from there on numerous trips to Africa and Asia. Interspersed with what he later called his "hoboing" and "seagoing" days (Loughmiller, 1980) were periodic college enrollments. He attended Weatherford College for a year followed by a stint at Texas Tech. When he retired from the sea in 1931, he enrolled at the University of California in Berkeley, taking first a bachelor's degree in philosophy and, soon after, a graduate certificate in social work. While on the West Coast, Loughmiller met and married Lynn, the woman who would give them a son and a daughter, who would co-author four of his books, and who would be his constant companion for the remainder of his days.

A series of public service jobs followed his studies. Loughmiller set up and administered the first County Welfare Department in Del Norte County, California, in 1935. That job led to a position with the Farm Security Administration in California and, shortly thereafter, a transfer to Dallas and his native soil. Three years later he accepted the directorship of the newly formed Dallas City-County Welfare Department, a position he held until the outbreak of World War II. During the war years he served as chief of the regional Farm Labor Program for the War Food Administration, a job that thrust him into a vortex of problems among the U.S. Army, the prisoners-of-war it maintained, and the farmers of the southwest who employed them as laborers. He held this position until 1946 when he received an offer to direct a new camp being set up by the Salesmanship Club of Dallas. Believing that it "might be developed into something worthwhile," Loughmiller accepted the offer (Loughmiller, 1980, p. 288).

As envisioned by the Salesmanship Club leadership, the camp was to operate seasonally and serve under-privileged boys. "At first," according to Loughmiller, "there was no thought of working with emotionally handicapped boys, but a few were accepted, more by accident than design. The progress they made suggested the idea of long-term camping for emotionally disturbed boys" (1965, p. v).

Campbell and Lynn Loughmiller's lives were to become inextricably bound with the life of the Dallas Salesmanship Club Camp over the next 20 years. One group of troubled boys and two intrepid counselors comprised the first, full-fledged experiment in therapeutic programming. In light of their success, that group was joined by two additional groups and later by two more, until a camp community, a total therapeutic milieu, took form. Although Loughmiller managed to find time to complete a master's program in Education at Southern Methodist University in 1951, most of his waking hours were spent at the center of the therapeutic community he had created. Lynn was also there every step of the way, as were their two children, Camelia and Grover, who grew up in the camp community. The commitment of the family to the camp endeavor was total and unequivocal. What free time they had was often spent in pursuits not unlike those that occupied them at the camp. An avid outdoorsman, conservationistm and photographer, Loughmiller took his family camping whenever he could break free. Although they traveled and camped throughout the country, most vacations were spent close to home. For 11 straight years, for example, the Loughmillers went to Big Bend National Park, camping and recreating there three weeks each year. Another favorite haunt was the Big Thicket area of southeast Texas, a crazy quilt of lowlands, pine forests, and bayous, where the Loughmillers would camp, canoe and chat with the old-timers who had spent all their lives there.

Back at the Salesmanship Club Camp, Loughmiller would often lead a group on what he called a ramble, a serendipitous pursuit that became a fixture of the program. "A ramble is a short trip of half a day or less which a group frequently takes by foot, usually within the camp property," he explained:

> It is primarily an exploration, subject to the whims of a boy's mind and the vagaries of his imagination. It is to see, speculate, wonder, and enjoy. It is for the spirit more than the muscles, though it is great for both. There is no destination. Such purposes as the group lightly proclaims for a ramble are more to get it under way than actually to achieve; to see if the dewberries are ripe at Box Spring, or if the deer still come to the salt lick in the pine grove. (Loughmiller, 1965, p. 56)

A ramble afforded the boys—and the man—opportunities that piqued their curiosity and stimulated their interest. A rotting log may be unworthy of notice to some, but to Loughmiller it was an opening to a discursive conversation on ecology, forest succession, and the web of life. Likewise, finding a box turtle could begin and end in a quick succession of catch, classification, and release. At camp, however, where the tempo of life was slower and more in accord with a boy's nature, this simple discovery alternately could serve as the first link in a chain of events that proceeds with questions and discussion, progresses to reading and research, and culminates in an expansive article for the camp newspaper. What do box turtles eat? Do they have any natural enemies? What is their lifespan? How is the male differentiated from the female, and how do they find one another at mating time? Does she bear her young live or in eggs? What chances does a newborn turtle have of making it to maturity? What, in fact, does it mean to be cold-blooded, and how do cold-blooded creatures survive temperature extremes? This mode of teaching and learning—what has since been called opportunity teaching or simply capitalizing on a teachable moment—came naturally to Loughmiller, and his ability to re-ignite a love of learning in those in whom it was all but extinguished was legendary. His secret, at least in part, was that his life at camp and his life away from it were mirror images of one another. In a sense, camp became the tableau for the delineation of his interests, and camp practices began to reflect his habits of a lifetime.

Rambles are a perfect case in point. Though he had traveled around the world three times, Loughmiller recounted with great fondness the joy of standing on the threshold of a three-month sabbatical:

> Our kids were in college so it was up to Lynn and me to decide what to do. We thought of going to Europe; we thought of going to Alaska, which we had planned to do on our honeymoon. We debated the merits of South America, but, finally, we bought a seventeen foot trailer and pulled out of the driveway with no idea in the world which way to go. It was April 1, and anywhere in Texas is good at that time of year. (Loughmiller, 1980, p. 1)

Loughmiller, in the third volume of his autobiographical work, proceeds to devote 50 pages to extolling the virtues of this meandering trip through east Texas, imparting one story after another of storekeepers, fox hunters, dog cemeteries, camellia patches, virgin timber stands, exotic birds, rattlesnakes, and eccentrics who lived off the land. He then sums up the trip this way: "Instead of going to Alaska or around the world, we had spent three months in traveling through a third of Texas, averaging fifty miles a day. It was one of the best trips of our lives. We've never abandoned our slow mode of travel" (Loughmiller, 1980, p. 49). In short, Loughmiller taught others as he himself learned, and led others as he lived. His opportunity teaching initiatives in the form of rambles at camp were not meant to be mere pastimes or diversions. They represented a concerted attempt at slowing down the pace of things so that life in all of its manifestations could emerge, take form, and exert its pull on all involved. "I went to the woods because I wished to live deliberately, to front only the essential facts of life and see if I could not learn what it had to teach…," noted Henry David Thoreau (Paul 1957, p. 62). So it was with Loughmiller in both his personal life and in his work with young people.

Writings

When the Loughmillers were not caught up in camp business and not traveling, they were often writing about either of the two pursuits. Their first publications appeared in the early 50s. Both *Camping and Christian Growth* (1953) and *Let's Go Camping* (1959) were modest affairs reflecting the Loughmillers' love of camping and, at least in the case of the former, their strong spiritual beliefs. Both booklets were co-authored by Campbell and Lynn.

By the mid-50s, the Salesmanship Club Boys Camp was beginning to achieve some national notoriety, and the publication of *The Worth of A Boy* (Smith & Loughmiller, 1958) really put it on the map. Written by Bert Kruger Smith "with the assistance of Campbell Loughmiller" (according to the title page), and published by the Hogg Foundation for Mental Health at the University of Texas, *The Worth of a Boy: Report on a Camping Program for Troubled Youngsters* was the most comprehensive review of the Texas program to date. With its emphasis on the camp's unorthodox, but highly effective treatment approaches, the results of early efficacy studies, and the success stories of the boys themselves, the Hogg Foundation report remained the definitive word on the program until the release of *Wilderness Road* seven years later.

Wilderness Road (1965) is the quintessential Loughmiller book. Its crafting at the behest of the Dallas Salesmanship Club allowed Loughmiller the opportunity to reflect upon and sum up his 20 years of work with troubled boys at the camp as he approached his retirement. In that book, he tells the story of individual boys and groups of boys, their successes and failures, and the program particulars that made it all possible. Out of it came emergent practices that were values based, practical and efficacious. In the foreword to that book, Nicholas Hobbs averred that "*Wilderness Road,* at its publishing, will be a classic" (p. xii), and so it has become. What the Dallas Salesmanship Club had hoped might be a blueprint for its own future programming, became a blueprint for others.

In the years following its publication, therapeutic camping programs proliferated in the United States. Loughmiller estimated in 1980 that there were at least 30 other camps in the country modeled on the Texas program (Loughmiller, 1980, p. 300). Despite some ebb and flow,[2] that estimate is probably an accurate reflection of the number of programs existing today. Loughmiller retired from day-to-day operations at the camp in 1966, the year after *Wilderness Road* was published. With his retirement came recalibration. While his interests remained the same, his priorities had shifted.

> Retirement years, enabled us to pursue our avocational interests, our hobbies, and gradually bring them into a pattern of living that also included a continuation of professional work as a consultant. Our main interests were travel, photography, conservation, nature study and people. Retirement years … made it possible for us to blend these interests together in the most satisfying way. (Loughmiller, 1980, p. 369)

His retirement years were also Loughmiller's most prolific. When he wasn't on the road, he was writing at his home on Lake Tyler in the little town of Whitehouse, Texas. The fruits of his labor included *Kids in Trouble: An Adventure in Education* (1979) and two books co-authored with Lynn, *Big Thicket Legacy* (1977) and *Texas Wildflowers* (1984). In addition, he produced over 1,000 pages of autobiographical material in the form of *These Fish Had Wings, Volumes I* (1980), *These Fish Had Wings, Volume II* (1980), and a third untitled and undated volume focusing on his extensive travels. All three volumes were prepared for family and friends only and were not intended for general distribution.

Kids in Trouble (1979) represents Loughmiller's final word on working with troubled youth. His years of consulting with the Salesmanship Club, Pressley Ridge, and other organizations prompted its creation. In it he picks up where *Wilderness Road* left off, amplifying, clarifying and extending ideas and concepts introduced in the earlier work. *Kids in Trouble* was intended for insiders, that is those working specifically in the realm of therapeutic camping, but its message is universal and its practices hold applicability and appeal for teachers, counselors, and others working in the youth care field generally.

Big Thicket Legacy (1977), produced with Lynn and released two years before *Kids In Trouble*, was a labor of love for the Loughmillers. Their frequent trips to the Big Thicket in the 60s and 70s had resulted in a growing appreciation for the heavily forested, bayou-laced wilderness area and the hardy people who lived there. Most were the sons and daughters, or the grandsons and granddaughters, of the original settlers, and all were in their 80s or 90s when the Loughmillers interviewed them. In *Big Thicket Legacy*, the Loughmillers allowed the people of the Big Thicket to tell their own stories. By capturing those stories, they preserved a piece of Texas history, folklore, and culture that otherwise might have been lost.

Texas Wildflowers: A Field Guide (1984), with its foreword by Lady Bird Johnson, has become a classic in its own right. Unquestionably the Loughmillers' most popular book, it came to be more by accident than design. Loughmiller was an inveterate nature photographer who rarely left home without his camera. He had been taking photographs of wildflowers for decades when some of his photos and word of his passion came to the attention of staff at the University of Texas (UT). Talks ensued and he and Lynn were prevailed upon to produce a book on Texas wildflowers. With thousands of photographs of wildflowers in hand, the project seemed less than daunting at the outset, but daunting is what it soon became. The sorting, classifying, and writing of scientific descriptions, even with considerable technical assistance from UT's Lynn Sherrod, took years. The end result though, is a beautiful book that has filled a niche in the scientific literature and continues in print since its release in 1984.

The Camp

The Dallas Salesmanship Club Boys Camp underwent a dramatic transformation in the years following World War II, and presiding over it all was Campbell Loughmiller. It was under Loughmiller that the camp shifted its focus from "underprivileged" boys to boys with serious adjustment issues and, concomitantly, its mission from one of providing summer recreation to one of providing year-round treatment. Its target population and therapeutic emphasis set the camp off from all but a few other programs in the country in the 40s and 50s—the University of Michigan Fresh Air Camp being the most prominent of the few that bore some resemblance to it (McNeil, 1957). What rendered it truly unique, however, was its move to year-round programming. At that point the camp became a residential treatment program like no other.

Working with troubled young people in any residential setting can be a difficult endeavor, so why take work that is challenging to the utmost when transacted in the confined environment of a treatment center or hospital, into an environment that is open, undifferentiated and out-of-doors? There is no simple answer to this question, although Loughmiller provides some insight into it in his opening to *Wilderness Road*:

> We find the camp environment good because it accords more fully with the child's nature and provides ample opportunity to satisfy the desire most boys have for adventure and exploration in the out-of-doors. Small group living in this environment encourages original experimentation and provides the widest possible variety of direct experience with the natural surroundings. (1965, p. 1)

The boys at Loughmiller's camp lived in small primary groups of 10 boys and two counselors each.[3] The groups were homogenous in that the boys were of similar age and level of social functioning, though their diagnoses and presenting problems differed greatly. The groups were continuous, moreover, with the comings and goings of boys entering the group and graduating from it spaced out so that the group culture, norms, values, and procedures, once fostered, could be maintained.

The program was unlike that which we normally associate with a typical camp environment. There were no ball fields nor tennis courts, no waterfront nor craft building. The program, instead, grew out of meeting life's demands. "The group must construct its own shelters, cut its wood, repair its equipment, arrange its own recreation, provide sanitary facilities, maintain the trails, and do all things necessary for safe and responsible living. These things in themselves provide objective discipline and play no little part in developing a sense of social responsibility" (Loughmiller, 1965, p. 1).

One can only wonder how 10 troubled boys can be persuaded to come together for any endeavor much less for activities that seem, by any measure, far more onerous than rewarding. In this revealing passage from *Kids in Trouble*, Loughmiller acknowledges the problem and how it is addressed:

> In an environment where there is no punishment, where a boy can run off when he chooses, our only hope of discipline is through satisfying experiences responsibly undertaken. We have to make sense to the boys. Structure comes from group goals in meeting life requirements. Discipline comes from group organization to accomplish them, on the basis of concrete, specific plans. Good plans, understood by each member, are the procedural means of achieving the maximum satisfaction from any undertaking. (1979, pp. 31–32)

Loughmiller always considered the outdoors to be a favorable setting for working with young people, according as it did with a "child's nature," but he was always quick to add that there was "no magic there unless we put it there" (Loughmiller, 1979, p. 24). How he put magic there, and how he was able to take the three ingredients of discipline, education, and democracy and mix them into a responsible living whole is the subject of the next section.

Philosophy and Practice

Relationship

For Loughmiller, nothing good happened with a youngster in the absence of a relationship with a trusted and trusting adult. His counselor ideal was a person of confidence, competence, worth, and integrity, someone capable of Rogerian "unconditional positive regard," deep empathy, and understanding. The beginning point for relationship was a belief on the part of the counselor in the inherent goodness of a youngster and in his or her ability to change. "The natural, inherent tendency of the organism is to grow and mature and, in the case of kids, to be wholesome and accepted," said Loughmiller, "but they get derailed by difficulties they do not know how to manage and get bogged down in conflict at home, or elsewhere, through an effort on their part to compensate for something they needed but did not get" (1979, p. 35). One of the most common characteristics of young people in treatment is that they do not trust adults. For many youth, distrust is an experience-based conviction born of innumerable hurts and disappointments at the hands of those whom they most trusted or most wanted to trust. Over time a wall goes up. The wall may take the form of withdrawal or aggression, but no matter what form it takes, the goal is the same—protection from harm. What protects isolates, however, and what stops hurt also interferes with healing. Therein lies the paradox. Children who have lost faith in adults, who have learned not to trust them, must find that faith in adults again by re-learning how to trust. There is no other path to recovery.

While the young person may have constructed the wall, onus for dismantling it resides with the counselor. It is he or she who must be at the child's side in good times and bad, who must weather whatever storms may come and guide the child back each time to safe harbor. A critical task for a troubled child is re-finding faith in adults by first re-establishing trust in one adult. For the counselor, faith in the child is equally critical.

> This simple development of faith in a boy is one of the greatest achievements a counselor attains in his work. It makes all the difference in the world whether he sees a boy as a hell-raiser who is trying to disrupt everything the group undertakes, or whether he sees him as a frustrated, insecure boy who is trying with all his might to find a satisfactory way of living with others. (Loughmiller, 1965, p. 11)

It is telling that Loughmiller prefaces his book, *Kids in Trouble* (1979), with a quotation from Goethe: "Treat people as if they were what they ought to be and you help them become what they are capable of being" (frontispiece). First comes faith, then comes action. Regarding the forging of the relationship, Loughmiller avers:

> The building of a genuine relationship with a boy need not, and should not, be centered around the handling of his negative behavior. Relationship is best achieved through action— helping a boy make his bed, showing him how to tie a hook to his fishing line, exploring the creek, paddling a canoe—anything that will help him toward new achievements or help him have fun and pleasure in his participation in the group life. (1965, p. 12)

"Catch 'em when the goose hangs high," Loughmiller was fond of saying, by which he meant that the most propitious times for making investments in the relationship were during the good times (personal communication, 1981). By making emotional bank deposits when the going was good, a counselor was positioned to make a withdrawal, that is to call upon the good will now on hand in the relational account, should the going get rough. So it is with any human relationship.

The Group

A counselor, no matter how good, cannot turn around 10 lives alone, nor could any number of counselors, no matter how skilled or well-intentioned they are. The group is absolutely essential to the endeavor. Learning to trust the group and use the group process is critical to a counselor's success. With such trust and skill, a counselor can surmount any problem. Without it, he or she is lost, and the group is adrift and rudderless.

> There are ten boys in a group and all of them are involved in every decision that is made affecting their life. The requirements of living constitute what we generally call "program"— food, shelter and recreation. The group decides what needs to be done and organizes to do it: the number and type of shelters they will need, the trips they will take, and hundreds of other things, big and little, that make up the requirements of pleasant living; but more important, they know the reason behind every plan they make. (Loughmiller, 1979, p. 28)

The norm in a therapeutic camping program is for a group to be together at all times. Group members gain a familiarity with one another and with their leaders rarely known outside of families. Such intimacy is important to a group's smooth functioning and essential to its success.

P-I-E

Activities, large and small, are framed by group discussions. A group makes plans at the outset of each four to six week camp session outlining what they intend to accomplish, what they need to do to perform optimally, and what kinds of fun they hope to have along the way. At the end of the session, they then review their performance in relation to the goals they had set for themselves. Only after an honest appraisal of past performance does the group look ahead and establish new goals and priorities for the next session. This same process—we call it P-I-E for Planning, Implementation, and Evaluation—is repeated continuously.

Individual weeks at camp begin with in-depth planning sessions out of which come detailed written plans that lay out what the group members will do to achieve their session goals, but these new plans are formulated only after performance over the past week is reviewed.

Individual days are similarly framed. Perhaps the most important time of the day for a group is the pow wow, the ritualized meeting that concludes each day, for it is at this meeting that the group looks backward and forward in a way that marks the passage of the day. The accent is always on the positive in the pow wow as the group discusses the day and the role each group member played in it. What did the group accomplish? Did it do what it set out to do and do it in a way that was satisfactory to all? Did their actions, both individual and composite, reflect well on the group and leave the world, or at least their little corner of it, better for their passing? After a short while in the pow wow, reflection on the day gives way to a look ahead to the morrow. What is it they have planned? How can they be even more successful tomorrow than they were today? As the pow wow draws to a close and the day concludes, there is genuine anticipation in the air for what awaits them in the morning.

Individual undertakings throughout the day are similarly framed, especially if they are new or novel or if they have been a source of friction in the past. Activities tend to begin and end with points of order, that is with the group coming together to discuss behavioral expectation on the front end of an activity, and to assess performance on the back end. The P-I-E process, used at this level, serves as a form of behavioral rehearsal for individual group members, bringing clarity to action beforehand and accountability to action after. When used repeatedly over time, the P-I-E process not only provides order and stability to the group, it provides a cognitive efficacy model for individual group members. Once internalized and habituated, this cognitive model of thinking before acting and reflecting afterwards can position the youngster for much success in real-world pursuits.

Treatment Is Teaching

The young people served in our therapeutic camping programs are typical of severely emotionally disturbed populations in general. Characteristically, they have emotional and behavioral problems, learning problems, and low self-esteem. It was Loughmiller's contention (as well as Hobbs's) that these problems were interrelated and that addressing one might well influence the others. While all lent themselves to some degree of direct address, learning opportunities abounded at camp at every turn. Loughmiller believed that camp presented "an unexcelled opportunity to teach" and that "almost every favorable condition known to man existed in the camp environment (Loughmiller, 1979, p. 44). Drawing upon the work of Drs. Paul Mort and William Vincent, Loughmiller affirmed that the six conditions essential to learning were omnipresent at camp and embedded in the program.

1. A person learns most quickly and lastingly what has meaning for him.
2. Before the facts and skills of teaching come friendliness, security, acceptance. No one learns well when he doesn't belong, any more than a plant can grow without roots in the soil.
3. Learning is more efficient and longer lasting when conditions are real and lifelike.
4. Facts and skills are best learned when they are part of a pattern, when we learn them in relation to their use—as a part of a job, project, or enterprise.
5. Students learn better if they see with the eyes, touch with the hands, hear with the ears, heft with the muscle, as they see with the mind's eye.
6. Behavior is controlled by the emotions as well as the intellect. Far more than a place to train the mind, the school is (should be) concerned with training the emotions also. (Loughmiller, 1979, p. 45)

At camp, the young people learned through direct experiences. "They built a fire for a meal they will eat two hours later; they cut poles for a tent they will build the next day; they write an article for the camp paper about a bobcat they saw thirty minutes ago. We try to capitalize immediately on those teachable moments when interest and enthusiasm are high," said Loughmiller (1979, p. 44).

Carl Rogers affirmed that successful living is healing, and Loughmiller's work strongly supports that contention. As the boys he served grew in competence, he saw their emotional and behavioral issues begin to fade. According to Loughmiller:

> In looking at our work with a boy we find nothing that is not educational in nature, and yet the symptoms that brought him to camp disappear. The dyslexia is gone, his schizoid condition has vanished, he is no longer hyperkinetic, his antisocial behavior ceases, and his 'learning disabilities' are overcome. Our contribution to his recovery consists primarily in providing a warm emotional climate where he feels accepted by peers and adults, where he is helped to acquire physical, social and educational skills related to his immediate environment but applicable anywhere. (1979, pp. 45–46)

Implications for EE Philosophy

According to the Association for Experiential Education (AEE) website, "experiential education is a philosophy and methodology in which educators purposefully engage with learners in direct experience and focused reflection in order to increase knowledge, develop skills and clarify values" (Association for Experiential Education, n.d., p. 1). Anyone familiar with Loughmiller's work knows that he deserves a place of honor at the table in the AEE Valhalla, for his practices foreshadow AEE practices and his philosophy prefigures AEE philosophy. His emphasis on relationship development; on capitalizing on teachable moments and on learning by doing; on providing developmental experiences both real and challenging, and on front loading and processing those experiences for the growth and benefit of all; on allowing young people to succeed or fail on their own merits and experience the unmediated consequences of their decisions and actions; and on programming that accentuated decision making, problem solving, direct experience, and personal accountability—all this and more mark Loughmiller as a pioneer in the experiential education field and a trailblazer for the therapeutic movement.

Notes

1. Re-ED here refers to the "Project for the Re-Education of Emotionally Disturbed Children," the eight-year demonstration project funded in 1961 by the National Institute of Mental Health (NIMH), and to the programs that emanated from it. Re-ED was the brainchild of psychologist and educator Nicholas Hobbs. Hobbs's NIMH proposal called for the creation of pilot schools to serve troubled children in Tennessee and North Carolina and for the establishment of a program at Peabody College (now part of Vanderbilt University) to train and staff the schools with a new type of mental health practitioner called teacher-counselors. Out of Project Re-ED came a treatment model for children that was both clinically efficacious and cost effective. Re-ED benefited considerably from the work of Campbell Loughmiller, often drawing upon practices that had proven effective in his Texas program. Hobbs and Loughmiller knew and respected one another throughout their professional careers, and it was Hobbs, at Loughmiller's request, who provided the forewords to both Loughmiller's professional books, *Wilderness Road* and *Kids in Trouble*.
2. While a number of new programs based on the Loughmiller model have come into existence in the last 25 years, the field has contracted commensurately. Misguided regulatory efforts and other attempts to force such programs to bend their practices to conform to ill-fitted standards, usually in the service of a cost shifting initiative, have resulted in the closure of several programs. Included in that number, sadly, is the original program, the Salesmanship Club Boys Camp, which closed in 2004, and the Pressley Ridge program which closed its doors in 2008.
3. Many programs utilizing the Loughmiller model have flexed these numbers through the years in accordance with regulatory dictates, standards, safety concerns, the age or presenting issues of the youngsters being served, or simply personal preference. The number of youngsters per group typically falls between 8 and 12, with 10 being the median. The number of counselors assigned to a group, meanwhile, is rarely less than 3 nor more than 8 or 9, depending upon whether a program uses a shift or live-in model and how much back-up support is assigned to a group.

References

Association for Experiential Education (n.d.). Retrieved July, 2007, from http://www.AEE.org/about/whatisEE

Loughmiller, C. (1965). *Wilderness Road*. Dallas, TX: Hogg Foundation for Mental Health, University of Texas.

Loughmiller, C. (1979). *Kids in trouble: An adventure in education*. Dallas, TX: Wildwood.

Loughmiller, C. (1980). *These fish had wings, Volume I* [autobiographical documents prepared for family and friends]. Author.

Loughmiller, C. (1985). *These fish had wings, Volume II* [autobiographical documents prepared for family and friends]. Author.

Loughmiller, C., & Loughmiller, L. (1977). *Big thicket legacy.* Dallas, TX: University of Texas.

Loughmiller, C., & Loughmiller, L. (2006). *Texas wildflowers: A field guide.* Dallas, TX: University of Texas. (Original work published 1984)

Loughmiller, L., & Loughmiller, C. (1953). *Camping and Christian growth* [Pamphlet]. Dallas, TX: Abingdon.

Loughmiller, L., & Loughmiller, C. (1959). *Let's go camping* [Pamphlet]. Dallas, TX: Abingdon.

McNeil, E. B. (1957). The background of therapeutic camping. *Journal of Social Issues, 13,* 3–21.

Paul, S. (1957). *Walden: Henry David Thoreau.* Boston: Houghton Mifflin.

Smith, B. K., & Loughmiller, C. (1958). *The worth of a boy.* Dallas, TX: Hogg Foundation for Mental Health, University of Texas.

31 Sidney B. Simon
Values Clarification Pioneer

Clifford E. Knapp

As a student at Paterson State College in Wayne, New Jersey, during 1958–1959, I enrolled in a Junior High School educational methods class taught by Sidney B. Simon. Sid had just earned his doctorate and had exciting ideas to share about how to teach potential teachers. That turned out to be one of the most memorable associations with a teacher of my life. Why was this so? Sid had a warm personality and a way of showing me that he cared about who I was as a person, as well as a potential teacher. His excitement about teaching was contagious. He taught by structuring class experiences so that the students could get to know him and each other. He also wanted to know about our lives outside of the classroom and he invited us to share this by writing a "Thought Card" (TC) each week. On a 4" × 6" TC we could write about anything we wanted —information about the course, our life in general, our questions, or any other topic we wanted to share. He then responded nonjudgmentally to our comments and returned the index card during the next class. I vividly remember anticipating his written responses because he seemed interested in who I was and what I thought.

He made use of values clarification strategies during most of the classes. One exercise involved asking us to list 20 things we loved to do and then we were to code this list according to certain questions. One example was: "How much did it cost to do?" Another was: "Whom did we like to do it with?" A third was: "When did we do it last?" The discussions we had in small groups were alive and personal because we were examining our own lives. Sid also did a lot of rank order exercises. For example, he asked: On a Saturday night would you rather go dancing, to a movie, or be alone doing something creative? Every time he led a rank order strategy, we were reflecting on our experiences. He would also have us draw a continuum line on paper with two different extremes on either end. Then we were asked to locate where we were on that line. For example, at one end was a person who hated seat belts, so much that he used scissors to cut them out of people's cars. At the other end of the continuum was a person who believed in them so much, he/she wore them while driving through the car wash. You can imagine the engaging discussions that went on in our small groups.

Another memory of Sid's teaching was the way he grouped us into pairs, trios, or quartets and asked us to comment on a particular educational dilemma or issue related to teaching in a junior high school. To this day, over 50 years later, I correspond with Sid Simon and we share our common interests in teaching and learning. Because Sid Simon was important to thousands of others during his teaching career and because he made significant contributions to the field of education, I chose to write this chapter so others could be introduced to his philosophy and instructional methods.

On March 5, 1998, I visited Sid at his home in Sanibel, Florida, and recorded an interview with him. This was later published in *Values Realization Journal* (2000, pp. 6–11). Some of the following material for this chapter was selected from that interview and from an e-mail received from him on July 25, 2007. Other text content was excerpted from some of Simon's publications or from those of his colleagues.

Brief Biography

Sid Simon was born in Pittsburgh, Pennsylvania, in 1927 where he was formally educated until his graduation from high school in 1944. He attended the Pennsylvania State University and earned Bachelor of Arts and Master of Education degrees there. He earned his Doctor of Education degree in Core Curriculum at New York University in 1958. From 1950 until 1957 he taught English, dramatics, and social studies at the high school level. In addition to teaching at Paterson State College, where I met him, he has taught at New York University, Queens College of the City University of New York, Temple University, and the University of Massachusetts at Amherst. The University of Massachusetts appointed him as a Professor Emeritus in 1989 after 20 years of teaching in psychological education. He also taught summer courses at six other universities around the United States.

Although retired from university teaching, he continues to offer workshops and give presentations in this country and around the world. He has authored or co-authored over 100 professional articles and 19 books on a variety of educational and psychological topics. Perhaps he is known best for his early writings in values education. His books, *Values and Teaching* (with Raths & Harmin, 1966/1978); *Values Clarification: A Handbook of Practical Strategies* (with Howe & Kirschenbaum, 1972); *In Search of Values: 31 Strategies for Finding Out What Really Matters Most to You* (with Howe & Kirschenbaum,1993); and *Helping Your Child Find Values to Live By* (with Olds, 1991) have, in combination, sold close to 2 million copies.

What Did Sid Simon Say About Teaching?

Sid Simon was influenced by Louis E. Raths, a professor at New York University. Simon worked under Raths for almost three years while pursuing his doctorate and teaching high school English on Long Island. They first met when Raths presented an inservice teacher workshop and Simon was selected as the moderator for the lecture series. Simon noted:

> Raths was not well received by the faculty, because they thought he was "off the wall", but I thought he was magnificent. That was the beginning of my adventures in values clarification and perhaps the beginning of my pattern of not always agreeing with mainstream educators. (cited in Knapp, 2000, p. 6)

Simon continued to work with Raths after he received his doctorate and they collaborated on a classic book about values clarification, *Values and Teaching* (1966). Simon and deSherbinin explain where Raths got the idea of values clarification:

> The term values clarification was first used by Louis Raths while he taught at New York University during the late fifties. Working from John Dewey's book, *Theory of Valuation*, Raths refined Dewey's ideas and created values clarification strategies based on the recorded thought of the great philosopher. (1975, p. 680)

A third co-author of this best-selling book was Merrill Harmin who later taught at Southern Illinois University. In an article published in *Educational Leadership* Harmin mentions Louis Raths as one of his mentors also: This story starts with Louis E. Raths, my first values teacher and a genius educator. Raths was a master at getting inside the thoughts and feelings of students. And he was a genius at crafting penetrating teaching strategies (1988, p. 25).The underlying theory and teaching strategies in *Values and Teaching* are excellent indicators of how Raths, Harmin, and Simon thought students should learn about values in their lives. The authors define values "as those elements that show how a person has decided to use his life" (Raths et al., 1966, p. 6), but acknowledge, "one can find consensus for no definition. About the only agreement that emerges is that a value represents something important in human existence" (Raths et al., 1966, p. 9). The co-authors were more interested in the process of valuing and helping students clarify their values, rather than in finding an agreed-upon definition. The value theory in their book is presented as a teaching theory and other educators and psychologists are credited with having similar ideas:

> The reader who desires to see some writings in a related view or to examine different implications of this general approach might consider Dewey, and especially his 1939 essay "Theory of Valuation," and his "Moral Principles in Education;" Gordon Allport, *Becoming: Basic Considerations for a Psychology of Personality*; Gardner Murphy, *Human Potentialities*; Asch, *Social Psychology; the 1962 yearbook of the Association of Supervision and Curriculum Development, Perceiving, Behaving, Becoming*; Edgar Friedenberg, *The Vanishing Adolescent*; and Carl Rogers, *On Becoming a Person*. (Raths et al., 1966, p. 9)

When explaining the process of valuing, Raths et al. (1966) describe seven requirements that must be met before they consider a behavior as a genuine value. These are:

1. Choosing freely
2. Choosing from among alternatives
3. Choosing after thoughtful consideration of the consequences of each alternative
4. Prizing and cherishing
5. Affirming
6. Acting upon choices
7. Repeating (1966, pp. 28–29)

They consider these seven criteria for a value as a beginning place for a teacher to help students clarify their values. For example, if a teacher or student identifies a particular value choice, such as how to spend free-time hours after school, the teacher can plan strategies (activities) related to this topic to help students think through the seven criteria in order to eventually consider this as a value in their lives. Teachers can encourage students' free choices when appropriate, help them discover and examine alternatives in choosing, assist them in considering the consequences of selecting each alternative, encourage them to consider what they prize or cherish, encourage them to live in accordance with their choices, and help them examine repeating patterns related to this value in their lives. Simon recognizes the complexity of this approach: "Too many people who are promoting values education are not willing to help students go through the difficult process of acquiring genuine values. They want to give them values" (cited in Knapp, 2000, p. 6). He would agree with Plato who said, "Knowledge which is acquired under compulsion has no hold on the mind (quoted in Kilpatrick, 1926, p. 299).

In summary, a value, according to Raths et al. (1966), results from the application of the process of thoughtfully choosing, prizing and acting after reflecting upon life experiences. They believe strongly in providing safe, alternative choices for students to consider whenever possible. With choice comes the responsibility to consider the consequences of these decisions. When students do that: "They must reflect and choose if values are to emerge" (Raths et al., 1966, p. 35). This reflection component was usually built in to the valuing strategy (activity) or teachers helped students with the processing for personal meaning after the strategy was completed. The co-authors shared the belief that many youth and adults need instructional help in becoming aware of their values and clarifying their thinking about them.

Some critics eventually questioned this values theory as the values clarification movement became more popular in schools and colleges in the 1970s. Some of the critics accused the authors of wanting to apply values clarification theory to all life situations involving value formation. Raths et al. (1966) believed that in some instances teachers should take a more traditional stance and prohibit students from choosing certain antisocial activities. Harmin made this more explicit in his article, "Value Clarity, High Morality: Let's Go for Both" (1988) written later in response to those critics. All of these authors recognized the traditional approaches to values guidance such as setting examples, persuading and convincing, limiting choices, inspiring, making rules, adhering to cultural or religious dogma, and appealing to conscience, but they wanted to present a new approach because they thought it would be more effective in creating a better society. Simon commented on the critics of values clarification:

> I still maintain that the critics were afraid to allow children to raise value questions, speak their truths, and ask for clarification about real life issues. They preferred to tell children what to think and how they should feel about issues. I wish I had had the courage and wisdom to know how to argue those points better. My forte was to create the strategies and teach these tools and techniques, not to publicly defend them. (cited in Knapp, 2000, p. 10)

What Are Some More Examples of Values Clarification Strategies?

Another values clarification strategy for helping students think through the seven criteria required for a value is named the "clarifying response." After explaining that there are at least 10 criteria to consider for giving an effective clarifying response, Raths et al. provide 30 selected responses in the form of questions (1966, pp. 55–62). Experiential educators familiar with the literature on leading reflection (processing or debriefing) sessions will identify these questions as part of the art and science of helping students reflect on experiences. For example: "Is this something that you prize?"; "Are you glad about that?"; "How did you feel when that happened?"; and "Did you have to choose that; was it a free choice?" (1966, pp. 56–57). As with values clarification strategies in general, the authors mention that the clarifying response should be used only under certain conditions: "The point here, then, is that a teacher would be wise to begin using clarifying responses only in situations that will prevent students from equating those responses with criticism or rebuke" (Raths et al., 1966, p. 79).

The co-authors provide descriptions of many other strategies in chapters six and seven and then outline guidelines for getting started and problems to attend to in chapter eight. Readers who want more details about how to implement values clarification techniques are urged to read the entire book.

In my interview with Simon, he told me that he uses journaling as a way of helping students become aware of their full potential and teaching them how to give helpful feedback to others.

> Another tool is something I use in my workshops all the time. I call it "Progoffian Writing," dedicated to Ira Progoff who developed the intensive journal-writing process in which people learn how to write by free association and to do it as rapidly as they can get it on paper. They write about what they are trying to be clear about. (cited in Knapp, 2000, p. 7)

In response to my question about how Simon would help first-year teachers become more effective, he said:

> I'd want them to learn the tools of working effectively in small groups so they don't get stuck in excessive lecturing and in expecting memory regurgitation from their students. It is amazing for me to think back and realize, that until I studied with Raths, in the late 1950s,

I had NEVER been in a class that put students into groups to talk to each other. Isn't that incredible? (cited in Knapp, 2000, p. 7)

When I was a student in Simon's class, I remember him talking about teaching only that which was worthwhile—giving students quality experiences. He drew a piece of Swiss cheese on the board to represent a student and asked how we would go about filling the holes with useful information. Simon elaborates:

> There is a danger that teachers may become so information driven that they become confused about the role of information in the learning process. I think of something that Raths said over 40 [now almost 50] years ago. He said that the function of information is to inform. He then asked, 'To inform what?' His answer was, "To inform our values."
>
> If it is gathering information for information's sake alone, then it becomes just like an overcrowded AOL chat room. Until the information focuses on helping youth to change, to clarify and to act on their values, then it is useless decoration, and we might as well memorize the telephone directory. (cited in Knapp, 2000, p. 9)

As my interview was drawing to a close, I asked Simon what he would most like to be remembered for as an educator. He replied:

> My first thought was that I provided an environment where people could move towards becoming more of their inherent selves. I know how to provide that environment. I would like to be remembered for the writings that have rippled out into other people's lives. I'd like to be remembered for contributing instructional techniques, tools and strategies to the field of education. (cited in Knapp, 2000, p. 9)

Sid Simon's teaching was transformative for me because of the environment he created in that one course I took in 1959. Since that time I have participated in many other workshops that he has led and have become very familiar with how he creates humane climates and with a variety of valuing strategies and methods he uses. I will always remember that he was the first college teacher who seemed to genuinely care about me and take an interest in my life. He loved to teach and he showed it. Because he engaged the class in small group activities and helped us to make more sense out of the topics we discussed, he made a deep impression on me. Later, I remembered some of these lessons and applied them to my own teaching.

How Does Simon's Philosophy and Practices Relate to Experiential Education?

In a personal correspondence (personal communication, July 25, 2007) with Sid Simon, he mentioned experiential education:

> I didn't invent it, but my I did spread it. How do I know? My students tell me. I know that all my students took two important things from me. One, they learned to put their students into pairs, trios, and quartets. You can't imagine, or maybe you can, how many students told me that. My classes were the first ones they were ever in, where they worked from a strategy, an exercise, or a situation I set up for them. Two, I invested or reframed dozens of structured experiences over the years for teachers to use with their students. Some of the best are in *Values Clarification: A Handbook of Practical Strategies For Teachers and Students*. (Simon et al., 1972)

Simon Elaborates on the Value of Experiential Education

> Learning must be experiential. I think John Dewey was right when he said that we learn by doing. Raths was a student of Dewey's and was very familiar with his work. Dewey developed a theory of valuation in the 30s and Raths took it further. We have to put more focus on students' learning out of the classroom, and becoming involved in community issues and projects. When at Temple University, I became very excited about an idea I called 'Sensitivity Modules.' They were a series of experiences students could choose and go into the community to explore. For example, having students spend the night in a shelter for the homeless or trying to eat on the monthly food allotment of a welfare mother were two on the list. These experiences were very meaningful. (Simon, as cited in Knapp, 2000, p. 8)

Implications for EE Philosophy

As I reviewed the 12 principles of experiential education practice adopted by the Association for Experiential Education (Proudman, 1995, p. 1ff. 21), I thought of Sid Simon and how he implemented all of them with our class. He engaged us in carefully chosen, structured experiences and supported them by reflection, critical analysis, and synthesis. These strategies required us to make decisions and be accountable for the results. We were usually actively engaged in posing questions, solving problems, and constructing meaning. These authentic activities involved us intellectually, emotionally, socially, and soulfully as young students preparing to be teachers and the resulting knowledge became personal and formed the basis for future learning experiences. We developed many close relationships with our classmates and with the teacher. Because of the uncertainty of the outcomes of many of the valuing strategies, we felt success, failure, adventure, and risk at various times. We explored our values about teaching as Sid Simon set clear boundaries, insured our physical and emotional safety, and facilitated the learning process. He also recognized and encouraged spontaneous learning opportunities and was apparently aware of how his personal judgments and pre-conceptions influenced us. Simon's consistent use of small groups as a primary tool to promote intimate discussions helped members of our class to get to know each other and bond. Perhaps his greatest contribution to experiential education was his focus on clarifying responses as ways to encourage reflective thinking about a topic. Because of my exposure to this technique, I developed a strong interest in how to lead reflection sessions after providing engaging experiences to my students. In addition, Simon's writings gave me many concrete examples of how to help my students make more meaning from what they learned. I learned from Sid how to create safe environments in my classes so students could feel comfortable and learn. I have carried his ideas of using a "thought card" and journaling into my teaching at the university level as ways of establishing a more personal relationship with my students. Using the power of writing to reach clarity on confusing issues repeatedly has been demonstrated and validated in my personal and teaching life.

Sid Simon was influential in my development as an experiential and environmental educator, although I didn't realize what those terms meant at the time I was his student. He created a model of teaching that made sense and set a high standard for me as I actively engaged my students in meaningful activities, both inside and outside the classroom. In 1973 I published a chapter in *Clarifying Values Through Subject Matter: Applications for the Classroom* (Harmin et al., pp. 116–134). The contents, related to environmental education situations, demonstrated all I had learned about values clarification from Sid. I'm sure that even today my educational philosophy and practice are clear reflections of that young, energetic professor I met a long time ago in New Jersey.

References

Harmin, M. (1988). Value clarity, high morality: Let's go for both. *Educational Leadership, 45*(8), 24–30.

Kilpatrick, W. H. (1926). *Source book in the philosophy of education.* New York: Macmillan.

Knapp, C. E. (1973). Using the values strategies with subject matter. In M. Harmin, H. Kirschenbaum, & S. B. Simon (Eds.), *Clarifying values through subject matter: Applications for the classroom* (pp. 116–134). Minneapolis: Winston.

Knapp, C. E. (2000). An interview with Sid Simon: Values education pioneer. *Values Realization Journal, 13*, 6–11.

Proudman, B. (1995). AEE adopts definition. *The AEE horizon: Newsletter of the Association for Experiential Education, 15,* 1ff., 21.

Simon, S. B., & deSherbinin, P. (1975). Values clarification: It can start gently and grow deep. *Phi Delta Kappan, 56*(10), 679–683.

Simon, S. B., Howe, L. W., & Kirschenbaum, H. (1972). *Values clarification: A handbook of practical strategies for teachers and students.* New York: Hart.

Simon, S. B., Howe, L. H., & Kirschenbaum, H. (1993). *In search of values: 31 strategies for finding out what really matters most to you.* New York: Warner Books.

Simon, S. B., & Olds, S. W. (1991). *Helping your child find values to live by.* Hadley, MA: Values Press.

Raths, L. E., Harmin, M., & Simon, S. B. (1978). *Values and teaching.* Columbus, OH: Charles E. Merrill. (Original work published 1966)

32 Eliot Wigginton

Foxfire—No Inert Ideas Allowed Here.

J. Cynthia McDermott and Hilton Smith

> In training a child to activity of thought, above all things we must be aware of what I will call "inert ideas"—that is to say, ideas that are merely received into the mind without being utilized, or tested, or thrown into fresh combinations.... Education with inert ideas is not only useless: it is, above all things, harmful. (Whitehead, 1916, pp. 1–3)

Alfred North Whitehead, philosopher, mathematician, and educator, in his Presidential address to the Mathematical Association of England in 1916 challenged the status quo of the prevailing educational model. In response to Whitehead's challenge to keep knowledge alive, and spurred by John Dewey's ideas about learning by doing, many brilliant educators and creative educational programs brought alternatives to conventional schooling throughout the 20th century. Perhaps none has created such an effective marriage between all aspects of outdoor and experiential education and the traditional classroom than Eliot Wigginton and Foxfire. Wigginton's imagination and experimentation took form 40 years ago with *The Foxfire Magazine*. This chapter will offer a brief overview to Wigginton's pedagogical perspective and some introductory information on the evolving Foxfire program.

Biography

Brooks Eliot Wigginton (a.k.a. "Wig") was born in West Virginia in 1942. Wig's father was a professor of landscape architecture who inspired his appreciation of nature and natural settings for human uses. His mother died early in Wig's life, so he was reared by a step-mother who seemed to have been the embodiment of all the stereotypes about the evil step-mother. Family life, in short, was not nearly the enjoyable experience it could have been. Wig's schooling could be described as "conventional," with the usual mix of memorable and less-than-memorable teachers. Although he gave little thought to what he was going to do after college, he settled on teaching as a fallback career start. We know that until he happened upon cultural journalism he almost decided that he was not cut out to be a teacher.

Wig graduated from college ready to begin his career as a high school English teacher. Without much planning and after writing a few letters to find a job, he ended up in the southern Appalachian town of Rabun Gap, Georgia, an area he knew because he had grown up in Athens, some 80 miles away. He began his professional career in August 1966. Teaching at the Rabun Gap Nacoochee School (RGNS) turned out to be an odd job; it was a private high school where most students were in residence while the local school board paid a token tuition for public school students to attend from the northern end of the county. In addition to his teaching assignment (all ninth- and tenth-grade English and one section of geography), he was also an assistant house parent. Wig was busy! Unfortunately, things did not go very well for him and his classes.

On one of the bleakest fall days in 1966, I walked into my first-period class, sat down on top of my desk and crossed my legs and said, very slowly and very quietly, "Look, this isn't working. You know it isn't and I know it isn't. Now what are we going to do together to make it through the rest of the year?" The class was silent. (Wigginton, 1985, p. 32)

After some time had passed, and with fits and starts, the students began making suggestions. Some ideas were accepted and others were rejected. Wig worked with any ideas that seemed promising to him and the students.

For several weeks, we experimented. Seasoned teachers, had any been watching us, would say we floundered, but I prefer the sound of *experimented*. (Wigginton, 1985, p. 46)

Many hours and discussions later, when Wig related his personal experience with magazine writing, the classes decided to move forward with a magazine project, determined that it would contain work by Rabun Gap students, work by students from other schools, and work by professional writers and authors from the surrounding community. This last insightful decision produced the response from the community that affirmed the students' work and became the basis of the teaching methodology that Wigginton and the Foxfire program developed.

What was it that allowed Wig to take this kind of educational risk? What did he have in mind that would allow students the kind of freedom necessary to make decisions? What supported his thinking to allow the practices of democratic teaching to prevail? Wig gives us something of a sense of the kind of personal perspective that was at work:

I sincerely feel that this cautiousness stifles all individuality even more than the machinery of society. People are no longer willing to live dangerously, try things that may hurt them or possibly knock them flat. We think too damn much and don't rely on impulse anymore. In a way that's too bad. I think. Millions of little aspects enter every decision and we see all the aspects and it scares us off from making any decision at all except to forget the whole thing. April 1963. (Wigginton, 1985, p. 47)

Thus began the teaching career of Eliot Wigginton, who was to be involved with a creative experiential education approach for the next 25 years. In 1984 he was honored as an outstanding alumnus from Cornell University and as a Kurt Hahn presenter at the national conference of the Association for Experiential Education. In 1989 he received a MacArthur Fellowship and in 1992 he received an Honorary Doctor of Humanities from Princeton University. He currently resides in Florida.

Foxfire

Born on that impulsive day in 1966 was the start of what has come to be known as the Foxfire approach. No formula, no teachers' manuals, no curriculum guide, no in-service from the visiting expert—just one teacher believing that children could make decisions and take responsibility for carrying them out and figuring out the skills they needed in the process was all it took.

When the students decided to publish a magazine, Wig was stirred to action. Of course, it was not easy. There was no money for the production of a magazine and no equipment except an old WWII camera that had been handed down to him, but the interest, excitement, and commitment from the students (and support from Wig and the principal) made it happen.

The most complete record of the history of the development of Foxfire is found in Wigginton's personal narrative, *Sometimes a Shining Moment: The Foxfire Experience, Twenty Years*

Teaching in a High School Classroom (1985). Six years in the writing, it chronicles Wig's thinking beginning in 1963 during his college years at Cornell. Wig shows us how his dissatisfaction with inert education generated his willingness to try something different.

One of the authors of this chapter, Hilton Smith, worked with the Foxfire program for many years. He joined Foxfire as an "editor/educator" to assist with editing of the J. P. Dutton series of Foxfire books about single topics, such as *The Foxfire Book of Toys and Games* (Page & Smith,1993), and assisting with the *Foxfire* magazine class when Wigginton was away—which was very often at the time. After two years, he began teaching social studies courses at Rabun County High School, using the Foxfire approach. When Foxfire received a grant from the Binghamton Trust to disseminate the approach through a "Teacher Outreach" program, he became the coordinator of that project.

Smith has maintained a friendship with Wigginton, and he visited with him for an interview in preparation for this chapter. The two authors then sat down to discuss Wig's ideas about Foxfire. The remainder of this section of the chapter will proceed as an interview/dialog between the two authors, a procedure that is consistent with the methods of the *Foxfire* magazine which students would use if they were writing this chapter.

〜〜〜

McDermott: The magazine was a huge risk, even though he had the support of the principal. Why do you think he was able to take that risk?

Smith: His passion about the potential value of language arts skills served as a kind of keel for his teaching. Wig did not see the magazine as a risk, but he did recognize the risk to his students if they did not acquire the necessary skills to produce the magazine. Keep in mind that since RGNS was a private school, with a student population consisting mostly of underachievers at that time, there was less chance of parents questioning the efficacy of the magazine as a worthy endeavor. When the local community responded so positively to the published interviews of local people, the project had all the support it needed to deal with any naysayers.

McDermott: What was it about Wig that allowed him to have such trust in the students?

Smith: Initially, he had no more trust in students than any other teacher at that school. But once he noticed how well students handled the responsibilities entailed in creating issues of the magazine—and how quickly their language arts skills advanced—he connected the dots and realized that they craved that trust and that he had to extend the trust for the venture to continue past a one-time project.

Also, his trust is not a matter of either/or sentiment. To some teachers the prospect of that much trust comes across as giving up "control." Wig is not naive about adolescents, so his classroom management involves anticipation of the students' responses to challenges and opportunities. Control becomes a collaborative responsibility, with the teacher being vigilant about the possibilities of things going off the rails.

McDermott: Outdoor Education and other experiential programs are designed to help students grow and mature in ways that "inert" education can't. What benefits did the Foxfire approach have for students?

Smith: Students acquired an enhanced sense of themselves as learners, along with some durable skills in and appreciation of literature and composition. That tends to translate into what we'd now call metacognition (thinking about thinking), in the sense that they approached other learning situations more aware of how to cope with them.

Along with those gains, his students began to realize that the culture of the southern Appalachians had many aspects to be proud of. They moved away from that sense of being hillbillies and therefore something inferior, toward more positive attitudes about themselves as part of that culture. The fact that about half the members of his classes were residential students from other parts of the nation added to that development as they, too, looked on that culture with more appreciation. This enabled Wig to work to dissolve the endemic racial and ethnic prejudices of the local students, an aspect of the Foxfire approach that continued when the program later moved to the public comprehensive high school.

Finally, Foxfire students learned that much of what is worthy to be learned is in venues other than the school building. That, too, became part of the Foxfire approach and was applied in other situations, including Native American communities and inner-city neighborhoods.

McDermott: As a community-based process, did Rabun County change as a result of Foxfire?

Smith: With the publication of the Foxfire books, there was a discernable increase in cultural pride in the region. Foxfire became a kind of reference point for the people. The instructional program at Rabun County High School changed, eventually including five Foxfire-influenced teachers (magazine, video, music, outdoor education, and social studies). We have to suspect that had a residual impact on the local area, but documenting that would be very difficult.

McDermott: Wig had to be encouraged to teach others about the process, partially because he knew that Foxfire was more than just the magazine. Was he satisfied with the national expansion and did it maintain its integrity as an approach?

Smith: The first Foxfire book, was called *The Foxfire Book: Hog Dressing, Log Cabin Building, Mountain Crafts and Foods, Planting by the Signs, Snake Lore, Hunting Tales, Faith Healing, and Moonshine* (Wigginton, 1972). Through the years, the Foxfire series grew to over 20 books; the most recent was published to celebrate the 40th anniversary of the program (Foxfire Fund, 2006). Once the books came out, teachers from all over sought Wig out to learn how to initiate similar "projects" with their classes. When I joined Foxfire in 1984, we kept track of about two dozen magazine projects around the United States involving what had become known as "cultural journalism." The fact that very few of them survived more than a few years—and that none of them caught on with other teachers in their schools—informed our later work with teachers.

McDermott: Wig avers that he first grasped the possibility that Foxfire was more than a magazine when he wrote *Sometimes a Shining Moment* (Wigginton, 1985). Did he understand the educational significance of the evolving Foxfire approach?

Smith: By his own acknowledgment, Wig did not have a deep background in education, so many of the experiences and encounters during these years served to fill in his knowledge about schooling. John Dewey's work, for example, was not part of the picture until Foxfire accepted the challenge of systematic dissemination of the approach on a larger scale. During that time various advisers, such as Junius Eddy, suggested things for Wig to read so he would be more conversant in the discourses he would now enter. That's how Dewey's *Experience and Education* (1938/1997) came into his view.

But the pivotal period for Wig and the whole Foxfire organization was from 1984 to 1987, when Foxfire received $1.5 million from the Bingham Foundation to mount a major Teacher Outreach program. What had been an almost casual sideline for Foxfire had to be tooled up for a systematic initiative to bring the approach to teachers in all demographic settings, all grade levels, all subjects, and all types of students. And we had to do it so that the results were more durable and would develop a momentum of their own rather than fading away as most initiatives tend to do.

Wig remembers that he approached the pilot course, summer 1986, at Berea

College in eastern Kentucky, "with trepidation." He included Experience and Educa-tion as a required reading to provide philosophic grounding for the approach—as he had experienced it. The course was not going well, and there was whining about the Dewey book. One member of the class, an archetype of the Appalachian American Gothic woman, sat stoic through the first week of the class, unresponsive even to the other women in the class, and seemingly indifferent to Wig. In the middle of the sec-ond week, she suddenly addressed the whining majority of the class with a 30-minute oral dissertation relating Dewey and Wig's commentaries to the miseries of school-ing in eastern Kentucky. It was a "shining moment" and the turning point in that class. It encouraged Wig's sense that we could really do this. That teacher returned to the Berea course in 1987 with some of her students to share what they were doing and learning. That set that course on track and established the link between Foxfire's Core Practices (n.d.).

Dewey's theory, and classroom teachers' own practices. That linkage continues essentially unmodified today in the Foxfire courses for teachers.

McDermott: Anecdotes like that characterize the experiences of all of us working with teachers on the Foxfire approach, because the approach is defined by the Core Practices, not principles; and it is an approach, not a technique nor a method, Foxfire becomes the accumulated experiences and reflections of all its practitioners. That gives it both durability and integrity.

Smith: Wig recognized that, and accepted that Foxfire had spiraled into something beyond the parameters of the Foxfire magazine and cultural journalism. It is significant that he continued to focus on his work at the high school, while accepting invitations to present at various events that aided the overall effort.

McDermott: The most difficult aspect of the history of Wig involves his conviction to a charge of molesting a minor. How did Wig's conviction affect the organization?

Smith: Having the founder plead guilty to a charge of molesting a minor would have killed many education programs. Foxfire survived for several reasons. In the minds of most people in northeast Georgia, Foxfire's contributions to students and to the appre-ciation of the regional culture weighed more than Wig's transgressions. This was manifested by the willingness of store owners to put "Foxfire Still Glows" signs in their front windows. Of course, there was dismay and some anger, but support for the organization remained strong.

Wigginton had little involvement with the Foxfire teacher regional networks that we had developed as the primary Teacher Outreach vehicle. Most of those teach-ers had never met Wig, so he was more of a mythic figure to them. At the time of the transgression and guilty plea, Foxfire was very fortunate to have Billy Parrish as CEO. He had come from the Trust for Historic Preservation to manage the organiza-tion when Wig moved his work to the University of Georgia. Billy handled all aspects of the situation with calm determination to not let it sink Foxfire. To that end, he and I made a point of traveling to the teacher networks and giving them the story straight up, no dissembling. So we sustained trust. In fact, in many ways the Foxfire organiza-tion was strengthened by the whole ordeal. Much of the credit goes to Billy Parrish.

McDermott: What is Wig doing now?

Smith: After Wig's incarceration he wrote an article from prison (Wigginton, 1993–94) in which his years of teaching took a deeper turn. Wig compares, in rather tragic ways, the parallels between public schools and the prison system, as he describes a project that the inmates attempted which was to build a library. After 26 years of teaching, Wig makes frightening comparisons between education and prison. He quotes Vik-tor Frankl, Nazi death camp survivor and world-renown psychiatrist who wrote:

[What] exists in nearly all humans; is the desire to make a difference, to be involved in work that matters, to feel a sense of belonging and efficacy. Man's search for meaning is the primary motivation in his life. [What he needs is] the striving and struggling for a worthwhile goal, a freely chosen task. (Wigginton & Bennett, 1984, p. 68)

∽∽∽

In his book *Refuse To Stand Silently By: An Oral History of Grass Roots Social Activism in America, 1921–1964* (1993), Wig writes with clear understanding of the problems associated with Whitehead's "inert learning." He writes about the challenge of building a learning community that involves non-inert learning:

In the absence of an environment that inspires and engages, inmates and students soon ask, "Is this all there is?" For inmates it comes after the shock of incarceration is replaced by a numb throbbing in the soul. Having suffered as much self-loathing as he or she can stand, an inmate finally asks, "Now what do I do? Spend the next five years staring at a wall?" For students it comes with the realization that most courses are driven by the same flat gray routines. The student says, "I'm supposed to spend how many years doing this? You ARE kidding, right?" (Wigginton, 1993, p. 70)

Foxfire's Core Practices of Education

Though the parallel Wig draws may be uncomfortably clear, the reader can find some optimism in the continuing work of Foxfire. The task of a non-inert learning community has at its center goals of involvement, inclusion, shared decision making and utilizing the strengths of each individual. This is exemplified by Foxfire's 10 Core Practices, which have at their root the understanding that work must be meaningful and engaging. In order for students to feel committed to the learning, the teacher and students must collaborate in the creation of the work.

The Core Practices

1. **From the beginning, learner choice, design, and revision infuses the work teachers and learners do together.** Learners' interests and concerns guide all decisions. Most problems that arise during classroom activity are solved in collaboration with learners, as learners develop their ability to solve problems and accept responsibilities.
2. **The work teachers and learners do together clearly manifests the attributes of the academic disciplines involved, so those attributes become habits of mind.** Through collaborative planning and implementation, students engage and accomplish mandated curricula. In addition, activities assist learners in discovering the value and potential of the subject matter, including connections to other disciplines.
3. **The work teachers and students do together enables learners to make connections between the classroom work, the surrounding communities, and the world beyond their communities.** Learners' work will "bring home" larger issues by identifying attitudes about and implications of those issues in their home communities.
4. **The teacher serves as facilitator and collaborator**. Teachers provide curricular "givens," then attend to each learner's developmental needs, monitor each learner's academic and social growth, and lead each learner into new areas of understanding and competence.
5. **Active learning characterizes classroom activities**, including the use of learning technologies that complement other modes of instruction. Teachers and learners manage the

learning process, posing and solving problems, creating products, and building under-standings. Because learners engaged in these kinds of activities are risk takers operating on the edge of their competence, the classroom environment provides an atmosphere of trust where the consequence of a mistake is the opportunity for further learning.

6. **The learning process entails imagination and creativity.** Classroom activities encourage learners to observe and investigate, then express to others what has been learned. In that process, learners experience the affective "tingle" which, in turn, leads to durable learning and a continuing thirst for understanding.

7. **Classroom work includes peer teaching, small group work, and teamwork.** Every learner is not only included, but needed. In the end, each can identify here or his specific stamp upon the effort. In the process, learners acquire the knowledge, skills and dispositions needed to fulfill roles in society that require collaboration and cooperation.

8. **The work of the classroom serves audiences beyond the teacher, thereby evoking the best efforts by the learners and providing feedback for improved subsequent performances.** An audience may be another individual, a group, another class, organizations, or the community.

9. **The work teachers and learners do together includes rigorous, ongoing assessment and evaluation.** Teachers and learners employ a variety of strategies to demonstrate their mastery of teaching and learning objectives, which then guides subsequent work toward higher levels of achievement.

10. **Reflection, an essential activity, takes place at key points throughout the work.** Teachers and learners engage in conscious and thoughtful consideration of the work *and* the process. It is this reflective activity that evokes insights and gives rise to revisions and refinements. (Foxfire, n.d.)

These Core Practices were tested and refined by hundreds of teachers working mostly in isolated and diverse classrooms around the country. When implemented, the Core Practices define an active, learner-centered, community-focused approach to teaching and learning. When the Core Practices guide learning, new activities spiral out of the old, incorporating lessons learned from past experiences, building on skills and understandings that can now be amplified. Regardless of a teacher's experience, the school context, subject matter, or population served, the Foxfire approach can be adapted in meaningful and substantial ways, creating learning environments that are the same but different—environments that grow out of a clearly articulated set of beliefs and, at the same time, are designed to fit the contour of the landscape in which they are grown.

Considered separately, the Core Practices overview 10 tenets of effective teaching and learning. Verified as successful through years of independent study, teachers begin their work through any number of entry points or activities. The choices they make about where to begin and where to go next are influenced by individual school and community contexts, teacher's interests and skills, and learners' developmental levels.

As teachers and learners become more skilled and confident, the Core Practices provide a decision-making framework which allows teachers to tightly weave fragmented pieces of classroom life into an integrated whole. When they are applied as a way of thinking rather than a way of doing, the complexities of teaching decisions become manageable, and one activity or new understanding leads naturally to many others. If teachers choose the Foxfire approach to guide their teaching decisions, it is not important where they start, only that they start. The adaptability and room for growth in skill and understanding make the Core Practices a highly effective, life-long tool for self-reflection, assessment, and ongoing professional development.

Implications for EE Philosophy

The Association for Experiential Education (AEE) defines experiential education as a philosophy and methodology in which "educators purportedly engage with learners in direct experience and focused reflection in order to increase knowledge, develop skills, and clarify values" (AEE, n.d). The principles of experiential education as described by AEE are quite parallel to those stated in the Core Practices of the Foxfire approach. The goal of any experiential education program, including the Foxfire approach, is in direct opposition to the teaching of inert ideas that is so common in most educational programs. There can hardly be disagreement with a conclusion that the Foxfire approach is experiential education.

Gardner found that "scholastic knowledge [inert ideas] seems strictly bound to school settings" whereas outdoor education fosters "connected knowing where education is part of, rather than separate from life" (1991, p. 122). Unlike most conventional classroom learning, outdoor education uses the students' whole environment as a source of knowledge. The community, rather than the classroom, is the context for learning where real experiences can occur. Experiential learning theory defines learning as the process whereby knowledge is created through the transformation of experience. Knowledge results from the combination of grasping and transforming experience (Kolb, 1984, p. 41).

Foxfire's founder, Brooks Eliot Wigginton, did not consider himself as an outdoor-adventure-experiential educator. Yet, the Foxfire approach can be clearly linked to the principles of outdoor and experiential education. When asked what kind of practices he saw as important, Wig answered with reference to three "common denominators" that had gained definition as he led workshops for teachers. He suggests that these three practices served as the forerunners of the Core Practices (Smith, personal interview, August, 2007). These common practices paralleled the three approaches to outdoor education overviewed by Boss (1999).

The first is outdoor adventure education, which aims to develop interpersonal competencies and enhance leadership and decision-making skills. Outdoor education nurtures a respect for our connectedness with nature and the environment, and this connectedness flows over into an awareness of our relatedness to others in the community. Kurt Hahn, in an address in 1965, eloquently described his hope for Outward Bound and what it could accomplish for society at large.

> The tragic history of continental countries transmits the warning that we should take heed of Napoleon's words: 'The world is not ruined by the wickedness of the wicked, but by the weakness of the good.' Again and again when disastrous decisions were taken by German governments in the last 50 years, wise men retreated in noble helplessness, lamenting events which they could have influenced. If we take to heart the lessons of history, we will regard it as a very serious responsibility of schools to build up the nervous strength in the vulnerable, the imaginative, the sensitive by methods which will harden yet spare them so that they will be better able to stand the strain which responsible citizenship imposes. (p. 4)

The second practice, cultural journalism, helps students understand their community and their place in it. Gathering community resources through interviews and research is an historic process that takes many forms, such as journalism courses, magazines, newspapers, anthologies, and various nonprint forms, such as video, radio, and theater. It may be community-based or may portray a culture for a general audience. Even though the process is not new, the term—cultural journalism—was first used to describe publications inspired by Foxfire (Olmstead. 1989). Olmstead (1989) states that as the world grows smaller, the mutual understanding of diverse groups of people becomes more important to peace and cooperation. Cultural journalism promotes such understanding. This was an essential concern for Wig because he found a deep level of prejudice and mis-information not only about those outside their community but also about their own community. Cultural understanding is a powerful way to help students understand their role in our democracy.

> We see decent people commit unthinkable acts. We see decent people silent in the face of unthinkable acts.... The survival task of humanity is clear; it is to envision and create institutions, from our schools to our media to our businesses that foster our democratic selves—people able to feel and express empathy and to see through the walls of race, culture and religion that divide us, people who know how to exert power while maintaining relationships. We've blinded ourselves to the most powerful tool we have. That tool is democracy. (Moore-Lappe, 2006, p. 4)

The third approach involves participatory research, and can be exemplified by Myles Horton and his work with the Highlander's Center. Participatory research is done by members of a community who want to solve (and resolve) a problem that affects them personally using a philosophy similar to that of Paulo Freire (1970). Horton engaged the community in ways that supported their own skills and capacities providing lasting change. Horton describes the efforts of three liberatory programs and says that they "were based on the democratic principle of faith in the people, and trust in the people's ability to govern themselves and make decisions about their lives. The underlying purpose was the same: to empower people. "That is the common denominator" (Jacobs, 2003, p. 185).

What is clear from the over 40 years of work of the Foxfire Fund, is that all three of these practices are part of the Foxfire approach. The location where the learning takes place is both the community and the classroom. Students interact with people from their community who farm and harvest the land, who hunt and fish and understand the "way" of nature, and who create personal environmentally friendly practices. Cultural journalism is a key component as the students interact with the community not only to preserve elements of the culture but to understand their place in that culture. Participatory research, yields numerous opportunities for the students to work with the community (both within the classroom and outside of its four walls). What is significant about Foxfire is the transformation that it allows. Foxfire learning is a fine example of experiential learning. No inert learning is accepted at Foxfire. While Eliot Wigginton is no longer involved with the program, the Foxfire approach continues to be an important alternative for educators. More information on Foxfire can be obtained by contacting the Foxfire Fund, Inc. (www.foxfire.org/index.html).

References

Association for Experiential Education (AEE). (n.d.). Retrieved from http:/www.aee.org

Boss, J. (1999). *Outdoor education and the development of civic responsibility.* Charleston, WV: Appalachia Education Laboratory. (ERIC Document Reproduction Service No. ED 425051)

Dewey, J. (1991). *Experience and education.* New York: Touchstone. (Original work published 1938)

Foxfire Fund, Inc. (2006). *The Foxfire 40th anniversary book: Faith, family, and the land.* Mountain City, GA: Author.

Foxfire Fund, Inc. (n.d). Foxfire's core practices. Retrieved from http://www.foxfire.org/teachi.html

Freire, P. (1970). *Pedagogy of the oppressed.* New York: Continuum.

Gardner, H. (1991). The tensions between education and development. *Journal of Moral Education, 2,* 113–125.

Hahn, K. (1965). Harrogate address on Outward Bound. Retrieved July 15, 2007, from http://www.kurthahn.org/writings/gate.pdf

Jacobs, D. (Ed.). (2003). *The Myles Horton reader: Education for social change*. Knoxville: University of Tennessee.

Kolb, D. (1984). *Experiential learning: Experience as the course of learning and development*. Upper Saddle River, NJ: Prentice Hall.

Moore-Lappe, F. (2006). *Democracy's edge: Choosing to save our country by bringing democracy to life*. San Francisco: Jossey-Bass

Olmstead, K. (1989). *Touching the past, enroute to the future: Cultural journalism in the curriculum of rural schools*. Charleston, WV: Appalachia Educational Laboratory. (ERIC Document Reproduction Service No. ED 308057)

Puckett, J. (1989). *Foxfire reconsidered: A twenty-year experiment in progressive education*. Urbana: University of Illinois.

Page, L. G., & Smith, H. (1993). *The Foxfire book of Appalachian yoys and games*. Raleigh, NC: University of North Carolina.

Wigginton, E. (1972). *The Foxfire book: Hog dressing, log cabin building, mountain crafts and foods, planting by the signs, snake lore, hunting tales, faith healing, moonshine*. Durham: University of North Carolina Press.

Wigginton, E. (Ed.). (1976). *I wish I could give my son a wild raccoon*. New York: Anchor Books.

Wigginton, E. (1977). The Foxfire concept. In D. Mielke (Ed.), *Teaching mountain children* (pp. 273–290). Boone, NC: Appalachian Consortium.

Wigginton, E. (1985). *Sometimes a shining moment: The Foxfire experience, Twenty years teaching in a high school classroom* New York: Anchor Books.

Wigginton, E. (Ed.). (1992). *An oral history of grass roots social activism in America 1921–1964*. New York: Anchor Books.

Wigginton, E. (Ed.). (1993). *Refuse to stand silently by: An oral history of grass roots social activism in America 1921–64*. New York: Anchor Books.

Wigginton, E., & Bennett, M. (Eds.). (1984). *Foxfire 8*. New York: Anchor Books.

Wigginton, E. (1993–94). A song of inmates. *Educational Leadership, 4*, 64–71.

33 Tricia Yu
The Tao of Experience

Gloree Rohnke

The Journey

The system and lessons of Tai Chi unfolding over generations can be likened to an ancient system of experiential education long before the term was coined or the concept created. The developmental process for Tai Chi in ancient China was a spiral of learning driven by cultural tradition, nature, natural experiences, practice, the search for meaning, and applications to life. In *Experience & Education*, author and theorist John Dewey, describes experience as "a moving force" (1938/1963, p. 38), involving "a transaction between the individual and whatever constitutes his or her environment" (p. 43). Experiential educators embrace two fundamental experiential learning processes. One form of experiential learning refers to the arranged or structured learning sequence used by leaders that are guided by a multi-stage learning model "which encourages continuity from one experience to another" (Greenaway, 1999, p. 1). The other process, however, is the unintentional learning that is inherent in everyday life events, when we learn directly from our experiences (Rohnke, 2001, p. 33). Tricia Yu, a certified Tai Chi master teacher, has been learning and developing through experience all her life. Her "solid roots" (Yu, 2007, interview with author) and innovative spirit forged the way to launch the ancient Chinese martial art of Tai Chi into the Western culture and as a somatic art into the allopathic medical system.

Tricia hails from a family of pioneers. Born in 1944 on a midwestern farm in Champaign, Illinois, she is the 12th generation of colonial Americans arriving from England and Holland. Her peripatetic family kept relocating westward, eventually moving from Pennsylvania and Indiana to be among the first families to settle in Illinois.

After World War II ended, Tricia's parents followed family custom and moved to Colorado Springs, Colorado. Sharing her youth with a sister and younger brother, Tricia describes herself as having healthy family ties built on a practice of kindness, family values, and a traditional sense of community (Yu, 2007, interview).

Currently the owner of Tai Chi Health and Uncharted Country Publishing, Tricia was the founding program and administrative director of the Tai Chi Center in Madison, Wisconsin, one of the oldest renowned schools of its kind in the United States. She received a Bachelor of Arts degree in psychology from DePauw University of Indiana and her Master of Arts in education from California's Claremont Graduate University. Tricia had an early interest in the outdoors: hiking, riding horses, climbing trees, and enjoying hours of exploring. She admits to a competitive spirit with sports, although she didn't like the guided path then and still sees herself as a "totally independent, free spirit" (Yu, 2007, interview). Tricia believes the discipline she received in her teens from her music background in piano and choirs taught her how to focus her attention and learn how to learn.

Although Tricia professed being a "tomboy" as a child, she also described herself as observant and insightful. "As a little kid, I thought a lot about how short life was; how you can die at any moment." At 14, an epiphany that "the only thing you know for sure is what is in the moment" became the life wisdom that would set her on the road toward Tai Chi (Yu, 2007, interview).

In 1970, while living in Taiwan with her husband, Tricia began her study of Tai Chi and Taoist meditation with renowned Master Liu Pei Ch'ung, who required 40 minutes of daily Tao Kung meditation. This practice involves mental focus on energy points within the body for inner harmony, attuning with the earth and the larger universe. According to Tricia, its teaching included reflection upon the Taoist perspectives of, "How do we live in harmony with the way things are? How can we be in the world now in a peaceful way, the "middle way"? "How can we cultivate our personal life force, and nourish and energize the body during its journey through life?" (Yu, 2007, interview). The practice of Tai Chi provides training in bringing this meditative awareness into action.

Tricia remains a living model of the Tao philosophy she teaches to others through her Tai Chi classes—living simply, the unity of purpose and mind. "To this day I have a lot of quiet time. I sit; notice the tea I am drinking. I live a quiet life and keep everything as simple, natural and local as possible." She does Tai Chi daily, gardens, preserves food, shops at a local farmers market, and "reads a ton, at one point mostly Chinese literature" (Yu, 2007, interview). Tricia exemplifies quiet elegance, confidence, physical strength, and fluidity, all benefits gained by a dedicated Tai Chi practitioner of well over 30 years. The influence of Taoist philosophy was apparent, as she has moved like water with the flow of life to promote a harmonious environment for herself and to meet the needs of the students she served.

Initially, Tricia followed Chinese tradition, teaching as she was taught, "No talking, just do it and everyone followed along" (Yu, 2007, interview). The model included visual learning with no verbal instructions and no corrections. Basically, the classes were taught in silence, tendering the philosophy that, to cultivate healthy energy called *Qi* (pronounced chee) in Chinese, you bring your attention into the present moment, where life is happening. Tricia acknowledges her introduction to the Chinese martial arts for this focus which she feels has been significant for her, and for her students.

Tricia remembers the traditional Asian teaching methodology as "hierarchical: a good student follows, asks no questions, helps no one else, follows the master, shows up, practices diligently, and does a good job" (Yu, 2007, interview).

> The model has provided a wonderful basis for learning. The best part was the silence, the nonverbal teaching. Americans don't have this valuable learning process reinforced in their education. It trains focus, and, I think, it helps access more subtle levels of perception. Learning movements nonverbally also fosters a great sense of connection with others. I try to include moments of silence in all my classes. (Yu, 2007, interview)

During the early years of teaching Tai Chi, Tricia intuitively developed a sense of self-trust in spontaneity. Honoring her true nature, she learned by experience that she had to become comfortable with possibly appearing foolish, inappropriate, or making mistakes. "I am fine with that. It's worth the risk to be spontaneous and so many incredible things happen when we trust the moment" (Yu, 2007, interview). Meanwhile, her classes underwent a perceptual spiral of transition motivated by her teaching, observing, experimenting, and exploring. Tricia became "as the open cup into which the new 'tea of learning' was poured" (Huang & Lynch, 1995, p. 29). Continuing her own studies with various masters, Tricia eventually connected with Master Benjamin Lo. Mirroring his example, Tricia began to include explanations during her classes about movements and to offer immediate feedback with hands-on corrections. Tricia's interest was in the extraordinary gifts that Tai Chi practice can bring to each person, rather than its martial arts application. "Possibly the biggest value of Tai Chi practice is that it brings us into the present" (Yu, 2007, interview).

Traditional Tai Chi is an intricate sequence of fluid movements called a form. Observing her classes, Tricia saw that older students, who could derive great benefits from the strengthening, balance, coordination, flexibility, and self-awareness that Tai Chi offered, were finding it difficult to learn. Stepping aside from tradition, Tricia sought to modify the form and its presentation, empowering people with a wide-range of abilities to access Tai Chi (Tai Chi Health with Tricia Yu, 20051).

Awareness of Tai Chi began to ripple through the American population in the 1970s. Rather than just popularizing the ancient system, Tricia became interested in communicating with those that had science-based training. "Science is considered the ultimate truth in our culture. Our belief systems are influenced by scientific research possibly more than any other one factor" (Yu, 2007, interview).

It became her passion to integrate Tai Chi into the medical model, and to help educate health care professionals about its somatic applications for therapy, wellness, and physical function. Thomas Hanna, founder of Hanna Somatic Education, depicts somatic learning as a body that experiences itself from within, and then learns to change itself (1990, p. 9). A somatic movement or exercise is a sensory-motor event that results in the increased voluntary control of the contraction and relaxation of muscles and helps to expand the range of motion (Bennett, 1992). The essentials of Tai Chi—self-focus, breath awareness, slow circular movements that involve the entire body, and a central equilibrium—are ideal as a vehicle for helping integrate useful training into exercise therapies.

Tricia entered research and development collaborations with occupational and physical therapists co-creating programs that "seamlessly put the two together for use therapeutically" (Yu, 2007, Interview). In 1981, she collaborated with occupational therapist Diane Harlowe to develop the innovative ROM (Range of Motion) Dance exercise and relaxation program for people with chronic pain and other physical limitations. The Tai Chi Fundamentals Program, a simplified form that maintains the integrity of the Yang style tradition, was created by Tricia with physical therapist, Jill Johnson in 1996 to "create a bridge between Tai Chi practice and the allopathic medical model" (Yu, 2007, interview).

These successful programs led to stress reduction models, seminars, and eventually to certification testing for health and fitness professionals and Tai Chi instructors as Tricia moved along her personal and professional continuum of experiential learning. This pathway transformed her original silent teacher-centered instruction to a more inclusive and student-centered approach. She matured as a teacher throughout the years as she blended the Chinese philosophy, lessons, and health benefits of the ancient marital art with modern Western values, contemporary schedules, and multiple learning styles. During her public classes and professional workshops, Tricia created a compassionate and sacred community that nurtured the spirit of the learner. The intertwining of science, spirituality, and health shaped programs that validated and affirmed learners, promoted self-reliance, confidence, and self-realization as the outcome. As she explained:

> I incorporated all that I have learned from watching others and developed on my own. I became aware of different learning styles—verbal, motor, visual—and began to incorporate them into my awareness when teaching. Having people interact with each other by working with a partner, helping others as you learn, having people talk about their experiences, and incorporating interactive principles. I integrated all the learning and teaching processes that 'spoke to me'. (Yu, 2007, interview)

Way of Contemplation

Tai Chi originated in China around the 13th century as a combination of the ancient meditation called *Dao Yin* (now *Qigong*) and martial arts exercises. Tai Chi means "Supreme Ultimate" or "the common source that unifies all apparent opposites" (Yu, 2003, p. 8). It is the ancient form of non-impact self-defense training and conditioning that has become a profound "physical activity for integrating mind, body, and spirit to function in harmony with the external world" (Yu & Johnson, 1999, p. 9).

The basic principles of the Tai Chi system include: posture alignment, diaphragmatic breathing, and mindfulness. The Tai Chi form is a choreographed sequence of postures or positions executed in a purposeful yet relaxed manner. Each posture is performed in "slow continuous movement" (Chewning, Yu, & Johnson, 2002, p. 2), with self-control and intention. The movements are designed to increase circulation, concentration, balance, endurance, and sense of personal well-being. Tai Chi can be performed almost anywhere without special equipment or clothing. Mastering Tai Chi is not necessary to acquire its benefits.

The methodology of Tai Chi was influenced by the Chinese philosophy of Tao (Dao) which fosters individual potential (Crider & Klinger, 2000, p. 2) by maintaining mental and physical balance during all circumstances. In her book, *Tai Chi Fundamentals: For Health Professionals and Instructors* (Yu & Johnson,1999), Tricia describes Tao as the "path" or "road" for "living in harmony with the earth and other humans" (p. 9). This ancient Chinese perspective evolved through the observations of early naturalists and astronomers who observed their inner processes. They recognized the body as a microcosm of the universe, its health influenced and interconnected with the rhythms of life on earth, the patterns of the larger universe, and in relationships with other individuals (Yu & Johnson, 1999, p. 9).

According to ancient Chinese ideology, Tao is the foundation of life made up of two primal cosmic forces called yin and yang. These natural forces are in a constant cyclical process of complementary opposites, each opposite generating the other. Day changes to night, emptiness to fullness; an eternal cycle as one returns to the other. Qi is the energy or "life force" that moves these forces and sustains life. This bioenergy, is identified in other mythology, philosophy and spiritual practices—*Rei Ki* in Japan, *Ka* in Egypt, *Prana* in Hindu, *Ruah* in Hebrew, *Maban* by the Australian Aborigines, the *Holy Spirit* by Christians, and the *Great Mystery* by Native Americans for example (Wikopedia, 2007). Greek tradition called it *pneuma* and Western science has recently identified bioelectricity or biomagnetism in research of "what is now being referred to as the *biofield*" (Jahnke, 2002, p. 242).

According to the ancient Taoist, everything has its own energy: animals, plants, the natural environment, the earth, and the universe. Each, then provokes an energetic response from another energy that comes within its reach (Dougherty, 2007, p. 7). Chinese tradition teaches that from birth, each of us is infused with Qi. It is always present, bathing us "internally and externally, constantly fueling, cleansing, healing, rejuvenating, and enlightening" (Jahnke, 2002, p. 11). Qi is free, is everywhere, and can be cultivated purposefully—easily, if you let it be—to improve health and vitality. Stimulating the flow of Qi is the underlying premise of performing Tai Chi.

Traditional Chinese medicine claims that thoughts and emotions as well as other external factors affect our overall health. Centering, "a basic skill of Tai Chi," brings the mind and body into harmony, improving health and well-being. In her book, *Tai Chi Mind and Body*, Tricia explains that "it begins with a few moments of quiet while focusing on slow, natural breathing to help calm the mind, relax the body, and bring the attention into the present moment" (2003, p. 12). A process of seeking inner stillness is seldom included in Western exercise [or educational] systems. Its significant wellness applications, beyond Tai Chi practice, have only become recognized for their potential in the last decade. "Learning to relax and quiet your mind helps you to connect with other people and your surroundings and to feel more responsive to what is occurring around you" (Yu, 2003, p. 12).

"May the force be with you," is the popular phrase of the famous Star Wars movie saga (Lucas, 1977). It embodies the benevolence of the bioenergy that is at the core of our lives. We tend to dwell in hectic lives filled with stress, often so absorbed with events of the past and worries of the future that the present becomes a cloud passing by unseen. According to Tai Chi principles, this unawareness depletes our personal Qi. When you learn to focus your attention and practice "conscious breathing or breath awareness" (Lewis, 2004, p. 13) in silence or with calming music as your background, you begin to integrate this centering practice into the open moments of your day, for example: while waiting in line, traveling in a car, or taking a walk. "Being aware of the present moment, in touch with your body's signals, and more sensitive to others and to your surroundings—this enhances your Qi" (Yu, 2003, p. 12). When we help our students experience the benefits of natural breathing and the phenomenon of silence, we guide them to align themselves with the energy around them, expanding their capacity to increase their bioenergy and improve their behavior and health.

The Way of Application

"Experiential learning can be described as a term for how learners translate personal and collective experience through social and cultural filters into personal discovery, performing a process of viewing the experiential components from different angles, perceptions, and vantage points" (Rohnke, 2001, p. 33). John Dewey was one of the first to draw "an organic connection between personal experience and education" (1938, p. 27). "Further," he wrote, "wholly independent of desire or intent, every experience lives in further experiences" (1938, p. 27). Thus, each experience impacts the next and the learning continues as in a continuous spiral (Rohnke, 2001, p. 34).

Tai Chi is a natural metaphor for the experiential process of the Experiential Learning Cycle (ELC) formulated by David Kolb in 1984 at the Massachusetts Institute of Technology. Kolb determined through observations that learning regularly followed a pattern that could be divided into four stages: an actual experience, reflective thinking on the experience, creating connections with past knowledge and future possibilities, and applying ideas and theories in a new situation (Rohnke, 2000, p. 34). His thesis about how people learn became the foundation for the evolving methodology of experiential education.

Training in traditional Tai Chi or the modified forms that Tricia developed begins an experience of learning and commitment unlike many others in the Western culture. "The practice of the Tai Chi form lends itself to self-reflection, inner thought, and potential for spiritual enhancement" (Crider & Klinger, 2000, p. 2). Formed in complex simplicity, as the nature it reflects, Tai Chi and the lessons of the Tao allow one to fulfill the balance of yin and yang, flowing from the physical activity to a deeper awareness of the systems of the body. Each movement, coordinated into the next, storing and releasing energy and searching for the intuitive and universal truths in the act of being in the present is the lesson of the senses, as when one sips a cup of tea to replenish the body and soul.

The lessons of Tai Chi are profound. Experiential educators strive to stimulate metaphorical thinking and design experiences to provide opportunities for their populations to search for meaning. Learning opportunities abound when using parables that explore: viewing the implications of white rain wearing through a single stone of a waterfall; deliberating the relaxed alertness of the snake; or discovering the quieted mind, endurance, and balance as one stands like a tree.

"Silence and stillness mask the tree's persistence work" (Chuen, 1991, p. 116). In preparation to commence a Tai Chi form, one learns to stand in postural alignment. Stability is achieved through the concept of rooting, planting ones feet firmly to the earth and remaining there, as if having grown roots in the earth. The solidity and strength of rooting can be introduced experientially to students by contrasting the traditional activity "boop" in a group circle (Rohnke, 1987, p. 49). As members are assigned to clasp hands to "boop" (tap) the balloon and keep it from falling to the ground, they experience a play interaction which is often erratic, unbalanced and self-serving. By reframing the experience, we observe the change to self-directed management as the learner's feet are planted firmly in contact with the earth's surface, focused on being inter-connected and interacting with other group members to keep the balloon aloft.

Passing beyond the joy and laughter of the playful activity, the mentor offers opportunity for reflection and insight: Who has given thought to how each person remains rooted to the earth and universe by cooperating thoughtfully in a community of others doing the same? How does the balloon's movement aloft and its speed of projection indicate the personal and group com-mitment to task accomplishment, and their awareness of being in the moment? Exploring the metaphor as if "living imagery" (Gendlin, 1980, p. 2). How deep are one's roots? How does one move and act from this connection to the earth? How is one nurtured by the connection to the earth? Finally, when holding a leaf in your hand, what is revealed about the cycles of life?

Each question is a cognitive assignment, providing another opportunity for cultivation of self-knowledge, being mindful of the interwoven levels of meaning that facilitates experiential learning. Mindfulness, which author Jon Kabatt-Zin, explains, "has to do with examining who we are, with questioning our view of the world and our place in it, and with cultivating some appreciation for the fullness of each moment we are alive. Most of all it has to do with being in touch" (in Anodea, 2004, p. 425). Being in a state of awareness creates circumstances for natural learning, which, when blended with an experiential curriculum, creates a learning environment that balances physical movement, metacognitive processes, and enlightens the human spirit.

Balance in curriculum, like balance in life, "alternates between action and reflection, com-munal and personal, social and solitary" (Hutchinson, 2000, p. 5). The yin and yang of learn-ing is central to the transformation guided by Tai Chi. Lessons arrive when the time is right. Learning is a continuing process, a spiral of guided lessons. This "dynamic balance" (Simpson, 2003, p. 95) of intentional actions is in constant motion and remains in equilibrium, creating outcomes. Similar objectives of balance and aptitude are sought by the holistic processes of experiential education utilizing designed curriculum that relates content to family, community, the earth, and the universe as a whole.

Reaching one's potential in the martial arts coincides with the theory of self-actualization originated by Maslow (Crider & Klinger, 2000, p. 1). It is when people reach self-actualization, the ultimate state in human development, that they reach a state of spiritual feeling. "Here peo-ple pour out playfulness, creativity, joyousness, sense of purpose, with a mission to help others" (Beard & Wilson, 2002, p. 138). This state of being, and its emotional and ethical gains can be identified as spiritual intelligence (Beard & Wilson, 2002, p. 138).

Implications for EE Philosophy

Tai Chi is an experiential exercise system that cultivates wellness and is simultaneously a con-veyer of meaning. Though based in the Eastern Tao philosophy, it lends itself to self-reflection and is adaptive to individual or group spiritual practice. The student learns the challenge and satisfaction of intrinsic motivation, self-acceptance, and self-confidence in addition to gaining the value of body and breath awareness, silence, and harmony with nature and with others. Learning each posture and sequence requires self-discipline, perseverance, and responsibility to practice daily. Respect for history and tradition prevails as students follow the ancient guiding principles.

Tai Chi offers opportunities for social interaction, giving and accepting feedback, learning how to help others, and cooperation in the Western classroom environment. Students can con-struct meaning from each movement and meditation, or search for the significance of being in the present, or ponder the state of emptiness glimpsed at the brief point between the inhaling and exhaling of each breath. Competency and confidence derived from accomplishing a pos-ture or form generally transfers to other aspects of the student's life. To augment practice and understanding, students can take the initiative to do outside investigative research to increase the depth of their experience.

Tricia Yu became an experiential facilitator and master teacher by blending Asian and Western ideology as she learned from experience. Pondering how the lessons of the Tao and Tai Chi can influence future educational experiences, Tricia summarized:

> Traditionally, in our learning as children … most of how we have been taught to do things has not included a process for accessing what is true for us. The piece I see in Tai Chi (and many other disciplines) is that it trains us in a simple practical way to be present and to remember our connection to the larger universe and take that into action. It teaches us to be aware of our bodies, our thoughts and emotions, aware of the environment, aware that we are connected to the earth, to all of life on earth and with the cosmos. Tai Chi practice can give us a little piece of our day to remind ourselves of that. It also helps train us in taking that awareness into action in our daily life. (Yu, 2007, interview)

The ancient Tai Chi technique of Push Hands honors the cooperation and synergy between willing partners (Huang & Lynch, 1995, p. 5). It is a dance of giving and receiving, blending movements in a circular pattern to create an empty space that exists between two people, a place that is the essence of the relationship. Tai Chi, similar to experiential education, nurtures the connection between mentor and student; the empty space between them being where truth and the path to wisdom guides the process of teaching (giving) and learning (receiving) in a dynamic interaction of natural movement that sustains the expansion of both.

Tricia Yu has lived this model and her journey demonstrates that incorporating Tai Chi as an experiential program will support and enhance life skills, expand inner wisdom, and contribute to general wellness. Tai Chi practice brings us into the present, a journey of transformation rather than an end result.

References

Anodea J. (2004). *Eastern body western mind: Psychology and the chakra system as a path to the self.* Berkley, CA: Celestial Arts.

Beard, C., & Wilson, J. (2002). *The power of experiential learning: A handbook for trainers and educators.* Sterling, VA: Kogan.

Bennett, B. C. (1992). Tai Chi, a somatic movement art. Retrieved June 2007, from http://somatics.org//library/bbc-taichisomatic.html, pp. 1–7

Chewning, B., Yu, T., & Johnson, J., (2002). T'ai Chi: An ancient exercise for contemporary times. Retrieved May 2007, from http://krapu4.com/taichi/research

Chuen, L. K., (1991). *The way of energy: Mastering the Chinese art of internal strength with Chi Kung exercise.* New York: Fireside.

Crider, D. A., & Klinger, W. (2000). *Stretch your body and your mind (Tai Chi as an adaptive activity).* ERIC #440080. Retrieved June 2007, from http://eric.ed.gov/ERICWebPortal/home portal

Dewey, J. (1963). *Experience and education.* New York: Colliers Books. (Original work published 1938)

Dougherty, P. (2007). *Qigong in psychotherapy: You can do so much by doing so little.* Minneapolis, MN: Spring Forest.

Gendlin, E .T. (1980). Imagery is more powerful with focusing: Theory and practice. Retrieved July 2007, from http://www.focusing.org/fot/gendlin_imagery.html

Greenaway, R., (1999). Experiential learning cycles: Active reviewing. Retrieved July 2007, from http://www.Reviewing.co.uk/ research/learning.cycles.htm

Hanna, R. (1990). Clinical somatic education: A new discipline in the field of health care. Retrieved August 2007, from http://www.somatics.com/hannart.htm

Huang, C. A., & Lynch, J., (1995). *Mentoring: The Tao of giving and receiving wisdom.* New York: Harper.

Hutchinson, D. (2000). Over the edge: Can holistic education contribute to experiential education? Association of Experiential Education. *Journal of Experiential Education*. Retrieved June, 2007, from http://findarticles.com

Jahnke, R. (2002). *The healing promise of Qi: Creating extraordinary wellness through Qigong and Tai Chi.* New York: McGraw Hill.

Kolb, D. (1984). *Experiential learning: Experience as the source of learning and development.* New York: Prentice-Hall.

Lewis, D. (2004). *Free your breath, free your life.* Boston: Shambala.

Lucas, G. (Director). (1977). *Star wars I, The original trilogy.* USA: 20th Century Fox.

Rohnke, K. (1987). *Silver bullets: A guide to initiative problems, adventure games, stunts and trust activities.* Hamilton, MA: Kendall/Hunt.

Rohnke, K. (2000). *Funn stuff.* Dubuque, IO: Kendall/Hunt.

Rohnke, G. (2001). Introducing the experiential learning spiral. *KAHPERD (Kansas Association of Health, Physical Education, Recreation, Dance) Journal, 72*(2), 33–37.

Simpson, S. (2003). *The leader who is hardly known: Selfless teaching from the Chinese tradition.* Oklahoma City, OK: Wood 'N' Barnes.

Tai Chi Health with Tricia Yu. (2005). Retrieved July, 2007, from http://www.taichihealth.com

Wikipedia. (2007) Qi. Retrieved June 2007, from http.//en.wikipedia.org/wolo/Qi

Yu, T. (2003). *Tai Chi mind and body.* New York: DK.

Yu, T., & Johnson, J. (1999). *Chi fundamentals: For health professionals and instructors.* Madison, WI: Uncharted Country.

Appendix I
Deserving a Closer Look
Other Thinkers and Suggested Readings

As we pondered the philosophical and programmatic roots for experiential education, our list of influential people grew to over 200 names. We first thought about having our peers choose the 25 to 30 most important, and then solicit authors to write about those historic and contemporary people. We decided instead to have interested experiential educators choose one or more people of significance that they had a passion to write about. The end result was 32 of the chapters included in this book. There are obviously many others who deserve a closer look. This appendix offers brief descriptions and starting references for people from history who the editors of this book think are important. A chapter about any of these people would certainly have been considered for this collection.

John Amos Comenius (1592–1670) was a Moravian theologian who is often considered as the father of modern education. He advocated that there should be free, universal education for both boys and girls of all social classes, and that put him in conflict with the Catholic Church. He believed in experiential learning, having students see things, touch things, and make things; and he was one of the first to suggest that much could be learned from playing.

Suggested Reading

Comenius, J. A. (1957). *Selections of John Amos Comenius* [foreword by Jean Piaget]. New York: UNESCO.
Sadler, J. E. (2007). *J. A. Comenius and the concept of universal education*. New York: Routledge.

David Hume (1711–1776) was a Scottish philosopher and historian, and is considered one of the important figures of modern philosophy. He published *A Treatise on Human Nature* in 1739, and his ideas about all valid knowledge coming from our senses was the foundation for what came to be known as "empiricism." Since all knowledge is believed to be based on experience, information passed from others must be doubted—until the recipient can test out that knowledge through real experiences. The goal of education should be to lead students to believe and trust their own experiences and to mistrust propositions that are based on reason and deduction. Hume's philosophy influenced Rousseau, Pestalozzi, William James, and John Dewey. Since he did not write much about education, secondary sources may prove more valuable.

Suggested Reading

Passmore, J. (1952). *Hume's Intentions*. New York: Basic Books.
Stroud, B. (1977). *Hume*. London: Routledge & Kegan Paul.

Mary Wollstonecraft (1759–1797) was a British writer, philosopher, and early feminist who challenged the educational belief of Rousseau about women not needing a rational education. She suggested that experiential interaction with men in schools would make them better teachers for their children, and that education should be related to the real lives of the students.

Suggested Reading

Todd, M., & Butler, M. (Eds.). (1989). *The complete works of Mary Wollstonecraft*. London: William Pickering.

John F. Herbart (1776–1841) was a German philosopher and educational theorist who developed a pedagogy of education suggesting that the process of instruction involved five stages: preparation, presentation, comparison, integration, and application. In his book, *Outlines of Educational Doctrine* (1835), he wrote about the value of instruction being adapted to the child's experience. Like Rousseau and Pestalozzi, he thought natural experience was valuable in learning, but, in contrast to those two important educational theorists, he believed that literary endeavors were also valuable.

Suggested Reading

Blyth, A. (1981). From individuality to character: The Herbartian sociology applied to education. *British Journal of Educational Studies, 29*(1), 69–79.
Parker, S. C. (1912). A *textbook in the history of modern elementary education*. Boston: Ginn.

Fredrich Froebel (1782–1852) was the founder of early childhood education. He loved the outdoors and studied to be a forest ranger as a young man. After studying with Pestalozzi, he founded the "Play and Activity Institute" in Germany, and later coined the term "kindergarten." He said learning involved free self-activity, creative expression, social interaction, and motor expression; and he thought play could help children become aware of their place in the world.

Suggested Reading

Bruce, T., Findlay, A., Read, J., & Scarborough, M. (Eds.). (1995). *Recurring themes in education*. London: Paul Chapman.
Froebel, F. (1967). *Fredrich Froebel: A selection of his writings* (I. Lilley, Ed. & Trans).. Cambridge, UK: Cambridge University.

Ralph Waldo Emerson (1803–1882), famous American essayist, poet, and leader of the transcendentalist movement in the 18th century. He advocated that government should provide sound educational programs for all citizens, and was in favor of a classical curriculum of instruction. His own teaching involved very traditional lecturing, but his descriptions of the learning process made it clear that he thought life experiences were very important. He suggested that learning from "country labors," and interaction with others, was very important and once wrote that "life is our dictionary."A summary of his thoughts on education was compiled from his notes and lectures after his death, and is included in many of the collections of his works.

Suggested Reading

Emerson, E. (Ed.). (1929). *Ralph Waldo Emerson Lectures: Emerson on Education*. New York: William Wise.
Sullivan, W. (1972). *New England man of letters*. New York: Macmillan.

Max Stirner (1806–1856) was a German philosopher who started out as a schoolteacher. He wrote *The False Principle of Our Education* (1844) in which he suggested that society often implants ideas and values into the minds of the young which then become "wheels in the head" making alternative views difficult. He believed that the only way to counteract domination by such "wheels" was for people to gain knowledge and beliefs through action experiences.

Suggested Reading

Spring, J., (1994). *Wheels in the head.* New York: McGraw Hill.
Stringer, M. (2002). *The false principle of our education.* New York: Ralph Myles.

Karl Marx (1818–1883) did not write much on education, but his ideas had influence on academics and educators who followed him. One of his central themes was that consciousness was determined by the actual living of everyday events. He believed that all people should have the same opportunities for life experiences that would enrich their consciousness. He also believed that the educational system, as part of the superstructure of society, tended to reflect the erroneous values of society, and would be improved when those values were changed.

Suggested Reading

Allman, P. (2001). *Critical education against global capitalism: Karl Marx and revolutionary critical education.* Westport, CT: Bergin & Garvey.
McLellan, D. (1973). *Karl Marx: His life and thought.* New York: Harper & Row.

Leo Tolstoy (1828–1910) is known mostly as a novelist, but he was also a teacher and he published a number of papers on education. One of his arguments was that it was not the intellectuals who should teach the peasants, but the peasants who should teach the intellectuals because their knowledge was based on experiences in the real world.

Suggested Reading

Pinch, A., & Armstrong, M. (Eds.). (1982). *Tolstoy on education.* New York: Fairleigh Dickinson.
Tolstoy, L. (2000). *Tolstoy as teacher: Leo Tolstoy's writings on education* (B. Blaisdel Ed). New York: Teachers & Writers Collaborative.

Francis Parker (1837–1902) was a prominent educator during the last quarter of the 19th century, considered by John Dewey as the "father of progressive education." He was influenced by progressive European educators like Pestalozzi and Froebel, and integrated activities of play, physical motor instruction, and field trips into the curriculum. He believed in integrating reading with other subjects and today his methods are considered as an early form of whole-language learning. He was a colleague and mentor of Wilbur S. Jackman at the Cook Country Normal School in Chicago, and encouraged him to become dean at the School of Education of the University of Chicago, where John Dewey was to develop his laboratory school.

Suggested Reading

Hlebowitsh, P. S. (2001) *Foundations of American education: Purpose and promise* (2nd ed., pp. 306–309). Belmont, CA: Wadsworth Thomson Learning.

William James (1842–1920) was a noteworthy American scholar of the 19th century. He was influential in the development of the philosophy of Pragmatism, and the approach to psychology called Functionalism. He wrote about thinking, learning, and the development of the human mind, and suggested that educational theory has to unravel the opposition between the idea that development is from within and from without. He argued that it was introspective observation (reflection) which was the basis of learning. In his famous "Talks to Teachers" in later life, James suggested "good habits are the stuff of which behavior consists."

Suggested Reading

James, W. (n.d.). Retrieved June, 2006, from http:www://des.emory.edu
Richardson, R. (2007). *William James: In the maelstrom of American modernism.* New York: Houghton Mifflin.

G. Stanley Hall (1844–1924) was a psychologist and leader in the child study movement at the end of the 19th century. He observed child development in what many consider as the first psychology laboratory in the United States, resulting in his study of individual differences. He recommended that children be given opportunities to move away from their desks and experience large muscle development. He was the first president of the American Psychological Association, and is considered as a founder of the field of Educational Psychology. His writings on the psychology and education of adolescents are of value in understanding and teaching youth in that period he called "storm and stress," after the German *strum und drang* movement.

Suggested Reading

Hall, G. S. (2004). *Adolescence: Its psychology and its relationship to physiology, anthropology, sociology, sex, crime, religion and education.* New York: Adamant Media Corporation.
Partridge, G. E. (1912). *Genetic philosophy of education: An epitome of the published writings of G. Stanley Hall.* New York: New International Encyclopedia.

Wilbur S. Jackman (1855–1907) was the first dean of the University of Chicago's School of Education, and director of the elementary school. He recommended that children study things in natural settings, and advocated a continuous nature study program from the earliest grades through college. He published his first book, *Nature Study for the Common Schools*, in 1891. The book was organized around a series of questions that could be answered by observation or experimentation throughout the year. He went on to write many books and teaching manuals on nature study. At his death it was written: "It is doubtful whether any man in the country has done so much for the cause of rational nature-study and elementary science."

Suggested Reading

Jackman, W. S. (1895). *Nature study for the common schools.* New York: Henry Holt.
Palmer, E. L. (1944). *Cornell Rural School Leaflet, XXXVIII,* 20–22.

Robert Baden-Powell (1857–1941) is best known as the founding father of the Boy Scout Movement in England, but he was also an innovative educator. He had earned his reputation as a soldier in the Boer War, and his book on army scouting brought him celebrity status in England. He thought that the essential purpose of education should be character development, leading to making manly, good citizens. His notions that education should involve experience, including adventure and community service, were most likely very influential when Kurt Hahn developed Outward Bound. It is reported that when he prepared for writing the founding text on Scouting he looked at a diversity of educational theorists, including Pestalozzi, Montessori, and Ernest Thompson Seton—all of whom were advocates of learning by experience.

Suggested Reading

Baden-Powell, R. (1908). *Scouting for boys: A handbook for instruction and good citizenship*. London: Horace Cox.

Liberty Hyde Bailey (1858–1954) is often considered the father of the nature study movement. He was a horticulturist, botanist, and professor of agriculture. He was an advocate of life-long learning, especially from experiences in the outdoors in rural areas, and he championed adult education. He had a long career as director of the College of Agriculture at Cornell University, and wrote many books on the importance of experiences with nature.

Suggested Reading

Bailey, L. H. (1903). *The nature study idea: Being an interpretation of the new school movement to put the child in sympathy with nature*. New York: Doubleday.

Rudolph Steiner (1861–1925) was an Austrian philosopher and advocate of educational reform. He believed that education should have a developmental point of view, and attend to each child's "natural rhythms of everyday life." In many ways, his educational concepts parallel those of Maria Montessori, for he believed that learning in early childhood was largely based on sensory and experiential events. Although he had lectured on education for many years, the first Waldorf School, which was organized around his principles, did not open until 1919 when Steiner was almost 60 years old. Today, there are over 1,000 Waldorf Schools around the world, and his ideas have also had impact on programs of special education and home-schooling. Much information of Steiner and the Waldorf methodology is available on the Internet.

Suggested Reading

Edmunds, F. (2004). *Introduction to Steiner education: The Waldorf school*. New York: Rudolph Steiner Press.
Lachman, G. (2007). *Rudolph Steiner: An introduction to his life and work*. New York: Tarcher.

Rabindranath Tagore (1861–1941) was a Bengali poet, musician, novelist, playwright, and educational reformist. He had early childhood experiences of education in the outdoors under the tutelage of his own father. He later studied in England, and while there he became aware of the European new school movement. His concern about providing meaningful education for all the children of India led him to start an experimental school in 1901—*Shantiniketan*. Cecil Reddie and others who were concerned about developing holistic education programs that could bring mind-body-soul-life to every child later visited the school. Tagore was awarded the Nobel Prize for literature in 1913, and he was knighted by the British Crown in 1913. His efforts for educational reform were limited, until Ghandi picked them up in his program of "Unity Education."

Suggested Reading

Narmadeshwar, J. (1994). Tagore. *Prospects: The Quarterly Review of Education*, xxiv (3/4), 603–619.
Radhakrishnan, S. (1918). *The philosophy of Rabindranath Tagore*. London: McMillan.

Nicholas Black Elk (1862–1950) was an Oglala Sioux and a respected interpreter of the wisdom of Wakan Tanka (great spirit). He was interviewed by John C. Neihardt shortly before his death, and the ensuing book, *Black Elk Speaks*, became very popular in the 1960s because it was an important account of Native American traditions. Black Elk also collaborated with Joseph Epes

Brown on a book about Native rituals. Native wisdom is certainly worthy of close study when searching for theoretical foundations for experiential educational practices.

Suggested Reading

Black Elk, & Brown, J. (1989). *The sacred pipe: Black Elk's account of the seven rites of the Oglala Sioux.* Oklahoma City: University of Oklahoma.
Black Elk, & Neihardt, J. (2004). *Black Elk speaks.* Winnipeg, Canada: Bison Books.

George Herbert Mead (1863–1931) was a sociologist/philosopher who studied with William James, became a life-long friend of John Dewey, and joined Dewey at the University of Chicago. Although his writings about education were limited, he laid groundwork for a social interaction theory which suggests that the individual's concept of self and self-in-society emerges from social interaction. His student, Herbert Blumer, later coined the term "symbolic interactionism" for the process, and it has since been explored by a number of social psychologists. The concept can help explain how intensive small group interactions affect the individual.

Suggested Reading

Blumer, H. (1969). *Symbolic interactionism: Perspective and method.* Berkeley: University of California.
Mead, G. H., & Morris, C. (1934). *Mind, self and society.* Chicago: University of Chicago.

Marietta Johnson (1864–1938). In 1907 she founded the School of Organic Education in Fairhope, Alabama. John Dewey visited the school and later wrote about it. There were no tests or grades at the Organic School, and no homework assignments until the high school years. Johnson believed in children living natural lives, and studying both in and about the outdoors. The school had animals and gardens, and the children's learning was guided by their interests. She believed in helping children learn to think for themselves and saw the ultimate goal of education to be self-discipline and living a life of involvement with the arts and with social issues.

Suggested Reading

Johnson, M. (2005). *Organic education: Teaching without failure..* Fairhope, AL: Marietta Johnson Museum of Organic Education.

Luther Gulick (1865–1918) & **Charlotte Gulick** (1866–1928). Luther Gulick was a medical doctor and educator who advocated camping and physical fitness for young people. He worked with the YMCA and his idea about development of the whole child (body, mind, & spirit) became their triangular logo. He also helped found the Boy Scouts in America. His wife, Charlotte, was also an advocate of camping and outdoor experiences, and she founded the Camp Fire Girls organization.

Suggested Reading

Finch, I. (Ed.). (1996). *The life and letters of Luther Halsey Gulick.* Berkeley: University of California Press.

Hermann Leitz (1868–1919) graduated with degree in theology and philosophy in Germany, and then took a teaching position at Cecil Reddie's Abbotsholme School in England. He admired the "new school" approach, and wrote a book criticizing traditional education in Germany. As an educational reformist, he founded country boarding schools that emphasized learning by experience. International travel was an important part of the Leitz schools; his students were highly visible decked out in knickers and red hats, climbing in the Alps, hiking the countryside in England, or walking the streets of Paris. He recognized that significant learning is based on personal experiences, and he criticized teachers who attempted to put their own thoughts into the heads of their students.

Suggested Reading

Breckman, W. W. (1964). Some review of the history of German education. *Comparative Education Review*, 8(3), 281–284.
Koerrenz, R. (1989). *Hermann Leitz: A biography* (in German). Berlin: Peter Lang.

William H. Kilpatrick (1871–1965) was a student of John Dewey's, and became one of the leaders of the progressive education movement. He taught at Teacher's College, Columbia University, for over 40 years, where he developed the concepts of project learning and purposeful activity for his students. The project method involved students choosing and directing their own studies. This, along with his emphasis on breaking the large group down into interactive small groups, made him a very popular teacher, and he had an impact on thousands of teachers. Kilpatrick was criticized by the McCarthyites in the 1950s because his teaching methods were contrary to traditional practices in higher education.

Suggested Reading

Bieneke, J. A. (1998). *And there were giants in the land: The life of William Heard Kilpatrick*. New York: Peter Lang.
Kilpatrick, W. H. (1952). *Philosophy of education*. New York: Macmillan.

Homer T. Lane (1875–1925) was one of the most radical and controversial educators of the first quarter of the 20th century. He was a proponent of self-government and character building for institutionalized children, and advocated giving them free choice about what to study—and whether to study at all! He took Dewey's ideas about the value of learning democratic processes to an extreme. Some educational historians suggest that Lane's ideas gave rise to free school movement that was to follow. A. S. Neill admitted that his ideas on self-government at Summerhill came from Lane. He built and directed a residential school in England (the Little Commonwealth), which was soon recognized as a truly alternative school.

Suggested Reading

Lane, H. (1928). *Talks to parents and teachers*. London: George Allen & Unwin.
Swartz, R. (n.d.). John Dewey and Homer Lane: The odd couple among educational theorists. *Education Revolution Magazine*. Retrieved May 2010, from http://www.educationrevolution.org/archieves
Wills, W. D. (1964). *Homer Lane: A biography*. London: George Allen & Unwin.

Teilhard de Chardin (1881–1955) was a French Jesuit priest (criticized by the order) and a paleontologist (he discovered the Pekin man), who became a reconstruction philosopher with a humanistic and globalistic orientation. His concept of personalism involves evolution of self from interaction with others and the world, and differs from individualism which too often results from traditional education. His optimistic philosophy centers on an evolutionary process that is taking humankind to increasing global and planetary consciousness.

Suggested Reading

Teilhard de Chardin, P. (1995). *The future of man*. New York: Harper & Row.
Teilhard de Chardin, P. (2000). *Building the earth*. Wilkes-Barre, PA: Dimension Books.

A. S. Neill (1883–1973) was a British educator who founded the Summerhill School which had a philosophy guided by student self-government and self-development. He advocated letting students follow their own desires and interests in seeking experiences that had personal meaning for them. Because many of the students at Summerhill had behavioral problems, Neill functioned as both a classroom teacher and a individual tutor providing "private lessons," which were in reality counseling sessions. Erich Fromm wrote the foreword to Neill's book on Summerhill. Neill admitted that he did not have a systematic educational philosophy, but his ideas had influence on many other educators, and were important to the "free school" movement of the 1960s.

Suggested Reading

Neill, A. S. (1960). *Summerhill: A radical approach to child rearing.* Oxford, UK: Hart.
Neill, A. S. (1996). *Summerhill school: A new view of childhood.* New York: St. Martin's Press.

Susan Issacs (1885–1948) brought psychoanalytic ideas to progressive education in England. Her essential argument was that the educational development of children was tied to their emotional well-being, and in her early years of teaching she thought it important that there was freedom in the classroom and on the playground so that students could express, and not repress, emotionality.

Suggested Reading

Isaacs, S. (1930). *The intellectual growth of young children.* London: Routledge.
Issacs, S. (1933). *Psychological aspects of child development.* London: Routledge.

May T. Watts (1893–1975) was a naturalist and teacher of teachers. She was an experiential educator who did most of her teaching by taking students outside to hike in nature. One example of her activism was writing a letter to the *Chicago Tribune* in 1963 that inspired the movement to use abandoned railroad right-of-way to be used as hiking and biking trails throughout Illinois. She worked for many years developing and mapping nature trails and nature centers in Illinois.

Suggested Reading

Watts, M. (1975). *Reading the landscape of America.* New York: Collier Books. (Republished in 1999 by Nature Study Guild, PO Box 1048, Rochester, New York)

George Counts (1894–1974) was a progressive educator who advocated changes in the educational system to take into account the emergence of a world society. He was considered as one of the founding fathers of global education. His proposal involved replacing the traditional American emphasis on rugged individualism and the competitive spirit with a more humanistic/socialistic curriculum. He was a strong advocate for empowering individual teachers to take stands against the traditionalists, and was an early advocate of teacher unions. Conservative champions of democratic capitalism are typically very critical of Counts.

Suggested Reading

Counts, G. (1978). *Dare the school build a new social order.* Carbondale: Southern Illinois University Press.
Gutek, G. (1970). *The educational theory of George Counts.* Columbus: Ohio State University.

Jidda Krishnamurti (1895–1986) was a religious philosopher from India who traveled the world for over 60 years teaching that holistic growth and life satisfaction required individuals to focus on their inner truth; the most important book to read is the "book of self." He was critical of modern education because it involved passing along outer wisdom instead of enhancing inner wisdom. He said that modern education tends to cultivate a dependence on the state and other institutions, and a craving for success measured in terms of outside criteria. He recommended that teachers attend to the wisdom within each child, and that they facilitate experiences which will help students find self-realization.

Suggested Reading

Krishnamurti, J. (1981). *Education and the significance of life*. San Francisco: Harper & Row.

Jean Piaget (1896–1980) was a Swiss psychologist who is considered by many as the father of educational constructivism. His lifelong concern was with the question of how knowledge develops and changes. He suggested that learning is a progressive construction of logically embedded cognitive structures that change through time, and thus the prior learning experiences of children are important to how they react to, and learn from, their present situations. He believed that children's modes of thinking are different from those of adults, and that development involves building sequential blocks of knowledge.

Suggested Reading

Piaget, J. (2001). *Language and thought of the child*. London: Routledge & Kegan Paul.
Piaget, J., & Inhelder, B. (2000). *The psychology of the child*. New York: Basic Books.

Reynold E. Carlson (1901–1997) was responsible for the early development of Indiana University's curriculum in outdoor education and recreation, and the establishment of the Bradford Woods Outdoor Center. Prior to that, he worked as a teacher, principal, coach, and part-time Yosemite National Park ranger. He was president of the American Camping Association for a time, and was one of the pioneers in educating teachers and recreation specialists about the value of outdoor experiential learning.

Suggested Reading

Smith, J., Carlson, R., & Donaldson, G . (1965). *Outdoor education*. Englewood Cliffs, NJ: Prentice-Hall.

Julian W. Smith (1901–1975). After serving as a secondary school teacher and principal, Julian Smith became Director of the Outdoor Education Project of the American Association for Health, Physical Education and Recreation at Michigan State University in 1953. He taught thousands of teachers about the value of outdoor education. He suggested that outdoor education would not only help in the conservation of natural resources and restoring the earth's ecological balance, but because of its focus on direct outdoor experiences, it would also serve to prevent "human erosion."

Suggested Reading

Smith, J. W. (1972). *Outdoor education for American youth* (2nd ed.). Englewood Cliffs, NJ: Prentice-Hall.

Erik Erikson (1902–1994) was a Jewish German developmental psychologist who studied to become a psychoanalyst and became one of the prominent Neo-Freudians. In 1936 he left

Germany to join the Institute of Human Relations at Yale University. He developed a theory of the eight stages of psychosocial development, focusing on resolving the typical life conflicts (e.g., identity-crisis, trust vs. mistrust, ego integrity vs. despair). He is best known for his book *Childhood and Society* (1950), but the complexity of his ideas is best summarized in a biography by Robert Coles.

Suggested Reading

Coles, R. (1970). *Erik Erikson: The growth of his work*. New York: Atlantic Little Brown.

Theodore Brameld (1904–1987) was an American educational philosopher who took John Dewey's ideas about progressive education to a higher level. While Dewey had emphasized the importance of education for learning about democracy, Brameld thought the goal of education should be to create critical, justice-seeking, citizens of the world. He laid groundwork for education as important to global economics, global environmentalism, and preparation for a multicultural world. Like Dewey, he thought there should be changes in the processes of education, but he also thought there should be changes in curriculum content. He was considered to be an educational reconstructionist.

Suggested Reading

Brameld, T. (1956). *Toward a reconstructed philosophy of education*. New York: Dryden Press.
Brameld, T. (1965). *Education as power*. New York: Holt, Rinehart & Winston.

Myles Horton (1905–1990) was an adult educator and social activist known as "the radical hillbilly." He was founder of the Highlander Folk School in Tennessee, which emphasized learning by doing—including storytelling, folk music, dramatic arts, and creative expression. He emphasized close, democratic interactions between teachers and students, as opposed to the traditional model of teachers telling students what to learn. Highlander was a rallying point for training leaders for the civil rights movement of the 1960s.

Suggested Reading

Horton, M., Kohl, J., & Kohl, H. (1990). *The long haul: An autobiography*. New York: Teachers College.

Abraham Maslow (1908–1970) was a humanistic psychologist whose concepts about the hierarchy of needs and self-actualization were important in the founding of the "third force" in American psychology. He saw education as important for both learning and the personal development of students. He believed that teachers must consider the student's needs, and adjust their practices to the interests and motivations of the students. Although he did not write a great deal about education, his thoughts on human development and interaction are important. In his later years, Maslow became interested in a "fourth force" for psychology, opening the door to what is now called "transpersonal education."

Suggested Reading

Maslow, A. (1968). *Toward a psychology of being*. New York: Van Nostrand.
Maslow, A. (1971). *The further reaches of human nature*. New York: Viking.

Paul Goodman (1911–1972) was a poet, writer, social/political critic, educational reformist, and Gestalt counselor whose friendship with Fritz Perls led to the first textbook on Gestalt Therapy in 1951. His next book, *Growing Up Absurd*, brought him attention from educators and the youth counter-culture. He suggested that more learning occurs from "incidental process" than from formal classroom instruction, and advocated that students be given more choice about what, when, and whether to learn. He argued that most teachers were ineffective in trying to pass on cultural values via lectures and reading assignments; his message promoted learning from experience.

Suggested Reading

Goodman, P. (1962). *Growing up absurd*, New York: Vintage.
Perls, F., Goodman, P., & Hefferline, R. (1951). *Gestalt therapy*. New York: Julian.

Jack Gibb (1914–1994) was a psychologist who first became involved with small group processes at the National Training Laboratory (NTL), and he was the co-author of a book on training group methodology. His interest in the importance of trust in interpersonal relationships led him to develop TORI theory (trust, openness, realization, & interdependence), and to establish TORI communities. His analysis of the dynamics of trust in small groups should be valuable to experiential educators. His biographical trilogy summarized his life's work. Gibb's theory and practice has been kept alive by his followers, and most of his work is available on the web.

Suggested Reading

Gibb, J. (1995). *Trust: A new vision of human relationships for business, education, family and personal living*. North Hollywood, CA: Newcastle.

Nicholas Hobbs (1915–1983) was a child-centered psychologist and educator who spearheaded project Re-ED, a National Institute of Mental Health program to develop a learning program for emotionally disturbed children. The project gave rise to his book outlining 12 principles of education/counseling with the troubled child, and a network of special schools around the country that operate under Re-ED principles. Most programs utilizing this model are quite experiential, and many of them take place in outdoor residential school facilities.

Suggested Reading

Cantrell, R., & Cantrell, M. (2007). *Helping troubled children and youth*. Memphis, TN: Jaco Bryant Printer.
Hobbs, N. (1982). *The troubled and troubling child*. San Francisco: Jossey-Bass.

Virginia Satir (1916–1988) was an American psychologist, best known for her approach to family therapy. She completed her formal education at the University of Chicago when Carl Rogers was there, and there are parallels in their ideas about personal growth and development. Her most famous book was *Conjoint Family Therapy*, published in 1964; but the main focus of her career was the process of helping others with the task of "becoming fully human." Her books on the process of personal growth, and her ideas about the Change Process Model for organizations, have relevance to the field of experiential education.

Suggested Reading

Nerin, W. F. (1986). *Family reconstruction: Long day's journey into light*. New York: Norton.
Satir, V. (1988). *The new peoplemaking*. New York: Science and Behavior Books.

Ivan Illich (1926–2002) was an Austrian philosopher and social reformer. His criticism of social institutions, including the schools, earned him an international audience in the 1970s, but his work is still not part of most higher education programs in educational philosophy. In his celebrated book, Deschooling Society (1971), he argued that formal schooling was not feasible because the learning was too remote from the real world. He suggested that learning outside the schools was more important and predicted that the new technologies would someday connect parallel learners in different places.

Suggested Reading

Hansom, P. (2001). *Twentieth-century European cultural theorists*. Detroit, MI: Gale Group.
Illich, I. (1999). *Deschooling society*. London: Marion Boyers.

Lawrence Kohlberg (1927–1987), an American psychologist, is best known for his work on moral development. He was a close follower of Jean Piaget's theory of the stages of cognitive development, and transposed this view to the development of morals. Like Piaget, he believed that life experiences carried the child through the various stages. While many experiential educators are familiar with Kohlberg's theory, its relationship to the goals of many outdoor-experiential programs has not been fully explored.

Suggested Reading

Kohlberg, L. (1981). *The philosophy of moral development: Moral stages and the idea of justice, Vol. 1*. New York: Harper Collins.
Power, F., Higgins, A., & Kohlberg, L. (1991). *Lawrence Kohlberg's approach to moral education*. New York: Columbia University.

Thomas Hanna (1928–1990) is the founder of somatology, which involves a philosophy of psychology and education. Hanna defines somatology as "the science of experience," and he recognizes experience as both a mind and body process. He speaks of whole body learning, and he believed that the goal of the educator should be to help students become aware of their mind-body totality in order to integrate these two aspects of being. To achieve this goal, education has to include action learning, wherein the student moves his/her body in space. Hanna's ideas support the use of movement like Tai Chi in educational programs, and can help in understanding the complexity of the mind-body process in activities such as climbing.

Suggested Reading

Hanna, T. (1970). *Bodies in revolt: A primer in somatic thinking*. New York: Holt, Rinehart & Winston.
Hanna, T. (1993). *The body of life*. New York: Healing Arts Press.

Neil Postman (1931–2003) was a media theorist and critic of television and education. He authored 18 books and hundreds of magazine and journal articles. In 1969 he gained nationwide popularity when he paired with Charles Weingartner on a book criticizing modern education. He suggested that education is consumed by technological advances which dehumanize the learning process. He believed that information flows from the media without context and the learner does not connect it to underlying theory, meaning, or purpose. According to Postman, the cure lies in more direct human interactions.

Suggested Reading

Postman, N. (1995). *The end of education*, New York: Vintage.
Postman, N., & Weingartner, C. (1987). *Teaching as a subversive activity*, New York: Laurel.

Appendix II
Editors' Dialogue

Introduction

The following dialogue between the co-editors is designed to help you, the reader, to reflect on some of the ideas presented in this book. Our hope is that the contents will stimulate your thoughts and feelings about experiential education, and that through this process, your philosophy of teaching and learning will be sharpened and clarified. We believe that these brief "peeks" into the lives of the people included between the covers of this volume will take your philosophy and practice to higher levels.

Tom: My first thought as we finish our work on this volume is about it being another great adventure—an adventure in exploring the ideas and words of great thinkers and doers. That made me recall our earlier conversation about how significant learning can come from seemingly passive experiences, not just from active ones. I've had many significant and important experiences with books, lectures, and conversations. While I may remember much more about more active somatic experience than just my encounters with words, I think experiential educators have to recognize that adventures with words and other symbols can be important as triggers to remember past experiences.

Cliff: I've had many engaging experiences with words—both spoken and written. I've thought a lot about whether a lecture can be an example of an event that leads to a meaningful experience. Most of the lectures I've heard have gone in one ear and out the other. Why haven't I retained much from them? However, there are some I've heard that still linger in my memory, although I can't quote many of the specific ideas. I'm a sensory learner and the more senses I can engage at the time, the more I can retain of the event. If reflecting on events results in producing an experience of lasting value, then maybe the reflection component has to be present; it must be done with thoroughness and care. I also have to be interested and engaged in the topic, see some future application, and have some past experiences that relate to the lecture.

Tom: Those are good points. Reflection on the experience may be the key, and perhaps we tend to reflect more on whole body experiences than simple word input from a lecture or a book. Many recognize that experiences have significant impact only if we reflect on them, so experiences with words have to be accompanied by or followed by reflection if meaning is to be expanded.

Cliff: I also need some knowledge about the topic I am learning and about to "hang" these new ideas upon. I think of prior knowledge as kind of a coat rack on which I hang the new "facts-hats" I receive in a lecture or from reading. I remember Caine and Caine (1994) writing about two kinds of memory. The first is called taxon memory. This kind of retention requires that I rehearse the content several times. There has to be a reason to remember particular facts. These facts are usually isolated from other facts I've memorized. I work at remembering these facts only when there is good reason to do so, and I can link them together somehow. For example, if I want to order a video I've seen offered on TV by calling a phone number, I work at remembering it until I can find a pencil to write it down. Most lectures afford opportunities to apply taxon memory, but often the information comes too fast and furiously for me to remember much of it. As a result, I have learned to take notes and refer to them afterwards if I want to retain the information. Most of the time, however, I never look at my notes again. The other kind of memory is called locale or spatial. When we learn something in a wider context through more of our senses, we have to construct mental maps so we can find our way around and remember. Caine and Caine (1994) use the example of remembering what we ate for dinner last night. This is often easier to do than to recall something someone said around the table. Locale or spatial memories always exist in relationship to our location in a place, how we feel, and what we are doing in that place. This memory system is constantly comparing our new place to other places we've been and new events to similar ones we've had. We are usually trying to figure out what is happening around us and how it relates to our life. If we are motivated about being in a certain place, it is easier to recall more of what happens to us. I can remember being so interested in a lecture on discipline given by Alfie Kohn that I perched on the edge of my chair waiting for his every word. I wanted to know about his topic, I found him a dynamic speaker, and I was looking for tips to help me become a better public speaker. Yes, Tom, words can stimulate our memory system and sometimes we can consider lectures a powerful and meaningful experience. We don't have to canoe a whitewater stream in order to get an experiential education and a flow of meaning from an event.

Tom: Before we started this book, we discussed the question of how experiential education can gain greater acceptance in the educational mainstream. In researching the book, I ran across an article by Frederick Wertz about the field of humanistic education once facing the same problem. Let me quote a few lines from that paper (Wertz, 1998):

> Although well understood and respected by some, it is inadequately understood and dismissed by many. (p. 42)

> Many of these problems are attributed to the movement's large proportion of practitioners. (p. 49)

> The most crucial task for humanistic psychology is to find more effective ways of infusing established institutions, upgrading its own institutions, and perhaps even creating new kinds of institutions. (p. 68)

That last statement made me wonder about the possibilities of creating new institutions that emphasize experiential education. I know that the Old Folks and Allies (OFA) group of AEE has had some discussions about creating a national institute on experiential education. Do you have any brainstorms on that?

Cliff: If the OFA group has the energy and desire to start a national institute to promote experiential education, I would encourage them to do that. I do wonder if another institution is the answer to the issue of how to raise the visibility of the experiential field. We have some good institutions for that purpose now. We just need to strengthen them. Experiential education is a theory of instruction that demands some radical changes in how we think about the student-teacher relationship. We tend to teach in the ways we were taught, so perhaps we have to unlearn some of the methods and values that were used to teach us. I still get caught up in trying to guess what the participants in my workshop will "need" or "want". The best way to determine these student learning desires is to ask them, but when I'm planning a workshop my students aren't usually around. If we want to spread the gospel of experiential education, we need to get others excited about the ways in which we teach so they will say, "Hey, this is really the best way to teach a particular concept, skill, value, or habit of mind."

Tom: As I listened to you, I thought "we don't need more institutions, we need better solutions." Maybe our efforts should go into teaching others, one by one, the power of experiential education. If there is to be a central Institute for Experiential Education, I wonder what it would involve? I wonder how it would be different from the Association for Experiential Education (AEE)? Would it employ direct teaching to demonstrate those alternative teacher-student interactions, or just be a clearinghouse of ideology and methodology? I would think that such a program should involve lots of action, not just lots of words.

When you said, "gospel of experiential education," I had a momentary association of your word "gospel" to a paper I did some years back on the need for experiential educators to understand how the experiences they facilitate often impact on the student's spiritual quest. You and I have talked other times about how EE programs relate to spirituality and life's great mysteries.

Cliff: I have thought about how experiential education might incorporate some characteristics of spirituality. Spirituality is not an easy concept to define and explain. To me spirituality is my deep connection to the great wonder and mystery of the planet and universe. I remember that someone famous said, "To be spiritual is to be amazed," but I can't remember who said it. The Latin root means breath or breathing, which is essential to our living and being in touch with our surroundings. Many experiential educators have thought about the connections between their work and the evolving spirituality of their students. I recall the importance of blending the heart, hand, and head as we teach others.

Tom: Often during the past months, as I sat at the computer having experiences with all the words and ideas expressed in this book, I remembered a bumper sticker that says, "I'd rather be fishing." I would close my eyes, remember my many wonderful experiences in the northern boundary waters, and think, "I'd rather be canoeing." Now, in retrospect, I realize that I have learned much from these experiences with words, although I doubt that they will bring those in the field of experiential education any closer to a consensus about the basic definitional and philosophical foundations. Perhaps they only represent our attempt to do what Bill Proudman recommended: "Experiential educators need to continue to grapple with the question of just what is experiential education, and similarly, what is good teaching" (1992, p. 23).

Cliff: The AEE umbrella has many spokes supporting it, and that's why some people can't put their minds around a simple definition of experiential education. We are united by a desire to provide practical, lasting, and useful learning experiences to our students, and we want them to want what we know how to teach. We are also united in our belief that our role as teachers is to help our students learn by creating rich learning environments and nurturing emotional climates.

Tom: Maybe what holds us together is not an encompassing educational philosophy but an appreciation of the value of experiential learning in our own lives.

Cliff: We may be tired of teachers going through the motions and students not coming away with the intended messages. Some would say that teachers aren't teaching if their students aren't learning, and I would agree with that. Sometimes, students come away with a completely different message than what is intended for that lesson. Maybe that's called learning, but I can't call it teaching in the conventional sense. Teachers want to make a positive difference in the lives of their students. Experiential educators want their students to want to learn what they have to teach. That's why I like to teach by receiving and giving questions. When a question sparks a student, then I want to help them find a satisfactory answer for themselves. Good teachers don't have to answer every question their students raise, but they can help in creating the right conditions for an adventurous search for the answer. Teaching to me is attempting to create the right conditions for learners to find the answers to questions that they deem important. That's why we invited the authors of this book to select a person to write about whom they had a passion to learn more about. Experiential educators want to respond to student needs and interests in the way that progressive educators of the past did. They see no problem in combining fun and learning or combining challenge or even confusion with learning. You raise a good point when you state that the commonalities of experiential educators is what connects us philosophically. Maybe the desire to engage our students in exciting and meaningful learning experiences is our common mission.

Tom: When I present ideas to the variety of professionals who make up the field of experiential education, I often try to show them that they are connected because of a common mission. I have them ponder the question, "Why do we do what we do?" Then I suggest an answer: "We do what we do in order to enhance people's awareness and understanding of self, others, environment, the Other, the self-other interdependency, the self-environment interdependency, and the self-other-environment-other oneness." Some of us may focus on awareness of self, in terms of self-esteem and empowerment, while others follow the earth-awareness goals of the historic naturalists and outdoor educators. Many of us are concerned with guiding people to awareness of the self-other interdependency through activities of trust, communication and cooperation, and there are some who see their roles as enhancing the spiritual development of participants. I think this broad overview helps people see their place in a bigger picture. I wonder if an awareness of the inter-relatedness of seemingly unconnected goals is what provides the supportive spokes for the AEE umbrella? Maybe there is no common philosophical orientation, and maybe not even an agreement on the methodology—but there seems to be commonality of mission and intent.

Cliff: I'm not sure that the goal of experiential education is about how to learn as much as it is about how to teach. That would make it more of a theory of instruction than a theory of learning. As soon as I thought about my words I wondered if I can ever teach without learning or ever learn without teaching (or thinking about how I would teach what I'm learning). The terms "teaching" and "learning" may be a senseless dichotomy. Ideally, they are two sides of the same coin. I believe in an old Latin proverb. By learning you will teach; by teaching you will learn (Quotes on Education, n.d., p. 16).

Tom: Or teaching and learning are two unrelated concepts. Rogers used to tell us that he often observed teachers doing lots of teaching even though the students did not seem to be doing lots of learning. Maybe, as you said, if there is no learning going on then whatever that teacher is doing can't really be considered as teaching, at all.

Cliff: Many in the Western world seem to want to create too many false dualistic divisions or dichotomies. I like the idea of creating continuums rather than either/ors. The content of experiential education is whatever an eager student wants to or should learn about. This raises some questions in my mind: What, if any, are the limitations of experiential learning? Is experiential learning only one kind of learning among many others? If so, what are the other kinds of learning? Is there such a thing as non-experiential learning? How can we learn about abstract ideas such as love, justice, or compassion through concrete experiences? I lean toward the idea that all learning results from having experiences in our world. In some of these, we are just not using as many senses or modes of engagement as in others in some type of experiences teachers are mediating what is learned by the use of words, pictures, or some other symbols. You suggested that perhaps the term "experiential learning" is redundant. Maybe we can't have an experience without having some form of learning occur.

Tom: Jasper Hunt's chapter on Alfred North Whitehead discusses the distinction between process and content in education, arguing that the two are interdependent. When I think about that distinction, I ask the question, "What is the content of experiential education?" I don't know that there is a definable content. Even if we came to an agreement about the goals of experiential educators, they might be achieved with different processes and by focusing on different content. That's why I find your idea about experiential education being a theory of instruction, a philosophy about how to teach, interesting. Related to that, I think any theory of experiential education also has to include ideas about the nature of the teacher-student relationship. Experiential education is about how to be a teacher with one or more students, not what to teach.

Cliff: Perhaps experiential educators are just as interested in the process as in the content of the lesson. If the process of learning some important content is painful or boring, they would opt for improving the process in some way more suited to the student's learning style. If the content is meaningless to the learner, they would opt for asking learners to choose alternate content that would be more interesting or necessary in their lives. Most experiential educators care about their students and want to make knowledge acquisition the intrinsic reward, rather than an extrinsic grade, a pat on the back, or words of praise.

Tom: There are two contemporary movements in education that experiential educators may want to think more about, reconstructionism and transpersonal education. The first has been around for many years and suggests that the purpose of education should be to achieve social reform. This movement dates back to the reconstructionists in education who stretched Dewey's ideas, especially Theodore Brameld and George Counts. Richard Kraft challenged the membership to develop and operate programs that followed Counts' hope that educators should have a "vision of a just, moral, and responsible society" (Kraft, 1981, p. 3). I think this challenge is similar to the goals of those who call themselves "global educators," and are interested in creating a more just, moral, tolerant, and responsible world. Those who find value in the critical theory of Paulo Friere could be called educational reconstructionists. In an article about implementing the philosophy of the 21st century as a vehicle of change, Christian Itin (1999) speaks of "change in an individual" (p. 92), but does not mention the broader goals of changing the world. Do you think experiential education should move beyond Dewey's progressivism, and define goals more like the reconstructionists and social activists? I guess I would echo the challenge that George Counts set down more than 75 years ago in his provocative essay, "Dare the Schools Build a New Social Order?" (Counts, 1978).

Cliff: I agree with Counts that schools and their teachers should try to change the world and make it better. This is especially true in the areas of achieving world peace and maintaining a non-toxic sustainable environment. Not everyone agrees that teachers should encourage students to become social activists; many want young people to follow the social order and not change it. One principle of experiential education approved by the AEE Board of Directors in 1994 speaks to this idea of global change: "Relationships are developed and nurtured: learner to self, learner to others, and learner to the world at large" (Proudman, 1995, p. 21). The problem with the schools changing the world is that teachers, principals, and school board members must have courage, take risks, and work very hard to achieve this goal. Accomplishing change in the local community is hard enough; changing the world on a global scale is a complex and difficult challenge. Despite facing barriers to resistance and change, I'd encourage others in our field to not "just do it," but to know why they think this goal is important. This is one reason we wrote this book. Maybe some of the people we introduce in these pages will inspire experiential education professionals to be social activists and make the world a better place. The one big problem with this approach is agreeing on the actions that will eventually improve the world.

Tom: Perhaps, because the experiential education movement dovetailed with the human potential movement and the environmental education movement, we often have emphasized goals of personal growth, group development, and earth consciousness. Maybe the realities of present-day globalization make it important for us to consider even more encompassing goals. The eco-psychologists would argue that the health of people and the health of the planet are interdependent.

Cliff: We are what we eat, breathe, and drink. I think many people are realizing that our quest for riches and convenience poisoned or depleted much of the earth's raw materials needed for long-term survival. I think all experiential educators should also be environmentalists and health and nature "nuts." I'm afraid that this stance is very unpopular with people when their jobs are threatened, when it costs too much to use earth-friendly technology, or when it is too expensive to buy organic food. I do see some signs of hope. One example is a new organization founded in 2006, The Children & Nature Network, which is a movement to reconnect children and nature. It was started by people who are concerned about the future of the world and the present health and well being of our youth.

Tom: That's a great network for experiential educators to check out. Richard Louv (2005/2008) has made a wonderful contribution with his discussion about "nature-deficit disorder." I love his slogan based on the weaknesses of "no child left behind legislation"—he said, "leave no child inside." Others later restated that as "no child left inside."

I sometimes get discouraged by the fact that there have been so many movements aimed at improving the human condition, and such little evidence of real change. Another of these movements has been called "transpersonal education." It is based on transpersonal psychology, which is often considered as the fourth force in psychology (after psychoanalysis, behaviorism, and humanism). Maslow became a transpersonal psychologist in the latter years of his life. Gay Hendricks, who wrote a book on centering activities for the classroom became an advocate for transpersonal education, as did Jack Canfield. The transpersonal approach puts more emphasis on the spiritual dimension of humankind, and on body processes of relaxing, breathing, centering and meditating. In some ways the goal is similar to that of the reconstructionists, in that transpersonal educators want to guide the student to a higher-order consciousness about self, others, environment, and the Other. One chapter in our collection that directly relates to this transpersonal educational perspective is Gloree Rohnke's. Do you think experiential educators should attend to the ideas and practices of transpersonal education?

Cliff: I know that I have moved my thinking and teaching closer toward transpersonal goals in the past decade. My interest in Native American cultures, living today and in the past, reflects my desire to live a life more connected to indigenous people and the rest of nature. I realized that I have only one body/mind during my life on earth, and that I'd better take good care if it. I have begun to participate in indigenous ceremonies, and to travel to meet tribes all over the world. I need these direct experiences as well as the knowledge from books. I guess my focus on Native cultures means that the transpersonal education movement is alive and well, at least in my life.

I recently reread an interesting article in the November Phi Delta Kappan (Keefe, 2007). It was titled, "What is Personalization?" Keefe defines personalized education as "a systematic effort on the part of a school to take into account individual student characteristics and effective instructional practices in organizing the learning environment" (p. 219). He mentions a 1999 review of 24 existing school renewal efforts and notes that about one-third of those demonstrated strong elements of personalization, and another one-third exhibited some features of personalization. Among some of these renewal efforts mentioned were: The New American Schools project, the Coalition for Comprehensive School Improvements, Expeditionary Learning Schools, Outward Bound, and The Foxfire Fund's Core Practices. Keefe explains the philosophy of personalization as including learner-centered teaching, building on the learner's strengths, reducing cognitive deficiencies leading to learner satisfaction and success, stressing the uniqueness of the individual student, accepting student responsibility for self-direction, including a curriculum connected to the student's real life whenever possible, and requiring interactive learning environments designed to foster collaboration and reflective conversation.

Tom: That sounds a lot like experiential education to me.

Cliff: Yes, and such components of a personalized education philosophy are supported by some of the papers in this book. Keefe admits that "antecedents of personalization have been known in the past under different names: nongraded education, continuous progress education, individualized education, and so forth" (Keefe, 2007, p. 218). Maybe we are missing the fact that many aspects of experiential education have already filtered into American school renewal projects, but have not been labeled as such. I've often said that I'm not very concerned with what the label of an educational field is as much as what the philosophy and mission are. We have to look beyond labels and examine what happens to individual students as they learn about their lives and the world around them.

Tom: I like the notion of self-directed learning; I think that's an important alternative to the authoritarian education models which define the knowledge students should have and then compel them to learn it. Plato said, "Knowledge which is acquired under compulsion has no hold on the mind" (Kilpatrick, 1926, p. 299).

That's a personal bias, of course, and some of our personal biases are reflected in this book. One of those is our bias toward having authors choose a person to write about who they see as potentially important to experiential education, or who they feel influenced their thinking. I think back to one of our early discussions about whether we should create our own list of significant figures and find people to write on them, or just solicit authors and let them choose somebody they were passionate about. We opted for the latter alternative, and I'm glad we did. Indeed, that process did leave a few very significant people behind. I think especially of William James, Jerome Bruner, Liberty Hyde Bailey, A. S. Neil, Ivan Illich, Jidda Krishnamurti, and Nell Noddings. These omissions present a challenge for others.

Cliff: I agree that by selecting the authors in this book and then having them choose an influential person to write about, we did the right thing. We want these experiential educators to write with passion about one or more people who really affected their philosophy and practice. Of course, our biases show in whom we selected to write the papers for the book. I know it's impossible to be completely objective as an educator.

We have tried to balance the genders of the authors and the people they wrote about, but we weren't perfect in attaining this goal. We tried to select the most important people who influenced present-day experiential education, but we omitted many other significant players. We tried to examine some key issues in experiential education and we probably missed many others along the way. We tried to help the authors write in as clear a manner as possible, but there may be some confusing or unclear statements in this book. We did our best under the conditions of living the other parts of our lives.

Tom: As we were organizing these chapters, we discussed the fact that there were so many naturalists and outdoor educators who seemed important to us. Does this suggest a bias stemming from our personal appreciation for outdoor experiences? Of course, your background is in outdoor and environmental education, and mine is that combination of psychology (the wilderness within) and outdoor adventure (the wilderness beyond), so that is the direction that our minds go. If there is a bias in the collection, how would you defend it?

Cliff: I'm not embarrassed to admit a bias in favor of outdoor activities and nature involvement. The first classroom was the outdoors. Sometimes people get too hung up on seeking an objective position in life. I don't think that's possible. We are all thinking people with our biases hanging out all over the place. We are all subjective people sometimes trying to appear objective for some reason. One of my pet peeves is to hear environmental educators say that we must be value free when we are teaching about an environmental issue. That's difficult, if not impossible. In selecting an environmental issue to study, we are applying a value judgment. Of course, we can't make our students share our values willingly. Maybe we can coerce younger students into complying with our values, but unless they give up their self-power completely, they usually will be able to hold to what they value.

Tom: I'm glad that we have some chapters about people who represent thinking that is not typically thought of as important to EE. I mentioned Gloree Rohnke's chapter on the influence of somatic activities; other examples would be Sean Blenkinsop's chapter on Martin Buber, and yours on the two Native Americans, Charles Eastman and Luther Standing Bear. I think chapters like that can truly expand our thinking. If there was a narrow definition of experiential education, and greater agreement on the scope of the field, then it might be valuable to lock our sights on a few significant people; but until that exists I think it valuable to expand our thinking by reading about a wide variety of contributors.

Cliff: Expanding awareness of the field of experiential education was one of the reasons we edited this book. Our hope was that by reading how people—other than John Dewey and Kurt Hahn—practiced some of the principles of experiential education in their lives, today's professionals would clarify their philosophies and expand their tools to get their jobs done more effectively. I wonder if that will happen? Personally, I have grown a great deal by reading all these chapters.

Tom: I feel that our book is an exciting first step toward expanding and refining the theory and practice of experiential education. There could certainly be additional volumes written to cover more of the people who are of potential importance. I would challenge those who ask, "Why isn't X included in your book?" to write a paper on him/her. As you know, there are people who have contacted us about writing chapters for another volume. We will have to take time to re-energize before we decide whether or not to tackle that task.

Cliff: We did our best. I think we have collected chapters on some very interesting folks, and hope that reading about them stimulates the thinking of many experiential educators. The project also led us to examine some key issues in experiential education. This was also just a first step, and there are certainly issues in the field that we did not address. I guess that also calls for a follow-up book, too.

Tom: I guess it's time to finish this dialogue. When I search for a parting thought of wisdom, I guess it would be to tell professionals in the field of experiential education to always keep their hearts and minds open to new experiences, and to recognize that spending time reading about the life and wisdom of other thinkers and doers can certainly be a wonderful experience. And, of course, that experience can stimulate personal growth and learning only if is followed by spending time in the reflective process. So, I say to experiential educators—"Here's our book. Read. Reflect!"

Cliff: My parting thought to experiential educators is to encourage them to find a hero or heroine who can help them expand their philosophy of teaching and learning. I hope that the readers of this book will find at least one or two people who really stimulate their thinking, and then go deeper into investigating their lives. The more complete and thought-out our philosophy of education becomes, the better it will serve as a guide to our practice. I think we are both interested in making a contribution to experiential education by helping others clarify why they do what they do. If this happens to more professionals in the field, I'm convinced experiential education will become more integrated into mainstream practice.

References

Caine, R., & Caine, G (1994). *Making connections: Teaching and the human brain. Association for Supervision and Curriculum Development Yearbook* (rev. ed.). New York: Dale Seymour.

The Children & Nature Network. (2006). Http://www.childrenandnature.org

Counts, G. (1978). *Dare the schools build a new social order.* Carbondale: Southern Illinois University.

Hendricks, G. (1975). *The centering book: Awareness activities for children, parents and teachers.* Englewood Cliffs, NJ: Prentice-Hall.

Itin, C. (1999). Reasserting the philosophy of experiential education as a vehicle for change in the 21st century. *The Journal of Experiential Education, 22,* 91–98.

Keefe, J. W. (2007, November). What is Personalization? *Phi Delta Kappan, 89*(3), 217–223.

Kilpatrick, W. H. (1926). *Source book in the philosophy of education.* New York: The Macmillan Company.

Kraft, R. (1981). A call to action and reflection. *Journal of Experiential Education, 4*(1), 1–3.

Louv, R. (2005/2008). *Last child in the woods: Saving our children from nature-deficit disorder.* New York: Algonquin.

Proudman, B. (1992). Experiential education as emotionally-engaged learning. *Journal of Experiential Education, 15*(2), 19–23.

Proudman, B. (1995). Experiential education as emotionally engaged learning. In K. Warren, M. Sakofs, & J. Hunt (Eds.), *The theory and practice of experiential education* (pp. 240–247). Boulder, CO: Association for Experiential Education.

Quotes on Education. (n.d.). Retrieved July 19, 2007, from http://www.escotet.org/web/quotes.html

Wertz, F. (1998). The role of the humanistic movement in the history of psychology. *Journal of Humanistic Psychology, 38*(1), 42–70.

Appendix III
Words of Wisdom
Selected Quotations About Experiential Education and Experiential Learning

All sorts of things can happen in a walk, not the least being experience itself, to write about or talk or draw about. Then the Golden Section becomes inseparable from writing and reading and drawing and conversation. Three ducks on the wing we like better than three ducks on a number card with a static three beside them.

Silvia Ashton-Warner (1964)
Teacher
New York: Bantam (p. 70)

Educators wishing to promote learning from experience...have to revive in their students learning styles which may have been discouraged since primary school—learning from experience depends on learning how to learn from experience.

N. C. Boreham (1989)
Continuing the Dialogue: New Possibilities for Experiential Learning
In S. W. Weil & I. McGill, *Making Sense of Experiential Learning: Diversity in Theory and Practice*. Bristol, PA: The Society for Research into Higher Education & Open University Press (p. 258)

For meaning...remains rooted in the sensory life of the body—it cannot be completely cut off from the soil of direct, perceptual experience without withering and dying.

David Abram (1996)
The Spell of the Sensuous: Perception and Language in a More-Than-Human World
New York: Vintage (p. 80)

Man has nothing at all but experience, and everything he comes to, he comes to only through experience. All his thinking, be it loose or scientific, common or transcendental, starts from experience ultimately in view. Nothing has unconditional value and significance except life. All other thinking, conception, knowledge has value only in so far as in some way or other it refers to the fact of life, starts from it, and has in view a subsequent return to it.

Werke Fichte. Quoted in W. H. Kilpatrick (1926)
Source Book in the Philosophy of Education
New York: The Macmillan Company (p. 19)

The only ground for anticipating failure in taking this path resides in the danger that experience and the experimental method will not be adequately conceived.

John Dewey. Quoted in J. W. Roberts (2005)
Disney, Dewey, and the Death of Experience in Education
Education and Culture, 21 (p. 12)

It stands to reason that in open education the teacher cannot work from a pre-established set of objectives. His or her role is first and foremost to have the students undergo enriching experiences, then help them analyze what they might have learned. Obviously, this pedagogical context leads to questioning certain key elements, such as curriculum, school timetable, and the relationship between student and teacher.

Claude Paquette. Quoted in Y. Bertrand (1985)
Contemporary Theories and Practices in Education
Madison, WI: Magna Publications (p. 49)

Learning involves interaction between the learner and his environment, and its effectiveness relates to the frequency, variety, and intensity of the interaction.

George Leonard (1968)
Education and Ecstasy
New York: Delacorte (p. 77)

Students' abilities to acquire organized sets of facts and skills are actually enhanced when they are connected to meaningful problem-solving activities, and when students are helped to understand why, when, and how these facts and skills are relevant.

J. D. Bransford, A. L., Brown, & R. R. Cocking (Eds.). (2000)
How People Learn: Brain, Mind, Experience, and School
Washington, DC: National Academy Press (p. 23)

Knowledge gained at second hand from books or hearsay is infinitely inferior in quality to knowledge gained at first hand by direct observation and experience with nature.

Aldos Huxley
Quoted in E. Kiley, (Ed.) (1990)
Adventures of a Nature Guide and Essays in Interpretation:
Enos Mills. Friendship, WI: The New Past Press (p. 161)

Before a thing can be learned, it has first to be lived. If it is a feeling, I can't learn it until I have first felt it. If it is a thought, I can't learn it until I first think it. If it is a skilled movement, I cannot learn it until I first make that movement. I learn only and exactly what I live.

W. H. Kilpatrick (1942)
The Role of Camping in Education Today
Camping Magazine, 14(2) (p. 15)

That which can best be learned inside the classroom should be learned there. That which can best be learned in the out-of-doors through direct experience, dealing with native materials and life situations should be learned there.

Lloyd B. Sharp
Quoted in J. Smith (Ed.). (1957)
Outdoor Education for American Youth
Reston, VA: American Association for Health, Physical Education, and Recreation (p. ix)

The traditional way of education was by example and experience and story telling. The first principle involved was total respect and acceptance of the one to be taught. And that learning was a continuous process from birth to death.

> Arthur Solomon
> Quoted in B. Horwood (Ed.) (1995)
> *Experience and the Curriculum*
> Dubuque, IA: Kendall/Hunt (p. iv)

Young animals and plants are given rest, and arbitrary interference with their growth is avoided, because it is known that the opposite practice would disturb their pure unfolding and sound development; but, the young human being is looked upon as a piece of wax or a lump of clay which man can mold into what he pleases.

> Fredrich Froebel (1907)
> *The Education of Man* (translated by R. Hailmann)
> New York: Appleton (p. 8)

We boast of our system of education, but why stop at schoolmasters and schoolhouses? We are all schoolmasters, and our schoolhouse is the universe. To attend chiefly to the desk or schoolhouse while we neglect the scenery in which it is placed is absurd.

> *Henry David Thoreau's Journal*
> October 15, 1859, (XII) (p. 387)

On giving children guidance in their learning: Let it be very little, and avoid the appearance of it. If he goes wrong, do not correct his errors. Say nothing til he sees them and corrects them himself; or at most arrange some practical situation which will make him realize things personally. If he never made mistakes he would never learn properly.

> Jean Jacques Rousseau
> *Emile* (translated by A. Bloom)
> New York: Basic Books (p. 13)

No man's knowledge can go beyond his experience.

> John Locke
> Quoted in the *Oxford Dictionary of Quotations,* 3rd edition (1980)
> New York: Oxford University Press (p. 43)

Learning to see small groups as transcending environment in an organic situation very different from a dyadic relationship, we tried small groups in team building, therapy, education, social planning, organizational development, political action—almost any relationship could be improved by creating intense, organic, intimate, transcending small groups.

> Jack Gibb (1995)
> *The Passionate Path*
> Los Angeles, CA: Omicron Books (p. 44)

It is through and by means of education that individuals can be provoked to reach beyond themselves in their intersubjective space.

> Maxine Greene (1973)
> *Teacher As Stranger: Educational Philosophy for the Modern Age*
> Belmont, CA: Wadsworth (p. 12)

What we have to learn to do, we learn by doing.

> Aristotle
> Quoted in J. Miner & J. Boldt. (1990)
> *Crew Not Passengers*
> Golden, CO: Outward Bound, USA (p. 87)

Learning is influenced in fundamental ways by the context in which it takes place. A community-centered approach requires the development of norms for the classroom and school, as well as connections to the outside world, that support core learning values.

> J. D. Bransford, A. L., Brown, & R. R. Cocking (Eds.). (2000)
> *How People Learn: Brain, Mind, Experience, and School*
> Washington, DC National Academy Press (p. 25)

Much significant learning is acquired through doing. Placing the student in direct experiential confrontation with practical problems, social problems, ethical and philosophical problems, personal issues, and research problems is one of the most effective modes of promoting learning.

> Carl Rogers (1969)
> *Freedom to Learn*
> Columbus, OH: Merrill (p. 162.

Do you know that even when you look at a tree and say: 'This is an oak tree', or 'that is a banyan tree', the naming of the tree, which is botanical knowledge, has so conditioned your mind that the word comes between you and actually seeing the tree? To come to contact with the tree you have to put your hand on it and the word will not help you to touch it.

> Jidda Krishnamurti (1969)
> *Freedom From the Known*
> New York: Harper & Row (p. 25)

Real curriculum integration occurs when young people confront personally meaningful questions and engage in experiences related to those questions—experiences they can integrate into their own system of meanings.

> James Beane (1991)
> The Middle School: The Natural Home of Integrated Curriculum
> *Educational Leadership* 49(2) (p. 9)

Learning is experience. Everything else is just information.

> Albert Einstein
> Quoted in K. Carroll. (2007)
> *A Guide to Great Field Trips*
> Chicago: Zephr Press (frontispiece)

Experiencing things enlightens us and enables us to affirm life in a profound way. Without such experiences, we are apt to maintain superficial standards and fail to win through to deeper experiential truths.

> David Strong (1995)
> *Crazy Mountain: Learning From Wilderness to Weigh Technology*
> Albany: State University of New York (pp. 155–156)

Knowing is not enough; we must apply. Willing is not enough; we must do.

Johann Wolfgang von Goethe
Quoted in M. A. Ledger (2007)
Pew Prospectus
Philadelphia, PA: The Pew Charitable Trusts (p. 7)

Interest gives the ability and energy to see accurately and the incentive to watch for things that may happen around us; added purpose to every outdoor day. Such happy experiences based on interest truly enrich life.

Enos Mills
Quoted in E. Kiley (Ed.). *Adventures of a Nature Guide and Essays In Interpretation: Enos Mills* (1990)
Friendship, WI: The New Past Press (pp. 111–112)

The symbols don't render the experience, they suggest it. If you haven't had the experience, how can you know what it is? Try to explain the joy of skiing to somebody living in the tropics who has never even seen snow. There has to be an experience to catch the message, some clue— otherwise you're not hearing what is being said.

Joseph Campbell
In B. S. Flowers (Ed.) (1988)
Joseph Campbell: The Power of Myth with Bill Moyers
New York: Doubleday (p. 61)

Our real-life experiences and practices should constitute the starting point, not the repository of theory.

L. Peterson (2006)
Toward A Materialist Environmental Ethic
Environmental Ethics, 28(4) (p. 387)

The traditional way of education was by example and experience and by story telling. The first principle involved was total respect and acceptance of the one to be taught. And that learning was a continuous process from birth to death.

Arthur Solomon
Quoted in B. Horwood (Ed.). (1995)
Experience and the Curriculum
Dubuque, IA: Kendall/Hunt (p. iv)

Experience must be the basis of our knowledge of anything, because it is all we have. We deeply believe that all understanding of nature, of which we are a part whether it be physical, biological, chemical, sociological, ethnological or psychological, will be congruent.

T. P. Malone, & P. T. Malone (1987)
The Art of Intimacy
New York: Prentice-Hall (p. 102)

In essence then the human race does have an instinct or impulse for adventure and exploration. There is an inbuilt drive to journey with a degree of uncertainty. The problem of Western man is to reduce the anti-social journeys and challenges in which he can get out of his proper responsibilities. This can best be done by making the self reliant adventure journey in the outdoors a fundamental part of the education of all young people.

Colin Mortlock (1964)
The Adventure Alternative, 2nd edition
Milnthorpe, England: Cicerone Press (p. 64)

Let me define more precisely the elements involved in significant or experiential learning. One element is the quality of personal involvement… Self-initiated involvement is another element… Another element is pervasiveness… Yet another element relates to the learner's evaluation of the event. She knows whether it is meeting her needs, whether it leads toward what she wants to know, whether it illuminates her dark area of ignorance… When such learning takes place, the element of meaning to the learner is built into the whole experience.

Carl Rogers (1994)
Freedom to Learn, 3rd edition
New York: Macmillan (p. 36)

Play is not an isolatable function of childhood that can be localized in playgrounds. It is a pervasive characteristic of all child activity in the total environment.

Paul Goodman (1969)
The Open Look
New York: Funk & Wagnalls (p. 17)

When students are encouraged to make more decisions, especially important ones about meaning, interpretation, and content, the learning is more directly experiential. When important decisions are to be made, and the students make fewer of them and the teacher more, the experiential base for learning tends to diminish. It is possible to have students be very active, but not make any decisions. "Active" does not translate into "experiential".

Tom Herbert
Experiential Learning: A Teacher's Perspective
In B. Horwood (Ed.). (1995). *Experience and the Curriculum*
Dubuque, IA: Kendall/Hunt (p. 21)

What has to be done must be learned by practice. Artisans do not detail their apprentices with theories, but set them to do practical work at an early stage; thus they learn to forge by forging, to carve by carving, to paint by painting, and to dance by dancing. In schools, therefore, let the students learn to write by writing, to talk by talking, to sing by singing, and to reason by reasoning. In this way schools will become workshops humming with work, and students whose efforts prove successful will experience the truth of the proverb: 'We give form to ourselves and to our materials at the same time'.

Comenius
Quoted in W. H. Kilpatrick (1926)
Source Book in the Philosophy of Education
New York: Macmillan (p. 309)

It is not enough to insist upon the necessity of experience, nor even of activity in experience. Everything depends upon the quality of the experience which is had.

John Dewey (1963)
Experience and Education
New York: Collier Books (p. 27)

I know that you, ladies and gentlemen, have a philosophy, each and all of you, and that the most interesting and important thing about you is the way in which it determines the perspective in your several worlds. You know the same of me… The philosophy which is so important in each of us is not a technical matter; it is our more or less dumb sense of what life honestly and deeply means. It is only partly got from books; it is our individual way of just seeing and feeling the total push and pressure of the cosmos.

William James (1907)
Pragmatism
New York: Longmans (p. 3)

'He leadeth me by still waters' was to us only a phrase in a book until we nosed our canoe through the green lagoons.

Aldo Leopold (1966)
A Sand County Almanac
New York: Oxford University (p. 142)

Everything that happens to you is your teacher. The secret is to learn to sit at the feet of your own life and be taught by it.

P. B. Berends (1975)
Whole Child, Whole Planet
New York: Harpers Magazine Press (p. 43)

Skill instructions can rely, therefore, on the simulation of circumstances in which the skill will be used. Education in the exploratory and creative use of skills, however, cannot rely on drills. Education can be the outcome of instruction, though instruction of a kind fundamentally opposed to drill. It relies on the relationship between partners who already have some of the keys which give access to memories stored in and by the community.

Ivan Ilich (1970)
Deschooling Society
New York: Harper & Row (p. 25)

As I began to trust students… I changed from being a teacher and evaluator, to being a facilitator of learning.

Carl Rogers (1982)
Freedom to Learn for the 80's
Columbus, OH: Charles Merrill (p. 26)

We hear and apprehend only what we already half know... Every man thus tracks himself through life, in all his hearing and reading and observation and traveling. His observations make a chain. The phenomenon or fact that cannot in any way be linked with the rest which he has observed, he does not observe.

Henry David Thoreau
Quoted in T. Owen-Towle (1996)
Sauntering
San Diego, CA: Bald Eagle Mountain Press (p. v)

Education is such an ordering of individual experience in the light of past experiences that through the resulting character modifications richer experience occurs to all concerned... Education is a process by which the individual comes into continually increasing possession of himself and his powers...

W. H. Kilpatrick (1942)
Sourcebook in the Philosophy of Education
New York: Macmillan (p. 273)

Briefly, it is his [Eugene Gendlin] view that at all times there is going on in the human organism a flow of experiencing to which the individual can turn again and again as a referent in order to discover the meaning of those experiences.

Carl Rogers (1980)
A Way of Being
Boston, MA: Houghton-Mifflin (p.141)

In a large political science class at a state university, three-fourths of the students were assigned a normal syllabus while the remainder were assigned all of that plus a field placement. One might think that the latter students would suffer academically; after all, they had to spend extra time and energy on field assignments and might even have resented that fact. But those students did better academically and became more personally and substantively engaged with the course because the great things they met by being involved with the community made their bookwork more real.

Parker Palmer (1998.
The Courage to Teach: Exploring the Inner Landscape of a Teacher's Life
San Francisco, CA: Jossey-Bass (p. 118)

Houston Smith recounts the frustration of the Zen teacher who accuses his student of "philosopher's disease" —the compulsion to analyze and reduce the world to rational terms. But then the teacher reconsiders his own assessment of the student, saying, "However, reason can only work with the experience that is available to it. You obviously know how to reason. What you lack is the experience to reason wisely from. For these weeks put reason aside and work for experience.

Houston Smith
Quoted in J. A. Lockwood. (2004)
Prairie Soul
Boston, MA: Skinner House (p. 38)

Our real-life experiences and practices should constitute the starting point, not the repository of theory.

L. Peterson (2006)
Toward a Materialistic Environmental Ethic
Environmental Ethics, 28(4) (p. 387)

To cultivate transformations and prepare adolescents for transition and societal change, learning situations should give full attention to personal and interpersonal as well as academic content. The treatment of content in each domain should be as concerned with intense firsthand experiences and challenging productive activities as with relevant theoretical studies.

Maurice Gibbons. (1990)
The Walkabout Papers: Challenge Students to Challenge Themselves
Vancouver, B.C.: EdiServ, Inc. (p. 37)

How many things do I say, of which I have no experience, only 'knowledge'?

Barry Stevens (1970)
Don't Push the River: It Flows By Itself
Moab, UT: Real People Press (p. 68)

People who talk about education and personal growth and group process are not denying that challenge and adventure are the bedrock of Outward Bound. They are not seeking verbalization and reflection instead of action, but in addition to action, as an enhancement and not as a substitute.

Thomas James. (1980)
Can the Mountains Speak for Themselves
Colorado Outward Bound School
Retrieved January, 2005, from www.wilderdom.com/facilitation

The more information we consumed, the more our mental lives were dominated by direct experience with information representing the world rather than direct experience with the world itself. And the more we grew accustomed to experiencing the world indirectly, by means of our more complex representations, the more we hungered for information of all kinds—and the more we turned our attention to inventing new ways to create it.

Al Gore (1993)
Earth in the Balance: Ecology and the Human Spirit
New York: Plume (p. 199)

We may misunderstand, but we do not misexperience.

Vine Deloria, Jr.
Quoted in N. S. Hill (Ed.). (1995)
Words of Power: Voices From Indian America
Golden, CO: Fulcrum Publishing (p. 31)

About the Editors

Thomas E. Smith, co-editor, began considering himself a "Psychologist/Wilderness Guide" in the 1960s, shortly after receiving his PhD in Clinical Psychology, when he guided groups on journeys to "the wilderness beyond and the wilderness within." Along the way he has been a college professor, the director of a community mental health center, a special education psychologist, and private practicing therapist. He has been "retired" for 20 years, but is still active in writing, teaching and presenting workshops. He has authored 10 books related to experiential education. His own journey to the wilderness beyond and wilderness within continues as he advocates the process, as well as the goal.

Clifford E. Knapp, co-editor, has been an experiential educator since working as a camp counselor in college. He became a teacher and taught all grades levels. Most of his career was spent teaching at two universities. He earned his bachelor's degree in junior high education, a master's degree in administration, and a doctorate in curriculum and instruction. He retired from Northern Illinois University in 2001 and continues to write, travel, and present workshops. He has interests in environmental ethics, indigenous cultures, processing experience, and history. He is a life-long learner who thrives on creating new ways of teaching and learning about nature and human nature.

About the Contributing Authors

Pete Allison works at The University of Edinburgh and is responsible for guiding graduate students in Outdoor and Experiential Education. He has a PhD in moral philosophy and outdoor education and has been involved in outdoor and experiential education throughout his life. Pete's research interests are in moral and ethical issues, wilderness, epistemology, and the construction of knowledge in different fields. Much of his interest in outdoor and experiential education is the result of expeditions and his experiences with traditional education. He maintains active interests in mountaineering, skiing, cycling, and canoeing in wilderness areas.

Sean Blenkinsop is an assistant professor in the Faculty of Education at Simon Fraser University in Vancouver, Canada. He has a doctorate in the philosophy of education from Harvard University and master's degree in experiential education from Minnesota State, Mankato. His current research interests include ecological education, existentialism, and issues of imagination in education, but he really wants to get out and paddle more.

Andrew J. Bobilya graduated from the experiential education program at Minnesota State University in Mankato, and then attended the University of Minnesota to earn his doctorate. He is currently an assistant professor in the Outdoor Education Department at Montreat College in North Carolina. His research interests include the impact of experiential education orientation programs for college students and the role of solitude in wilderness programs. He has served as an instructor, trainer, and facilitator of many outdoor education programs, and has worked with Wheaton College's High Road Wilderness Program. He has been an active member of the Association for Experiential Education (AEE) for over a decade.

Mary Breunig has been involved in outdoor and experiential education for 20 years. She started her career as a wilderness trip guide and did that full time for seven years. Mary is currently an assistant professor at Brock University in Ontario where she teaches courses in outdoor and experiential education and leadership, in addition to a number of field-based courses. Her research interests include the intersections between experiential education and issues of social justice, critical pedagogy and Freirean praxis, and wilderness trips and the psychological sense of community. Mary is currently the co-editor of the *Journal of Experiential Education*.

Julie Carlson teaches experiential education and educational leadership at Minnesota State University, Mankato. With nearly three decades of experience in elementary education, residential outdoor environmental education, and adventure education, she estimates she is just past the mid-point of her evolutionary journey as an educator. Her highest interests lie in the history of outdoor education, experiential learning theory, philosophy of leadership, qualitative and life history research methods, and power issues relating to group process and social exchange theories.

David Carr is professor of Philosophy of Education at The University of Edinburgh. He is author of *Educating the Virtues* (1991), *Ethics in Teaching* (2000), and *Making Sense of Education* (2003), as well as numerous philosophical and educational papers. He is also editor of *Education, Knowledge and Truth* (1998), co-editor (with Jan Steutel) of *Virtue Ethics and Moral Education* (1999), and (with John Haldane) of *Spirituality, Philosophy and Education* (2003). He has recently been interested in the significance of the arts for moral education in general and for environmental education in particular.

Brad Daniel is professor of Environmental Studies, Biology, and Outdoor Education at Montreat College in North Carolina. He holds a master's degree in Outdoor Teacher Education from Northern Illinois University, and a PhD in Environmental Studies from Antioch New England Graduate School, where he serves on the adjunct faculty. He has led wilderness expeditions with students at Montreat for more than 20 years. He has interests in significant life experiences in outdoor settings, environmental theology, and field-based environmental education. He has been honored as "Distinguished Professor" and "Teacher of the Year" at Montreat a number of times.

James Doncaster is currently the Senior Director of Organizational Development at Pressley Ridge, a Re-Education program for troubled children based on the work of Nicholas Hobbs. He has over 35 years of experience in both public and private programs working as a teacher-counselor, a supervisor, a program director, and a director of training. He has published papers on the principles of the Re-Ed approach, and a chapter in the book *Helping Troubled Children and Youth* (2008). He joined a distinguished group of professionals that included his friends and mentors Nicholas Hobbs and Campbell Loughmiller when he received the 2008 Lifetime Achievement Award from the American Re-Education Association.

Laurie S. Frank is a former public school teacher who has worked in the adventure and experiential education arenas for more than 25 years. Laurie is the owner/director of GOAL Consulting, working with school districts, camps, and non-profit organizations around the country to create environments where students, faculty, staff, and families are invited into the educational process. She is committed to playing her small part in school transformation, and looks forward to the day when "No Child Left Behind" is a distant memory. When not doing consulting work, she roots for the Green Bay Packers.

Mathew Gingo is a doctoral student in the Cognition and Development program at the University of California, Berkeley. His research focuses on adolescent social development, especially social opposition, moral resistance, and subversion of authority. Prior to his return to the classroom as a student, Matt served as the director of UC Berkeley's outdoor education program for several years, earning a master's degree in equity and social justice along the way.

Bob Henderson has taught Outdoor Education at McMaster University, Hamilton, Ontario, Canada. He began his passion for outdoor life as a camper at an Algonquin Park summer camp and soon was guiding long canoe trips for camps, schools, family, and friends. He is the author of *Every Trail Has a Story: Heritage Travel in Canada* (2005), and *Nature First: Outdoor Life the Friluftsliv Way* (with Nils Vikoader) (2007), both published by the Natural Heritage Books in Toronto.

Peter Higgins, PhD, holds a Personal Chair in Outdoor and Environmental Education at The University of Edinburgh, and heads an academic section with an international reputation for practical and academic teaching and research. His university training and early career was in environmental sciences and freshwater ecology before training to teach outdoor education. He holds high-level teaching qualifications in canoeing/kayaking, free-heel skiing and mountaineering, and has taught at UK outdoor education centers and overseas. He is active in research and consultancy, a member of national and international (EU and UN) advisory groups, and serves as advisor to national governments on outdoor and environmental education.

Jasper S. Hunt has been professionally involved with experiential education since 1970. He was a field instructor for three Outward Bound or Outward Bound adaptive programs in the 1970s. He has taught at the University of Colorado, Boulder; Western Washington University, Bellingham; and Minnesota State University, Mankato. He is currently Professor of Experiential Education and Leadership Studies in the Department of Educational Leadership at Minnesota State University in Mankato.

Christopher S. Leeming has been working with groups since he was a teenager. After earning a Bachelor's degree in Psychology, Chris spent 10 years working as an instructor and administrator for Outward Bound, and especially enjoys working programs in an expeditionary setting. Chris has completed two master's degrees, one in Higher Education Administration and one in Recreation Administration. He is constantly exploring and learning more about the interplay of group dynamics and the power of wilderness experiences. Chris currently lives in Ithaca, New York, and serves as Lands Programs Coordinator at the Outdoor Education Center for Cornell University.

Tom Lindblade has been a counselor and experiential educator for over 40 years. For 25of those years he taught in and coordinated a community college experiential learning program. He has led field studies for students to 50 countries and many of the wilderness areas of North America. Since retirement, Tom continues to teach and lead field studies, trains canoe instructors for the American Canoe Association, and serves on several advisory boards. Tom has a lifelong love for waters and for paddling, and spends as much time as possible in one of his five boats.

Cynthia McDermott has been a teacher since 1971 and has taught all grades. Her most recent teaching has been at the university level in teacher education, and she currently serves as the program chair in Education at Antioch University in Los Angeles. A passionate advocate for student-centered learning, she conducts her classes in ways that encourage inquiry. One of her main interests is children's literature, and she has recently created a national award for books that encourage children to take a stand for what they believe in. She is committed to creating just classrooms in the urban environment.

Robbie Nicol lectures in outdoor environmental philosophy at The University of Edinburgh, and has previously worked for various organizations within the public, commercial, charitable and voluntary sectors. His PhD thesis is titled "Outdoor Education for Sustainable Living?: An Investigation into the Potential of Scottish Local Authority Residential Outdoor Education Centers to Deliver Programs Related to Sustainable Living." This investigation examined the meaning of environmental, personal and social education in relation to theoretical, policy and operational perspectives. He recently undertook a 28-day solo canoe and kayak journey in Scotland to raise awareness of environmental issues and the role of the outdoors as motivating factors for environmental thinking and action.

Tim O'Connell, PhD, is an Associate Professor in the Department of Recreation and Leisure Studies at Brock University, St. Catharines, Ontario, Canada. Tim has been involved with outdoor and experiential education for more than 20 years. He teaches and conducts research in the areas of outdoor leadership and group dynamics. Tim has been a professional wilderness guide, and enjoys a wide variety of outdoor recreation activities. He is currently co-editor of the *Journal of Experiential Education.*

Steve Pace taught his first course using experiential techniques at Antioch College in the mid-1970s. This led to many exciting years of designing and facilitating curricula enlivened with the philosophy and methodology of experiential education, first at Outward Bound and then at Prescott College where he chairs the Adventure Education Program and the Human Development and Psychology Program. Steve recently finished a term as president of the Association for Experiential Education (AEE) . He loves working with groups of all ages and hopes to continue learning and teaching for many years to come.

Edward O. Raiola, PhD, is the Carol Grotnes Belk Chair of the Outdoor Leadership Studies Department at Warren Wilson College, Asheville, North Carolina. He teaches courses in outdoor leadership, organizational leadership, and international and cross-cultural experiential education. His research and writing interests have focused on outdoor leadership education and experiential education.

Gunnar Repp practiced teaching *friluftsliv* (open air life) in Norwegian primary schools from the late 1960s. He tutored *friluftsliv* at the Norwegian University of Sports and Physical Education, and earned his doctorate by investigating the thinking of explorer Fridtjof Nansen. He was a lecturer/tutor and associate professor on the faculty of Art and Physical Education at Volda University. He has a strong ambition to continue practicing, thinking, and learning about *friluftsliv*. He also has interests in drawing and painting, woodcut printmaking, and other graphic arts, exploring humanitiy's relationship to nature from artistic perspectives.

Gloree Rohnke was involved in the early years of Outward Bound and Project Adventure, and eventually earned a master's degree in Education and a second master's degree in Elementary Teacher Certification. She has worked with the High Five Adventure Learning Center, and consulted for the non-profit Play-for-Peace program. An Ecuadorian adventure steered her towards energy-based healing practices, and she has been a Reiki Master Practitioner for the past decade. She currently resides with husband Karl in Galena, Illinois, where she gardens, kayaks, paints, and teaches Tai Chi at the Galena Yoga Center.

Jayson Seaman is currently assistant professor of Kinesiology, in the Outdoor Education option at the University of New Hampshire. He holds a PhD in Education and a master's degree in Kinesiology from the University of New Hampshire. Prior to working at UNH, Jayson was a high school English teacher, an experiential program manager for a rural school district, and a director of statewide service learning programs for New Hampshire. His practical and scholarly interests center on the links among individual, social, and academic learning, especially among ethnically and socioeconomically diverse students involved in experiential programs in and out of schools.

Steven Simpson is a professor of recreation management at the University of Wisconsin-La-Crosse. In the early 1990s he taught at National Taiwan University, and his years in Asia provided the seed for his book, *The Leader Who is Hardly Known* (2003). His interest in John Dewey and Kurt Hahn led him to write a chapter on environmentalist Aldo Leopold, because each spring he takes his university students to the grounds of Leopold's "shack" to conduct conservation projects.

Hilton Smith taught history and the social sciences at several high schools in the Atlanta metro region, then joined with like-minded colleagues to start an alternative secondary program in Atlanta (The Downtown Learning Center). After nine rewarding years there, he pursued a PhD in education leadership, and then joined the Foxfire program in Rabun County, Georgia, as an editor-educator. As Foxfire went national, he gradually moved out of the classroom and into the role of Coordinator of Foxfire Teacher Outreach. After 10 years at Foxfire, he accepted a position at Piedmont College to develop graduate-level secondary education programs. In 2005 he became the Coordinator of Programs for Teachers for the newly formed Foxfire-Piedmont Partnership.

Paul Stonehouse has long been inspired by curiosity and a penchant for asking questions. His education has ranged from biology to seminary. After pursuing an experiential education degree, Paul moved from Minnesota to Scotland where he began his work on a PhD, studying character formation on wilderness expeditions through a virtue-ethical lens. He currently lives and teaches at Simpson University in Redding, California. His interests lie in moral philosophy, theology, wilderness travel by foot and canoe, and his new son, Findley.

Michael J. Swiderski, PhD has been an experiential educator since 1972. He has taught and administered at the college and high school levels. As a passionate adventurer, he continues to guide sea kayak expeditions in the Florida Keys and Everglades, skippers international sailboat deliveries, and tours via bicycle along the Eastern seaboard. When not on his boat or bike, you can often find him in his workshop building wooden boats. Michael is the former Book Review Editor for the *Journal of Experiential Education*.

Karen Warren, PhD, has been an experiential educator and trip leader since 1974. She has taught in the Outdoors Program/Recreational Athletics Department at Hampshire College, Amherst, MA, for over 25 years. She enjoys teaching and writing about outdoor leadership, experiential education, wilderness studies, and social justice in the outdoors. She is the editor of *Women's Voices in Experiential Education* (1996), and a co-editor of *The Theory of Experiential Education* (2008). Karen has been involved for many years with the Association for Experiential Education (AEE). She has received the AEE's 1998 Michael Stratton Practitioner of the Year Award, and the 2006 Experiential Teacher of the Year Award as well as the Blair and Carol Brown Outstanding Staff Member Award at Hampshire College.

Lorene Wapotich is the director and lead instructor for Her Feet on the Earth, an organization dedicated to supporting women and girls in creating stronger relations with nature, their authentic selves, and a community of women mentors and role models. Lorene is an experienced wilderness guide, educator, and herbalist in the Wise Woman Tradition. She holds a bachelor's degree in Wilderness Leadership and Natural History Education, and a master's in Education with a focus on female development, nature-based mentoring, and rites of passage. Lorene is a dynamic teacher who is passionate about connecting women and girls with nature and their inner power and wisdom.

Christopher D. Wells' career path has crossed a number of fields. He has served in the U.S. Navy as an electrician onboard a nuclear submarine, and has worked in technology-related fields such as aerospace, telecommunications, and information technology. His strong interest in the outdoors led to a career shift to outdoor environmental education that eventually resulted in his becoming the executive director of a YMCA camp. Through his work at the camp, he learned about experiential education, a methodology he now uses to teach technology courses to students of all ages. Chris is currently pursuing a doctorate in Sustainability Education through Prescott College in Arizona, and teaching at a private high school in Illinois.

Janice L. Woodhouse, EdD, received her doctorate in Adult & Higher Education at Northern Illinois University. Jan has worked at all levels of education including K–12, adult, community-based, and higher education for over 25 years. Her current interest and research focus is on place-based pedagogy and education for ecological and cultural sustainability. Experiential education has been first an intuitive endeavor and later a studied and deliberate foundation of her work. She also has lived and studied the history of women in science. Jan passed away on July 1, 2010. This earth has one fewer supporter for creating a more sustainable future now.

Maureen Zarrella has been a special educator for more than thirty years, always incorporating outdoor environmental and adventure education programming into her work with special needs children. She has led students on ropes courses, backpacking trips, and caving and climbing expeditions. Her most recent outdoor teaching was at Chief Leschi School in Puyallup, Washington, where she worked with Native American students. She has a bachelor's degree in Science, Elementary Education, and Special Education, and a master's degree in Outdoor Teacher Education from Northern Illinois University. She is now working at East Aurora High School in Aurora, Illinois, as a Transition-Coordinator for special needs students.

Index

eBooks – at www.eBookstore.tandf.co.uk

A library at your fingertips!

eBooks are electronic versions of printed books. You can store them on your PC/laptop or browse them online.

They have advantages for anyone needing rapid access to a wide variety of published, copyright information.

eBooks can help your research by enabling you to bookmark chapters, annotate text and use instant searches to find specific words or phrases. Several eBook files would fit on even a small laptop or PDA.

NEW: Save money by eSubscribing: cheap, online access to any eBook for as long as you need it.

Annual subscription packages

We now offer special low-cost bulk subscriptions to packages of eBooks in certain subject areas. These are available to libraries or to individuals.

For more information please contact webmaster.ebooks@tandf.co.uk

We're continually developing the eBook concept, so keep up to date by visiting the website.

www.eBookstore.tandf.co.uk